BIOCHEMICAL
SYSTEMATICS

PRENTICE-HALL BIOLOGICAL SCIENCE SERIES

William D. McElroy and Carl P. Swanson, *Editors*

BIOCHEMICAL SYSTEMATICS,* by Ralph E. Alston and B. L. Turner
CLASSIC PAPERS IN GENETICS, by James A. Peters
EXPERIMENTAL BIOLOGY, by Richard W. Van Norman
MECHANISMS OF BODY FUNCTIONS, by Dexter M. Easton
MILESTONES IN MICROBIOLOGY, by Thomas D. Brock
PRINCIPLES OF BIOLOGY, by Neal D. Buffaloe
SELECTED BOTANICAL PAPERS, by Irving W. Knobloch
A SYNTHESIS OF EVOLUTIONARY THEORY, by Herbert H. Ross

CONCEPTS OF MODERN BIOLOGY SERIES

BEHAVIORAL ASPECTS OF ECOLOGY,* by Peter H. Klopfer

FOUNDATIONS OF MODERN BIOLOGY SERIES

ADAPTATION, by Bruce Wallace and A. M. Srb
ANIMAL BEHAVIOR, by Vincent Dethier and Eliot Stellar
ANIMAL DIVERSITY, by Earl D. Hanson
ANIMAL GROWTH AND DEVELOPMENT, by Maurice Sussman
ANIMAL PHYSIOLOGY, by Knut Schmidt-Nielsen
THE CELL, by Carl P. Swanson
CELLULAR PHYSIOLOGY AND BIOCHEMISTRY, by William D. McElroy
HEREDITY, by David M. Bonner
THE LIFE OF THE GREEN PLANT, by Arthur W. Galston
MAN IN NATURE, by Marston Bates
THE PLANT KINGDOM, by Harold C. Bold

* These titles are also in the Prentice-Hall International Series in Biological Science. Prentice-Hall, Inc.; Prentice-Hall International, United Kingdom and Eire; Prentice-Hall of Canada, Ltd., Canada; Berliner Union, West Germany and Austria.

BIOCHEMICAL

SYSTEMATICS

Ralph E. Alston

Associate Professor of Botany
University of Texas

B. L. Turner

Professor of Botany
Director of the Herbarium
University of Texas

Prentice-Hall, Inc.

Englewood Cliffs, N.J.

Dedicated to the memory of

Professor Donald Walton Davis

late Professor of Biology at the College of William and Mary. His devotion to academic and scientific principles and his human qualities represented a continuous inspiration (R. E. ALSTON).

33289

PRENTICE-HALL INTERNATIONAL, INC., *London*
PRENTICE-HALL OF AUSTRALIA, PTY., LTD., *Sydney*
PRENTICE-HALL OF CANADA, LTD., *Toronto*
PRENTICE-HALL FRANCE, S.A.R.L., *Paris*
PRENTICE-HALL OF JAPAN, INC., *Tokyo*
PRENTICE-HALL DE MEXICO, S.A., *Mexico City*

Library of Congress Catalog Card Number: 63–14907

Printed in the United States of America
C

PREFACE

Although hundreds of thousands of words have already been written about biochemical systematics its actual impact upon formal systematics is still trivial. So far, no significant taxonomic dispositions of higher plants rest primarily upon biochemical criteria. We consider that an important objective of this book is to develop, more fully an appreciation of the diversity of applications of biochemistry to systematics.

The present treatment is oriented towards botanical systematics. Many of the readers of this book will be: (1) plant taxonomists with only slight background in biochemistry and (2) chemists with little background in classical plant systematics, possibly unacquainted with certain concepts on which the field is founded and with limited knowledge of modern work in systematics. Chapters II through IV are written primarily for the nonsystematist. We ask the indulgence of the well-informed if this introductory matter reiterates much that has already been written on the subject.

At the present stage of development, plant biochemical systematics is a difficult field to survey. It will be noted that nowhere in the book is there a phylogenetic tree constructed out of chemical correlations. Perhaps contrary to the expectation of some readers, we do not see that even the beginnings of such a system are justified. Thus the decision to organize the chapters about major groups of chemical constituents rather than to focus upon taxonomic systems of categories is based upon our firm belief that it is more useful to consider various "natural" chemical groups somewhat critically relevant to their present and *potential* systematic value than to draw a series of taxonomic judgments out of the usually fragmentary biochemical data at hand. The latter approach has been used, at least eclectically, by others, to no great advantage.

The writers cannot regard present limited biochemical data as favoring one or another of the systems such as those of Engler and Prantl, Bessey, Hutchinson, etc. Much of the literature in biochemical systematics includes references by the authors to competing systems when the data bear upon the systematic relationships of higher categories, but in general the individual issue concerns only a small part of the taxonomic whole, and the chemical data now available are often quite limited.

Some readers may be puzzled by the fact that we speak elsewhere of taxonomists who have no interest in phylogeny. The nontaxonomist may be least capable of understanding this situation. Nevertheless, professional taxonomists exist who favor the exclusion of phylogeny from taxonomy. Similarly, although authoritative documentation from the literature is not available we have heard prominent biologists express the belief that biochemistry could never make a contribution to systematics since, e.g., nicotine and certain other substances occur in obviously unrelated plant groups. Such arguments as the latter may be transparent, but they are not fictitious, and therefore some attention is given to answering them in the text.

We believe that the intellectual, technical and perhaps even psychological gap (not intended to be construed as hierarchical in nature) between systematics and chemistry has been the main factor in delaying the maturity of biochemical systematics as a natural discipline. Biochemical systematic studies of the present are often not markedly different from those of 30 years ago. Modern statements

(Constance, 1955; Gibbs, 1958) are hardly distinguishable from those of a generation ago (Redfield, 1936) or nearly a century ago (Abbott, 1886).

Classical cytogenetic methods, which offer far less, potentially, than does comparative biochemistry in over-all application to plant systematics, were quickly assimilated into the discipline, and as a result some of the highest intellectual achievements are represented by classical cytogenetical investigations (e.g. Cleland, 1949, 1954; Clausen, 1953). Therefore, the conspicuous retardation of real progress in the development of sound principles of biochemical systematics is considered to reflect, in part, the wide technical and intellectual separation of taxonomy and chemistry. Partly because of the emergence of new research tools, and partly because a relentless and natural trend toward molecular biology will otherwise turn the field of biochemical systematics over to biochemists by default, the writers believe that a reappraisal of biochemical systematics and the development of a strongly positive attitude toward the field by taxonomists is desirable.

In our judgment the chief weakness of biochemical systematics has been and remains the threat of superficiality. If the present book serves merely to foster a host of superficial shotgun chromatographic comparisons miscellaneous irresponsible correlations and naive interpretations, we will have failed completely in our purpose. We hope that it will encourage an approach to biochemical systematics which is reflective and cautiously optimistic.

The book is offered with humility in recognition of our individual and collective limitations. We have tried to avoid both pedantry and oversimplification. In numerous instances we have taken the liberty of professing a personal evaluation or criticism, always with the objective of establishing a better perspective for viewing biochemistry in its relation to systematics.

To our knowledge, there is no precedent for this book. Consequently, it is based almost entirely upon research contributions from technical journals. Because of the breadth of subject matter encompassed it is virtually impossible to cover the literature completely, and it is likely that some work of major significance was not detected. The words of Sir Francis Galton* come to mind:

> I trust the reader will pardon a small percentage of error and inaccuracy, if it be so small as not to affect the general value of my results. No one can hate inaccuracy more than myself, or can have a higher

* Galton, Francis. 1869. Hereditary Genius. 1st Edition. Reprinted, 1952. Horizon Press, New York.

idea of what an author owes to his readers, in respect to precision; but in a subject like this, it is exceedingly difficult to correct every mistake, and still more to avoid omissions.

Perhaps most importantly we regard this book as an effort to consider perspectives in biochemical systematics. In this sense it is written for the future. An encyclopedic compendium of biochemical data organized in a taxonomic framework is badly needed. However, the writers see no relationship between such a work and our present endeavor.

RALPH E. ALSTON
B. L. TURNER

TABLE OF CONTENTS

ix

1
INTRODUCTION

The great advances in biochemistry which have
come in a few decades have impressed both the informed layman and scientist. The scientist who has
made an effort to acquire more than a passing
acquaintance with the subject is appreciative of not
only the elegance of method and the intellectual
challenge of the field but in addition the implications, sometimes of even a philosophical nature, of
these discoveries to other subdivisions of biology.
For instance, the biochemical unity disclosed
incidentally along with the elucidation of basic pathways of metabolism is as effective support for Dar-
winian evolution as is comparative anatomy. Without a fossil record, and assuming that evidence from
comparative anatomy were in some way unavailable,

comparative biochemistry would have already established unequivocally the same concepts of evolution which now exist.

Four levels of biochemical unity may be recognized which, collectively, provide a framework for evolutionary theory. Starting with the most fundamental they are: (1) biochemical unity as expressed in the basic similarity of the hereditary material of all organisms; (2) biochemical unity as expressed in the group of co-enzymes which are essential to many of the basic biochemical processes; (3) biochemical unity as expressed in the similarity of metabolic pathways, particularly those involved in energy exchange, of different organisms; and (4) biochemical unity as expressed within major taxonomic groups in the common presence of certain structural components such as chitin, cellulose, and so on. At all of the levels there is also some degree of diversity. For example, while deoxyribonucleic acid is present in the chromosomes of diverse species, the same sequence of nucleotide subunits is unlikely to be expressed even in two individuals of a single species. All of this knowledge has a direct bearing upon phylogeny in its broadest meaning. At least, all of the facts have potential phylogenetic significance; those which emphasize unity, to relate species, and those which emphasize diversity, to separate species.

In recent years a number of books have been written about various aspects of the broad subject of biochemistry in relation to evolution. *The Molecular Basis of Evolution* by Anfinsen (1959), and the six volume work in preparation edited by Florkin and Mason (1960) are especially noteworthy. There are also numerous individual articles on the subject of biochemical evolution, treating various aspects of the subject. Speculation upon the origin of life itself is now centered almost entirely upon questions relating to molecular evolution (Oparin, 1959).

Dating back many years before the beginnings of enzyme chemistry and studies of metabolic pathways are numerous investigations of the distributions of various substances, initially in higher plants and now including fungi and bacteria as well. Such investigations often had pharmacological and other economic objectives, but some of the earliest workers were interested in correlations between the distributions of substances and the taxonomic treatments of the species investigated. Subsequent workers have continued to note such correlations or even to make a tentative taxonomic judgment based on their chemical results. Periodically, belief in the utility of biochemical data for systematic purposes has been reiterated. Biochemistry has not yet been responsible for any major advances in our knowledge of phylogenetic relationships. Yet, inexorable progress in the accumulation of biochemical data, many of which are already seen to be of phylogenetic importance, points to an obligatory integration of these data in systematics. The systematist does not have the prerogative of evaluating the purely chemical aspects of data, but he has a responsibility to be alert to progress in biochemistry, particularly when discoveries bear potentially upon phylogenetic considerations. Biochemistry relates to phylogeny at several levels, only one of which involves the taxonomic distribution of specific compounds. Certain approaches discussed in Chapter 4 may seem to be remote or even irrelevant, but the writers believe that no approach should be discouraged provided it is theoretically sound though its practical value may eventually prove to be slight.

It is not the purpose of this book to develop a case for the use of biochemical data in systematics but rather to establish a better perspective concerning the place of biochemistry in systematics. There is a need for an exploration of some theoretical and intellectual aspects of the subject, the development of a basic rationale, an integration of certain chemical and biological aspects, an analysis of the advantages and limitations of the biochemical approach, a broad and essentially critical analysis of existing work. We have attempted to accomplish this series of objectives.

We do not believe that biochemistry represents a panacea for all systematic problems. If anything, the writing of this book has modulated our initial enthusiasm which even in the beginning did not lead us to conceive of present biochemical data as providing more than supplementary data for phylogenetic considerations. However, profound and far-reaching new insight into phylogenetic relationships is potentially available in biochemistry, ultimately, we predict, from intensive study of the comparative chemistry of macromolecules.

Nowadays, much is spoken and written about what is popularly known as molecular biology and its relationship to descriptive or classical biology. It is possible that some individuals regard these two categories as mutually exclusive. It is true that in this age one person rarely acquires eminence in both areas. However, there are many who can excel in performance in one area and be intellectually in contact with the other. It is the purpose of this book to contribute to an integration of these disciplines by providing the groundwork for a more effective utilization of biochemical data in systematics than has previously existed.

2 TAXONOMIC PRINCIPLES

Taxonomy is one of the oldest fields of biological science. Organisms, and their relationships to other organisms, have occupied man's thinking for hundreds, if not thousands, of years. In order to classify, even at the most elementary level, man had to recognize (or identify) organisms. To do this he was prone to observe, make comparisons, and to some extent, integrate data, and develop generalizations therefrom. It can be argued that taxonomy was almost synonymous with biology in its beginning as a science. The identity of organisms occupied the thinking of early biologists. To derive order out of the multitude of forms in existence, these biologists were primarily concerned with writing descriptions and giving names.

Many non-taxonomists, including biologists and other scientists, believe that the sole function of the taxonomist is to describe and name species. While this is still an important function of taxonomy, it is not its beginning or end. Taxonomy, like other areas of biology, has kept pace with the mainstream of biological progress.

A well-trained worker in taxonomy today must have a broad background in the fundamental concepts and basic working techniques of a number of disciplines. He not only has to be familiar with the special disciplines of his own field, but also should have some familiarity with cytology, genetics, statistics, anatomy, and, it is hoped, biochemistry. Without such breadth the worker is often confined to a rather narrow avenue with much diminished perspective. If he is to synthesize and integrate the data provided by classical methods and augment this knowledge with new kinds of evidence he must be, as he was in the beginning of the natural sciences, one of the better informed and widest-read of all biologists.

Taxonomic thought, as indicated in more detail below, changed radically with the advent of Darwinism. Taxonomists not only have incorporated various new morphological approaches (for example, embryology and palynology), but also have accepted enthusiastically the contributions from genetics and cytology. In the present text we are attempting to inform the interested taxonomic worker of some present trends and developments in biological thinking which are or may become relevant to taxonomy.

Certain biologists attempt to discredit taxonomy as a "classical" or dead field. This is unfortunate since taxonomy offers a conceptual approach to biology at the organismal level such as chemistry offers at the molecular level. Both taxonomy and chemistry are unifying fields. The former, based on evolutionary principles, provides a framework to account for morphological variation and its mechanisms at the organismal and populational level, while classical and theoretical chemistry provide a systematic framework to describe and in part comprehend variations in the organization of elementary particles.

While the term taxonomy has long been used to cover systematic work in the inclusive sense, more recently a number of new approaches has occasioned the advent of new names, such as systematics,[1] biosystematics, neosystematics, and so on. Regardless of

[1] Simpson (1961) defines systematics as "the scientific study of the kinds and diversity of organisms and of any and all relationships among them," while taxonomy is defined as "the theoretical study of classification, including its bases, principles, procedures, and rules." In the present text we have used the terms interchangeably and in the inclusive sense.

their appellation, all such workers are, in fact, taxonomists; perhaps a bit more modern by employing experimental procedures but otherwise attempting to solve the same problems, namely, to show relationships and to classify accordingly.

Constance (1960) in reviewing the book of Takhtajian (1959) was impressed enough with certain statements made by this author to quote in his review the following section:

> Among many biologists of experimental aim the notion is widespread that Systematics is a branch of knowledge that is absolutely outmoded. This conception of Systematics is profoundly false and the result of a certain narrow-mindedness of thought associated with one-sided specialization. . . . The fundamental general-biological significance of Systematics consists in that millions of facts that have no sort of scientific value in themselves find their place in the construction of Systematics. Systematics is consequently not only the basis of biology, but also its coronation.

Placed in its proper perspective then, taxonomy becomes the framework or the ordered arrangement of innumerable observations and bits of information. This order is as useful for biochemical data as it is for morphological features. Indeed, it would seem almost indispensable for the former since the seemingly unlimited number of molecular configurations might lose much of their interpretative significance without such a foundation.

Taxonomists generally fall into one of two sorts: (1) those who are primarily interested in the biological units, particularly with respect to their identification, distribution, and proper description, and (2) those who are less concerned with the names and descriptions of categories and more concerned with evolutionary histories and the mechanisms of speciation. In taxonomy, as in most other fields, there are specialists, some who are involved with floristic work, some with identification, some with phylogeny, and some with evolutionary mechanisms. There is room for all, in spite of the fact that different approaches might seem to be more significant at different periods of time. Ultimately all of the information must be consolidated into any unified system of classification.

THE CATEGORIES

FORMAL CATEGORIES

There has been much misunderstanding about the nature of biological categories. Such terms as species, genus, tribe, family,

"Lord, what a day!"

Fig. 2-1. From the systematic point of view, the original caption might have read, with equal humor, "You mean they're not all dogs?" (Drawing by George Price, 1954, The New Yorker Magazine, Inc.)

order, and division have no specific meaning to most non-biologists and frequently disputed meaning among biologists. The categories may be regarded as highly arbitrary. Any attempt by man to categorize natural variation must be arbitrary with respect to a terminological system. This does not mean that the natural entities which are being classified are, in themselves, arbitrary or subjective. If Darwin's theory of evolution is accepted as the general mechanism for the origin of extant taxa, it necessarily follows that the hierarchy of formal categories erected by man do stand in certain positions relative to each other.

It is often argued that the biological categories, in that they are classified by man, are completely subjective in nature. What is often overlooked here is that the subjectiveness is in applying the terminology; the objectiveness of the category under consideration, from a biological point of view, is real. If the biological entity were completely subjective, then, to use a far-fetched analogy, one might well expect the dog-catcher to bring into the pound occasionally lions, orang-outangs, pelicans, and on rare occasions, snakes (cf. Fig. 2-1).

Fortunately, however, the dog-catcher is not concerned with semantic problems, and, though not trained in taxonomy, he finds no difficulty in recognizing *Canis familiaris* despite its modern polymorphism.

The professional biological classifier has been said to arrive at his classification through a process popularly known as the taxonomic method. Several attempts have been made to define or otherwise explain the taxonomic method, but most definitions or descriptive attempts fall short of their mark. While most taxonomists have a fairly good idea what is meant by this method, they find it difficult to express. Essentially, it can be defined as an attempt to make taxonomic interpretations using pattern data from any source. Rogers and Tanimoto (1960) among many others have clearly recognized the inherent complexities of this multiple correlate method and hence have suggested the use of computer programs,[2] using punch cards, for classifying plants, since in making comparisons of many variables when he studies his specimens the taxonomist is often unable to convert his mental picture of these variables into a system which can be communicated readily.

Anderson (1957) attempted to evaluate the objectivity of the "taxonomic method" (he used the term "taxonomic intuition") by sending pressed plant material to several specialists in different parts of the world and asking these workers to classify the material as to the number of taxa involved, particularly as concerned their designation as genus, species, and variety. The results of the study are significant in that most of the workers were in essential agreement as regards the *degree* of relationships expressed, and, in particular, there was remarkable extent of agreement as to the generic status of the material considered. To most taxonomists the nature of this experiment would appear rather trivial. We think it can be fairly stated that most taxonomists working today who might be working with the same biological entities and using basically the same data will come to essentially the same conclusions with respect to the recognition and relative rank of the biological entities considered. The differences that one might expect are the actual hierarchies assigned to the categories recognized. For example, one worker might recognize ten or fifteen genera in a given family, while another might designate only a single genus for the same group, but recognize, instead, ten or fifteen species within this major taxon. They both agree as to the number of biological entities involved. The difference is one of rank

[2] Grant (1959) has expressed little hope "at the prospects of purely mechanical methods in systematics, such as the punching of cards and their classification by IBM machines. . . . If the more obvious characters are selected for scoring . . . [then] . . . Convenience is apt to go hand in hand with artificiality in the classification of complex groups."

which involves a subjective judgment. The biological status of these taxa would not be changed if they were called families or, for that matter, orders. However, one should understand that any changes in the nomenclature of the categories of a portion of a taxonomic system or arrangement should be followed consistently throughout that portion of the system under consideration.

It is evident that the taxon which lends itself most readily to experimental techniques, that is, the species, is also the taxon which is most likely to intergrade morphologically and genetically with some closely related taxon. Thus the species is the most difficult taxon for which to discern discontinuities and to establish parameters for recognition purposes. As one proceeds from the species to the genus, family, order, and so on, though the discontinuities between these various taxa becomes increasingly large, and consequently easier to circumscribe and identify, nonetheless the subjectiveness of these categories increases.

Or, stated another way, it is easier for the taxonomist to circumscribe and hence recognize the major taxonomic categories in spite of the fact that the lesser specific and infraspecific categories are better defined biologically and lend themselves to experimental genetical and populational studies.

EXPERIMENTAL CATEGORIES

The development of cytogenetics and its application to taxonomy made possible a quasi-experimental approach to plant classification. It was natural that early workers in this area of systematics felt that a panacea was in the making and that with detailed (cytogenetical) study much of the difficulty in defining or circumscribing formal categories would soon become a matter of the mere accumulation and application of such data. Unfortunately, this has not proven to be the case. It soon became apparent that sometimes obviously closely related taxa would not hybridize while morphologically more distinct taxa hybridized with ease, often both in the experimental garden and in nature. Many studies which were conceived to establish genetic affinities between taxa of given groups more often succeeded in showing degrees of reproductive success or failure rather than demonstrating comparative genomic differences.

Such reproductive data are often difficult to obtain, and even where assembled the data may contribute little to the solution of the species problem since, at least in the higher plant groups, taxa show all degrees of reproductive affinity, depending on the time and circumstances under which hybridization occurs (either artificial or natural).

Even such a promising criterion as chromosome number was often found to be a poor guide for the identification or circumscription of certain plant taxa. For example populations, and even individuals within populations, of *Claytonia virginiana* (Rothwell, 1959; W. Lewis, 1962) and *Cardamine pratensis* (Banach, 1950; and others) tolerate a wide range of chromosome numbers. While polyploids of a normally diploid entity are often ecologically, if not morphologically, distinct, they are sometimes interspersed *within* populations which appear to be fairly uniform from an ecological and morphological point of view. Examples of diploid and tetraploid populations or individuals which can be distinguished in no other way than by their chromosome number are becoming increasingly common in the taxonomic literature, and this fact has understandably diminished the hopes of many workers who would wish to use cytogenetical data as the final criterion for categorical disposition.

Fortunately, most workers, while recognizing the value of cytogenetical data for systematic purposes, have been aware of the taxonomic chaos that might ensue at the specific and infraspecific levels if any attempt were made to define rigidly the formal categories in terms of reproductive affinity or chromosome number. The formal categories, which are established by international agreement under an appropriate code, have been erected and modified subsequently by several generations of taxonomists. The taxa are usually circumscribed by discontinuities, and more often than not they are natural biological entities classified according to their relative morphological similarities or differences (which presumably is a reflection of their genetical similarities or differences).

The "experimental categories" (see below) are in reality no better defined than the formal categories and, as indicated above, they suffer an inherent classificatory deficiency in that they may or may not reflect relative genetic differences between and among taxa. Lewis (1957) has clearly set forward the value of experimental systematics from the standpoint of taxonomy by pointing out that while such approaches do not permit an objective definition of the species, they do provide an orientation for the concept. Hecht and Tandon (1953) have appropriately stated that:

> The delimitation of two species upon the basis of their failure to form a hybrid is untenable wherever single or few gene differences or simple structural heterozygosity leads to the formation of nonviable combinations. Incipient species may owe their origins to differences such as these, but the accumulation of further differences must follow before what was once a single species may be considered as two.

Lewis (1957), in a brief and excellent paper dealing with the relation of genetics and cytology to taxonomy, has stated,

> Highly interfertile geographical races of a species may be genetically far more different and phylogenetically much more distant than morphologically comparable but, intersterile populations. . . . Consequently, we should not attempt to reflect in our formal taxonomy evidence of discontinuity in the genetic system unaccompanied by corresponding genetic differentiation.

Unfortunately too few of the early experimental workers recognized the limitations of their approaches, and, instead of accepting a modicum of rationale in the classical approaches, they were often overanxious to submerge or erect a species on the basis of rather limited or questionable cytogenetical data.

The most widely used series of experimental categories are the *ecotype, ecospecies,* and *cenospecies* which are based on an

Table 2-1. Analytical key to the experimental categories. (After Clausen, 1951.)

MORPHOLOGY	ECOLOGY	GENETIC RELATIONSHIPS		
		Hybrids Fertile. Second Generation Vigorous	Hybrids Partially Sterile. Second Generation Weak	Hybrids Sterile. or None
Distinct	In distinct environments	Distinct subspecies (or **ecotypes**) of one species	Distinct species (**ecospecies**)	Distinct species complexes (**cenospecies**)
Distinct	In the same environment	Local variations of one species	Species overlapping in common territory	Distinct species complexes (**cenospecies**)
Similar	In distinct environments	Distinct **ecotypes** of one species	Genetic species only (autoploidy or chromosome repatterning)	Genetic species only (autoploidy or chromosome repatterning)
Similar	In the same environment	Taxonomically the same entity	Genetic species only (autoploidy or chromosome repatterning)	Genetic species only (autoploidy or chromosome repatterning)

ecological-genetic classification (Grant, 1960). Table 2-1 shows the characteristics and relationships of these informal groups. These and similar categories are becoming increasingly common in the systematic literature. They are useful additions to the vocabulary in that they enable the experimental worker to describe more accurately the kinds of biological entities with which he is concerned. Information conveyed in this form avoids any cumbersome explanatory extrapolations to the formal categories. In addition to the experimental categories shown in Table 2-1, many additional informal descriptive terms have been proposed by numerous workers (Camp and Gilly, 1943; Grant, 1960; and others).

BIOCHEMICAL CATEGORIES

With the accumulation of chemical data from various plant groups it seems likely that some serious attempt will be made to erect a special nomenclature to deal with those categories so delimited. Tétényi (1958) has already proposed a series of infraspecific categories such as *chemovar, chemoforma,* and *chemocultivar,* and so on to designate appropriate races or forms of chemically defined taxa. We are inclined to agree with Lanjouw (1958) "that chemical strains or varieties formed in the wild should be treated as ordinary infraspecific units"; however, we doubt that these groups, unless accompanied by sufficient morphological divergence, should bear formal names according to the International Code of Botanical Nomenclature. It is already apparent that chemical components may show variation just as do morphological features, and any effort to encourage a formalized nomenclature would only invite a deluge of names which would further extend the lists of synonymy and in other ways increase the nomenclatural burden. For the present, it appears wiser to develop informal descriptive categories, much as has been done by the cytogenetical workers. As an example, one could speak of the chemical races of a given taxon using the distinguishing constituents as adjectives—thus, cyanogenetic race or acyanogenetic race, and so forth. There seems to be little merit in a formal system along the line suggested by Tétényi (1958) and Mansfeld (1958). If we are to believe in the biochemical individuality within *Homo sapiens* (Williams, 1956), there would be nearly as many formal "varieties" or forms as there are people.

The field of biochemical systematics is too poorly developed to predict accurately its long-term effect on plant taxonomy. We are certain that it will add greatly to the data with which to develop further our system of classification. However, any changes in the nomenclatural system will surely be incidental to its more important contribution, that of providing a biochemical basis for showing relationships and ultimately the recognition and incorporation of *molecular evolution* into the over-all, synthetic concepts of taxonomy.

PHYLOGENETIC CONCEPTS AND TAXONOMIC SYSTEMS

Crow (1926) has presented an excellent argument in defense of phylogenetic approaches to taxonomy, the following exerpt being typical:

> The relationships of organisms with one another are not theoretical interpretations at all, but descriptions of the actual facts of the relationship of parts of one organism to another. Phylogeny consists of theories and hypotheses formed from these facts. . . . Phylogeny can give little satisfaction to those who desire absolute truth, but those who hold a partial view to be better than none at all may find it an interesting study.

Theories and hypotheses, essential to analytical science, while often rejected ultimately in the light of unfavorable subsequent evidence, are symbolic of progress, and failure of a new theory or a new hypothesis to emerge is perhaps indicative not of vitality but rather stagnation in that instance. No scientific discipline, unless it is purely descriptive, can afford to discourage or impugn the erection of rational hypotheses from available knowledge. Nevertheless, in systematic biology, which is an analytical science, those attempting to erect phylogenetic systems of classification, particularly those treating groups at higher taxonomic levels, often must defend not only their particular hypothesis, but even the utility of hypotheses per se. Doubtlessly many of those who object to phylogenetic classifications (Gilmour, 1961; Russell, 1962; and others) have, in part, acquired such an attitude as a result of the multiplicity of differing systems which have been proposed for particular groups. All of the systems are stoutly defended by their proponents, and, among the comprehensive systems, all are constructed from more or less the same available data. Even some taxonomists have argued that systematists should not strive to arrange and classify plants on an evolutionary basis but rather should classify only on the basis of total similarities (such a system may be referred to as "natural" even though not implicitly phylogenetic). However, such a position cannot possibly be defended on philosophical or even pragmatic grounds, and the writers consider it axiomatic that phylogeny is the intellectual forte of systematics.

Any hypothetical arrangement purporting to show phyletic relationships, whether based on cytogenetical, biochemical, morphological, or a combination of such data, although of limited value in itself, may be catalytic in the sense that it elicits further speculation and wider associations or suggests preferred additional investigation. In fact, it has succeeded if it has merely received sufficient attention to persuade its declaimers to crystallize their own position and reappraise the total evidence. Of course, a parade of tenuous and vacuous theories of trivial nature is to be discouraged, but most of this type are rather easily perceived by the competent systematist.

Prior to Darwin's publications there were few, if any, purportedly phylogenetic systems of classification proposed by the serious plant taxonomist, for so long as taxonomists accepted the idea of special creation, they were not likely to be concerned with phylogeny. While several outstanding taxonomists during the 1800's classified plants by a "natural" system, they often made no serious or conscious attempt to place the major taxa together according to their evolutionary relationships. For example, such outstanding workers as Bentham and Hooker, in their classic *Genera Plantarum,* placed the gymnosperms between the dicots and monocots instead of placing the latter two together as most phyletic workers have done since that time. Nonetheless Bentham and Hooker's work remains to this day a useful system, mostly "natural," but not phylogenetic.

Much has been written about the speculation involved in numerous attempts by taxonomists to show phylogenetic relationships at various taxonomic levels. While most workers concede that it is possible to hypothesize with considerable assurance at the generic and specific level, mainly because these lower categories are suited to experimental, cytogenetical, and populational study, they also recognize that attempts to construct phylogenetic classifications at the higher taxonomic levels often involve highly subjective judgments. The fact that it becomes more difficult to position taxonomic groups with respect to each other at the higher taxonomic levels in no way invalidates the objectives sought, and the admission that this can be done at the lower levels, in principle at least, assures the worker that attempts to do this with the higher categories are fundamentally sound.

Some workers have despaired of ever achieving any stable[3] or useful phylogenetic classification and have argued for a system that is both reasonably "natural" and useful but without phyletic

[3] Many persons concerned with taxonomic problems, not necessarily taxonomists themselves, deplore the repeated rearrangements of taxa that appear necessary as new information accumulates. Let us suppose a species, long placed in a particular genus, after careful study is found to belong to some other genus. Under a set of international rules,

overtones. Whatever the argument against the incorporation of phylogeny in classificatory systems, it seems obvious that if plants are arranged in as close a phylogenetic order as possible, along somewhat practical lines,[4] the taxonomist has performed a service, however small, to the biochemist interested in natural plant products, to the geneticist interested in making realistic crosses, or to the pharmaceutical worker in his efforts to locate new sources of drugs. In addition to these factors, as noted previously, phylogeny provides intellectual vitality to taxonomy.

Actually, most phylogenetic workers are cognizant of the speculative nature of their various systems, but many outside of the field are not fully aware of the tentative nature of differing and often contending systems. The fact that evidence is not available to prove or disprove one of two contending hypotheses concerning a particular relationship does not invalidate the system as a framework for future investigations. As new evidence accumulates, one of two competing systems may increase in favor. Indeed, the two may be replaced by a third which, while perhaps incorporating parts of both previous systems, may be substantiated with new evidence and information which were not available to previous workers.

SYSTEMS OF CLASSIFICATION

Lawrence (1951) in an excellent treatment of the history of classification stated that:

> Many different classifications of plants have been proposed. They are recognizable as being or approaching one of three types: artificial, natural, and phylogenetic. An artificial system classifies organisms for convenience, primarily as an aid to identification, and usually by means of one or a few characters. A natural system reflects the situation as it is believed to exist in nature and utilizes all information available at the time. A phylogenetic system classifies organisms according to their evolutionary sequence, it reflects genetic relationships, and it enables one to determine at a glance the ancestors or

---

the taxonomist now must make a formal name change, replacing the generic name, and, if necessary, the specific name. But, why make the change? Changing the name doesn't change the plant. What is gained by such action?

The answers should be obvious. The previous position of the species was unnatural and phylogenetically unsound. The scientist must recognize natural relationship or phylogenetic position by making the appropriate transfer and resulting name change. The latter is only incidental to the primary purpose in this redisposition.

[4] Other systems might be easier to erect, maintain, and use for identification purposes, but the utility often ends there.

derivatives (when present) of any taxon. The present state of man's knowledge of nature is too scant to enable one to construct a phylogenetic classification, and the so-called phylogenetic systems represent approaches toward an objective and in reality are mixed and are formed by the combination of natural and phylogenetic evidence.

In the discussion below we will confine our attention primarily to those systems of a phylogenetic nature. Artificial systems are no longer used by the professional taxonomist, and since as indicated earlier truly natural and truly phylogenetic systems are theoretically synonymous, there is little need to prolong a distinction between the two except in a historical-philosophical sense such as Lawrence has done.

After Darwin's work there began to appear numerous and varying systems of classification, nearly all of which were based on phylogenetic considerations. Turrill (1942) has perhaps justly criticized much of this speculation as has Lam (1959). The latter author, in particular, emphasized the necessity of fossil evidence before any substantial phylogenetic classification might be achieved, and he distinguishes between systems erected on the basis of "static taxonomy" (proposed without paleobotanical data) and systems based on "dynamic taxonomy" (utilizing fossil data).

Since, in the case of most flowering plants, nothing resembling a progressive fossil sequence exists equivalent to the classic zoological examples (for example, horse, ammonites, and so on), nearly all systems of classification for the group are based frequently on arbitrary principles as to what constitutes primitiveness or, in turn, advancement.

Over fifty such principles have been advanced, some of a contradictory nature depending on the point of view of the systematist (Just, 1948; Constance, 1955). For example, Engler and Diels (1936) considered that the majority of plants with simple unisexual flowers were primitive, while Bessey, Hutchinson and others have considered these same floral types indicative of advancement, the condition having developed by reduction processes from complete, bisexual flowers. The bases for some of the principles are well documented by extensive, detailed correlative studies on both living and extinct groups (for example, the derivation of vessels from tracheids; Bailey, 1944), while other principles are based more or less on a priori judgment (for example, the assumption that free petals are more primitive than connate petals, and so on). It should also be emphasized that any evaluation of the various principles must be considered with respect to the group under examination. Thus Hutchinson

(1959), in setting forth his views on the phylogeny of angiosperms, adopts the principle that "the spiral arrangement of leaves on the stem and of the floral leaves precedes that of the opposite and whorled type." However, Cronquist (1955), in considering the phylogeny of the family Compositae, considered opposite leaves to be the primitive condition for the family, but this need not mean that he considers this to be a primitive character for the angiosperms generally. Similarly, Hutchinson's view that the herbaceous habit is primitive in the Ranunculaceae does not conflict with his supposition that woodiness is a primitive condition for the angiosperms generally.

Practically all of these principles concern morphological features, but it is not unlikely that as studies of "molecular evolution" (Anfinsen, 1959) develop there will be as many, if not more, principles formulated from purely chemical data. At least one worker (McNair, 1945) has ventured, though prematurely, into this field of conjecture, and others are sure to follow.

Many of the more recently proposed classificatory systems are accompanied by schematic diagrams showing the relative taxonomic positions of the taxa treated. Lam (1936) has written an excellent summary of such presentations, some of which are rather bizarre. Little advance in this type of symbolization has occurred since Lam's review of the subject. Most workers have presented their diagrams in a two-dimensional framework, mainly because fossil data are lacking to substantiate speculations in time. However, some workers, on the basis of several other kinds of evidence, have sought to reconstruct the chronological phyletic history of a given group and thus have added a third dimension, time, to their scheme. Diagrams of the sort mentioned have been constructed for taxonomic groups at all levels from the species to the kingdom (Fig. 2-2 to Fig. 2-7). Most two-dimensional schemes are presented merely to show relative similarities and differences between taxa, although attempts are sometimes made to include the "lines of evolution" for the taxa concerned, usually without time connotations.

Two-dimensional Phylogenetic Diagrams

The two-dimensional presentation is popular because it is simple to construct and need not reflect phylogeny, though it would usually imply that the presentation was the best approximation from the data at hand. One popular form of the two-dimensional scheme is that shown for the genus *Dicentra* (Fig. 2-4). While phylogenetic lines are shown in this scheme and the relative positions of the

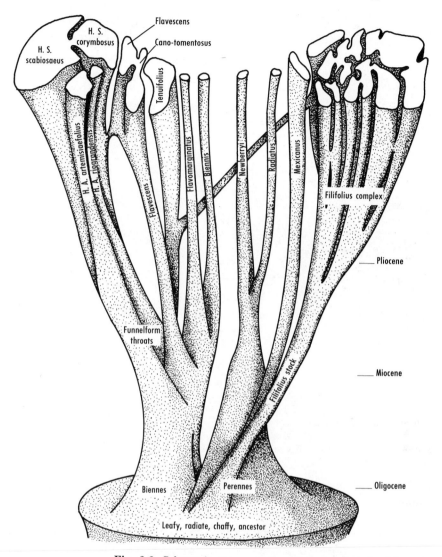

Fig. 2-2. Schematic representation of the suggested origin and evolution of present day *Hymenopappus* species (Turner, 1956).

various taxa, as determined from degrees of specialization, are indicated, the factor of time for the assumed branching is not indicated.

The diagram indicates that *D. torulosa* is morphologically the most specialized, or advanced, and that *D. chrysantha* is the most primitive. In terms of position, as determined from the morphology of the characters selected, *D. torulosa* is closer to *D. scandens* than it

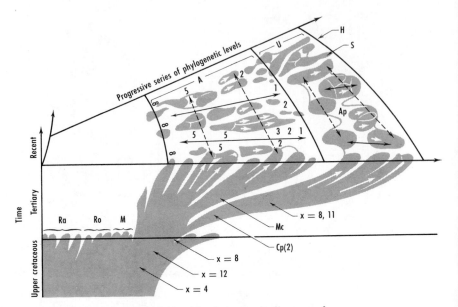

Fig. 2-3. Diagram showing relationships between Araliaceae and Unbelliferae. Horizontal lines mark beginning and end of Tertiary; dotted lines connect morphological levels; solid lines indicate typological relationships; long double arrows signify actual relationship; short double arrows indicate homologous (parallel) evolutionary lines; ∞, 5, 4, 3, 2, 1 = number of carpels; O = genus or tribe; x = basic chromosome numbers; A = Araliaceae, Mc = Myodocarpus, U = Umbelliferae, Ap = Apioideae, H = Hydrocotyloideae, S = Saniculoideae, M = Myrtales plexus, Ro = Rosales plexus, Ra = Ranales plexus. Adapted from Baumann (Just, 1948); copyright (1948) by the University of Chicago.

is to *D. chrysantha,* but its actual phyletic relationship might be closer to *D. chrysantha,* its extreme specialization being a result of more rapid evolution from the phyletic line culminating in *D. chrysantha. D. scandens* possibly diverged earlier from the *chrysantha* stock, but diverged at a much slower rate (Fig. 2-5a and 2-5b). As indicated by Stern (1961), "the angles of divergencies, etc. are strictly diagrammatic and are not designed to denote constant rates of divergencies of evolution."

The *Dicentra* diagram was constructed primarily from interpretations of exomorphic features. It is sometimes possible to construct two-dimensional phyletic diagrams with assurance, often with experimental support, when working with species groups where hybridization, autoploidy, and amphiploidy have been major immediate factors in the speciation process. The diagram for the genus *Clarkia* by Lewis and Lewis (1955) is one of the better documented

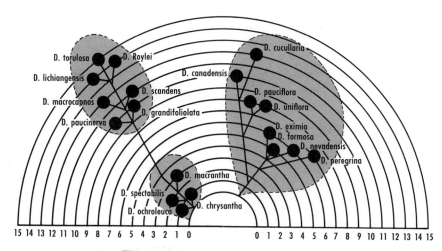

Fig. 2-4. Graph based on specialization indices indicating the probable phylogeny of *Dicentra*. Upper left: Subgenus *Dactylicapnos*. Lower left: Subgenus *Chrysocapnos*. Right: Subgenus *Dicentra*. Higher values indicate a greater degree of specialization (Stern, 1961).

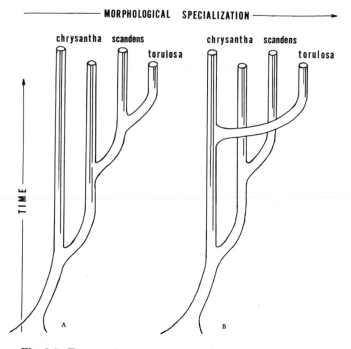

Fig. 2-5. Two possible phyletic interpretations of portions of the diagram shown in Fig. 2.4.

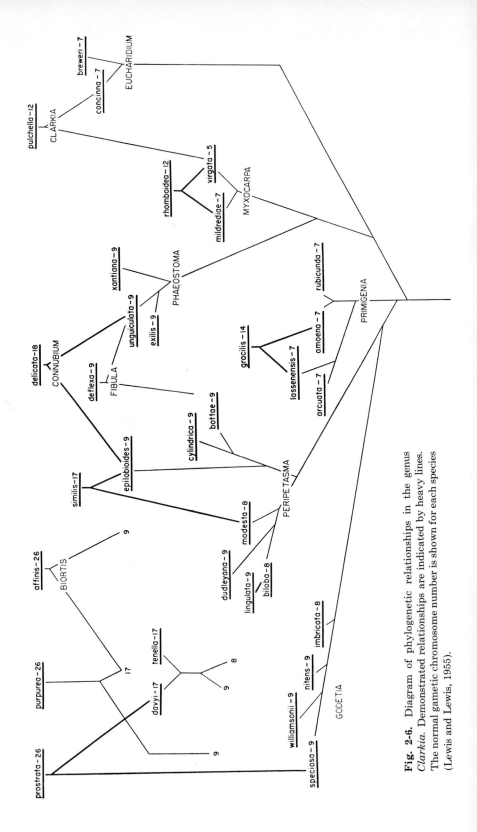

Fig. 2-6. Diagram of phylogenetic relationships in the genus *Clarkia*. Demonstrated relationships are indicated by heavy lines. The normal gametic chromosome number is shown for each species (Lewis and Lewis, 1955).

cases utilizing such information in conjunction with exomorphic features for phyletic evaluation. As is obvious from this diagram (Fig. 2-6), putative diploid species must have preceded the derived polyploids, but again the relative time of such divergences is not shown in the diagram.

THREE-DIMENSIONAL PHYLOGENETIC DIAGRAMS

For higher plant groups where fossil data are mostly lacking, three-dimensional schemes are usually purely speculative. Nonetheless, some monographers have ventured to reconstruct the phyletic past using geomorphological, phytogeographical, ecological and other lines of subtle evidence. If, for example, a North American genus with five species is critically studied and it develops that two of the species occupy mesic habitats which are believed to be floristically old (such as extant remnants of the Arctotertiary flora; Chaney, 1938), while the remaining species occur in grassland and desert habitats (which, on paleobotanical grounds, are believed to be more recently derived vegetational types; Axelrod, 1950, and others), then this information can be used to give relative time dimensions to any appropriate phylogenetic diagram. Phylogenetic schemes constructed from such data are often severely criticized, but, as indicated elsewhere, as a framework for future investigation they are often of definite value.

Time-dimensional phyletic diagrams have been proposed for the evolution of organic matter and organisms for the planet Earth (Fig. 2-7), for the relationships between and within several families (Fig. 2-3), for species within a genus (Fig. 2-2), and so on.

CLASSIFICATION OF VASCULAR PLANTS

Because of the complex morphological variation of the vascular plants, this group has been the most extensively and successfully studied from a phylogenetic standpoint. This is particularly true of the flowering plants, and a number of systems of classifications, usually to the level of family, have been proposed for this group (Lawrence, 1951, for review; Cronquist, 1957, 1960; Benson, 1957; Hutchinson, 1959; Takhtajian, 1959; and others). However, only a few phylogenetic systems have gained wide acceptance or attention, the more important being the systems of Engler, Bessey, and Hutchinson. Certain aspects of these three systems are discussed briefly below, mainly to acquaint the nontaxonomist with their nature and objectives.

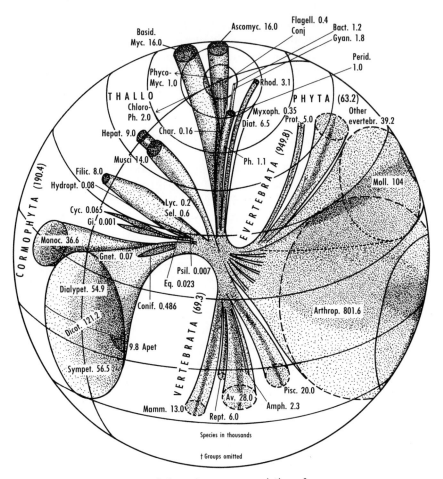

Fig. 2-7. Spherical system of the microcosm, consisting of an
infinite number of concentric "Time spheres." Adapted from
H. J. Lam, 1936, with the authors permission.

1. ENGLER SYSTEM.

As indicated by Lawrence (1951, pp. 118–120), Engler
"attempted to devise a system that had the utility and practicality of
a natural system based on form relationships and one that was compatible with evolutionary principles." However, Engler considered the
angiosperms to be polyphyletic, and his arrangements are more an
attempt to show progressive complexity in structure rather than a
phylogenetic sequence. This system has gained wide acceptance, primarily because of its broad and detailed coverage, and the plants in
many of the world's major herbaria are arranged according to this sys-

tem as are the treatments in numerous floras and texts. Engler's system is not ordinarily displayed in schematic form, mainly because its author did not claim his treatment to be phylogenetic (Turrill, 1942), and the system is recognized by most taxonomic workers as a useful but partly artificial arrangement.

2. BESSEY SYSTEM

Bessey was one of the most astute and prolific American taxonomists to put forward a system of classification for the higher plants. His system (Fig. 2.8) differed considerably from that of Engler in that, instead of emphasizing progressive specialization from the superficially simple flowers of both monocots and dicots, such as Engler proposed, Bessey felt that progressive differentiation has proceeded along a number of lines, one of these being the loss of parts from a relatively simple but multicarpellate perfect flower such as is found in the families Ranunculaceae and Magnoliaceae. This system was not elaborated nearly to the degree that Engler's system was, and, in addition, it suffered certain shortcomings resulting from the fact that Bessey had only fragmentary knowledge of the families indigenous to other parts of the world. In any case, Bessey's system did not receive wide acceptance outside of the United States, although, as is apparent from the Hutchinson system (discussed below), the principles on which Bessey's system was erected have received wide approval elsewhere.

3. HUTCHINSON SYSTEM

Hutchinson's system of classification for the flowering plants was formulated on about the same principles as Bessey's system with one important exception: Hutchinson thought that there occurred early in the evolutionary history of the group a major phyletic dichotomy, resulting in an herbaceous offshoot which produced both the herbaceous dicots and the predominantly herbaceous monocots of today. The ancestral woody plexus was believed to have given rise to those dicot families with mainly woody species. When the herbaceous habit is found in otherwise essentially woody families such as the Leguminosae, it is assumed by Hutchinson to have an independent origin. The same is believed to be true for those semi-woody groups which occur in essentially herbaceous families (for example, *Clematis* in the Ranunculaceae).

Hutchinson's scheme allows for the wide separation of what heretofore have been looked upon as fairly closely related taxa (for example, the Umbelliferae and Araliaceae; see Baumann's phyletic diagram for these groups, Fig. 2-3). Hutchinson ascribes much of this

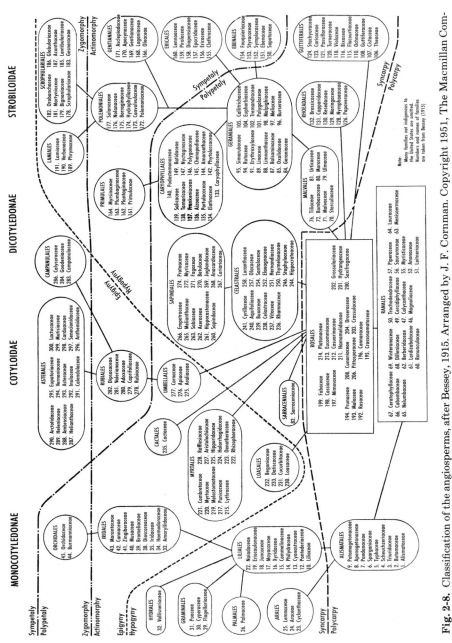

Fig. 2-8. Classification of the angiosperms, after Bessey, 1915. Arranged by J. F. Cornman. Copyright 1951, The Macmillan Company. From G. H. M. Lawrence, *Taxonomy of Vascular Plants.*

similarity to convergent evolution (discussed below). Hutchinson contends that there is a considerable and fundamental phylogenetic gap between a buttercup and a magnolia tree and that, although the herbaceous habit has developed independently in several woody families, the preponderance of morphological evidence supports his arrangement.

Figures 2-8 and 2-9 do not show the arrangement of all the families within the orders recognized by Bessey and Hutchinson, but this information is included in their original presentations. It is important to remember that these systems, while agreeing in parts, are contending hypotheses. The authors recognized this, for, as Hutchinson (1959) stated in the preface of his latest work,

> Botanical systems can never remain static for long, because new facts and methods of approach are liable at any time to modify them. Like other things in this changing world, that which seems to be a probability or even a certainty one day may quite well prove to be a fallacy the next.

Diagrams of the type mentioned above enable the interested worker to tell at a glance the presumed phyletic relationships within the groups concerned; however, it cannot be overemphasized that these are, at the most, hypothetical in nature and only in the rarest instances are they free of gross oversimplifications. For the experienced taxonomists such schemes may prove more irksome than instructive, but to the systematically inclined organic chemist (possibly even for specialists such as palynologists, embryologists, floristic cataloguers, and so forth) they might provide some insight not apparent from the more formalized monographic treatments.

PARALLELISM AS A FACTOR IN CLASSIFICATION

Grant (1959) attributes to two principal factors the main responsibility for the differing generic treatments accorded the phlox family (Polemoniaceae) by several workers on the basis of facts available. These are: reticulate relationships following ancestral hybridization and parallelism in evolution. As indicated in Fig. 2-10, the two phenomena are often concomitant. Several workers have felt that convergence and parallelism per se make it difficult, if not impossible, to erect meaningful phylogenetic classificatory schemes, and some discussion of these phenomena will be included here.

Parallelism may occur as a result of hybridization and subsequent backcrossing (Fig. 2-10b). This type of parallelism, whether

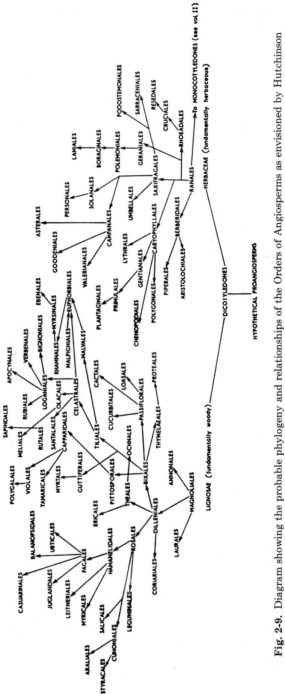

Fig. 2-9. Diagram showing the probable phylogeny and relationships of the Orders of Angiosperms as envisioned by Hutchinson (1959). Copyright 1959, Oxford University Press, *The Families of Flowering Plants*.

detected or not, would hardly affect classificatory systems since, in both the phylogenetic and typological approaches, the taxa concerned would be grouped in about the same relative systematic positions. The type of parallelism shown in Fig. 2-10a poses a more difficult problem, but, except where one or only several criteria are selected for emphasis over other kinds of data, such cases are apparently uncommon. When autonomous parallelism[5] following "convergence" has been a factor in the evolution of a plant group, its discovery is more likely to reflect the soundness of a broad, synthetic (albeit predominately morphological) approach to higher plant classification.

The case for convergence in most closely related taxonomic groups usually rests upon the quantitative features in one or at most only a few characters. If these characters are important "key" characters (discussed below), then any systematic treatment based on such features is likely to be more artificial than natural, and to cite such examples as instances of erroneous phylogeny resulting from convergence and parallelism is to stretch the case. If two taxa have diverged sufficiently to be recognized by their phenotypic differences, reflecting multiple gene differences, then, on a priori grounds, the chance for absolute genetical convergence seems most unlikely in view of our present knowledge of mutational rates and the subtleties involved in the selective forces having to do with character fixation.

Several workers have mentioned examples of what appear to be autonomous convergence and parallelism *for certain characters* of different taxa of higher plants (Bailey, 1944). An even more striking parallelism has been described for some chemical components of otherwise widely differentiated taxa. One rather striking example is the occurrence of the hemoglobin molecule in cells of fungi and in the root nodules of legumes (White, *et al.*, 1959). Several additional examples of chemical convergence and parallelism will be discussed elsewhere in the present text more fully.

The argument that convergence and parallelism make it impossible to achieve a meaningful phylogenetic system can be appropriately countered with the following remark from Crow (1926):

> The problem of the cause of convergence and parallel development is, of course, an extremely important one. But inasmuch as convergence itself was discovered by systematic and morphological investigations, and is itself a phylogenetic conclusion from the systematic and anatomical facts, the necessity of making more detailed study of phylogeny is all the more necessary. . . . To use the polyphyletic origin

[5] As distinguished from parallelism due to hybridization and subsequent backcrossing.

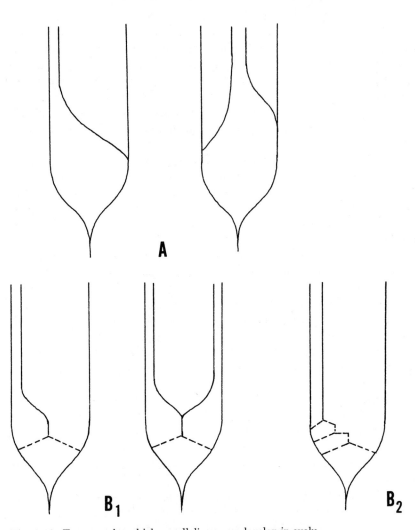

Fig. 2-10. Two ways by which parallelisms can develop in evolution. Parallel selection is assumed in each case. (A) Independent parallel mutations at homologous loci. (B) Hybridization followed by segregation in the direction of one or both parental species (B_1), or followed by backcrossing, viz. introgression (B_2), V. Grant, *Natural History of the Phlox Family. Systematic Botany.* International Scholars Forum A Series of Books by American Scholars, Sciences 1. The Hague: Martinus Nijhoff, 1959.

of a group formerly supposed to be a natural (monophyletic) one as an argument against the possibility of constructing a natural system is nothing more nor less than to use the conclusion of phylogeny to disprove phylogeny.

THE FALLACY OF THE "FUNDAMENTAL" CHARACTER

Most workers today are aware that any ultimate system of classification must be based upon the available data from all fields. To assemble these data is difficult enough, but to assess their phyletic significance often appears impossible. This is particularly true with respect to morphological features (as opposed to chromosomal or genetic data). For example, what genetic (or phylogenetic) significance does an inferior ovary versus a superior ovary have? How does one evaluate the genetic significance of separate carpels as opposed to fused carpels? Of course the answer is sometimes obvious when one is considering the mere presence or absence of a given character (other characters being similar), but when two taxa are separated by a combination of morphological features, all of which vary, both quantitatively and qualitatively, there is no simple solution.

Because of the complexities involved, many workers set arbitrarily certain "fundamental" or technical characters to mark given groups. Consider the largest angiosperm family, the Compositae, with over 30,000 species. All of the species are more or less alike in that most contain an involucrate head, four or five united petals, a modified calyx-like structure (the pappus), an inferior ovary and two carpels, a single style with two branches, and so on. In spite of the extraordinary similarity of all of the species in this family, most workers have grouped the species into twelve or thirteen tribes. The tribal groupings are mostly natural, but occasionally certain taxa are misplaced as to tribe, mainly because of the too rigid adherence to the so-called "fundamental" features used to delimit the tribes initially. For example, the genus *Hymenopappus* had long been placed in the tribe Helenieae because of the absence of chaff. However, more recent investigation has shown this genus to be unnaturally placed in the Helenieae, since its most closely related taxon, *Leucampyx*, an obvious prototype for the chaffless *Hymenopappus*, is apparently correctly placed in the tribe Anthemideae. The presence or absence of chaff in this case appeared to be sufficiently "fundamental" to some workers to separate two very closely related taxa, not only into separate genera, but even into separate tribes. However, Turner (1956), on the basis of total data, united the groups in a single genus and suggested that their proper tribal disposition should be in the Anthemideae. Numerous similar cases could be cited.

Of course, the term "fundamental" as applied to such characters is misleading. They are more appropriately called "key" characters in that they usually furnish an easily observed, mostly constant feature by which to recognize the affinities of a given taxon. It often takes the beginning student many years to appreciate this distinction, and even today some otherwise well-informed professional taxonomists still think of certain single characters as "making" a given specimen and/or population a member of this or that species, tribe, family, and so forth.

Cronquist (1957) has appropriately emphasized this point in stating:

> Every taxonomic character is potentially important, and no character has an inherent, fixed importance; each character is only as important as it proves to be in any particular instance in defining a group which has been perceived on the basis of all of the available evidence.

Stated otherwise, there is no inherent value in a selected single character. As will be indicated in more detail elsewhere, this is as true for chemical characters as it is for megamorphic features.

Most systematic work of a biochemical nature has been directed towards the evaluation and construction of phyletic schemes for the higher taxonomic categories. For example, the detailed serological work of Mez eventually resulted in the creation of his now famous "Stammbaum" (Fig. 2-11). It seems apparent that Mez' diagram was influenced by previous work which was based essentially on exomorphic features. A critical discussion of the objectives and limitations of serology will be presented in Chapter 5 of the present text.

With the development of rather rapid chromatographic techniques which allow rapid detection of numerous chemical constituents of organisms, it is now possible to make considerable *new* use of the many phyletic diagrams which have been prepared by various monographers. Most chemotaxonomic studies of a correlative nature have dealt with presumed phyletic relationships at the family level or higher, reflecting, no doubt, the textbook familiarity of such systems to many non-biologists. Interpretations of relationships at this level are perhaps no better than the data on which they are based, and at the present time these data are still quite limited.

With present knowledge and techniques, a more meaningful application of biochemical data towards classificatory schemes may be

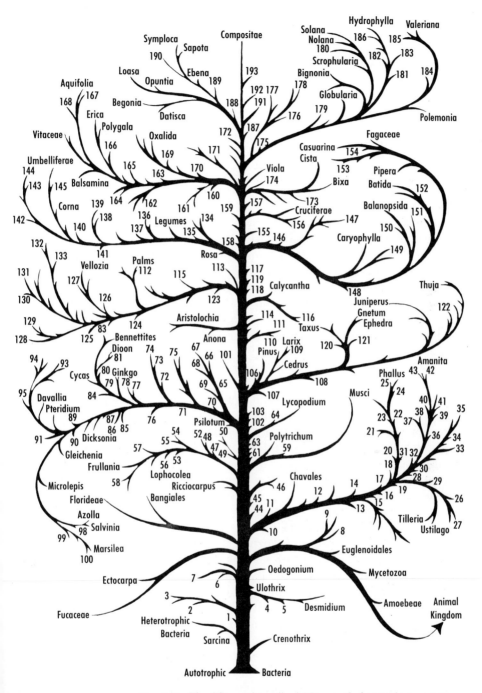

Fig. 2-11. The "Stammbaum" of Mez, a phylogenetic tree pur-portedly constructed, in part, from serological data; adapted from Gortner, 1929, Outlines of Biochemistry, John Wiley & Sons, Inc. The ending "aceae" is omitted from many of the families. For the names of taxa that correspond to the numbers indicated in the diagram, see Appendix I, p. 345.

made at the family level and lower. Carefully constructed phylogenetic systems have been prepared for numerous generic groups, but only in a few instances (for example, Baker and Smith, 1920, on *Eucalyptus*) has there been any concentrated effort to evaluate such systems with purely biochemical data. For example, detailed chemotaxonomic work of this nature on the phylogenetic groupings proposed within the genus *Crepis* (Babcock, 1947) should prove exceedingly rewarding, and might provide new data for relationships yet undetected. The hypothetical phyletic diagram for the genus *Hymenopappus* (Fig. 2-2) could be used profitably for the orientation of a purely chemotaxonomic study; for example, will biochemical data further support the basic dichotomy indicated by the Series Biennis and Perennis, or will new data come to light that might indicate a much more reticulate relationship between the species of these two series than is indicated? It might even be possible to test by chemical data the validity of some of the time speculation indicated in the *Hymenopappus* diagram. For example, it has been demonstrated in numerous instances that certain molecular configurations must occur before some more "advanced" reaction is possible (cf. Ch. 11, p. 197, rotenones). If the latter molecular configuration was found only in the morphologically more advanced desert species, then this would correlate with the evidence from both morphology and paleobotany as to the time of origin of desert habitats and the plant types which must have become adapted to such regions after or concomitant with their development. By the same reasoning, species which have retained certain hypothetical ancestral morphological features and ecological associations might be shown to have one or several of the metabolic precursors necessary for the molecular advancement indicated.

The approach to systematics of genera and lower categories using biochemical patterns has not been vigorously pursued, but as indicated by Alston and Turner (1962) it is capable of sufficient refinement that not only are species detectable but also *degrees* of hybridity for individuals from hybridized populations. Furthermore, it appears likely that with appropriate controls biochemical patterns can be constructed which permit rather objectively determined visual presentation of numerous chemical features for inter- and intrapopulational comparisons. Data obtained chromatographically can also be expressed mathematically with a minimum of interpretative effort so that considerable exactness in the presentation of relationship data can be achieved. Limitations involved in this type of comparison are obvious, of course, and further discussion will be devoted to evaluation of biochemical data in a later chapter.

The present categorization of vascular plants was developed

by several generations of taxonomists, each generation adding observations and concepts to the preceding. Descriptive data were compiled
for the lower taxa first and their significance and limitations determined before meaningful interpretations and circumscription of the
higher categories could be made. Many errors were forthcoming in the
extrapolations and interpretations incidental to its construction, but,
over-all, the resulting taxonomic structure rests on a solid foundation
of observational fact as opposed to mere conjecture.

　　Phylogenetic knowledge of both the major and minor categories of classification is certain to advance as our knowledge of
biochemistry advances. To be sure, the ultimate proofs of the system
must depend on the evidence from all fields, mainly paleobotany, but
we can no longer tacitly assume that ". . . a natural classification must
in the main be based on external characters, simply on account of the
much larger number of these and their much more restricted inci-
dence" (Sprague, 1940). There is a wealth of biochemical data awaiting
exploration, and, while the gross examination of leaves and floral parts
might be the most practical method for the classification of most
plants today, the chemical approach is certain to add significantly to
any ultimate phylogenetic system. Even at the level of identification
there is a significant advantage to the biochemical approach, for if an
exomorphic taxonomist were asked to identify a plant from a leaf or
petal fragment he might despair, but given chemical data he might be
able to identify the fragment to species. This can be done with
certainty in the case of the species of *Baptisia* so far examined
chemically.

3
PLANT TAXONOMY

A BRIEF HISTORY OF
MAJOR DEVELOPMENTS IN THE FIELD

The history of civilization, or indeed all time-dependent phenomena, can be divided into a number of major chronological periods according to the intellectual imagination or disposition of the recorder. Thus one might partition historic time into one-hundred-year periods and graphically treat each unit with equal systematic coverage as if history were a straight line whose ascending time-event path was devoid of significant event fluctuations. Fortunately for students of history, most historians have found it more appropriate to divide recorded history into large or small time periods according to the importance or significance of the events surveyed.

Botanical historians have also recognized the special signifi-cance of certain contributions in making possible the development of new vistas in botany. Greene (1909) in his *Landmarks of Botanical History* emphasized the major early descriptive developments in taxonomic botany, particularly as related to specific individuals and their contributions to systematics. Beginning with prehistoric time, he recognized as foremost (1) the descriptive contributions of Aristotle and Theophrastus (followed by a long quiescence up to the fifteenth century), (2) the significance of the observations of the herbalists Tragus, Brunfels, Bauhin, *et al.* of the sixteenth century, (3) the first distinction of the monocots and dicots by John Ray in 1703, (4) recognition of sexual characters and their significance by Linnaeus and others in the mid-eighteenth century, and so on. Greene purposely selected the word "Landmarks" in his published title since he recog-nized "the impossibility of any such thing as a complete and faithful history of any period when once that period is past."

While such a treatment of botanical history might be sufficient to show the major descriptive phases, it seems that from a dynamic-developmental point of view (in the historical sense) taxonomic history, beginning with Aristotle, can be logically divided into four or five major periods, each of which is terminated (or initiated as the case may be) by some major "breakthrough" in scientific thought or through the development of techniques which have permitted the acquisition of new data (Table 3.1).

Different writers might recognize yet other "breakthroughs" than those listed below, but we believe that few readers will argue about the impact of each on taxonomic practice and thought.

It should be obvious that the present treatment of taxonomic history in no way supposes that the valid techniques or methods of any prior period give way to those of another. Rather the methods and ideas of succeeding periods are usually superimposed on the pre-existing framework; and all are necessary (or at least have so far been found necessary) in our efforts to obtain an "ultimate" phyloge-netic system of classification.

These periods of botanical history have been treated exten-sively by a number of writers. Greene (1909) treated essentially the **Megamorphic Period;** Sachs (1890) treated, among others, the **Micro-morphic Period;** a number of workers have recently reviewed the **Evolutionary Period** (Constance, 1955; Tax, *et al.,* 1960; among others); certain aspects of the **Cytogenetical Period** have been adequately reviewed by several workers (Stebbins, 1950; Clausen, 1951; Heslop-Harrison, 1953; Constance, 1955; Darlington, 1956;

Table 3-1. The major historical or developmental periods of systematic biology.

Period	Time	Characterization of the period
1. Megamorphic	ca. 400 B.C. to ca. 1700 A.D. (Beginning with Aristotle's time and continuing to Leeuwenhoek's invention of the microscope.)	A terminological-descriptive period characterized by the development of formal group concepts (e.g., families, genera, species, etc.) and the establishment of a descriptive language to define these groups better.
2. Micromorphic	ca. 1700 to ca. 1860. (Beginning with Leeuwenhoek and continuing to Darwin's published views on evolution.)	Leeuwenhoek's microscope and lens systems made possible the recognition of hitherto unknown microorganisms, the recognition of sexual features, and their significance and made possible the acquisition of new morphological data (viz., anatomical embryological, palynological, etc.).
3. Evolutionary	ca. 1860 to ca. 1900. (Beginning with Darwin's evolutionary theory and extending to the rediscovery of Mendel's laws of inheritance.)	Darwin's theory profoundly affected systematic thinking. Hereafter most classification systems were constructed on a phylogenetic basis.
4. Cytogenetical	ca. 1900 to ca. 1960(?). (Beginning with the rediscovery of Mendel's laws and extending to the present time.)	This period is characterized by the detailed application of cytogenetical data and populational statistics to plant taxa, mostly at the generic, specific, and infraspecific levels. These techniques permitted the first truly experimental approach to systematics.
5. Biochemical	ca. 1950(?) to —— (?). (Beginning with the biochemical approach, made possible by the development of rapid and relatively simple techniques such as chromatography, and possibly extending to the determination of the sequences of subunits of polynucleotides such as DNA and RNA and of proteins. Techniques are already available whereby nucleotide and amino acid sequences can be analyzed.)	Characterized in its early stages by the establishment of "biochemical profiles" for various plant taxa and their comparative use in solving taxonomic problems; in later stages by a comparative biochemical approach that takes into consideration metabolic pathways, protein evolution, and comparative enzymology.

Lewis, 1957; Hedberg, 1958; and others), and it is probable that this period has not yet made its total contribution (i.e. in terms of broad principles and ultimate potential).

The following questions may be raised: Are we really at the beginning of a new period of taxonomic history? Will taxonomically oriented biochemical investigations yield data that make possible a better phylogenetic scheme? Will they give answers to taxonomic questions that previous methods did not permit? Will chemotaxonomy become as significant in the next half-century as cytotaxonomy has during the last? Is the time at hand for this molecular approach?

We believe that plant taxonomy is now entering this new phase of biochemical investigation. The purpose of the chapters that follow is to document (though selectively) the present state of our knowledge in this field, to give our interpretations of the significance of certain approaches already in use, to evaluate critically the limitations as well as potential of the field, and, finally, to develop philosophical concepts that might lead to increased activity and more important contributions in the future.

4 INTRODUCTION TO BIOCHEMICAL SYSTEMATICS

If there are any biologists who deny the evolution of metabolic pathways in plants, they must certainly constitute a small minority. At our present state of knowledge the evolution of metabolic pathways may be considered axiomatic. It is self-evident that certain fundamental pathways such as those involved in energy transfer and the synthesis of basic protoplasmic constituents appeared before the seed plants evolved, probably even before the origin of cellular organisms. However, there are numerous plant components, broadly classified as secondary substances, which have undoubtedly evolved late in the evolutionary progression. Pertinent questions concerning each of these substances are related to when and in what group of plants they first occurred and how often they have arisen independently. Not only are the secondary substances proper subjects for such considerations, but important structural components, such as lignin, which are of relatively restricted distribution, also have an evolutionary history which may be informative. Finally, it is highly probable that innovations have appeared even in the fundamental pathways, from time to time, which have been preserved in the descendants of the organisms in which the change occurred. Thus it is not gross exaggeration or mere wishful thinking to assert that a natural system of classification is potentially available based on comparative biochemistry. Actually, comparative biochemistry, itself, may be studied at several levels. At one level emphasis is upon the distribution of certain classes of substances, such as, for example, the isoquinoline type alkaloids. Ultimately, comparative biochemistry will likely be represented by comparative enzymology or perhaps even the comparative chemistry of RNA and DNA. It may well be that such studies will yield the most accurate image of phylogeny, but the first level approach must precede these more technically exacting ones or at least be pursued concomitantly.

The distribution of a substance will not necessarily have positive phylogenetic significance in all cases. Sometimes the compounds may have clearly evolved independently in several plant groups and will thus be phylogenetically useless at major taxonomic levels. Nevertheless, those compounds may be valuable in pointing out relationships within a given taxonomic group where they are found. The authors have heard a prominent biologist state that biochemistry can never make any contribution to systematics because certain substances, such as nicotine, are found in such obviously unrelated plant groups as *Equisetum* and *Nicotiana*. It is tempting to dismiss this type of argument summarily as not worthy of rebuttal. It follows from such reasoning that the person making such a statement believes that the vast majority of compounds have evolved again and again throughout the plant kingdom or that chemical substances appear, somewhat capriciously, via a mechanism that transcends the usual order so that their appearance has no real phylogenetic meaning. Since the latter argument has been decimated through biochemical genetics, it need not be taken seriously. As for the first, it is probably that the mode of evolution of biochemical characters roughly parallels that of morphological characters in that certain characters evolve repeatedly (for example, pubescence) and are thus inconsequential at major category levels, or they may arise once (or appear to have arisen once) as in the case of double fertilization in the angiosperms. Frequently, even after intensive study, one does not know whether a given morphological character represents convergent evolution or phylogenetic affinity. Should it come as a surprise or disillusionment to find that the same problem may confront one who is attempting to evaluate a biochemical character? Hänsel (1956) has discussed some of the problems raised in this paragraph. He illustrates clearly the point that the same basic problems are involved in the phyletic interpretation of biochemical as well as morphological data. The "percentage of frequency rule," illustrated with an example from indole alkaloid distribution (Fig. 4-1) is often useful in the interpretation of the systematic significance of members of a related series of substances.

At the present time there is no phylogenetic system based on the distribution of biochemical constituents, nor is there likely to be one, at least one derived out of the first biochemical level referred to previously. What comparative biochemistry has to offer is supplementary evidence which, when added to other systematic knowledge, may clarify or help to clarify a given situation. If comparative biochemistry seriously contradicted any part of the major structure of plant systematics, it would be equally as disturbing to the proponents of comparative biochemistry as to other biosystematists.

The matter of weighing equitably biochemical data, of evaluating it, and comparing it with a given unit of morphological, cytological, physiological, or anatomical data is so important that a separate chapter will be devoted to this topic. In the final analysis one would like to translate all differences into gene differences. It is difficult to do this in the case of most biochemical or morphological data, and unless hybridization is successful, it is impossible to analyze directly the genetic basis for a particular difference.

There is reason to believe that in special situations biochemical characters provide advantages if one is considering the question of the genetic basis for a particular difference. In work to be more fully described in Chapter 15, Turner and Alston (1959) have demonstrated recombination of species-specific characters in individuals from natural hybrid swarms of *Baptisia* species. Most species-specific substances of the parents were present together in the hybrids though often in reduced amounts. In order to translate these species-specific chemical characters into genetic units of differences one must produce an F_2 generation. Theoretically, if a particular substance required only one gene from one parent not present in the other parent, three-fourths of the F_2 generation should produce it, and if n genes were required to form the substance, $(\frac{3}{4})^n$ of the F_2 generation should contain that compound. Therefore, a moderately large F_2 generation should suffice to translate units of biochemical data into unlinked gene differences, assuming that pairing relation-

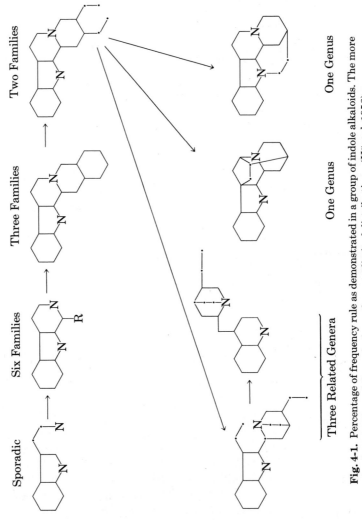

Fig. 4-1. Percentage of frequency rule as demonstrated in a group of indole alkaloids. The more complex members of the series have the more limited distributions. (Hänsel, 1956).

ships are regular. The advantage of the biochemical characters as opposed to morphological characters is presumed to lie in the fact that the biochemical characters are affected in general only in a quantitative way by modifiers while many morphological characters (for example, leaf form) may be influenced qualitatively by numerous modifiers, many of which exert their effect in a cryptic way. Perhaps this generalization may prove invalid, but it is offered tentatively on the basis of our personal experience with *Baptisia* hybrids to date and the much larger background of evidence from biochemical genetics in general.

Historically, interest in the application of chemistry to systematics goes back almost 150 years. In some of the writings of A. P. de Candolle, as Hegnauer (1958) has noted, considerable attention was given to the chemical properties of plants as correlated with their morphological characters. Examples from de Candolle cited by Hegnauer were the observations that all *Cinchona* species aided fever, all *Pinus* species produced terpenes, all Amentifera had astringent bark and all Convolvulaceae were laxative. However, since it was not possible before Darwin's time to accumulate any large amount of chemical data, and since the theoretical implications from the later fields of genetics, evolution, and comparative biochemistry were lacking, it is understandable why little interest was displayed. In fact, more often than not, chemical characters seemed to complicate the existing taxonomic systems. An example of what may have been the prevailing pre-Darwinian attitude is the statement by John Lindley in his preface to *Vegetable Kingdom,* quoted by Gibbs (1958):

> In the first place such matters belong to Chemistry, and not to Botany; secondly, it does not appear possible to connect them with any known principle of botanical classification; and, moreover, the extremely unsteady conditions of the opinions of chemists themselves upon the resulsts of their own researches, would render the introduction of the supposed results of chemists embarrassing rather than advantageous.

Yet, in 1886, twenty-eight years after the appearance of the Darwin-Wallace papers, Helen C. De S. Abbott[1] published a paper entitled, *Certain Chemical Constituents of Plants Considered in Relation to Their Morphology and Evolution.* After noting that Haeckel had divided the flowering plants into three groups: those with simplicity of floral elements, those with multiplicity of floral elements, and those with condensation of floral elements; she stated that

---

[1] Helen Abbott Michael's scientific and philosophical writings, including the reference cited, may be found in *Studies on Plant Chemistry and Literary Papers by Helen Abbott Michael.* The Riverside Press, Cambridge, 1907.

saponin-containing groups all belonged to the middle group of Haeckel and that saponin was a "constructive element in developing the plant from the multiplicity of floral elements to the cephalisation of these organs." She considered that saponin was "an indispensable principle" in those plants in which it occurred. Later, she stated that saponin was a "factor in the great middle realm of plant life when the elements of the individual are striving to condense and thus increase their physiological action and the economy of parts."

Such dogmatic assertions concerning the role of saponins as an "indispensable principle" in "cephalisation," are, at best, exceedingly tenuous, and she has resorted to an anathema to some botanists, namely, a teleological statement, but in the following remarks she expresses an idea that, in some circles, would be regarded as somewhat radical even today.

> The evolution of chemical constituents in which they follow parallel lines with the evolutionary course of plant forms, the one being intimately connected with the other, and consequently that chemical components are indicative of the height of the scale of progression and are essentially appropriate for a basis of botanical classification. In other words that the theory of evolution in plant life is best illustrated by the chemical constituents of vegetable form. (Sic.)

Further, in support of her proposal to utilize plant chemistry in the pursuit of phylogenetic relationships she called attention to the fact that disagreement among botanists themselves pointed to an inadequacy of morphological criteria. Also she noted that plant chemistry represented internal influences controlling function and modifying form rather than external forces. In addition to the preceding ideas which were basically sound, she concluded, rather naively (not, perhaps for the period) that "the percentage of any given compound in a plant would gauge the progress or retrogression of the plant, species or genus. . . ."

Abbott also pointed out that "albuminous compounds" and chlorophyll were not likely to be of much use in classification because they were necessary for the maintenance of life and presumably occurred in all species. A similar idea has been expressed, in substance, more recently by Erdtman (1956) and others who noted that secondary compounds are probably more useful in systematics than are basic metabolites, so that the idea which has been equated with modern thought, in reality, goes back to the previous century.

In the early twentieth century, some remarkably modern or progressive statements appear. For example, Greshoff (1909), in the

Kew Bulletin, used the term "comparative phytochemistry" which he defined as "the knowledge of the connection between the natural relationship of plants and their chemical composition." Greshoff advocated the use of a short chemical description as a part of the formal description of a new genus or species. This is none other than the "biochemical profile" which Alston and Turner suggested recently (1959).

As early as 1925 Munkner indicated full appreciation but premature optimism concerning the use of chemical data in the solution of phylogenetic problems when he noted that in the "older" systematics morphological characters alone, and later anatomical characters, served to relate plants, while in "recent" time comparative chemistry was being utilized in the determination of phylogenetic relationships.

It is reasonable to ask why, in the light of these early recognitions of the potential role of biochemistry, so little progress has been made. The question, of course, does not have a single answer, but the lack of progress in biochemical systematics may be explained partly through the developing interest in genetics and enzymology around the turn of the century. These fields may have lured some investigators who possibly would have turned to biochemical systematics.

Also, many of the early surveys of natural products were instigated from the more practical pharmacological approach. Biologists of fifty years ago were not generally cognizant of the relationship of chemistry to biology, and the biologist was, therefore, not likely to be trained in chemistry. If present circumstances reflect persistent viewpoints, the systematic botanists must have been even repelled by chemistry.

Until recently, techniques have not been available to yield the refined chemical information necessary for biochemical systematics to contribute greatly to systematics. A long and distinguished period of survey has provided vast amounts of information concerning the distribution of chemical substances among the plant species, and in some instances this has proved helpful, usually in a corroborative way to morphology, in systematics. Only in the last decade have techniques such as chromatography allowed the study of microquantities of substances from individual plants. The application of chemistry to individual plants has provided almost unlimited opportunity. Of paramount importance is the fact that it allows the study of populations —natural and otherwise. It allows biochemical systematics to become experimental. Among lower taxonomic categories it often may allow the natural affinity of phylogeny and genetics to be expressed through analysis in a new way—the genetic basis of the expression of chemical characters. It is not expected that knowledge derived from such techniques in higher plants will equal that gained from studies of certain microorganisms (in which the focus has been upon biochemical pathways rather than phylogeny), but important advances will undoubtedly be forthcoming.

Among some groups of organisms, whose simple organization limits a morphological basis of systematics, chemical criteria have long been utilized. Unfortunately for the present argument it seems that bacterial systematics is about as far away from "naturalness" as that of any group of organisms, and chemical criteria have failed to produce a natural system. According to Van Niel (1946):

> Now the fact that the bacteria also have gradually been assigned to families, orders, and classes does not imply that our understanding of their phylogeny is on approximately the same level as our understanding of the plants and animals, in spite of the close resemblance of the structure of the systems of classification. Bacterial taxonomy is far more similar to Linnaeus' original system of the plants, ...

However there are special reasons why this situation is to be expected in bacterial taxonomy.

Among certain groups of lower plants, notably the algae, biochemical criteria, especially the pigment complement and the principal photosynthetic products, have been given a considerable amount of weight, and it is probably correct to say that such criteria were important factors in the recent revision of algal taxonomy at the highest level. Even in this situation the biochemical information was usually applied negatively, that is, not to show relationship but to support non-relationship. It exposed problems too, for example, in the case of the siphonaceous alga, *Vaucheria,* now placed, somewhat conspicuously, in the Chrysophyta (Smith, 1950).

SOME PRELIMINARY CONSIDERATIONS OF THE
APPLICATIONS OF BIOCHEMISTRY TO SYSTEMATICS

Moritz (1958) in a review of plant serology called attention to the fact that serology may make contributions to both major and minor systematic categories; that is, at the family, order, or higher taxon level (major); or to the systematics of genera, species, and infraspecific categories (minor). What is true of serology, itself essentially a biochemical method, is true of biochemical contributions in general. Although these two taxonomic levels do not impose any absolute restrictions upon the particular biochemical approach, and there is no mutual exclusion, it is important to emphasize some fundamental differences.

Biochemical systematics at the major taxonomic category level involves the use of classical studies of such substances as alkaloids, and so on. For example, certain plant families tend to produce alkaloids, while others do not. Within those families which do, one is likely to find a certain class of alkaloid, and related genera are apt to form a particular example of this type of alkaloid. The basic rationale is that of associating specific secondary products of restricted occurrence with specific groups of plants. Some groups of secondary products, such as anthocyanins, are rather too widespread to be of great value although we shall find that, even here, the distribution of unusual types is meaningful in systematic terms.

Biochemical systematics as applied to minor categories may be approached in diverse ways. It is theoretically capable of the utmost refinement, as will be discussed later in this section. Experimental chemical systematics is most likely to make a contribution at this level. One form is the work by Turner and Alston on *Baptisia* which has been referred to earlier in this chapter. It may be assumed as a valid generalization that emphasis is shifting from the major to include the minor category level. It has only been within the last few years that certain ultimate goals have even been conceived. A few examples here will serve to illustrate that definite progress is being made in directions undreamed of ten years ago.

From the area of serology, an exceedingly interesting situation has been reported by Suskind (1957). In *Neurospora crassa* a number of tryptophan-deficient mutants (td series) have been studied. Evidence from serological studies indicates that a protein closely related to tryptophan synthetase (the functioning enzyme) is present in a tryptophan-requiring mutant. In fact, several td mutants have been studied serologically, and those which exhibit serological cross reactivity are referred to as CRM (cross reaction mutant). Some mutants (for example, td) show no serological difference from the wild type allele while others, although exhibiting a cross reactivity, demonstrate a degree of reactivity indicating a serological difference. It is particularly interesting to note that most CRM mutants can be suppressed while CRM-less mutants cannot be suppressed (Suskind, 1961).

The basic method is to obtain rabbit antibody (using partially purified preparations of tryptophan synthetase) which neutralizes enzyme activity. Tests, using td mutants, were conducted to determine whether or not they could yield a substance capable of combining with the antibodies to normal tryptophan synthetase, and it was discovered that certain td mutants did contain serologically active though enzymatically inactive material. This presumably represented an altered protein, formed in the presence of the mutant. It was sufficiently close to the normal enzyme to behave as a similar antigen, but the protein had not retained its catalytic property. Furthermore, the td mutant could elicit antitryptophan synthetase when injected into rabbits. If the inferences drawn from these studies are correct, classical genetics will be served at least to the extent of an elegant experiment suggesting indirectly the idea of mutation as a change, not a loss. Suskind and other workers are primarily interested in the study of an allelic series as applied to questions of intragenic structure. Adams (1942) and Markert and Owens (1954) have prepared antisera against a tyrosinase preparation from the fungi, *Psalliota campestris* and *Glomerella,* respectively. Antiserum for the tyrosinase of *Psalliota* was inactive against tyrosinase from a related genus, *Lactarius piparatus,* and antiserum for the tyrosinase of *Glomerella* was inactive against tyrosinase preparations from *Neurospora, Psalliota, Tenebrio,* and the vascular plant genus, *Solanum.* Therefore, the same enzyme from different species, by serological criteria, may be somewhat different. Novel applications of such serological methods are theoretically possible, though perhaps impractical at this time. For example, Birdsong, Alston, and Turner (1960), noting the absence of canavanine in seeds of certain species in a genus in which canavanine occurs, suggest that interspecific crosses of canavanine-less forms might yield a canavanine-producing hybrid, disclosing latent pathways in much the same way that complementary mutants in *Neurospora* are indicative of metabolic blocks affecting different steps. But what if the species are incompatible or even compatible but yield a canavanine-less hybrid? Serological tests of the type described above might be applied to disclose an enzymatically inert, but related protein. This result would imply that canavanine synthesis was a lost property, and such information would have definite taxonomic value.

Even now, it is apparent that the disclosure of homologous genes by serological tests is becoming feasible (Nisselbaum, *et al.,* 1961). Stimpfling and Irwin (1960a) have recently reported a study of gene homologies in species of the Columbidae (including doves and pigeons). Through extensive previous genetic and serological investigations, it has been possible to demonstrate in these species a series of species-specific antigens which segregate in backcross generations as simple Mendelian characters. If one thus produces an antiserum and adsorbs with appropriate mixtures of test sera, it is possible to produce a single-antibody-containing antiserum which can then be used to test a number of related species. Gene homology is implied in each case where such antiserum is active against the serum furnished by the test species. One series of species-specific antigens, through appropriate matings, has been defined as the product of genes occupying homologous loci in four different species (Stimpfling and Irwin, 1960b). The antigens behave as contrasting characters in backcross hybrids and are considered to be products of genes that had a common origin but underwent subsequent change. They then constitute a series of multiple alleles considered in this situation at the generic level. Additional complexity of the locus, at least in the serological expression, is indicated by the fact that, within a species, variants of the species-specific allele occur. Furthermore, another antigen, in this case from a different genus, has been shown to have some serological affinities with the series discussed above, and it may represent another allelic variant which, if confirmed, would elevate the character to the family level. In this last case, the serological affinities of the allelic series are greater among species of the same genus than with the extrageneric related antigen.

We hardly know where enzyme studies will have arrived by ten more years. The following discussion is indicative of the course of future progress, and discloses the potential refinements of biochemical systematics.

In recent years much progress has been made in the analysis of the amino acid sequences within certain protein molecules. The classic example is the work of Sanger on the insulin molecule. Application of these techniques to genetics appears in the work of Ingram on sickle cell anemia and altered hemoglobin. In a recent book by Anfinsen (1959), *The Molecular Basis of Evolution,* some of this work has been summarized. A few of the pertinent facts follow:

(1) Insulin from five different species has been studied (beef, pig, sheep, horse, and whale), and only insulins of pig and whale were found to be identical.

(2) Adrenocorticotropic hormone (ACTH) of sheep, beef, and pig has been examined, and that of pig differs from the other two.

(3) Sheep and beef ribonucleases differ.

(4) Vasopressin (with only eight amino acids) of beef has arginine while that of hog has lysine.[2]

(5) Ferriporphyrin peptides from cytochrome C of pig, horse, beef, and salmon are alike, but in chicken, serine replaces alanine.

[2] Addendum from A. C. Allison, 1959.

Even more remarkable than the facts listed above are the implications of recent work by Zuckerkandl *et al.* (1960) who have utilized trypsin lysis of hemoglobins of various animals and have then examined the patterns of the derived peptide mixture by means of combined electrophoresis and paper chromatography. Although it is admitted that comparison of individual spots is limited by the methods, the authors suggest that when two complex peptide patterns are generally similar the probability is high that most of the spots represent identical or highly similar sequences. Among several primates studied the basic patterns were very similar; other mammals showed less similarity to the primates than did primates to each other; three fish patterns (bony fish, lungfish, and shark) showed few similarities, and a cyclostome and Echiurid "worm" showed none. The three fish patterns differed among themselves more than did the mammals observed. Apparently most of the hemoglobin molecule has been subject to the effects of gene mutations which have been retained in the course of vertebrate evolution,[3] and probably mutations affecting the same peptide region have occurred repeatedly. The heterogeneity of these hemoglobins is remarkable in itself, but even beyond this, it suggests that this type of comparative biochemical study may be expected to make a major contribution in the not too distant future. Enzyme heterogeneity is now well established, and a major conference has already been devoted to the question of multiple molecular forms of enzymes (Wroblewski, 1961). Introductory remarks at this conference, held by the New York Academy of Sciences, by Gregory (1961) reflect the current lively interest and realistic possibilities of studies of the comparative biochemistry of enzymes:

> It is apparent that enzyme heterogeneity is a common phenomenon. More than 30 enzymes have been shown to exist in multiple forms within individual organisms. They have been observed in both plants and animals, in unicellular microorganisms as well as multicellular species. They have been distinguished on the basis of a variety of characteristics including electrophoretic and chromatographic behavior, serological specificity, differential solubility, and differential response with coenzyme analogues. . . . The importance of the study of multiple forms of enzymes stems in part from their frequent but by no means universal occurrence. Their study promises to expand our knowledge in a variety of fields ranging from embryology and the study of evolution to physiology and pathology.[4]

---

[3] For an interesting discussion of the evolution of hemoglobin and myoglobin, see V. M. Ingram, "Gene evolution and the haemoglobins." *Nature,* **189:** 704–708 (1961).

Although the exact wording of the quoted paragraph emphasizes variation within individual organisms, variations among individuals and among species occur. In the beginning, it is to be expected that enzyme differences within individuals will complicate taxonomic appraisals of interspecific differences, but as the bases for such differences are better understood, the problem should be simplified. An excellent illustration of the extent of variations in similar enzymes is to be found in Fig. 4-3.

Directly related to the remarks made above are implications from studies of the effect of partial degradation of enzymes upon their activity. Selected examples from those summarized by Anfinsen are the following:

(1) ACTH consists of 39 amino acid residues.
    (a) With carboxypeptidase, three C-terminal residues may be removed without loss of activity.
    (b) With limited pepsin digestion, eleven C-terminal residues may be removed without loss of activity.
    (c) With mild acid hydrolysis fifteen C-terminal residues may be removed without loss of activity.
    (d) Loss of even one or two N-terminal residues results in loss of activity.
(2) Papain consists of 180 amino acids.
    (a) About eighty residues from the N-terminal end may be removed without loss of activity.
(3) Ribonuclease consists of 124 residues. (Fig. 4-2.)

Figure 4-2 may be consulted to show the extensive modifications of ribonuclease which may be tolerated without loss of activity of the enzyme. Note that it is at the extremes of the protein chain wherein modification is permitted without loss of activity.

The discovery that enzymes may have a rather large number of nonessential amino acids (that is, nonessential with respect to the overt action of the enzyme) associated with them and also substitutions within the essential parts at some points without loss of activity supports the earlier implications of serological findings: that the same enzyme from two species may differ. This fact, again, provides for a

---

[4] Although enzyme heterogeneity is becoming recognized as commonplace, there are also examples of enzymes from different sources which appear to be identical, at least by serological criteria. For example, Fredrick (1961) has reported that a purified phosphorylase preparation from the bluegreen alga, *Oscillatoria princeps,* was serologically active against other blue green algae. Yet, as noted, serological activity may not indicate total similarity.

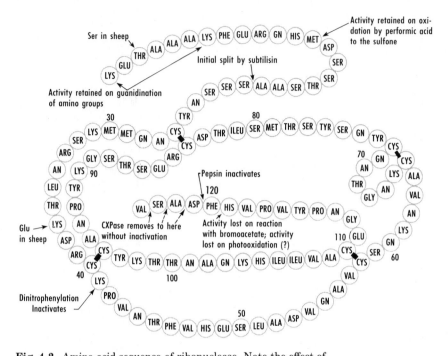

Fig. 4-2. Amino acid sequence of ribonuclease. Note the effect of specific modifications upon activity. Courtesy C. B. Anfinsen; the figure is a composite of results from the following: C. H. W. Hirs, S. Moore and W. H. Stein, *J. Biol. Chem., 235*:633 (1960). R. R. Redfield and C. B. Anfinsen, *J. Biol. Chem., 385* (1956). D. H. Spackman, W. H. Stein, and S. Moore, *J. Biol. Chem., 235*:648 (1960). J. T. Potts, A. Berger, J. Cooke and C. B. Anfinsen, *J. Biol. Chem.* (in press). C. Smyth, W. H. Stein and S. Moore, *J. Biol. Chem.* (in press).

comparative biochemistry of enzymes at the molecular level. This basis for potential enzyme heterogeneity, the extent of which is illustrated in Fig. 4-3, has been pointed out by Paul and Fottrell (1961).

Mutations that affect the amino acid sequence in nonessential parts of the enzyme can in all likelihood be preserved and will thus represent extremely subtle indices of relationship somewhat analogous to the system of reciprocal translocations of *Oenothera* chromosomes which have provided valuable insight into the phylogeny of this genus. Progress in comparative enzymology is accelerating now, and such investigations may play an increasingly important role in the study of evolution. Recently, Esser *et al.* (1960) studied twenty-five reverted mutants, presumably back mutations, of the tryptophanless (td$_2$) mutant of *Neurospora crassa*. Reaction rates for the specific reaction system governed by the gene differed among the reverted mutants, while reaction rates for six different wild strains were similar. These results suggest that the reverted mutants are not qualitatively identical and represent further evidence for enzyme heterogeneity, although simultaneously they emphasize the complexity of the problem of establishing the phylogenetic meaning of those differences which are disclosed.

Another important question which is more apropos now than ever before in the light of advances in biochemical techniques is raised by Anfinsen:

> One of the major questions to be answered in arriving at a clear understanding of the phylogenetic relationships between different forms of life is whether there exist identical, or closely homologous, genes in widely separated species, or whether similarities in phenotypes are due to analogous genes which determine equivalent appearance or function by different pathways.

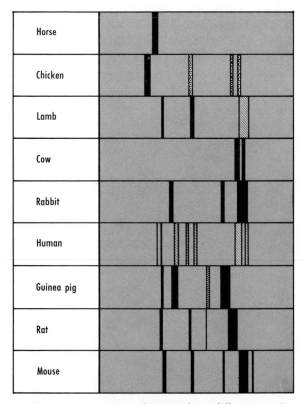

Fig. 4-3. Esterase zymograms of serum from different species. From Paul and Fottrell, 1961, "Molecular Variation in Similar Enzymes from Different Species." Ann. N. Y. Acad. Sci. 94:671

Actually, Anfinsen's question may be modified to apply to enzymes, which are generally assumed to be direct or indirect template products of genes, and further subdivided:

(1) Do widely separated organisms, which possess the ability to synthesize a certain substance, employ the same sequential order and precursor series, implying enzymatic homology, or do they travel different roads to the same destination?

(2) If two biochemical sequences are identical stepwise, to what extent are the enzymes involved homologous and thus identical or nearly so? The minor differences in, say, ribonuclease, of different organisms would not seem to suggest non-homology.

With respect to the second question, if only a small active site has critical spatial arrangement, then independent evolution of an enzyme might be expected to yield chemically different enzymes—unless new enzymes evolve by minor variations in a member of a pair of repeats. This last idea is expressed in detail by Demerec and Hartman (1956) following studies of non-random distribution of genes involved in histidine and tryptophan synthesis in *Salmonella*. Non-random gene distribution appears to be characteristic of amino acid synthesis in *Salmonella*. More recently it has been reported that 4-threonine and 5-isoleucine-valine loci are clustered in an order corresponding to the sequence of biochemical reactions they control (Glanville and Demerec, 1960). Nonetheless the examples of non-random gene distribution of which we are aware at present are found in only a few organisms and may not represent a widespread phenomenon. In Horowitz' words (1950):

> Biochemical mutants of *Neurospora* should provide excellent material for study of the possibility of non-random gene distribution. At present, all that can be said is that if such a distribution exists, it does not leap to the eye.

The situation, at present, in *Neurospora* is essentially unchanged although Wagner *et al.* (1958) have described a system involving valine and isoleucine synthesis wherein the gene sequence seems to be correlated with a sequence of metabolic steps.

In connection with the question of comparative enzyme chemistry, the following excerpt from a discussion at a recent symposium (Haslewood, 1959) illustrates the trend of thought among biochemists at present.

Bloch: "On the other hand you see no difficulty in assuming entirely separate pathways in the evolution of the specific bile acids?"

Haslewood: "No difficulty. If you were to tell me, as the result of researches on protein, that the enzymes making cholic acid in the cod are quite different substances from the enzymes making cholic acid in man, I would not be at all surprised."

When the time arrives at which amino acid sequences of individual proteins can be efficiently analyzed, this procedure will doubtlessly provide some of the answers to questions of enzyme homology versus analogy. At present the procedure is complex and tedious, and only a few laboratories are involved. Serological investigations may provide considerable circumstantial evidence, as has been discussed, for if two similar enzymes behave as a single antigen, they are best considered to be homologous. It is possible, of course, but not highly probable, that the enzymes have evolved independently as serologically identical molecules. There are some interesting possibilities for the study of enzyme systems which appear to be definitely non-homologous. For example, in the squid eye the prosthetic group of the visual pigment is described as neo-b-retinine (Hubbard and St. George, 1958), similar to the pigment of the vertebrate eye. Since the squid eye and vertebrate eye are generally regarded as one of the classic examples of convergent evolution in structure, the precise molecular configuration of the "enzymes" involved in the remarkable correlated biochemical parallelism is of interest. In another similar case Johnson *et al.* (1960) reported an interacting luciferin-luciferase system between a crustacean (*Cypridina*) and a fish (*Apogon*). There is reason to believe that the biochemical mechanisms of phosphorescence are similar in the two species and represent another example of convergent biochemical evolution. Surprisingly, the authors seem to interpret the discovery somewhat differently, however, "although the similarities in the luminescent systems of a fish and crustacean could represent a rare, evolutionary coincidence, they as likely indicate that more of a thread of unity exists in the comparative biochemistry of luminescence among diverse types of organisms than has been hitherto supposed." Anyway, serological comparisons of luciferase from the two sources would be of interest as they represent potentially analogous enzymes.

Dessauer *et al.* (1962) have compared certain iron-binding proteins (transferrins) of 150 reptiles and amphibians by electrophoresis. Large differences in migration rates were observed; in some instances there was considerable intraspecific variation, and also multiple transferrins were often found. In some cases the transferrins were quite constant and similar among related species. Dessauer speculated that variation in the transferrin pattern might be greater in species in a more active phase of evolution. The results in general, while they raised a number of questions, indicated that the iron-binding proteins might be of considerable value in direct systematic comparisons or in population studies when intraspecific variation is encountered.

Another method of studying comparative enzymology which appears to be very promising has been described recently by Kaplan *et al.* (1960), and Kaplan and Ciotti (1961). This technique involves a comparison of the catalytic properties of selected enzymes. Several related methods have been utilized by Kaplan's group. For example, they have shown that certain diphospho-pyridine nucleotidases of ruminants (for example, goat, beef, lamb, deer) are inhibited strongly by isonicotinic acid hydrazide while those of a number of other mammalian groups, as well as the frog, are relatively insensitive. This implies a distinctiveness in these enzymes in one related group of mammals which is systematically significant.

In the work reported by Kaplan *et al.* (1960) reaction rates were compared at high and low substrate concentration using the "same" enzyme from a relatively wide assortment of vertebrates. The specific enzyme reported on was lactic acid dehydrogenase, using both lactate and pyruvate as substrates. In addition to the normal diphosphopyridine nucleotide (DPN) cofactor they prepared specific analogs of the pyridine ring of DPN such as acetyl pyridine and thionicotinamide. These cofactors participated in the reaction either as electron donors (with pyruvate) or acceptors (with lactate). Table 4-1 presents some of Kaplan's results. The values reported could be duplicated, according to the authors, within a few per cent when a number of different individuals of the same species were analyzed.

One notable feature of the data from Table 4-1 is the fact that ratios for heart muscle and for skeletal muscle of the *same* species consistently differed. Also there were outstanding differences in the ratios of flounder, sole, and halibut (all flatfishes) as opposed to the other animals, including a number of other fishes. Differences, though somewhat less marked, were typical between the enzymes of most of the species examined, giving the impression that, if these reaction rate differences truly reflected enzyme structural differences, all of the animals possessed different enzymes. The authors were conservative, however, and did not stress the smaller differences in ratio. A few additional analyses were carried out with invertebrates, and extremely wide differences were observed, notably a greatly enhanced affinity of the enzyme with the pyridine analog, acetyl pyridine, in crustaceans.

Table 4-1. The ratio of the reaction rates for lactic dehydrogenases from heart and muscle of different animals, with high and with low concentrations of pyruvate or lactate. Kaplan *et al.* (1960). Reprinted from *Science* by permission.

Animal	$DPNH_H/DPNH_L$		$APDPN_L/TNDPN_L$	
	Heart	Skeletal muscle	Heart	Skeletal muscle
Man	0.4	0.7	0.7	1.8
Mouse	0.5	0.8	1.2	3.0
Rat	0.4	0.8	0.7	2.4
Guinea pig	0.4	0.8	0.9	2.8
Rabbit	0.3	1.1	0.4	5.1
Beef	0.5	1.1	1.1	2.9
Pig	0.5	0.8	0.7	2.4
Lamb	0.4	1.2	0.7	3.5
Pigeon	0.2	0.7	0.8	3.0
Chicken	0.5	0.9	1.1	4.4
Bullfrog	0.7	0.8	0.7	4.9
Grass frog	0.4	0.7	0.5	4.5
Salamander	0.9	1.3	1.6	4.1
Box turtle	0.6	0.7	2.3	4.8
Painted turtle	0.8	1.0	2.8	9.0
Herring	1.2	1.9	2.9	11.6
Mackerel	0.9	3.2	0.8	11.5
Flounder	2.0	1.9	28	45
Sole	2.1	3.2	30	45
Halibut	*	1.9	*	49
Sea bass	0.9	1.9	0.9	5.6
Butterfish	0.8	1.7	0.8	10.6
Scup	0.6	1.4	0.6	4.9
Sea robin	1.1	1.4	1.9	8.5
Puffer	1.2	1.3	7.4	14.0
Toadfish	0.9	1.3	1.4	9.5
Suckerfish	0.5	1.0	0.9	6.0
Dogfish	0.4	1.1	1.2	8.0

* Not available.

Kaplan *et al.* state, in summary that:

> The data presented indicate that it is possible to classify animals not only by their physiological and morphological characteristics but also by their enzymatic properties, and they also suggest that change in enzyme structure may have been of significance in the establishment of new species.

Boser and Pawelke (1961) have discovered that there are two malic dehydrogenases in potato. This finding is pertinent to Kaplan's work in that variations in the relative amounts of two enzymes could yield differences such as reported by Kaplan, among different species or within an individual. In this case, no qualitative difference in the enzymes is required and the implications of the results would differ.

Somewhat related to the work of Kaplan is that of Blagoveshchenskii (1955) who has emphasized in his writings the fact that the same enzymes from different organisms exhibit different activation energy thresholds and particularly that more advanced organisms have reduced in general the activation energy required for a particular enzymatic process (for example, legume catalase has lower activation energy requirement than does bacterial catalase) implying greater enzyme efficiency in the more advanced species.

So far the great achievements in biochemistry have been integrative and unifying in their influence. The metabolic similarities of all organisms, from bacteriophage (in their limited metabolic abilities), to higher plants, to man are emphasized. Examples of this are so well known that it is no longer necessary to cite them. There is already evident a turn of the tide, a focus upon minor category differences in biochemistry. This thinking is expressed succinctly by H. C. Crick (1958):

> Biologists should realize that before long we shall have a subject which might be called "protein taxonomy"—the study of the amino acid sequences of the proteins of an organism and the comparison of them between species. It can be argued that these sequences are the most delicate expression possible of the phenotype of an organism and that vast amounts of evolutionary information may be hidden away within them.

It is unfortunate that anyone should equate biochemical systematics merely with a survey of the distribution of a given chemical entity. Novel situations providing challenge and reward for ingenuity and perception abound in the area of biochemical systematics as in all areas of biology. An example of an ingenious use of biochemical data in *Drosophila* systematics is the work of Hubby and Throckmorton (1960). It has been shown that more primitive *Drosophila* species produce red pteridine pigments in various parts of the body while the more advanced forms have the distribution of such pigments restricted to the eyes. In the primitive forms, the red pigments are present in the testes of males. The red pteridine pigments of the testes are identical with the eye pigments, and the relationship suggests an evolutionary change in pteridine metabolism in *Drosophila* so as to restrict pteridine accumulation to the eyes where presumably functional significance may be attributed to the pigment. Hubby and

Throckmorton studied the pteridines of 156 species representing five sub-genera. Estimations of pteridine content were made visually from paper chromatograms of extracts. Their results indicated that primitive species from *each sub-genus* contained greater amounts of several pteridines in the body than did the more highly evolved forms. Even some of the colorless pteridines were reduced in amount in certain highly evolved forms. Notably, drosopterine and sepiapteridine have been almost eliminated in the testes of advanced forms of each evolutionary line, and the authors suggest that there is evidence that different mechanisms have arisen to bring about this decrease among the various evolutionary lines. It is obvious that this system offers an additional valuable key to *Drosophila* phylogeny with no indication presented that it contradicts or challenges the system established from genetic and cytological or morphological criteria.

Another interesting approach to comparative biochemistry with an essentially phylogenetic focus is represented by the work of Vogel (1959a, 1959b, 1960, 1961) on lysine synthesis. It has been known for some time (see Wagner and Mitchell, 1955, p. 203) that the biosynthesis of lysine proceeds via two different pathways involving either α-aminoadipic acid (in *Neurospora*) or diaminopimelic acid (in *E. coli*).

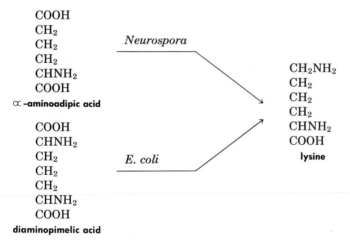

Vogel extended this knowledge to numerous plants representing various major taxonomic groups including bacteria, algae, fungi, and vascular plants. The results of his investigations are summarized in the table below (Table 4-2). Vogel utilized a technique involving radioactive tracers in which the labelling pattern of lysine was indicative of the pathway by which it was formed.

Conclusions from these data are that, by the criterion of com-

Table 4-2. Taxonomic differences in the synthesis of lysine.

Pathway Suggested

DIAMINOPIMELIC ACID	α-AMINOADIPIC ACID

Bacteria
  Bacillus subtilis
  E. coli
	Algae
	  Euglena gracilis

Algae *Chlorella vulgaris*	

Fungi
  Saprolegnia ferax
  S. parasitica
  Achlya bisexualis
  A. americana
  Hypochytrium catenoides
	Fungi
	  Allomyces macrogynus
	  Rhizopus stolonifer
	  Mucor hiemalis
	  Cunninghamella blakesleeana
	  Candida subtilis
	  Neurospora sp.
	  All other ascomycetes and basidiomy-
	  cetes studied.
	  3 species of chytrids

Higher plants
  fern (*Azolla carolina*)
  duckweed (*Lemna minor*)
  pollen tissue (*Ginkgo biloba*)
  leaf parenchyma (*Agave toumeyana*)
  habituated root tissue (*Melilotus*
    officinalis)
  petiole crown gall (*Helianthus annuus*)	

parative lysine synthesis alone, bacteria, some algae, and higher plants show a closer relationship to each other than to the majority of fungi and *Euglena*. However, among the fungi, the Saprolegniales and also *Hypochytrium catenoides* are atypical in that they utilize the diaminopimelic acid pathway. Such data are clearly of phylogenetic interest, though it is obvious that at present it is uncertain as to how much weight must be given this evidence.

That higher plants do synthesize α-aminoadipic acid is evident from work by Grobbelaar and Steward (1955) who found that this acid became radioactive after C[14] lysine was fed to *Phaseolus*. Fowden also (personal communication) has noted that α-aminoadipic acid is frequently encountered as a minor or trace component of many plants and that C[14] lysine and tritiated pipecolic acid give rise to radioactive α-aminoadipic acid in *Acacia*. How these facts will influence, ultimately, the assessment of the phylogenetic implications of

Vogel's work remains to be seen. Obviously absolute metabolic distinctions represent the most satisfactory types of criteria because they imply the emergence of a new synthetic ability or independent origins of alternative biosynthetic routes. When both systems are potentially available (as the formation of α-aminoadipic acid from lysine implies), the demonstration of a selection favoring one pathway over the other becomes the systematic criterion.

A final example illustrating the varied approaches to biochemical systematics is taken from the field of zoology. It is derived from a Harvey Lecture by Wald (1947) entitled "The Chemical Evolution of Vision." Some of the major points are summarized below:

It had been noted that extracts of fish retinas were purple-colored while those of mammals, birds, and frogs rose-colored. Subsequently, marine fish were found to yield extracts colored like those of mammals, birds, and frogs. The purple pigment (characteristic of freshwater fish) was found to be closely related but distinct from the rhodopsin of the second group and was named porphyropsin. The essential biochemistry of rod vision was strictly analogous, in the porphyropsin system, to the rhodopsin-retinene-vitamin A system, but biochemical studies suggested minor differences in the carotenoid moiety of the chromoprotein. Subsequently this difference has been found to reside in the ring of the retinene portion wherein, in the porphyropsin system, one additional double bond is present (Wald, 1960).

It is noteworthy that such a division between marine and freshwater fish receives no support from their taxonomy. Indeed, investigation of euryhaline fish showed that the visual system was related to their spawning environment.

(1) Anadromous types (spawning in freshwater) have the porphyropsin system.
(2) Catadromous types (spawning in salt water) have the rhodopsin system. Some yield mixtures of the two pigments.

Wald noted that it is with evolutionary migrations between freshwater and the sea that the patterns are associated. Since it is commonly believed that freshwater fishes provided ancestors of the amphibia, Wald investigated other pertinent species.

(1) The sea lamprey (spawning in freshwater, however), a primitive vertebrate type, has the porphyropsin system.
(2) The newt has porphyropsin.
(3) The bullfrog (*Rana catesbiana*) provides the most signif-

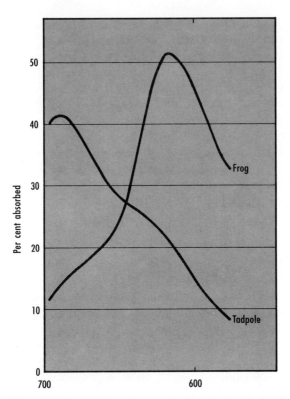

Fig. 4-4. Transfer from the porphyropsin to the rhodopsin system during metamorphosis of the bullfrog. Antimony chloride tests with extracts of bleached retinas from tadpoles approaching metamorphosis, and from newly emerged frogs. The tadpole retina contains a high concentration of vitamin A_2 with only a trace of A_1, the frog retina just the reverse pattern (Wald, 1945–46). Reprinted from the *Harvey Lectures* by permission of the Academic Press, Inc.

icant information, for tadpoles have mostly porphyropsin with only a trace of rhodopsin, while the frogs have mostly rhodopsin. Intermediate stages exhibit mixtures (Fig. 4-4).

Wald says, "It is difficult to view this [latter] phenomenon otherwise than as a recapitulation." This work is of unusual interest to biochemical systematics. In the first place, at the major systematic category level it provides modest further support for the argument that freshwater fishes are the most primitive and that they were the progenitors of amphibians.

However, at the lower systematic category level it provides

spurious biochemical evidence. That is, all marine fishes are linked to the rhodopsin system while freshwater fishes are linked to the porphyropsin system. Yet, certain groups of freshwater and saltwater fishes are obviously closely related by every other criterion.

The interpretation thus derived might better be that, for some unknown reason, there is rather strong selection pressure for the rhodopsin system in marine or terrestrial habitats, so that it evolved *independently* with each evolutionary emergence of a group from freshwater. There is no obvious reason why there should be strong selection for the rhodopsin system under such circumstances. In Wald's words, "there is an order here that goes with the ecology, but with the genetically determined rather than the causal ecology."

Subsequent work has supported the original data except that a few marine fishes are now known to utilize the porphyropsin system and not all frogs exhibit the conversion of the porphyropsin to the rhodopsin system associated with metamorphosis (Wald, 1960).

The lesson which may be learned from this is that data which provide valid support for a systematic interpretation at one level may be simultaneously misleading at another level. In this work one gains the impression that strong selection pressure may be present, when unexpected on a priori grounds. One must, therefore, be cognizant of cryptic selection pressure which could produce a biochemical correlation which might be deceptive in its implications.

The foregoing discussion has touched briefly upon several facets of biochemical systematics. The authors hope that some of the ideas expressed serve to indicate the need for an enlarged perspective from which to view the field. The scope of the subject greatly exceeds the somewhat sterile cataloging of compounds and their host species. There is scarcely any doubt that this broad field offers a tremendous potential to systematics. Its past near-neglect has stemmed almost certainly from limitations of technique, but instrumentation is advancing at an incredible pace, and techniques are now commonplace that were totally unavailable even ten years ago.

5 SEROLOGY AND SYSTEMATICS

Intensive serological investigations preceded sustained or general interest in other biochemical approaches to systematics. Since serology is, in application and methodology, fundamentally different from those approaches (for example, studies of specifically known chemical entities), treatment of serology precedes that of particular "natural" classes of compounds in subsequent chapters.

Although some interest in biochemical applications to systematics presumably developed as a result of the work of Abbott more than seventy-five years ago (1886, 1887a, 1887b), and indeed sporadically the subject was introduced even earlier, as indicated in the preceding chapter, only a handful of important contributions appeared prior to the classic work of Baker and Smith (1920) on the terpenoids of *Eucalyptus*. However, as early as 1901 Nuttall published his significant work on the use of essentially serological methods in establishing species relationships. These serological methods were, in turn, adopted by numerous workers and extended to include a wide variety of organisms, both plant and animal, over the succeeding several decades. In its period of greatest emphasis (that is, during the period of 1920–1930), the serological approach received mixed reactions. Some investigators embraced this development as a panacea which, almost alone, would provide a completely objective approach to systematics generally. One prominent group of plant serologists emerged at Königsberg, Germany, following the initial investigations of Gohlke in 1913. Later, Mez was the dominant figure in the Königsberg group. The Königsberg work culminated in the development of the much debated, but now often overlooked, "Serodiagnostiche Stammbaum" (Fig. 2-12) purporting to show a phylogenetic tree derived almost entirely from comparative serological investigations (Mez and Ziegenspeck, 1926). The serological data evoked in some quarters a considerable amount of skepticism and in fact some severe criticism. Most skepticism, as might have been expected, came from the classical morphological systematists while violent emotional criticism of Mez's contributions came surprisingly from other serological workers, such as the Berlin group represented by Gilg and Schurhoff (1927) who stated, "the serodiagnostic method is, for investigation of plant relationships, completely useless."

The controversy between the Berlin serologists and the Mez group at Königsberg was discussed by Chester (1937) in a series of three general reviews of plant serology. These papers were masterfully written, and they represent a classic summary of the early period of plant serological investigations. The present authors are indebted to Chester's review for much of the information on basic methodology presented in the succeeding pages. It is ironic that at about the time the Chester review appeared, interest and activity in plant serology waned. Plant serological investigations have subsequently revived somewhat, in Germany in the work of Moritz and in America by Johnson and Fairbrothers. The revival of interest in America in plant serology represents an offshoot from the animal serological systematic studies of Boyden and co-workers, begun in 1925 and continuing at Rutgers University. In the following paragraphs selected examples will be drawn from zoological studies when they illustrate, particularly well, a certain principle. In general, however, botanical studies will be emphasized.

It is doubtlessly recognized, by even the general reader, that serology concerns essentially antigen-antibody responses. That is, certain foreign substances (called antigens and formerly regarded as proteins though now it is recognized that other substances than protein may be antigenic), when injected into a host, may elicit the formation, in the host, of other substances (called antibodies, likewise generally regarded as proteinaceous) which may agglutinate or otherwise affect the foreign substance. Various species of domestic animals may serve as the host although rabbits are most frequently used.

Chester has listed the types of reactions which were utilized up to 1937. Since his review, the first method to be discussed below, the precipitin reaction, has become the most widely used. The precipitin reaction is probably the simplest of the various methods of evaluating antigen-antibody reactions. In this method, one mixes aliquots of the antigen in varying dilutions with the antibody preparation (antiserum); this mixture produces an amount of precipitate corresponding to the "strength" of the reaction, and the precipitate is appropriately measured. In addition to the precipitin reaction various reactions classified as anaphylaxis reactions have been utilized. In principle these last methods involve sensitizing a host, then later injecting into the host a second dose of antigen preparation. The second injection may induce some physiological response such as inflammation or spasms. An interesting modification of the anaphylaxis reaction is known as the Schultz-Dale technique. A sensitized virgin female guinea pig is killed, and the uterus removed, placed in Ringer's solution, and attached to a kymograph. The antigen preparation is added directly to the uterus, and the degree of uterine contraction is measured on the kymograph. A third type of reaction involves the destruction (or agglutination) of particulate antigen carriers such as bacteria, blood cells, pollen or other unicellular bodies by antisera from sensitized hosts. Complement fixation, a fourth type of reaction, utilizes the knowledge that a non-specific, heat labile substance (complement) which participates, essentially, in the antigen-antibody interaction, is used up in the process. Therefore, in principle one measures the presence or absence of residual complement, following the exposure of the antiserum to an unknown antigen preparation. Residual complement is measured by comparing the efficiency of a second reaction to a standard antigen preparation, for example sheep blood cells. Complement fixation would be suitable as an indirect indicator of an interaction which could not be followed visually. In another type of reaction, the Aberhalden reaction, the serum and the antiserum used to test it are mixed in a dialysis membrane. Subsequently one tests the external medium with ninhydrin for dialyzable cleavage products. Some other rather uncommon reactions have been utilized but so infrequently as to render them insignificant for present purposes.

As in any other biochemical approach, the validity of serological data depends directly upon the reliability of the techniques utilized. From the earliest investigations strong support for particular innovations of technique has been the rule, and often the attitude has been taken that other techniques, usually equally vigorously supported by their adherents, are, nevertheless, almost completely worthless. Controversy over technical procedure was particularly rife between the Königsberg and Berlin investigators, and it seems that they hardly agreed on anything. Subsequent improvements in technique, to be discussed later, indicate that the controversy could only disclose which group's technique represented the greater imperfection. Since the question of technique in serology is exceptionally relevant to a reasonably objective appraisal of the method itself, some details will be included below.

In botanical serology, seeds are most frequently used as a source of antigen. These may be ground in a mortar and pre-extracted with some non-polar solvent such as petroleum ether to remove lipids. The ground material may also be extracted with ethanol. The protein is finally extracted, most often with physiological saline, in proportions of about 100 ml per 10 gms of tissue. Extraction time is controlled, of course, and may represent several hours, or overnight. Sometimes expressed sap is used directly.

Considerable disagreement arose among earlier investigators as to whether individual plants were serologically homogeneous or whether different organs or even tissues from the same plant had different antigenic complements. Mez believed that plants were homogeneous, but the Berlin group disagreed. Chester noted, however, that comparisons between seed proteins and other plant parts were particularly distinctive and supported the Berlin viewpoint. Quite recently, strong evidence for antigenic heterogeneity has been adduced by Kloz, *et al.* (1960); this evidence will be presented in detail later, following some additional discussion of present methodology. If there is significant adaptive enzyme formation during development of higher plants, as a priori considerations and precedent from microorganisms suggest, then antigenic heterogeneity may be expected. Furthermore, present work on multiple enzymes, discussed earlier (Chapter 4), suggests strongly that large differences in antigenic composition may be expected within an organism.

Another important question of technique relates to the protein concentration of a particular plant extract. For example, if a protein extract from one plant is twice as concentrated as that of another, should they be adjusted to a standard concentration for valid comparison? Dissenters would note that it has not been established that there is a necessary correlation between total protein and antigenic activity. It has been suggested that a constant ratio of tissue to solvent is preferable.

Injection of the extract into the host is intraperitoneally, intracutaneously, or intravenously. A typical inoculation schedule might be 5 cc doses administered at three to four day intervals with a total of five to eight injections followed by a nine to ten day rest before bleeding (Chester, 1937). It may be noted that individual differences in the reactivity of different host animals, while reduced by careful breeding, can never be entirely eliminated. Consequently, some of the differences in serological reactions must represent variations in host reactivity. This factor is undoubtedly taken into account by workers in serology but is not often expressed. The complications stemming from the requirement of a supply of host animals have probably deterred many botanists otherwise receptive to serological investigations. If the "Kunstsera" (artificial serum from beef) reported by Mez had proven as reliable in the hands of other investigators as claimed by its developer, we might have witnessed a dramatic adoption of the serological approach.

In the earlier serological investigations, there were two different methods of reading the precipitin reactions. As usual, one was favored in Berlin and one in Königsberg. The first of these, the "flocculation test" was utilized by the Mez group in Königsberg. In this technique a carefully diluted antigen solution was mixed in a standard sized test tube with an aliquot of undiluted antiserum. The mixture was shaken, incubated for a standard time, and the height of the precipitate which had, in the interim, flocculated, was read. The observer, by design, did not know the identity of the serum being tested. The second method was called the "ring test." In this test the denser liquid was added to a test tube and the less dense liquid pipetted carefully onto its surface. Without disturbing the layers, the tube was incubated under standard conditions and the width of the ring of precipitate measured. The ring test is not used frequently at present, but Lewis (1952) has used this test in studies of the serological manifestations of pollen incompatibility factors.

A final commentary on the rather unfortunate controversy between the Königsberg and Berlin groups may be appropriate at this point before passing to the post-Chester period in plant serology. Chester felt that the controversy was to a considerable degree responsible for the failure of systematists to become receptive to the serological approach. In any event the serological data were in general ignored by the majority of systematists, though von Wettstein is said to have regarded serological data as useful, within limits, in phylogeny. Chester offers a quotation from the Swedish systematist Heintze as a reflection of the opinion of many systematists:

> Serodiagnostic investigations have hardly contributed to a clearing up of the relationships within the Cormophytes. By and large they only "confirm" the errors of Engler and Prantl.

With the passage of time details of the Mez "Stammbaum" have faded from the memory of most of the relatively few people who saw it. The illustration was copyrighted, and aside from its appearance in the original article, has been published only rarely. It is difficult to believe that the "Stammbaum" possesses much validity in view of the current recognition of certain limitations of the early serological methods. Yet, when higher taxonomic categories are compared serologically, correspondingly, the sensitivity of the method may not need to be as great to provide clues to relationships.

Boyden (1942), in an important general review of serology and systematics, discussed some of the methodological innovations in use at that time, particularly the "photronreflectometer," which is essentially a modified densitometer. The Rutgers serologists (botanical as well as zoological) are now using mostly densitometric measurements of the precipitin reaction (Boyden and De Falco, 1943), but Moritz, in Germany, is using a micromethod called micronephelometry in which a beam of light passes through a microscope slide, containing the test solution, mounted on a microscope. A photocell is attached to the ocular position, and light reduction resulting from turbidity is recorded through the photocell and an ammeter (Moritz, 1960). An interesting point brought out by Boyden concerns the phenomenon of optimal proportions. Briefly, it has been established that the amount of precipitate obtained with constant amounts of antiserum and increasing dilutions of antigen rises from zero to a maximum then falls off again to zero with considerable excess of antibody. As a result of this phenomenon (for which several hypothetical explanations exist), one must compare interactions over a series of dilutions. The optimal proportion for different antigen preparations may vary significantly, as indicated in Fig. 5-1. Since in most of the early serological work only one proportion of antigen and antibody preparations was utilized, it is obvious that the reliability of the method was accordingly lessened. This disclosure cannot help but reduce the value of much of the early serological work including, of course, that of Mez.

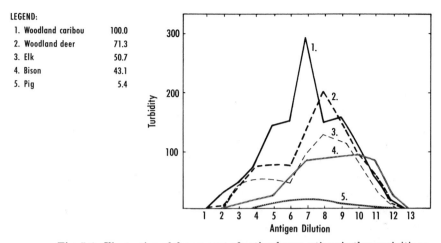

LEGEND:
1. Woodland caribou   100.0
2. Woodland deer   71.3
3. Elk   50.7
4. Bison   43.1
5. Pig   5.4

Fig. 5-1. Illustration of the concept of optimal proportions in the precipitin reaction. Note that the greatest amount of interaction occurs at different antigen dilutions for different species. Thus the total area under the curve represents, more accurately, the degree of interaction (Gemeroy, Boyden & De Falco, 1955).

The technique recommended by Boyden requires a measurement of the total area under the curve obtained by measuring the reaction with various antigen dilutions. Relationships are expressed as the per cent area of a particular heterologous reaction compared to the homologous reaction (in a homologous reaction, the antiserum is matched with its original inducing antigens, and the amount of reaction, or curve area, is denoted as 100 per cent). The higher the percentage of reaction obtained with a particular heterologous reaction the closer would be the presumed serological affinity.

Despite the improvements in technique such as described above, some workers question the validity of methods based on strictly quantitative reactions. Gell *et al.* (1960) have pointed out, for example, that when species A gives more precipitate in a heterologous reaction with B than it does with C, this may reflect varying amounts of a single protein which is abundant in B and not in C. However, species A and C may contain several common, non-cross-reacting substances and might reasonably be regarded as more closely related species, although the serological method utilized would obscure this relationship. The actual extent to which such theoretical objections, in practice, detract from the validity of serological data cannot easily be ascertained, but it does appear that such complications are sufficiently probable that every effort should be made to come to grips with some of the more fundamental aspects of the method.

Systematic applications of serology require more insight into the molecular basis of the phenomenon than now exists, yet there is no clear indication that this facet of the problem is being aggressively explored except by biochemists. No vigorous analytical treatment of the problem of the qualitative aspects of the reaction appears from the literature of systematic serology. The critical question of precisely what is being measured has not been faced. For example, what are the relative contributions of structural proteins, storage proteins, enzymatic proteins and non-proteins to the total reaction? Most proteins which have been tested are antigenic, but their effectiveness varies. What bearing, for example, does the disclosure that one may convert gelatin from a weak antigen into a potent antigen by the attachment of tyrosine, tryptophan or phenylalanine peptides (Sela and Arnon, 1960) have upon the question?

Granted that it is perhaps not required that systematic serologists establish, themselves, the precise molecular dynamics of the reaction, there remains nevertheless an obligation to attempt to establish some parameters with respect to the presumptive validity of the method through experimentation. Several possibilities are apparent. For example, it should not be difficult to obtain genetic stocks of different highly homozygous lines of intensively investigated species, such as maize. Hybrids could then be produced and back-crossed, in successive generations, to each parental type. By this method one could obtain, empirically, a graded series of genetic types from one parental extreme to the other. If a parental "standard" is utilized to prepare an antiserum, then the remaining lines would, if the technique is valid, be predicted to yield heterologous reactions of decreasing amount. Should a linear trend in the serological results appear, it would provide convincing corroboration of the method. Unfortunately, this type of experiment has not apparently been done. In hybrid populations, where morphological hybrid indices (and even biochemical indices in the case of *Baptisia*) are available, the serological data could be correlated with data of these other types. Unless experiments of these types are conducted, one cannot accept the taxonomic implications of serological data without considerable reservations. Actually, Moritz has undertaken a number of serological investigations of hybrids (for example, Moritz and von Berg, 1931), in which pre-adsorption with appropriate parental serum was utilized, among other devices, in establishing the hybrid nature of a putative hybrid. That is, if a putative hybrid is used to produce an antiserum, and following pre-adsorption with a serum from one and then the other parent, no reaction occurs with the homologous serum, it is concluded that the hybrid has no antigens not present in one or the other parent and is truly a hybrid. This work will be described more fully in Chapter 15 (Hybrid Studies).

In the older literature, there are some serological investigations which have been correlated with other criteria but not in a manner which is wholly capable of resolving questions such as those raised above. For example, Baldwin *et al.* (1927) studied the serological interrelationships of a number of cross-inoculation groups of legumes. Cross-inoculation groups are groups of species within which certain nodule-inhabiting strains of bacteria may be cross-inoculated. Generally, it may be assumed that the species belonging to a particular cross-inoculation group are rather closely related to each other. In some cases a particular cross-inoculation group may also be affected similarly by some pathogen; for example, in the cowpea group several genera are susceptible to the bacterial spot disease. Using a variety of reactions (including precipitin reactions and the Schultz-Dale technique) these investigators found that in general the serological responses were in agreement with cross-inoculation grouping. In the same paper a summary of previous serological investigations of some genera indicated agreement with the cross-inoculation group disposition of the genera, and these investigations offered some support for the validity of the serological method. A final precaution was taken to establish that the reaction involved host-plant antigens rather than bacterial antigens. Legume-seed antisera did not agglutinate the corresponding nodule inhabiting bacteria.

Recent botanical investigations in systematic serology at Rutgers University begin with the work of Baum (1954) on the Cucurbitaceae and by Johnson (1953, 1954) on the Magnoliaceae. Subsequently, Hammond (1955a, 1955b) reported on serological investigations in the Solanaceae and Ranunculaceae, and Fairbrothers (Fairbrothers and Johnson, 1959; Fairbrothers and Bouletta, 1960) has investigated some grasses and certain species of the Umbelliferae. Since these investigations are quite similar in methodology and approach, and in general do not introduce highly controversial interpretations, only the Johnson work and the Hammond work on the Ranunculaceae will be discussed.

In Johnson's serological investigation of the Magnoliaceae several genera were compared with *Magnolia* and then several species of *Magnolia* were compared to establish intrageneric serological relationships. The serological data are shown in Table 5-1. It has been noted that the precipitin reaction was, in the Rutgers laboratory, derived from calculating the area under the curve of photronreflectometer readings at various antigen dilutions. At the generic level the contention that *Magnolia, Michelia,* and *Talauma* form a natural

Table 5-1. Results of titrating, with the photronreflectometer, antisera against four species of *Magnolia* with antigens from several species of the genus (Johnson, 1953). By permission of the *Serological Museum.*

Antiserum	Species	Homologous Area	Heterologous Area	Het. Area Homol. Area per cent
M-14-1a (1 + 1)	*Magnolia kobus* DC.	353		
	M. acuminata L.		279	79.2
	M. tripetala L.		244	69.2
	M. virginiana L.		240	68.1
	M. portoricensis Bello		129	36.6
#3 (1 + 1)	*Magnolia tripetala* L.	332		
	M. obovata Thunb.		308	92.7
	M. kobus DC.		250	75.3
	M. virginiana L.		240	72.3
	M. acuminata L.		214	64.5
	M. portoricensis Bello		178	53.6
9-1 (1 + 2)	*Magnolia portoricensis* Bello	406		
	M. obovata Thunb.		274	67.5
	M. tripetala L.		267	65.8
R-1 (1 + 1)	*Magnolia obovata* Thunb.	327		
	M. tripetala L.		304	93
	M. portoricensis Bello		202.5	61.9

group is supported by the data, while *Liriodendron* is relatively distant, serologically, and *Illicium,* which has been removed from the Magnoliaceae by some investigators on anatomical grounds, gave no reaction. *Illicium* was shown to produce a highly reactive antiserum, when tested against homologous serum, so that the lack of reaction with *Magnolia virginiana* antiserum is not due to generally low antigen content. It is notable that McLaughlin (1933) placed the genus in the *Hamamelidaceae.* However, *Disanthus,* in this latter family, gave no reaction with *Illicium,* perhaps supporting its treatment by some taxonomic workers as a monotypic family, Illiciaceae.

At the species level the data suggest a closer serological relationship between the Asiatic species, *Magnolia obovata* and the American species, *M. tripetala* than between the latter and two other American species, *M. acuminata* and *M. virginiana. Magnolia portoricensis* (Table 5.1) is farthest removed from all species, and, according to Johnson, there is some morphological evidence to support its separation as a single species of a separate sub-genus.

Other data presented by Johnson indicate that inter-specific differences in *Magnolia* surpass the inter-generic differences in certain cases. For example, the heterologous reaction between *Magnolia tripetala* and *M. portoricensis* is 53.6 while the heterologous reaction between *Magnolia virginiana* and *Michelia champaca* is 83.0. In fact, the latter heterologous reaction is greater than many heterologous reaction among species of *Magnolia* tested against *M. tripetala* antisera. Since, apparently, similar procedure was used in all cases, it is difficult to account for this apparent paradox, even when it is recognized that different host animals were used which may differ in their antibody responsiveness. The same type of situation is noted in Baum's work. Unfortunately no explanation of this is presented in the original publications. In this connection an interesting statement in a discussion of serological work on songbirds seems pertinent:

> An additional point to consider in the interpretation of these [serological] tests is that the techniques used tend to separate more sharply species that are closely related, while species distantly related are not so easily separated. In other words, comparative serological studies with the photronreflectometer tend to minimize the differences between distant relatives and to exaggerate the differences between close relatives. (Stallcup, 1961.)

This remarkable statement provides for a somewhat confusing situation wherein, in the interpretation of data, one doesn't know whether to consider two species farther apart or closer together than the data indicate. If Stallcup's generalization is supportable, then certain taxa, of problematical familial alliance, such as *Hydrastis* (to be discussed below), would be almost incapable of placement by serological results.

Hammond (1955b) compared a number of genera in the Ranunculaceae on the basis of their serological interactions, and this criterion, together with cytological and morphological data, was used to produce a new systematic treatment of the genera. According to Hammond the family is "serologically close-knit," and he considers this observation to be in contradistinction to the generally held viewpoint that certain genera of the family are relicts of ancient evolutionary lines and thus genetically quite distinctive. The basis of Hammond's statement is, however, not clear, since only a few families of flowering plants had been studied at that time, and furthermore a number of genera which he tested gave no reaction to the antiserum. Hammond produced a three-dimensional model to depict the serological relationships within the Ranunculaceae. Notable among his conclusions is the placement of *Hydrastis* into the Ranunculaceae on the basis of a positive reaction with *Aquilegia* antiserum. *Hydrastis* has

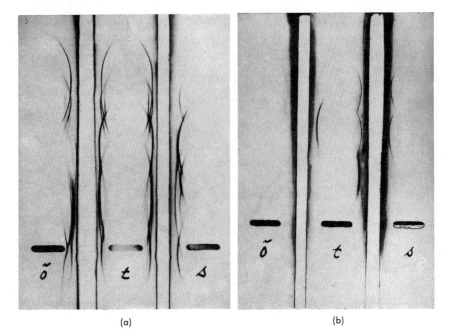

(a)   (b)

Fig. 5-2. Immunoelectrophoretic patterns: (a) unadsorbed anti-rye-wheat serum (in trough) against rye (right), rye-wheat hybrid (center), and wheat (left); (b) adsorbed antirye-wheat serum against rye (right), rye-wheat hybrid (center), and wheat (left) (Hall, 1959). By permission of *Hereditas*.

been placed by some systematists into the Berberidaceae. Alkaloid chemistry presents another line of biochemical evidence relevant to the placement of *Hydrastis,* but in this case the biochemical affinities are with the Berberidaceae. This question will be considered further in a subsequent chapter devoted to the alkaloids.

The immunogenetic studies of M. R. Irwin and his colleagues and students at Wisconsin are well-known, and these have been alluded to briefly in the preceding chapter. Further consideration of this significant work is included in the later chapter on biochemical studies of hybrids.

A serological method which, in contrast to the straight pre-cipitin reaction, is qualitative in nature has been utilized to advantage in animal systematic investigations and to some extent in plant studies. In principle this technique, known as immunoelectrophoresis, is similar to the other serological methods. Extracts of seeds or other plant material are prepared and then subjected to agar-gel electro-phoresis. As described by Hall (1959), in one modification, parallel troughs are cut into the agar along the electrophoretic track between each sample, and antiserum is poured in (Fig. 5-2). The antigens and antibodies diffuse into the agar, and when they meet, corresponding antigens and antibodies form stabilized precipitates in the shape of arcs which may be detected by appropriate methods.

A recent botanical study involving the immunoelectrophoretic technique is that of Gell, Hawkes, and Wright (1960) on the genus *Solanum*. They studied the gel diffusion patterns of fifteen Mexican and twenty-two South American species of this genus. Since the antisera were relatively ineffective in distinguishing the South American species, only the fifteen Mexican species will be discussed. The latter species are arranged into seven series according to Hawkes' systematic treatment. (He divided the tuberous solanums into seventeen series, some of which are listed below.)

III.   Morelliformia
          S. morelliforme

IV.   Bulbocastana
          S. bulbocastanum

V.   Cardiophylla
          S. cardiophyllum
          S. ehrenbergii
          S. sambucinum

VI.   Pinnatisecta
          S. pinnatisectum
          S. jamesii

XII.   Demissa
          S. demissum
          S. guerreroense
          S. semidemissum
          S. spectabile
          S. verrucosum

XIII. Longipedicellata
          S. polytrichon
          S. stoloniferum

XIV. Polyadenia
          S. polyadenium

In the preparation of the extracts from the tubers the crude juices were adjusted to yield a protein concentration of 0.5 per cent. Antisera were prepared from rabbits.

With an antiserum prepared from *S. tuberosum* the Mexican species could be divided into three groups: one gave four precipitin lines, another two lines, and the third one line. (All South American species give reactions similar to *S. tuberosum.*) One aberrant epiphytic species, *S. morelliforme,* yielded only one line, but in addition this line could not be further resolved into two lines as was the case with a precipitin line in a similar position in the other fourteen species. Therefore, serologically, *S. morelliforme* appeared farthest removed from *S. tuberosum.* In some comparisons, notably in strains of *S. polytrichon,* differences within a species proved greater than those between species.

Species of Series V and VI without exception yielded two lines with *S. tuberosum* antiserum and further showed a similar pattern against antiserum of one of the Series V species (namely *S. ehrenbergii*) and even a moderately close relationship to species of Series IV and XIII. Thus the authors consider Series V and VI to be a linking group between the two pairs of series mentioned.

All other species were grouped together when tested against *S. tuberosum,* but against *S. ehrenbergii* (preadsorbed with *S. tuberosum*) only *S. tuberosum, S. verrucosum* and *S. semidemissum* were placed together (showing no precipitin lines).

Series XII, XIII, and XIV, which gave four-line patterns against *S. tuberosum,* have in common an important morphological feature, the rotate or wheel-shaped corolla, while the other series have a stellate corolla type. (South American species have, also, the rotate corolla.) Furthermore, crosses within Series XII, XIII, and Series Tuberosa can be made as well as between Tuberosa and various South American species. Series Bulbocastana, which also gave a four-line pattern with Tuberosa, is exceptional in that it does not hybridize with species of the other Series readily. Finally, Series V and VI, giving the two-line spectrum, are fairly interfertile. Although the results should prove to be interesting, reaction patterns to specific antisera of all species concerned were not reported.

In general, the serological data from *Solanum* follow rather closely the patterns of morphology and hybridization. The fact that the type of serological methods used by these authors provides a pattern in accord with other lines of evidence lends validity to the use of the method in systematic studies. It is interesting that immunoelectrophoretic studies generally yield only a relatively few arcs of interaction, even though no preadsorption is carried out. From precipitin reactions one gains the impression that a large number of antigen-antibody interactions are involved in a single precipitin reaction. It is probably that in immunoelectrophoresis, when crude extracts are used, only the major constituents in the serum are in sufficient quantity to yield a visible reaction, and antigens of an enzyme nature are not detected.

Somewhat similar work on the legume genus *Phaseolus* has been done by Kloz (1962), but the number of species investigated at this time (four) is too few to allow significant conclusions. However, apparently significant serological differences exist, and it is likely that the more extensive analysis in progress will provide further insight into the relationships of the species in this genus.

Earlier in this section it was stated that even in the 1920's differences of opinion existed between the Königsberg and Berlin serologists as to whether there were serological differences within a plant, that is, whether different organs were serologically distinct. Recently Kloz *et al.* (1960) have demonstrated unequivocally that such differences exist and indeed often exceed inter-specific serological differences. These workers compared the antigenic substances from cotyledons, "subcotyledonous" parts (roots) of seedlings, and mature leaves in *Phaseolus vulgaris, P. coccineus, Glycine soja* and *Vicia faba.* They employed essentially the technique of the Rutgers group. Some of their precipitin results (in per cent) are given below.

Phaseolus vulgaris (antiserum of cotyledons against sera from cotyledons of the following species):

P. vulgaris	100
P. coccineus	88.2
Glycine soja	3.4
Vicia faba	1.8

Phaseolus vulgaris (antiserum of leaves against sera from leaves of the following species):

P. vulgaris	100
P. coccineus	89.7
Glycine soja	41.7
Vicia faba	19.9

Comparison between serological properties of individual organs of the same species, data taken from *P. vulgaris.*

Antiserum against cotyledons tested against sera from the following sources:

cotyledons	100
subcotyledons	8.9
leaf	5.2

Antiserum against subcotyledonous tissue of seedlings against sera from the following sources:

subcotyledons........................... 100
leaf.................................... 23.7

Antiserum against leaf tissue tested against sera from the following sources:

leaf.................................... 100
subcotyledons........................... 53.4
cotyledons.............................. 8

There is no question but that there are serological differences among the organs investigated. Kloz *et al.* stated that the protein characters of cotyledons (reserve proteins) showed weakest cross reactions between species of different genera, indicating that generic differences were more pronounced in these organs. These authors presented the hypothesis that the protein characters of the subcotyledonous and leaf tissues are phylogenetically older than storage protein of the cotyledons and therefore emphasize the common origin of taxa more than do characters which have undergone differentiation at later stages of evolution. Although the hypothesis is interesting and, if valid, of theoretical importance, it may be an oversimplification. Presumably, in this instance what one is measuring are differences which parallel and reflect the evolution of several genera of a single tribe at a time when the cotyledons had already made their evolutionary appearance. It is therefore possible that in some cases more subsequent specialization appeared in organs such as leaves than appeared in cotyledonous proteins. In any event, the major point, that serological differences exist among different tissues within a plant, should not be obscured by further attention to the second question.

Wright (1960) has refined, further, investigation of organ specific antigens. By combining ultracentrifugation and immunodiffusion he was able to demonstrate an antigen in the microsome fraction of three-day old coleoptile tissue of wheat. In order to exclude non-microsomal antigens, the antiserum was first absorbed with the supernatant of the microsome fraction. The precipitin band associated with the microsome fraction of three-day coleoptile tissue was absent from coleoptile tissue of a younger age and from root and leaf tissue. These data imply, in the words of the author, "that a non-organ specific meristematic pattern of antigens has superimposed upon it, during differentiation, a combination of proteins characteristic of differentiated cells."

In recent years there has been considerable interest in a modified serological method using relatively crude plant extracts to distinguish human blood types. Although an important motivating factor in this work is a rather practical consideration, namely, the commercial application of specific plant agglutinins in blood typing, there are in addition a number of intriguing problems of a fundamental nature involved (Boyd, 1960). Although this work is not widely known, even now, the first report of the existence of a plant agglutinin manifesting some degree of selectivity was made as early as 1888 when Stillmark noted that an extract from the seeds of the castor bean (*Ricinus communis*) agglutinated the red blood cells of animals selectively. Although occasionally some minor work was devoted to plant agglutinins, for the most part the subject was ignored until 1948 when Renkonnen at Helsinki revived interest in plant agglutinins with a survey of ninety-nine legume species, six of which showed definite affinity for either A or O blood types. Subsequently, numerous investigations have disclosed a large number of legume species which agglutinate red blood cells, sometimes with no antigenic specificity but frequently with definite specificity. No knowledge is available concerning the botanical function of the agglutinins which are usually, but not always, obtained from the seeds. By 1955 perhaps a thousand species of plants had been screened, and an overwhelming proportion of the species disclosed to be producers of "specific" agglutinins were in the family Leguminosae. The relevance of this work to biochemical systematics lies in the question of whether such investigations can disclose any meaningful patterns of distribution of agglutinins among the plant species.

Following the work by Renkonnen, selected examples of some important early surveys are those of Boyd and Reguera (1949) who studied 262 species from sixty-three families and Krupe (1953) who studied 167 species in the Leguminosae and, in addition, ninety-four different varieties of lima bean (*Phaseolus lunatus*). Krupe, for example, found some genera such as *Lathyrus* and *Phaseolus* which showed quite consistent agglutinin activity; that is, a large proportion of the species were active. Other genera, for example, *Caragana*, showed wide species differences. Species which specifically favored certain blood groups were recognized; for example, *Lotus tetragono-lobus* favored blood type O; *Vicia cracca* and *Phaseolus lunatus* favored blood type A; and *Sophora japonica* and *Coronilla varia* favored blood type B. By far the most comprehensive survey and general study of plant agglutinins, however, has been that of Mäkelä (1957), a student of Renkonnen, who studied 743 species of the family Leguminosae, including 165 genera. Thirty-seven per cent of the species studied contained agglutinins in their seeds, and a number of the agglutinins showed some degree of specificity. This work will be discussed in more detail later.

The technique used in testing for plant agglutinins is rather simple. Seeds are ground and extracted in saline, appropriately diluted, and then incubated at room temperature with a suspension of erythrocytes. The mixture is then examined for evidence of agglutination. Apparently the extracts are quite stable and may be retained for months without significant loss of activity. Mäkelä, who studied such parameters as temperature, salt content, and pH, reported a surprising tolerance for such an apparently specific reaction. For example, agglutination occurred over a fairly wide concentration of NaCl in the medium (though optimum results were obtained near the "physiological" range) and over a pH range from 5 to 11. Despite the simplicity of the technique there appears to be fairly good reproducibility, and some of the results are actually, in themselves, validation of the method. For example, Schertz et $al.$ (1960) reported that a specific hemagglutinating substance, "anti-A," from the lima bean is inherited as a simple Mendelian dominant. The F_1 of a cross between one high-activity parent and one inactive parent yielded seventy-two plants showing high activity, none showing no activity. The F_2 segregated essentially three active to one inactive. Furthermore, Morgan and Watkins (1956) have utilized specific plant agglutinins to show that the blood group antigen of type AB individuals is a unique molecule rather than a mixture of A and B substances.

There is no certain knowledge of the chemical nature of the plant agglutinins. Some investigators consider them to be mucoproteins. Rigas et $al.$ (1955) obtained a highly active mucoprotein fraction which, when hydrolyzed, yielded an inactive polysaccharide and a very active euglobulin. Presumably elimination of the polysaccharide enhanced activity of the protein. However, he does not believe that the term "antibody" is entirely appropriate and instead refers to the agglutinins as "lectins." Part of his objection to the use of "antibody" lies in the fact that their formation is not elicited as in the case of most animal antibodies. Some investigators consider that the plant agglutinins do not react with the same receptors as do the typical antibodies. The question is not completely settled, however. One argument in favor of a different mode of specificity for the plant agglutinins is that the plant agglutinins are neutralized in many cases by certain simple sugars while animal agglutinins are not. Mäkelä believes that the plant agglutinins accidently possess a configuration that is complementary to the chemical grouping of the blood group substances.

One point raised previously is of particular interest. It was stated that simple sugars may sometimes inhibit specific plant agglutinins. The first report of inhibition of this type was that of Watkins and Morgan (1952) who, in this case using anti-H agglutinin of eel serum, discovered that agglutination was inhibited by L-fucose. In addition to certain simple sugars, the sugar derivation N-acetyl-galactosamine inhibits anti-A, and anti-B agglutinins from a number of sources (Mäkelä, 1957). This observation acquires added signif-icance following the disclosure that N-acetyl-galactosamine is present in hydrolysates of blood (particularly high yields are derived from blood group A, lower yields in O, and practically none in B). It is suggestive of the presence of a carbohydrate-like terminal group on the antigen. A general theory to account for the inhibition of agglu-tinins by simple sugars is that the sugars resemble the reactive end group of a red blood cell receptor. The sugars then attach to the agglutinin complementary site blocking it and thereby preventing agglutinin-receptor contact. On the basis of the structural relation-ships of groups of sugars which are effective inhibitors as opposed to the ineffective sugars it has been suggested by Krupe (1956) that the configuration of carbon 3 and 4 is important in determining the ability of the sugar to inhibit agglutinins.

Four patterns available in placement of hydroxyl groups in carbons 3 and 4 of aldopyranoses.

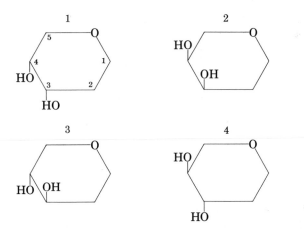

The more strongly inhibiting sugars fall into groups 1 and 2 above. For example inhibitors of anti-B extracts, such as L-arabinose and D-galactose, represent group 2. Inhibitors of anti-H extracts, such as D-arabinose, D-digitoxose, L-fucose, and L-galactose are of group

1. However, Mäkelä reported that some group 3 sugars such as D-glucose, D-mannose, and the ketose, D-fructose, strongly inhibited some other types of plant agglutinins.

In connection with the question of the systematic value of the plant agglutinins it is premature to attempt a final evaluation. Plant agglutinins have been found in a number of families of flowering plants, but it has already been noted that the Leguminosae have special proclivity toward the production of agglutinins. Yet the agglutinins are not common within the sub-families Mimosoideae and Caesalpinioideae of the family. The Mimosoideae are especially deficient (only a few species of the genus *Parkia* are positive). The extensive survey of the Leguminosae by Mäkelä has provided enough data to permit some generalizations to be made concerning the distribution of agglutinins within the legume family. It is obvious that only tendencies are disclosed by the data. That is, at most taxonomic levels the character tends not to be constant. For example, within the sub-family Papilionoideae only the tribes Podalyrieae and Trifolieae have not proved to have any agglutinins. The tribes Dalbergieae and Hedysareae are somewhat poor in agglutinins, but the rest of the tribes contain numerous agglutinin producers. In the tribes Phaseoleae and Galegeae, there is a great variation, but in the tribe Vicieae, which is particularly consistent, the large majority of species studied produce agglutinins. There is some apparent regularity of a qualitative nature with respect to the distribution of the agglutinins. For example, anti-H agglutinins are quite rare except in the tribe Genisteae where they are frequently encountered in the genera *Cytisus, Genista, Laburnum, Petteria,* and *Ulex,* though absent from some other genera in the tribe. Elsewhere, only the genus *Lotus,* of the tribe Loteae and *Virgilia* of the Sophoreae are known to produce anti-H agglutinins.

Mäkelä does not emphasize strongly the systematic aspect. He makes only a few general comments such as the following:

> The occurrence can be said to conform to the taxonomic plant system to some extent though by no means absolutely. Proofs of this are, in particular, the total absence of agglutinins in the seeds of certain tribes, e.g. Trifolieae, and the almost regular presence in the seeds of Viceae.

When data concerning the specificities of plant agglutinins are supplemented by further knowledge of their responses to various inhibitors, they may involve sufficient qualitative refinement to disclose a more meaningful pattern to the distribution of plant agglutinins than we now have. Some progress in this direction has been made, but the results so far have not given much cause for optimism.

For example, Mäkelä has combined specificities and inhibitor characteristics to distinguish two groups of genera as follows. Certain genera produce agglutinin which act upon rabbit cells but not guinea pig cells and are inhibited by certain sugars of group 2 (for example, D-galactose). Most of them contain also anti-A + B or anti-B agglutinins. Another group of genera produce agglutinins which act on rabbit cells but also on guinea pig cells. These agglutinins are inhibited by group 3 sugars (for example, D-glucose). Genera falling into the former class are *Bandeiraea, Sophora, Crotalaria, Cytisus, Caragana,* and *Coronilla.* Genera of the second group are *Lathyrus, Lens, Pisum, Vicia,* and possibly *Parkia.* It is evident to taxonomists that the two groups do not fall neatly into any systematic order. In fact, the groups individually overlap even the sub-family level, and each group includes a number of tribes, some of which are represented by species in both groups. There is reason, however, in the opinion of the writers, to expect the plant agglutinins to be systematically important, if not at the tribal level then at least at the genus level. Since it has been shown that the presence of at least one agglutinin is genetically controlled, by that fact alone there is established a rational basis for their distribution which is phylogenetic in principle.

In the preceding chapter an example from zoological studies and one from botanical studies were utilized to illustrate biochemical systematics approaches which provided significant information but which did not represent, entirely, correlations of the distribution of a compound with a taxonomic system (for example, Vogel's investigation of lysine synthesis and Wald's investigation of the visual pigments). Although it was not intended that this establish a precedent for later chapters, in a general discussion of the possible role (including the future role) of serology in phylogenetic studies it is useful to review briefly one or two special applications of serology which, although not directly relevant to systematics, nevertheless indicate some of the possibilities of the method. In general, some of the limitations of the gross quantitative serological method are obviated when refined genetic stocks are available and appropriate preadsorption is utilized. Since the genetic knowledge of the materials to be discussed below is more complete than that of earlier studies, the implications of the work seem to have greater validity. Again, one example is drawn from plant studies and one from animal studies.

The first example treats serological investigations of a series of four pollen incompatibility alleles (S_2, S_3, S_4, and S_6) of *Oenothera organensis* carried out by Lewis (1952). Preadsorption was utilized not only to precipitate common protein antigens not connected with the S-factors, but also to provide, artificially, what are referred to as "half-homologous" extracts. For example, if one wishes to form a half-homologous antiserum to a plant of the genotype S_{2-3}, an antiserum is prepared against S_{2-3} serum and pre-adsorbed with S_{2-4} serum. In the first reaction the common proteins, including the S_2 antigen are precipitated, leaving in the antiserum, presumably, only the S_3 antibodies. Another S_{2-3} pollen extract is then said to be "half-homologous" with the antiserum, and an S_{2-6} extract is said to be "heterologous." In the latter case no reaction, or at most a very slight reaction, may be expected. The results of a series of cross reactions are shown in Fig. 5-3. The figures within the squares represent the time, in minutes, required to form a precipitin ring; therefore the lower values indicate the stronger reaction. A blank indicates that the reaction was not recorded. Certain inconsistencies are presumed to result from extraneous genic differences in the material since the stocks were not isogenic. However, these gene differences were obviously not sufficient to prevent generally good correlations.

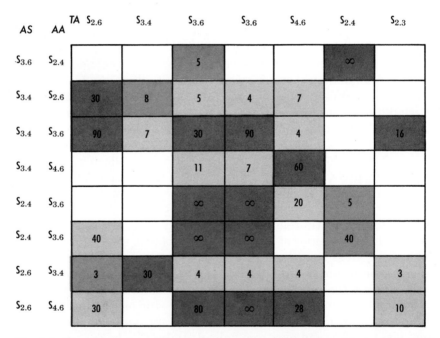

AS	AA	TA $S_{2.6}$	$S_{3.4}$	$S_{3.6}$	$S_{3.6}$	$S_{4.6}$	$S_{2.4}$	$S_{2.3}$
$S_{3.6}$	$S_{2.4}$			5			∞	
$S_{3.4}$	$S_{2.6}$	30	8	5	4	7		
$S_{3.4}$	$S_{3.6}$	90	7	30	90	4		16
$S_{3.4}$	$S_{4.6}$			11	7	60		
$S_{2.4}$	$S_{3.6}$			∞	∞	20	5	
$S_{2.4}$	$S_{3.6}$	40		∞	∞		40	
$S_{2.6}$	$S_{3.4}$	3	30	4	4	4		3
$S_{2.6}$	$S_{4.6}$	30		80	∞	28		10

Fig. 5-3. Time in minutes to form a ring precipitate at $\frac{1}{5}$ dilution of test antigen (TA). Antiserum is designated AS, and the adsorbing antigen is designated AA.

   ■ = Heterologous antigen, that is, no **S** alleles common to test antigen and adsorbed serum.

   ▨ = Completely homologous, that is, both **S** alleles common to test antigen and adsorbed serum.

   ▢ = Half-homologous, that is, one **S** allele common to test antigen and adsorbed serum.

   □ = Untested combinations.

The original purpose of the investigation was to discover, if possible, the nature of the mechanism by which diploid pollen (from tetraploids) carrying two different S alleles was not inhibited. If the interaction fails to produce the "S-substances" or if a new product with new specificity was produced under such circumstances, this might be disclosed by the serological method. However, Lewis did not consider the tests sensitive enough to yield valid results. Linskins (1960) reported results similar to those of Lewis in a study of three S alleles in *Petunia* hybrids. It is obvious that methods analogous to those of Lewis, and to some extent Irwin (that is, the gene homologies in certain birds), might be applied successfully to a study of gene homology in related species. The critical point is to be able to pre-adsorb in such a fashion as to leave in the antiserum a designated single antibody which can then be used to screen other species.

In the second example, Fox (1949) employed a serological method to study specific eye color mutants of *Drosophila*. Using isogenic stocks, he analyzed serologically various combinations of the mutants, ruby and vermilion, along with the wild type. By means of selective adsorption such as described above Fox showed that vermilion antiserum and the double mutant, ruby-vermilion, antiserum were serologically equivalent. He inferred that the normal allele at the ruby locus further modifies an "antigen" dependent upon the wild type allele of vermilion. Therefore, in the presence of the vermilion allele the normal allele at the ruby locus cannot effect the modification, and consequently in the vermilion phenotype no serological difference between Rb (normal allele of ruby) and rb could be detected. If the antigens are indeed enzymes and if the conclusions are valid, this is yet another example of gene interaction to produce a single enzyme, an exception to the classic one-gene, one-enzyme hypothesis. (Of course, in these days, when the gene is becoming almost as difficult to define as a species and virologists are threatening to reduce the "unit of crossing-over" to as little as two nucleotide pairs (Benzer, 1957) such aphoristic generalizations are inviting targets anyhow.)

The examples just discussed do not by any means represent all of the instances in which serological methods have been applied to the study of specific enzymes or genetic factors. Several other studies of this nature have been noted by Moritz (1958).

In summary, there is reason to believe that serological techniques, especially those utilizing immunogenetic methods (in general, restricted to the lower taxonomic categories), will make important contributions to systematics. Immunoelectrophoresis, however it may be applied, presents in addition a distinct advance over earlier techniques in that a qualitative element is introduced, and this technique may be expected to become increasingly significant. Modifications of the strictly quantitative precipitin tests, even with increased sensitivity, seem to possess some inherent limitations. As a general criticism it appears that proponents of the precipitin methods have expended tremendous effort in the development of techniques without exerting equivalent efforts to set up critical "test" experiments or to pursue the theoretical aspects of antibody-antigen reactions at the biochemical level.

6 AMINO ACIDS

Amino acids are generally recognized primarily in their role as structural units of proteins. The fact that amino acids may have additional important roles may not always be fully appreciated. There are already more non-protein than protein amino acids known, for example, and the ratio of non-protein to protein amino acids will increase as new amino acids are discovered (Fig. 6-1). Numerous ninhydrin positive substances, yet uncharacterized, are known. Most, if not all, of the protein amino acids are of little taxonomic value by virtue of their cosmopolitan distribution[1] while the non-protein acids are

[1] Eventually, however, as indicated previously, the structural sequence of protein amino acids may prove to be among the ultimate phylogenetic criteria.

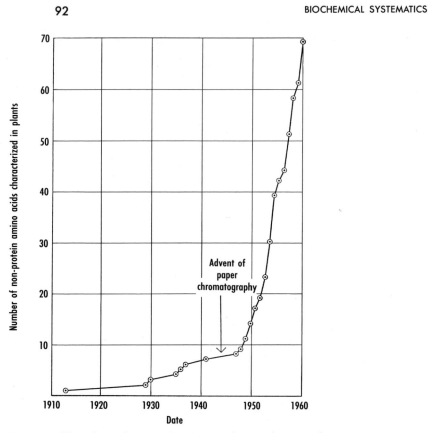

Fig. 6-1. The effect of paper chromatography on the rate of identification of new non-protein amino acids (Fowden, 1962).

often of somewhat more limited distribution and therefore may be effectively used as systematic characters.

Since the vast majority of the non-protein amino acids are probably not basic metabolites in the strict usage of the term, there is some question as to the appropriateness of including amino acids along with carbohydrates and lipids among basic metabolites. Whatever group of substances to which the amino acids may be more appropriately related, there are at least some historical reasons for beginning the treatment of specific classes of compounds with a chapter on amino acids.

The technique of paper chromatography, which has been primarily responsible for renewed interest in biochemical systematics, had its origin in studies of amino acids (Consden *et al.,* 1944). Partly because development of new techniques in chromatography and refinements of older methods proceeded most rapidly in amino acid chemistry, chromatographic investigations of amino acids have greatly outnumbered similar investigations of other classes of compounds. Consequently, more workers are aware of the possible application of chromatography to the study of amino acids than perhaps any other group of compounds. Therefore, it is not surprising that some of the earliest investigations into the application of chromatographic techniques to systematics involved amino acid patterns. There is no indication in these early studies that there was careful consideration of the question of whether amino acids were, on apriori grounds, likely to be of greater systematic value than other classes of substances. As has already been noted amino acids are among the least useful classes of substances if one concentrates upon the approximately twenty amino acids of protein. Not only are these protein amino acids nearly always present in tissues but, in addition their absolute and even their relative concentrations are so closely dependent upon the physiological state of the moment and so sensitive to metabolic disturbances that their quantitative as well as qualitative relationships are likely to be of little systematic value. This last point will be discussed further in a later paragraph.

Before the advent of paper chromatography, the study of amino acids contributed very little data of taxonomic importance. Chromatographic techniques, however, not only provided new dimensions of study of the common amino acids (for example, comparisons of amino acids of individuals and accurate measurements of the concentrations of various free amino acids in a single root apex), but inadvertantly disclosed the presence of a variety of "new" amino acids. Fowden (1959) describes these latter compounds as "products of the chromatographic revolution." It should not be inferred that all of the non-protein amino acids owe their discovery to paper chromatography. In lists compiled by Vickery (1941) and Dunn (1943), prior to the development of chromatography, a number of suspected non-protein amino acids were included (though they were reported simply as not known to be constituents of protein). Each of these lists contained approximately fifty compounds, about twenty of which were the ubiquitous protein amino acids.

Table 6-1 illustrates some of the non-protein amino acids of plants and relates them structurally to protein amino acids when possible. At least one acid of column two is found in protein (α-aminoadipic acid is found in the protein of corn seeds) though it is more typically associated with non-protein amino acids.

New amino acids continue to be reported, and since 1958 some twenty or more additional amino acids have been characterized. Several new amino acids have been discovered in the Mimosaceae,

Table 6-1. Structural relationships between some protein and non-protein amino acids (Fowden, 1962).

Protein amino acid	Related non-protein amino acid	Occurrence in plants
Acidic		
HOOC CH₂ CH₂ CH(NH₂) COOH Glutamic acid	HOOC C(=CH₂) CH₂ CH(NH₂) COOH γ-Methyleneglutamic acid	Peanuts, tulips, and other random occurrences.
	HOOC CH₂ CH₂ CH₂ CH(NH₂) COOH α-Aminoadipic acid	Many plants.
Amides		
H₂N OC CH₂ CH₂ CH(NH₂) COOH Glutamine	H₂N OC C(=CH₂) CH₂ CH(NH₂) COOH γ-Methyleneglutamine	Peanuts, tulips, and other random occurrences.
H₂N OC CH₂ CH(NH₂) COOH Asparagine	(C₂H₅)HN OC CH₂ CH(NH₂) COOH N-Ethylasparagine	Cucurbitaceae.
Basic		
CH₂(NH₂) CH₂ CH₂ CH₂ CH(NH₂) COOH Lysine	CH₂(NH₂) CH₂ CH(NH₂) COOH α, γ-Diaminobutyric acid	Solomon's seal (*Polygonatum* sp.).
Hydroxy		
CH₃ CH(OH) CH(NH₂) COOH Threonine	CH₂(OH) CH₂ CH(NH₂) COOH Homoserine	Peas and many other plants.
Aromatic		
[benzene ring] CH₂ CH(NH₂) COOH Phenylalanine	HO–[benzene ring, OH, CH₃]–CH₂ CH(NH₂) COOH 2,4-Dihydroxy-6-methylphenylalanine	Seeds of *Agrostemma githago*.
Heterocyclic		
[imidazole ring] C CH₂ CH(NH₂) COOH Histidine	[pyrazole ring] N CH₂ CH(NH₂) COOH β-Pyrazol-1-ylalanine	Cucurbitaceae, especially seeds.

Sulphur-containing
HS CH₂ CH(NH₂) COOH
Cysteine

$CH_3\ S\ CH_2\ CH(NH_2)\ COOH$
S-Methylcysteine — *Phaseolus vulgaris* seeds; *Neurospora crassa.*

Imino acid

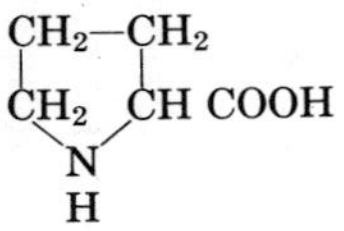

CH₂—CH₂
CH₂ CH COOH
  N
  H
Proline

CH₂
CH₂ CH COOH
 N
 H
Azetidine-2-carboxylic acid — Liliaceae.

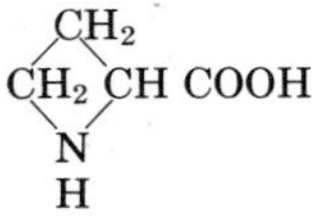

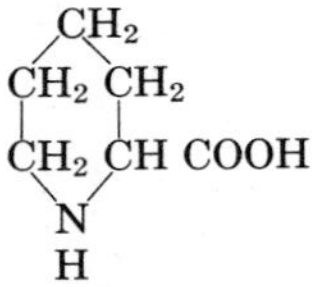

CH₂
CH₂ CH₂
CH₂ CH COOH
 N
 H
Pipecolic acid — Legumes and many other random occurrences.

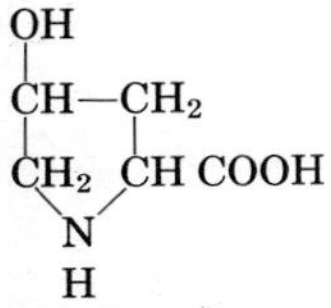

OH
CH—CH₂
CH₂ CH COOH
  N
  H
Hydroxyproline

CH₂
HO CH CH₂
CH₂ CH COOH
 N
 H
5-Hydroxypipecolic acid — Dates, ferns, and legumes.

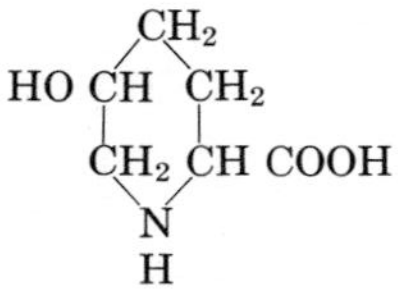

Cyclopropyl acids
No equivalent

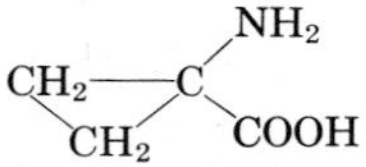

NH₂
CH₂—C—COOH
CH₂
1-Aminocyclopropane-1-carboxylic acid — Unripe fruits of apple and pear.

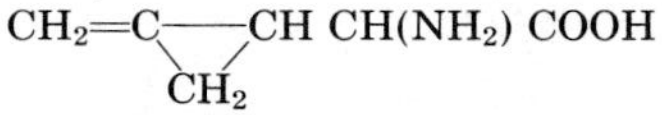

CH₂=C—CH CH(NH₂) COOH
   CH₂
α-(Methylenecyclopropyl) glycine — Seeds of litchi (*Litchi chinensis*).

particularly in the genus *Acacia* (Gmelin, 1959; Virtanen and Gmelin, 1959; Gmelin *et al.*, 1959; Gmelin and Hietala, 1960). New amino acids have been identified in *Lathyrus* species (Bell, 1961); in *Reseda* (Larsen and Kjaer, 1962); in *Allium* (Virtanen and Matikkala, 1960); in *Ecballium* (Gray and Fowden, 1961); in crown gall tissue (Biemann *et al.*, 1960); and in a red alga (Kuriyama *et al.*, 1960. Even a selenium-containing amino acid has been identified in *Astragalus* (Trelease *et al.*, 1960). These amino acids fall into several different chemical sub-types.

Although at present, the majority of these newly discovered non-protein amino acids are known to occur in only a few plants, Fowden (1962) has noted that one still cannot detect trace amounts, and it may be that their distributions are far more extensive than now suspected. Steward *et al.* (1955) stated that eighty-one ninhydrin reactive substances found in the non-protein portion of various plant extracts did not correspond to any of the known amino acids.

SYSTEMATIC STUDIES INVOLVING AMINO ACIDS

One of the first taxonomic studies employing chromatography of amino acids was that of Buzzati-Traverso and Rechnitzer (1953). In this brief paper the authors compared the chromatographic patterns of fish muscle protein hydrolysates from different species. The amino acids themselves were not identified, and the chromatograms showed few spots, but it was evident that differences in the patterns occurred. It is strange, in view of the general occurrence of twenty amino acids in protein that, in protein hydrolysates, many of the twenty amino acids were missing. According to the authors the amino acid patterns of species regarded as more closely related by other criteria were more alike chromatographically, and they further maintained that stocks from geographical races of the same species could sometimes be distinguished. Although the authors forecast wide use of chromatography in population and genetic studies, little work of this type on fish has appeared subsequently. Vismanathan and Pillai (1956) repeated, essentially, the work of Buzzati-Traverso and Rechnitzer, in a study of sardines, but the results contributed nothing to the systematics of the group.

Another paper by Buzzati-Traverso (1953) has gained considerable attention. The work is not primarily systematic and does not even treat exclusively the amino acids. However, implications of the work, if substantiated, bear directly upon the sensitivity of the chromatographic method and indirectly upon applications of similar types of investigations to systematics. Although Buzzati-Traverso's work included examination of fluorescent substances in addition to amino acids, the former class was probably a rather heterogeneous assemblage of undefined substances. These may be considered here since the principles concerned are independent of the nature of the compounds compared. Fruit flies (*Drosophila*) were studied intensively, but Buzzati-Traverso also included some plant studies, as will be disclosed. The flies were fed a standard diet and chromatographed by mashing the individual flies directly on paper. It was not stated that the *Drosophila* compared were isogenic. The ninhydrin patterns (revealing amino acids) of different *Drosophila* strains were said to be similar, but with respect to fluorescent spots, males and females exhibited distinct differences. Since later work by Fox (1956) on sex differences in *Drosophila* elaborates this point somewhat, and will in turn be discussed, no description of these sex differences is necessary here. Of more importance for this discussion are the results of Buzzati-Traverso's comparisons of a series of mutants with corresponding wild type flies. As a background, it should be noted that Hadorn and Mitchell (1951) had undertaken a chromatographic study of fluorescent patterns of *Drosophila* mutants in eye color and body color. Although conspicuous changes in the fluorescent patterns occurred in different developmental stages, Hadorn and Mitchell, in their early work reported no significant differences in the fluorescent patterns of either eye color or body color mutants, as opposed to wild type, at any stage examined. More recently, however, with improved chromatographic techniques for the separation of pteridines (which include the *Drosophila* eye pigments), distinctive chromatographic differences are now correlated with a number of eye color mutants (Hadorn, 1962). Buzzati-Traverso used a group of morphological mutants rather than biochemical mutants (that is, the overt phenotypic expression was morphological rather than biochemical). By Buzzati-Traverso's interpretation of his results each of the strains tested gave a distinctive fluorescent pattern, and each genotype had a characteristic biochemical pattern. According to the author the heterozygotes could always be detected, though the morphological expression of the gene indicated dominance. The present writers, after examining the illustrations in the Buzzati-Traverso paper, have some reservations concerning his interpretation. It appears possible, if not probable, that the pattern differences were in part artifact. In some cases, for example, two patterns may appear to be different, but by our interpretation the only difference that is apparent is a shifting of the Rf values of the same series of spots upward in certain cases. Perhaps, in the photographic reproduction the details were lost, but on the basis of the evidence presented, certainly no clear-cut differences can be detected.

On the basis of previous results and on theoretical grounds, differences such as those reported are indeed surprising, though Buzzati-Traverso did not indicate this to be so. For example, Hadorn and Mitchell did not detect differences in the heterozygote, and those authors were studying *biochemical* mutants.[2] In the Buzzati-Traverso work in which a series of *morphological* mutants were compared, it is remarkable that of a small number of unidentified fluorescent substances, one or more of them are invariably affected, quantitatively or qualitatively by each mutation. It is even more surprising that the heterozygotes could be detected chromatographically. In general when a biochemical mutant is dominant (for example, a flower color factor) one can scarcely detect the heterozygote even by sensitive quantitative methods. Dominance may be above 90 per cent in the majority of such cases.

Similarly Buzzati-Traverso reported that a recessive mutant of tomato had two fluorescing spots not present in the wild type strain. However, in this case the fluorescent pattern of the heterozygote was similar to that of the double recessive, but its ninhydrin pattern was intermediate. Finally, in a yellow-green mutant of muskmelon the chlorophyll content of the heterozygote could not be distinguished from the homozygous dominant, but the ninhydrin pattern of the heterozygote was indistinguishable from that of the double recessive. The writers consider that the interpretation given by Buzzati-Traverso to his results is not necessarily the only interpretation which is plausible, since the photographs resemble closely anomalies we have sometimes observed in our experiences with paper chromatography.

Interesting work on the comparative fluorescent patterns of male and female *Drosophila* has been reported by Fox (1956). He was principally concerned with whether any biochemical differences could be attributed to the presence of the Y chromosome. Therefore, he compared males and females chromatographically and then compared normal (XX) females and females carrying, in addition, a Y chromosome (XXY). These two types of females showed similar patterns, suggesting that the Y chromosome itself was not responsible for any overt biochemical effect. Of more significance to systematic investigations was the disclosure by Fox that, in isogenic stocks, striking differences in the fluorescent patterns of males and females occurred. Ten spots were common to males and females, but in all

---

[2] In the case of white eye, which is morphologically recessive, the chromatographic pattern of the heterozygote is distinguishable from the homozygote of either class, but this appears to be rather exceptional (Hadorn, 1962).

but one of these spots there were detectable quantitative differences. In addition there were seven spots peculiar to males and two spots peculiar to females. Some of these spots were probably the pteridines mentioned in Chapter 4.

Although Fox was not immediately concerned with potential systematic applications stemming from his work, it is possible that the comparative biochemistry of sex, could be extended profitably to other species and genera, or even higher taxa, of insects. In the present case a number of absolute sex-linked differences were recorded in one species, and a systematic extension of this comparison could hardly fail to provide valuable insight into relationships.

Micks (1954) applied amino acid chromatography to a study of certain mosquito species which are difficult to separate on morphological bases, and his illustrations of chromatographic differences are convincing. Later, Micks (1956) studied several different groups of insects, and again his illustrations of comparative ninhydrin patterns show distinctive differences at the order level (that is, in a comparison of certain Hemiptera, Diptera, and Orthoptera). Even three genera of cockroaches could be distinguished chromatographically. Within a single genus, however, any differences which were apparent were quantitative. Intrageneric qualitative differences in mosquito (*Culex*) had previously been reported by Ball and Clark (1953). These investigators found aspartic acid in *Culex quinquefasciatus* and *C. stigmatosoma,* though an extract five times as concentrated was used in the last named species. They also reported the unusual sulfonic amino acid, cysteic acid, in *C. tarsalis* and *C. stigmatosoma* but not in *C. quinquefasciatus.* Cysteic acid may possibly have arisen as an artifact by oxidation of cysteine. It is noteworthy that specimens of *C. quinquefasciatus* as widely separated as California and Texas were qualitatively identical, and Ball and Clark concluded that the interspecific differences were intrinsic, not environmental.

In other systematic zoological studies involving chromatography, Kirk *et al.* (1954) found that seven species of land snails could be distinguished by their fluorescent patterns. The pattern for a given species was the same regardless of diet or geographical location. A few other reports are scattered throughout the literature such as those of Möhlmann (1958) who studied fluorescent patterns of butterflies and Wright (1959) who studied mollusks of the genus *Lymnea* by similar methods. In summary, however, in the judgment of the present writers none of the papers in this series extends beyond the point of suggesting that chromatographic studies might be valuable in future taxonomic investigations. None was addressed to any specific problem or shed any light upon an actual systematic problem.

Botanical investigations of amino acid patterns, while initially lagging somewhat behind zoological studies, now seem to be providing even more information of direct taxonomic utility, probably because unusual amino acids are more often involved.

Bell (1962a) has recently examined forty-nine species of the legume genus, *Lathyrus,* and has presented data which appear to be potentially quite valuable in interpreting species affinities within the genus (compare the work of Pecket on the phenolics of *Lathyrus,* Chapter 11). A new guanidine amino acid (homoarginine) is present in seeds of thirty-six species; seven unidentified ninhydrin-reacting compounds in concentrations of the order of 1 per cent have been detected in the seeds of one or more species. Some of the substances are probably those responsible for the toxic condition known as neurolathyrism (Chapter 10), and others may be related to the lathyrus factors. Bell believes that these non-protein amino acids may constitute a highly concentrated form of nitrogen storage in leguminous seeds, and many of these amino acids, in fact, contain additional nitrogen. Although free amino acids are not typically found in the seeds of most plants in high concentration, the content of free amino acids in seeds of the Leguminosae is often high.

The most important immediately significant taxonomic conclusion from the work of Bell is contained in the following statement by the author:

> Within the genus there existed well defined groups of species that were characterized, not by the presence of an arbitrary concentration of one specific ninhydrin-reacting compound, but rather by the presence of associated groups of such compounds. These groups of associated compounds appeared as characteristic patterns after the seed extracts had been chromatographed or subjected to ionophoresis on paper. In the extracts of most, but not all, of the species examined the spots forming the characteristic patterns were of comparable size and intensity.

(Table 6-2 illustrates the grouping of *Lathyrus* species on the basis of the patterns described by Bell.)

Another recent systematic study of plant amino acids is that of Reuter (1957) who studied the principal forms of soluble nitrogen in various parts of sixty-six species representing forty-eight families (Fig. 6-2). Reuter did not exaggerate the systematic implications of the work. He noted that since the substances considered were frequently common metabolites of plants and animals, their relative quantities rather than strict presence or absence were of most significance. In some species the principal amino acids in various parts of

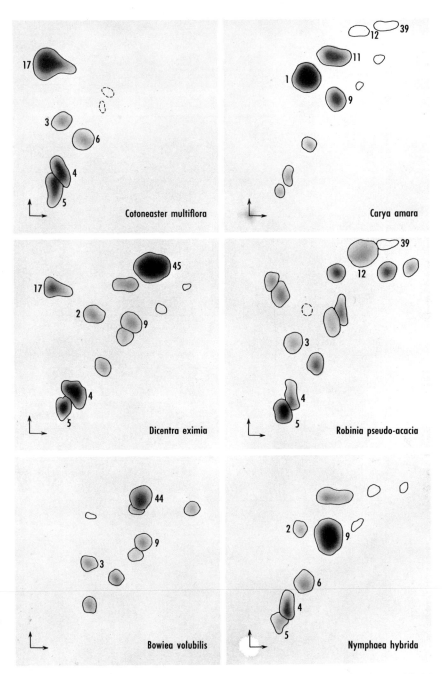

Fig. 6-2. Patterns of amino acids of storage organs of several plant species not considered to be closely related:

1. Citrullin	6. Serine	39. Piperidine-2-carboxylic acid
2. Glutamine	9. Alanine	44. Azetidine-2-carboxylic acid
3. Asparagine	11. Gamma-aminobutyric acid	45. Delta-acetylornithine
4. Glutamic acid	12. Proline	
5. Aspartic acid	17. Arginine	(Reuter, 1957)

Table 6-2. Ninhydrin-positive compounds present in seed extracts of *Lathyrus* species (Bell, 1962a). Reproduced from *The Biochemical Journal* with permission.

Group	No.	Name	$B_1{}^a$	B_2	B_3	B_4	B_5	N_1	N_2	N_3	A_1	A_2	A_3	Lathyrine	Arginine
1	1	*L. alatus*	++	.	.	.	.	.	.	.	++	.	.	.	T
	2	*L. articulatus*	++	.	.	.	.	.	.	.	++	.	.	.	T
	3	*L. arvense*	++	.	.	.	.	.	.	.	++	.	.	.	++
	4	*L. setifolius*	++	.	.	.	.	.	.	.	+++	.	.	.	T
	5	*L. pannonicus*	++	.	.	.	.	.	.	.	++	.	.	.	T
	6	*L. ochrus*	++	.	.	.	.	.	.	.	+++	.	.	.	T
	7	*L. clymenum*	++	.	.	.	.	.	.	.	T	.	.	.	T
	8	*L. sativus*	++	.	.	.	.	.	.	.	+	.	.	.	T
	9	*L. megallanicus*	++	.	.	.	.	.	.	.	T	.	.	.	T
	10	*L. quadrimarginatus*	++	.	.	.	.	.	.	.	T	.	.	.	T
	11	*L. cicera*	++	.	.	.	.	.	.	.	T	.	.	.	T
2	12	*L. sylvestris*	.	++	.	.	.	.	.	.	+	+	T	.	+++
	13	*L. latifolius*	.	++	.	.	.	.	.	.	+	+	T	.	++
	14	*L. heterophyllus*	.	++	.	.	.	.	.	.	+	+	T	.	++
	15	*L. gorgoni*	.	++	.	.	.	.	.	.	+	+	T	.	T
	16	*L. grandiflora*	.	++	.	.	.	.	.	.	+	+	T	.	T
	17	*L. cirrhosus*	.	++	.	.	.	.	.	.	+	+	T	.	++
	18	*L. rotundifolius*	.	++	.	.	.	.	.	.	+	+	T	.	++
	19	*L. tuberosus*	.	++	.	.	.	.	.	.	+	+	T	.	++
	20	*L. multiflora*	.	++	.	.	.	.	.	.	+T	+	.	.	+T
	21	*L. aurantius*	.	++	.	.	.	.	.	.	.	.	.	.	T
	22	*L. luteus*	.	++	.	.	.	.	.	.	.	.	.	.	T
	23	*L. laevigatus* subspecies *aureus*	.	++	.	.	.	.	.	.	.	.	.	.	T

Group	No.	Name	B_1	B_2	B_3	B_4	B_5	N_1	N_2	N_3	A_1	A_2	A_3	Lathyrine	Arginine
3	24	L. pratensis	++											T	
	25	L. laevigatus subspecies occidentalis	T											+	+
	26	L. varius	+												T
	27	L. niger	+											+	T
	28*	L. japonicus	+											+++	T
	29*	L. maritimus	+											++	T
	30*	L. aphaca	+		+									+	T
	31	L. sphaericus	+		+									+++	T
	32	L. tingitanus	+		+++									+++	T
	33	L. cyanus	+		+									++	
	34*	L. alpestris	+			+++			+++					+++	
	35*	L. variegatus	+			+++			+++					+++	
	36	L. venetus	+			+++			+++					++	
4	37*	L. incurvus	++						+					T	+
	38	L. vernus	+++						+					T	+
	39	L. montanus	+++						+++						+
	40	L. palustris	+++						+++						
	41	L. aureus	+++						+						T
	42	L. neurobolus	++						++						T
	43	L. nissolia	++						++						
5	44	L. roseus						T							T
	45	L. hirsutus						++							T
	46	L. odoratus	+					+						T	T
	47	L. venosus	+				+							T	T
	48	L. pisiformis	T												T
	49	L. annuus	T												T
	50	L. angulatus	T												T

ᵃThe letters B_1, B_2, etc., represent compounds whose isolation and identification are still incomplete. T, Trace. Glutamic acid and aspartic acid were detectable in all extracts. In the species marked with an asterisk glutamic acid occurred in more than trace amounts.

the same individual differed. Thus arginine was found to predominate in the lower stem in ash (*Fraxinus*), but moving toward the stem apex glutamic acid, asparagine, and glutamine in the order listed represented the main amino acids of corresponding positions.

The three acids found in high concentration in the stem apex (namely, glutamic acid, asparagine, and glutamine), plus asparatic acid, are consistently among the predominant amino acids of numerous plant species. These acids are probably among the first compounds into which amino nitrogen is incorporated. Asparagine is the amide of aspartic acid which, in turn is derived via transamination from the Krebs' cycle acid, oxaloacetic acid. Similarly, glutamine is an amide of glutamic acid, also derived via reductive amination of another Krebs' cycle acid, α-ketoglutaric acid.

Because of the metabolic position of these acids no special significance is attached to their prominant occurrence in a large number of species. Therefore, statements such as that by Korohoda *et al.* (1958) that glutamine, glutamic acid, and alanine are most characteristic of the genus *Brassica* have very little systematic significance. However, in certain cases less common amino acids appear to be consistently prominent in a family and thus are characteristic of the metabolism of that family. Some examples taken from Reuter (1957) are discussed below. It should be borne in mind, however, that rapid changes in amino acid content may accompany development, and the concept of "principal amino acid" should not be applied too vigorously.

Arginine, illustrated below, possesses the guanidine group:

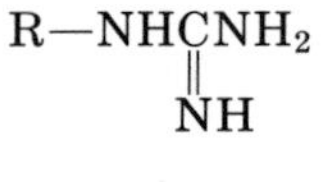

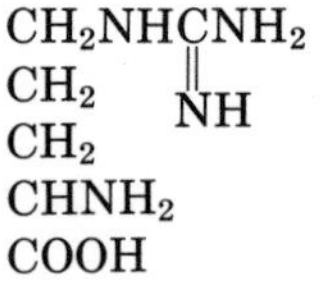

$$R-NH\underset{\overset{\|}{NH}}{C}NH_2$$

$$\begin{aligned} &CH_2NH\underset{\overset{\|}{NH}}{C}NH_2 \\ &CH_2 \\ &CH_2 \\ &CHNH_2 \\ &COOH \end{aligned}$$

Arginine is often present as a principal amino acid in the families Saxifragaceae, Hamamelidaceae, and Rosaceae, but its occurrence elsewhere as a principal amino acid is sporadic. It is noteworthy that other guanidine compounds are conspicuous in the family Rosaceae (Reuter also reported the presence of certain guanidine compounds) and in the one member of the family Hamamelidaceae which was tested, namely, *Parrotia persica*. Only a few members of the family Saxifragaceae were tested, and these were negative for guanidines other than arginine.

Citrulline, as indicated by its formula, is closely related to arginine. It was originally reported in the family Cucurbitaceae and is present in several members of the family. It rarely appears in Reuter's table except in the families Juglandaceae and Betulaceae wherein it is the chief acid in all eight genera tested. The former family is usually placed alone in the order Juglandales while the latter family is included with the Fagaceae in the order Fagales. Since citrulline is absent in the three genera of the Fagaceae tested, the distribution of this compound (as a principal amino acid) is significant.

$$CH_2NHCNH_2$$
$$CH_2 \quad \overset{\|}{O}$$
$$CH_2$$
$$CHNH_2$$
$$COOH$$

citrulline

A third acid, δ-acetylornithine, is probably the outstanding example cited by Reuter since it is restricted in the Papaverales to the sub-family Fumarioideae of the Papaveraceae where it was found to be present as the chief amino acid among all of the nineteen species (representing four genera) examined. It was not found as a principal amino acid in any of fifteen genera of the sub-family Papaveroideae tested although a small amount is present in *Hylomecon, Chelidonium majus,* and *Glaucium flavum.* In a later section, additional biochemical data bearing on the relationship between the Papaveroideae and the Fumarioideae will be presented and discussed (Chapter 9). δ-Acetylornithine also occurs in ferns (*Asplenium*) and grasses. Unusual amino acids which occur in widely separated taxa provide potential opportunities to study analogous enzymes or analogous biosynthetic routes as defined in a previous chapter, but they are not likely to have any direct systematic use at higher taxonomic levels.

$$CH_2NHCCH_3$$
$$CH_2 \quad \overset{\|}{O}$$
$$CH_2$$
$$CHNH_2$$
$$COOH$$

δ-acetylornithine

A fourth acid, proline, which was once considered to be somewhat rare, is now reported from a number of different species in the Leguminosae. Additional genera of other families, which have a high proline concentration, are *Taraxacum* (Compositae), *Mahonia* (Berberidaceae), *Eleagnus* (Eleagnaceae), *Tamarix* (Tamaricaceae), *Phellodendron* (Rutaceae), *Ailanthus* (Simarubaceae), and *Morus* (Moraceae).

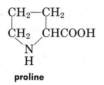

proline

Finally, azetidine-2-carboxylic acid which is a lower homolog of proline, seems to be typical of the Liliaceae where it is of rather widespread occurrence. This fact is not evident from Reuter's lists, but Fowden and Steward (1957a) reported the presence of this acid in seventeen of fifty-six genera of Liliaceae tested. Reuter also shows it as the principal amino acid in roots of *Convallaria majalis* (sometimes treated as a separate tribe [Hutchinson, 1959] or family [Gates, 1918] of the Liliaceae).

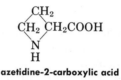

azetidine-2-carboxylic acid

Reuter has described a scheme of probable inter-conversion for the acids just considered which, if correct, suggests a rather close biochemical affinity for all. It is not likely that the distributions of these acids are of great taxonomic importance in themselves. The scheme of probable inter-conversion (slightly modified from Reuter) appears below:

```
                 ↗ glutamine                              ↗ citrulline → arginine
glutamic ↗→ glutamic semialdehyde → ornithine
       |                      ↘ proline          ↘ δ acetylornithine
       |
aspartic → aspartic semialdehyde → azetidine-2-carboxylic acid
       ↘ asparagine
```

When two acids such as proline and azetidine-2-carboxylic acid probably arise by analogous reactions of precursors differing by a single carbon, comparison of the enzymes involved should prove interesting. There is some likelihood that two enzymes responsible for such equivalent reactions are structurally related, perhaps even phylogenetically related (homologous). The same enzyme may catalyze both reactions, of course. Such a phenomenon exists in valine-iso-leucine synthesis in *Neurospora*.

A particularly interesting study of plant amino acids is that of Fowden and Steward (1957) who studied the amino acids of eighty-nine species representing fifty-six genera of the Family

Liliaceae (actually six genera were in the family Agavaceae and three in Amaryllidaceae, but all of these had at some time been placed in the family Liliaceae). Eighteen amino acids were of relatively common occurrence and need not be discussed beyond mention of the fact that methionine and histidine were notable by their absence. A total of fifty-four ninhydrin-positive but unidentified spots were detected. Most of these spots were restricted to one or at most only a few species, but little can be said concerning systematic implications of these distributions beyond the fact that they probably represent a reservoir of biochemical information to be utilized in the future.

Eight amino acids, representing a series of recently discovered types, all of which were identified, exhibit rather interesting patterns. Five of these represent an apparently related group, all of which may be conceived as derivatives of glutamic acid.[3]

$$\gamma\text{-Methyleneglutamic acid} \qquad \underset{\underset{NH_2}{|}}{\overset{\overset{CH_2}{||}}{HOOCCCH_2CHCOOH}}$$

$$\gamma\text{-Methyleneglutamine} \qquad \underset{\underset{NH_2}{|}}{\overset{\overset{CH_2}{||}}{H_2NOCCCH_2CHCOOH}}$$

$$\gamma\text{-Methylglutamic acid} \qquad \underset{\underset{NH_2}{|}}{\overset{\overset{CH_3}{|}}{HOOCCHCH_2CHCOOH}}$$

$$\gamma\text{-Hydroxy-}\gamma\text{-methylglutamic acid} \qquad \underset{\underset{OH \quad NH_2}{| \quad \;\;|}}{\overset{\overset{CH_3}{|}}{HOOCCCH_2CHCOOH}}$$

$$\gamma\text{-Hydroxyglutamic acid} \qquad \underset{\underset{OH \quad NH_2}{| \quad\;\; |}}{HOOCCHCH_2CHCOOH}$$

γ-Methyleneglutamic acid was reported from seven genera: *Tulipa, Erythronium, Haworthia, Lilium, Notholirion, Fritillaria,* and *Calochortus.* The acid is apparently characteristic of *Tulipa* wherein all species tested contained it. γ-Methylglutamic acid was found in six genera: *Tulipa* (most species), *Erythronium, Lilium, Notholirion, Calochortus,* and *Puschkinia.*

[3] γ-hydroxyglutamic acid, having a different carbon skeleton, may be excluded. The fact that its distribution pattern is also distinctive as opposed to the others of the group is then significant.

γ-Methyleneglutamine was reported only in the two genera, *Tulipa* and *Erythronium* but was present in all species of *Tulipa* examined.

γ-Hydroxy-γ-methylglutamic acid was found as traces in six genera including *Tulipa* (many species), *Erythronium, Littonia, Lilium, Calochortus,* and *Puschkinia.* γ-Hydroxyglutamic acid was found in only two genera: *Hemerocallis* and *Gasteria.*

The association of these unusual amino acids among certain related genera is of taxonomic significance. It is especially interesting that *Calochortus* contains two of the acids since Ownbey (1940) has stated that "the relationship of the genus [*Calochortus*] as a whole, although remote, is probably rather with the genus *Tulipa.*" Recently, Buxbaum (1958) established this genus as the single member of the new tribe, *Calochorteae.* However, Hutchinson (1959) retains *Calochortus* and related genera (*Erythronium, Fritillaria, Tulipa, Lloydia, Gagea, Notholirion, Lilium, Nomocharis,* and *Giraldiella*) in the more inclusive tribe *Tulipeae.* Using the amino acid criteria alone it would appear that Ownbey's comments are especially significant, and intensive chemical studies should contribute significant data to establish the phylogenetic affinities of the genera.

Two other acids, not derivatives of glutamic acid and hence not included in the natural group above, had a rather restricted distribution within the Liliaceae. One of these, hydroxyproline, was detected only in *Dracaena* (which is now placed in the family Agavaceae by many workers, Hutchinson, 1959). Another, azetidine-2-carboxylic acid, has already been discussed. Finally, pipecolic acid, the next higher analog of proline, appeared in nine genera, including *Hosta, Haworthia, Fritillaria, Chionodoxa, Hyacinthus, Muscari, Smilacina, Convalleria,* and *Maianthemum.*

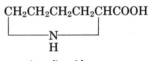

pipecolic acid

These distinctive glutamic acid derivatives seem to occur sporadically among widely separated taxa (for example, peanut, ferns, phlox). Fowden and Steward state that this distribution implies the genetic factors responsible do not operate at the generic or specific level; that is, "in short, the accumulation of any of these compounds may be determined by relatively few of the genes that characterize the organism." In other words, since the compounds are not restricted to a genus or species, their synthesis could not therefore depend upon the specific association of a large species-delimiting gene pool. A generation of studies of genetic control by biosynthesis has in fact already established this principle.

Fowden and Steward concluded from their study that numerous metabolic pathways, previously unexpected, existed. This conclusion certainly appears to be valid, since many yet unidentified compounds exist, and these offer further promise for comparative biochemical studies.

Birdsong *et al.* (1960) have reported on the distribution of the guanidine, canavanine, an amino acid found thus far only in the family Leguminosae. Within the family its appearance seems to be of definite taxonomic significance.

$$
\begin{array}{l}
\text{NH} \\
\quad \| \\
\text{ONHCNH}_2 \\
| \\
\text{CH}_2 \\
\text{CH}_2 \\
\text{CHNH}_2 \\
\text{COOH}
\end{array}
$$

canavanine

Prior to this study a total of sixty-eight species representing thirty-one genera had been analyzed by various workers, and Tschiersch (1959) was of the opinion that since canavanine appeared somewhat randomly in the family, its distribution had no taxonomic significance. Extension of the number of investigated species disclosed, however, that canavanine occurs only in the sub-family Papilionoideae, and of the tribes of that sub-family, it does not occur in Podylarieae and Sophoreae and is apparently rare in the tribe Genisteae. Canavanine is particularly common in the tribes Trifolieae and Loteae; all of seventeen species in these two tribes analyzed by Birdsong *et al.* contained canavanine. Przybylska and Hurich (1960) have reported the canavanine distribution in a few additional species, but the pattern of distribution is maintained. The lack of canavanine in the tribes Podylarieae and Sophoreae is interesting because independent chromosomal evidence suggests that these tribes are offshoots from the main Papilionoid stock (Turner and Fearing, 1959).

There is considerable circumstantial evidence that canavanine is an important metabolite in those plants in which it occurs; for example, it may be important in the storage and transport of nitrogen. If this is true, the distribution of canavanine should be more vigorously controlled by selection pressure, and therefore its distribution should have greater significance (that is, subsequent loss of ability to form canavanine would have negative survival value). The Birdsong *et al.*

study illustrates clearly the fact that in some cases a small sampling may not disclose a pattern of the distribution of a substance.

Another point of interest in the canavanine work is that certain large and diverse genera such as *Vicia, Astragalus,* and *Glycine* contain some species with canavanine present and some without. As noted in an earlier section, it is possible that those species lacking canavanine have, in certain cases, lost only one enzyme, specific for a single step. Therefore, two different species could have complementary deficiencies. Hybridization could produce individuals capable of forming canavanine. Canavanine would then appear as a hybrid substance in such a case. More will be said later about the formation of "new" substances in hybrids.

It now appears that another newly discovered amino acid, like canavanine, is restricted to the Papilionoideae of the family Leguminosae. This unusual acid, which gives a brilliant scarlet color with ninhydrin, was identified from *Lathyrus tingitanus* seeds by Bell (1962). It was reported to occur in only a few of many species of *Lathyrus* examined. We have now examined nearly 300 species in the family Leguminosae for the presence of lathyrine, and the acid has been detected only in several species of *Lathyrus*. Within the genus *Lathyrus* this amino acid is likely to be of definite systematic utility.

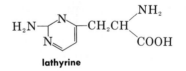

lathyrine

Alston and Irwin (1961) have reported on the relative variation in free amino acids and secondary substances in five species of *Cassia*. They noted that, although definite differences did appear in the amino acid chromatograms of different species, the extent of variation was far less than that of fluorescent substances. For example, from ten to twelve amino acid spots appeared, no more than nine of which were present in a single species. Superimposed upon the relative limitation in numbers of amino acids which are readily disclosed from crude extracts is the fact that the quantities of free amino acids present at a particular time tend to be quite sensitive to numerous external and, presumably, internal influences, for example, light and temperature, nutritional conditions, stage of development, and so on. Fowden (1959) has observed that certain amino acids such as histidine, tyrosine, cystine, and methionine are rarely detectable unless

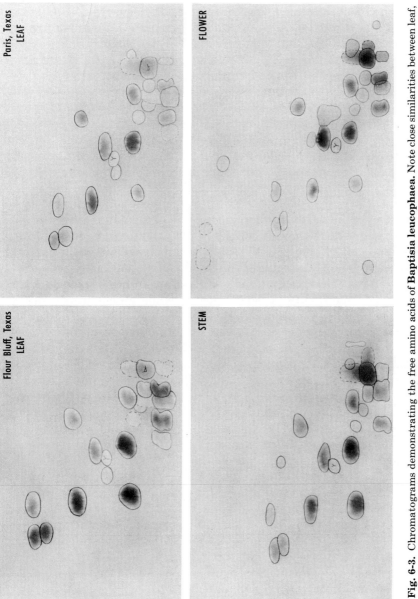

Fig. 6-3. Chromatograms demonstrating the free amino acids of **Baptisia leucophaea.** Note close similarities between leaf, stem, and flower extracts and between leaf extracts from a plant at Flour Bluff, Texas and Paris, Texas, sites nearly 400 miles apart. The chromatograms were not selected for similarities.

the plant is in circumstances which encourage protein breakdown. Additionally, the amides, glutamine and asparagine, are extremely sensitive to modifications of plant growth. Pleshkov *et al.* (1959) compared the free amino acid content of corn leaves and roots grown in a complete nutrient medium and grown in media minus nitrogen, phosphorus, or calcium, respectively. With prolonged deficiency in each case the amino acids decreased sharply, the greatest decrease being evident in aspartic and glutamic acids, alanine, serine, and glycine. In contrast to the nitrogen deficient plants, which responded by a drop in free amino acid content within twenty-four hours after removal from the complete medium, the phosphorus and potassium deficient sets showed a slight increase in the amino acid content during the first week, followed by a rapid decrease with prolonged deficiency. Possingham (1956) found that in tomato plants cultured in media deficient in copper, zinc, manganese, or iron, the free amino acid fraction actually increased while in molybdenum deficient plants the free amino acid fraction decreased. When molybdenum was added, there was a rapid upswing in free amino acid content interpreted to reflect the role of molybdenum in nitrate reduction and nitrogen uptake (Possingham, 1957). Although qualitative differences were not great, an example such as the appearance of pipecolic acid in iron and manganese deficient plants, while absent in controls, is notable. A similar situation reported by Coleman (1957) occurs in flax. In this plant citrulline, not previously found in flax, occurs in moderate concentration in sulfur deficient plants. Possingham (1956) noted that the relative amounts of amino acids changed in a different pattern with each type of deficiency. The systematic implications of these last observations are that, if one is interested in discovering whether the enzyme system leading to the production of a substance is present and not merely whether the plant normally accumulates the substance, exposure to various types of physiological stress may provide the opportunity in some cases.

There are other more recent studies, similar in principle to those of Possingham cited above; for example, Tso and McMurtrey (1960) found that, in general, mineral deficiencies other than N caused an increase in the free amino acids of tobacco plants and variations in the relative concentrations of amino acids.[4] Such evidence serves to support the concept that apparently metabolically labile substances such as amino acids provide less reliable data than do metabolic end products which accumulate.[5]

---

[4] Mineral deficiencies also affect the accumulation of other groups of substances, for example, alkaloids, anthocyanins, and so on, but generally not so directly, hence as quickly, as the common amino acids.

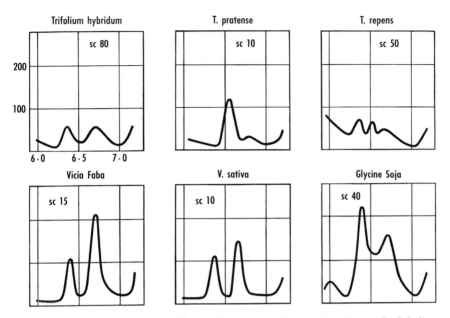

Fig. 6-4. Electrophoretic mobilities of major seed globulins (Daniellson, 1949). Reproduced from *The Biochemical Journal*, with permission.

In our comparison of the free amino acids of the seeds of *Baptisia* species we have noted very consistent results within a species and in fact quite similar patterns among all of the species examined to date. Thus, if free amino acids vary greatly during development as indicated and furthermore are easily affected by the environment, as indicated, the seeds at least provide a rather stable base for the analysis of developmental changes. We have found that even the patterns of the free amino acids of the stem, leaves, and flowers of *Baptisia* species are predictable and reliable although quantitative differences certainly occur. The patterns of free amino acids of the stem, leaves, and flowers are generally quite similar in *B. leucophaea* (Fig. 6-3).

Although most work has been devoted to single amino acids it is now evident that a variety of peptides may exist, and these may prove, eventually, of considerable taxonomic importance (Virtanen and Matikkala, 1960; Wiewiorowski and Augustyniak, 1960; Carnegie, 1961). Aside from the tripeptide, glutathione, and a recently dis-

[5] It should be noted, however, that appropriate populational sampling for chromatographic study should reduce the disadvantage of much of the individual variation which might occur in nature.

covered tetrapeptide, called malformin (Takahashi and Curtis, 1961), reported from *Aspergillus niger,* very little work on specific higher peptides is available.

Haas (1950) reported on the peptides from four species of marine algae. The breakdown of amino acids derived from the hydrolysis of these algal peptides follows:

Algal Species	glycine	alanine	arginine	histidine	aspartic	glutamine
Griffithsia flosculosa	+	+	+	+	−	−
Pelvetia canaliculata	+	+	+	+	−	+
P. canaliculata f. libera	+	+	+	+	−	+
Corallina officinalis	+	+	+	+	+	−

Since these peptides do not occur in detectable amounts in summer months, Haas proposed that lack of light in winter interferes with normal protein synthesis leading to the formation of mixtures of peptides (intermediates?).

It is possible that at some future time alteration of normal metabolism by exposure to stress will disclose abnormal but systematically enlightening metabolic pathways; that is, the accumulation of substances normally found only in small amounts, such as citrulline in flax described earlier, if enzymatically controlled, would provide clues to relationships. Hoffman (1961) observed that several species of the green alga, *Oedogonium,* could not be distinguished chromatographically until cultures were allowed to remain in stale media. Under these suboptimal conditions, a number of additional compounds then appeared, some of which were species-specific.

In the older botanical literature there are a number of studies of seed proteins. Some of the results are suggestive of taxonomic affinities. In general the studies are of rather slight value because the proteins are characterized somewhat crudely. One of the more recent comparisons of seed proteins (of grasses and legumes) is that by Danielsson (1949). His work consisted essentially of studying the globulin fractions by ultracentrifugation. The information yielded by such techniques relates to the number of major globulin types, their relative molecular weights and their relative abundance. The data may be expressed in the form of a graph (Fig. 6-4), each peak representing a component and the height of the peak its amount. To the right is the higher molecular weight. From the standpoint of systematics the legume data appear to be more interesting. Two major globulin components, vicilin and legumin (mol. wts. 186,000 and 331,000, respectively), are of widespread occurrence and two others were detected in certain species of Leguminosae.

Some of the curves obtained by Danielsson have been reproduced to illustrate the nature of the information in these tests. In the figure of *Vicia faba* (Fig. 6-4, lower left) two peaks are distinct. The peak at left represents vicilin, that at the right legumin. In contrast most species of *Acacia* show legumin either weakly or not at all. With the possible exception of *Trifolium repens, Acacia* is the only genus showing so little legumin.

In general, the curves of related species tend to show similar relative proportions of vicilin and legumin in their seeds. In the closely related genera *Lathyrus* and *Vicia* legumin always predominated, while in the less closely related *Phaseolus,* vicilin predominated. The distributions of the minor components seem not to be amenable to any systematic interpretation.

While this work is of interest, it is doubtful whether, in its present form, a large diversity of critical data may be acquired. Although the patterns definitely seem to bear resemblance at the generic level, they are not likely to succeed in clarifying taxonomic points in question or solving problems of phylogeny. Gerritsen (1956), however, has obtained amino acid analyses of five highly purified seed globulins of lupines, three globulins from *Lupinus angustifolius,* and two from *L. luteus.* The highest molecular weight protein of each species appeared to be identical; the next in size showed similarities but also definite differences. The smallest (mol. wt. ca. 25,000) had no counterpart in *L. luteus.* This type of investigation would seem to offer much promise particularly at the intrageneric level.

Blagoveshchenskii (1960), who also studied the seed proteins of various legumes, inferred from his results that in the "primitive" species alkali-soluble proteins predominated while the contents of albuminus and vicilin were low. In more "advanced" species vicilin predominated over legumin, and the content of alkali-soluble proteins was low. His illustrations were not very clear, however, and are therefore difficult to evaluate.

Sibley (1960) has utilized electrophoretic patterns of egg-white proteins in an extensive study of over 650 avian species. He has assumed that the electrophoretic patterns are representative, in part, of the genic complement of the species. It is indeed notable that serologically related substances are found in the embryonic and adult blood sera. The curves obtained from the egg-white proteins of

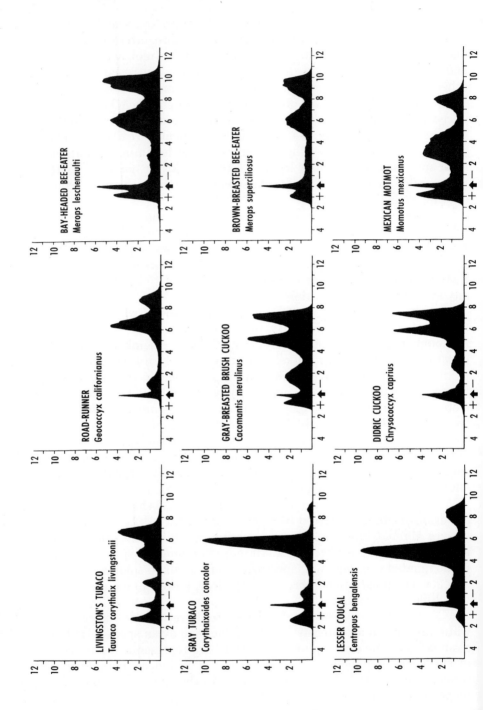

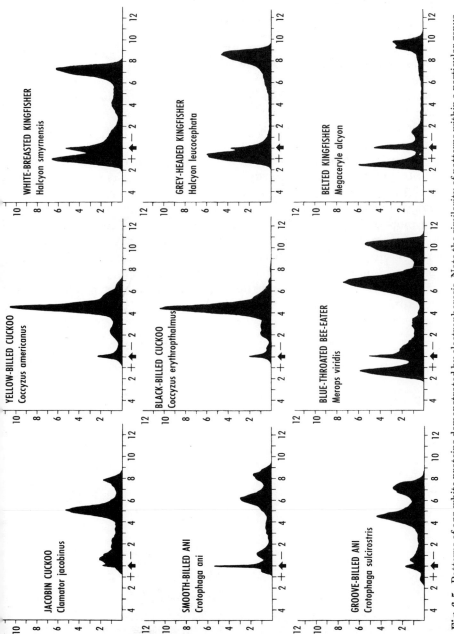

Fig. 6-5. Patterns of egg-white proteins demonstrated by electrophoresis. Note the similarity of patterns within a particular genus (Sibley, 1960). Reproduced from *The Ibis* by kind permission of the British Ornithologists' Union.

birds are considerably more complex than those obtained from seed proteins (Fig. 6-4). It would be interesting to compare the results of this approach with the serological data obtained by Boyden and others (Chapter 4). There is, however, some danger of circular reasoning whenever one engages in apriori deductive speculations concerning the systematic value of a character which is studied only superficially. This statement, which is not intended as a condemnation of Sibley's methods, needs some clarification. Sibley points out that the proteins are of particular significance since they are more or less direct gene products. While no one would dispute the general principle, the fact remains that electrophoretic data yield only patterns. They are accordingly a *cumulative* expression of the protein complement and do not provide evidence as to the particular structure of particular proteins. Therefore, it seems that the force of the argument is lost, and it is a mistake to assume that the electrophoretic patterns are more incisive indicators of phyletic affinity than the morphological pattern also evoked by those same agents (the genes) perhaps more indirectly. It is unnecessary to reaffirm the conviction that intimate knowledge of protein molecular structure is of profound phylogenetic importance and the statements above are not intended to refute this hypothesis.

7 FATTY ACIDS

The naturally occurring fatty acids, at least those to be found among the higher plants, provide an apparent mild paradox, insofar as their systematic implications are concerned. For example, Hilditch (1956), in his comprehensive treatment of the chemistry and distribution of natural fats, makes the following statement:

> The fatty (glyceride) compounds of seeds are specific and closely related to the families in which the parent plants have been grouped by botanists. It is, indeed, not an exaggeration to say that the component acids of seed fats could themselves be made the basis of a system of classification of plants.

Despite the preceding statement, there are no cases known to the writers in which data concerning the fat composition of species were applied to the solution of a taxonomic, or more specifically, a phylogenetic, problem. There are not even any contributions which attempt to infer relationships from such data, in contrast to, for example, Hegnauer's treatment of the isoquinoline alkaloids (Chapter 9). It is apparent that Hilditch was not necessarily implying that a *natural* system of classification could be constructed out of the distribution of seed fats. This may be ascertained from inspection of Table 7-1. For example, in Group A, whose major component acids are linoleic, linolenic, and oleic, families in the gymnosperm order Coniferae and the angiosperm families Juglandaceae, Labiatae, and Oenotheraceae among others are included; in Group D, whose major component acids are palmitic, oleic and linoleic, families such as Gramineae, Magnoliaceae, Solanaceae, and others are included; and in Group K, whose major components are stearic, palmitic, and oleic

Table 7-1. Distribution by family of some fatty acids (Meara, 1958).

Major Component Acids	Family	
(A) Linoleic Linolenic and/or Oleic	*Celastraceae* *Coniferae* *Elaeagnaceae* *Juglandaceae* *Labiatae* *Linaceae*	*Moraceae* *Oenotheraceae* *Passifloraceae* *Rhamnaceae* *Valerianaceae*
(B) Linoleic Oleic	*Amaranthaceae* *Asclepiadaceae* *Betulaceae* *Capparidaceae* *Compositae* *Dipsacaceae* *Fagaceae* *Hippocastanaceae* *Myrtaceae* *Olacaceae*	*Oleaceae* *Papaveraceae* *Pedaliaceae* *Plantaginaceae* *Scrophulariaceae* *Staphyleaceae* *Theaceae* *Typhaceae* *Ulmaceae* *Vitaceae*
(C) Linoleic Oleic or Linolenic Elaeostearic Licanic or Ricinoleic	*Cucurbitaceae* *Euphorbiaceae* *Rosaceae*	

Table 7-1. (*Continued*)

Major Component Acids	Family	
(D) Palmitic Oleic Linoleic	*Acanthaceae* *Anacardiaceae* *Anonaceae* *Apocynaceae* *Berberidaceae* *Bombacaceae* *Caprifoliaceae* *Caricaceae* *Caryocaraceae* *Combretaceae*	*Gramineae* *Lecythidaceae* *Magnoliaceae* *Malvaceae* *Martyniaceae* *Menispermaceae* *Rubiaceae* *Rutaceae* *Solanaceae* *Tiliaceae*

Families Elaborating Seed Fats Containing Characteristic Fatty Acids

Major Component Acids	Family	
(E) Petroselinic Oleic and Linoleic	*Araliaceae* *Umbelliferae*	
(F) Acetylenic Tariric Octadecenynoic	*Simarubaceae* (*Picramnia* sp.) *Olacaceae*	

(G) Eicosenoic
(Oleic, Linoleic)
	Olacaceae
	  (*Ximenia* sp.)
	Sapindaceae
		Buxaceae
		  (*Simmondsia* sp.)

(H) Erucic Oleic Linoleic	*Cruciferae* *Tropaeolaceae*	
(I) Cyclic unsaturated acids	*Flacourtiaceae*	
(J) Arachidic Lignoceric Oleic Linoleic	*Leguminosae* *Moringaceae* *Ochnaceae* *Sapindaceae*	
(K) Stearic Palmitic Oleic	*Gnetaceae* *Burseraceae* *Convolvulaceae* *Dipterocarpaceae*	*Guttiferae* *Meliaceae* *Sapotaceae* *Verbenaceae*
(L) Lauric Myristic Palmitic	*Lauraceae* *Myristicaceae* *Palmae* *Salvadoraceae*	*Simarubaceae* *Ulmaceae* *Vochysiaceae*

acids, the families Gnetaceae, Verbenaceae, and Dipterocarpaceae are among those included. Throughout the twelve groups listed, families with few or no affinities are placed together, though in some instances two or more families which are related on the basis of their classical treatment occur together.

Obviously, attempts to read phylogenetic implications from this pattern of distribution of fatty acids will avail nothing. Yet, fatty acids may prove useful to systematics since a fairly large number of fatty acids are known to have limited distribution (for example, the cyclic unsaturated acids of the Flacourtiaceae). However, two factors must be considered to bear upon the assessment of the systematic significance of the distribution of fats. There are about the same number of fatty acids known as there are amino acids, and many of the fatty acids, like many amino acids, are widely distributed. Secondly, as Hilditch has pointed out, in the formation of typical triglycerides the glyceride structure tends to be dependent upon the proportions of the various component acids. In other words the enzymatic esterification of the fatty acids with glycerol appears to be of low specificity so that the distribution of fatty acids in glycerides tends towards the maximum degree of heterogeneity. The effect of this is that a full range of variation, for a given fatty acid complement, is permitted. If two species have a similar fatty acid complement, they will both produce a similar fat complement. Doubtlessly, there are exceptions to this generalization, and more needs to be known about the precise control of fat synthesis.

One of the difficulties of the classification of Hilditch illustrated above is that it is based upon *major component* acids which in the majority of instances are of exceedingly wide occurrence. For example, oleic acid is included in nine of the twelve groups. It is not likely that the distribution of this acid offers much to chemosystematics. Another difficulty lies in the fact that since the groups are based on major components, not absolute distinctions, one is not measuring the presence of a given metabolic pathway but rather certain favored pathways. In effect it is not always clear what is actually being measured. Concentration on the unusual or the rare fatty acids is likely to prove more profitable.

Excellent treatments of the chemistry and distribution of fatty acids are available in the recent literature (Hilditch, 1956; Meara, 1958). No such comprehensive account is included here and in fact much of the information in these works is not strictly relevant to systematics. However, certain basic considerations of the chemistry of fatty acids, specifically the major variations, and a brief description of certain features of their biosynthesis may be useful in providing heightened perspective from which to evaluate their systematic significance. For example, it is pertinent to consider whether all fatty acids are synthesized via one or via several basic biosynthetic routes. Very little is known about the genetics of fatty acid synthesis, so one potentially valuable aspect of the subject is temporarily obscured. Finally, certain examples will be selected to illustrate the association of specific fatty acids with particular genera or families. Table 7-2 includes a list of fatty acids.

FATTY ACID BIOSYNTHESIS

In recent years the pathways involved in fatty acid metabolism have been rather well established, and it is now evident that fatty acid metabolism is linked directly to the oxidative breakdown of carbohydrate at the point of the formation of acetyl coenzyme A. Presumably all aerobic organisms possess the ability to form acetyl CoA. Since all fatty acids appear to be constructed from two-carbon units supplied from acetyl CoA, this mechanism accounts for the overwhelming predominance of even-numbered fatty acids found in nature. The first step in the building up of fatty acids is assumed to be a condensation between two molecules of acetyl CoA:

$$2 \ CH_3\overset{O}{\overset{\|}{C}}-S\ CoA \longrightarrow CH_3\overset{O}{\overset{\|}{C}}CH_2\overset{O}{\overset{\|}{C}}\ S\ CoA + CoA\ SH$$

Within the last few years a slight modification of this step has been recognized as a result of the demonstration that CO_2 is essential for fatty acid build up, yet CO_2 does not become incorporated into the fatty acid. To satisfy these requirements CO_2 is postulated to combine, with acetyl CoA to form malonyl CoA as an intermediate:

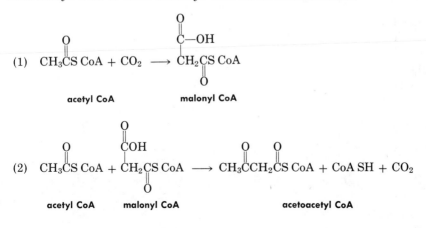

(1)   acetyl CoA   malonyl CoA

(2)   acetyl CoA   malonyl CoA   acetoacetyl CoA

Table 7-2. List of fatty acids. Reproduced by permission from THE CHEMICAL CONSTITUTION OF NATURAL FATS (3rd Ed.) T. P. Hilditch. Chapman & Hall (London).

SATURATED ACIDS, $C_nH_{2n}O_2$ or C_mH_{2m+1}:COOH

Molecular Formula	Common Name	Systematic Name	Structural Formula
$C_4H_8O_2$	Butyric	n-Butanoic	$CH_3.[CH_2]_2.COOH$
$C_5H_{10}O_2$	iso-Valeric	3-Methyl-n-butanoic	$(CH_3)_2.CH.CH_2.COOH$
$C_6H_{12}O_2$	Caproic	n-Hexanoic	$CH_3.[CH_2]_4.COOH$
$C_8H_{16}O_2$	Caprylic	n-Octanoic	$CH_3.[CH_2]_6.COOH$
$C_{10}H_{20}O_2$	Capric	n-Decanoic	$CH_3.[CH_2]_8.COOH$
$C_{12}H_{24}O_2$	Lauric	n-Dodecanoic	$CH_3.[CH_2]_{10}.COOH$
$C_{14}H_{28}O_2$	Myristic	n-Tetradecanoic	$CH_3.[CH_2]_{12}.COOH$
$C_{16}H_{32}O_2$	Palmitic	n-Hexadecanoic	$CH_3.[CH_2]_{14}.COOH$
$C_{18}H_{36}O_2$	Stearic	n-Octadecanoic	$CH_3.[CH_2]_{16}.COOH$
$C_{20}H_{40}O_2$	Arachidic	n-Eicosanoic	$CH_3.[CH_2]_{18}.COOH$
$C_{22}H_{44}O_2$	Behenic	n-Docosanoic	$CH_3.[CH_2]_{20}.COOH$
$C_{24}H_{48}O_2$	Lignoceric	n-Tetracosanoic	$CH_3.[CH_2]_{22}.COOH$
$C_{26}H_{52}O_2$	"Cerotic"	n-Hexacosanoic	$CH_3.[CH_2]_{24}.COOH$

UNSATURATED ACIDS

Mono-ethenoid acids, $C_nH_{2n-2}O_2$ or C_mH_{2m-1}:COOH

Molecular Formula	Common Name	Systematic Name	Structural Formula
$C_{10}H_{18}O_2$		Dec-9-enoic	$CH_2:CH.[CH_2]_7.COOH$†
$C_{12}H_{22}O_2$		Dodec-9-enoic	$CH_3.CH_2.CH:CH.[CH_2]_7.COOH$†
$C_{14}H_{26}O_2$		Tetradec-5-enoic	$CH_3.[CH_2]_7.CH:CH.[CH_2]_3.COOH$†
$C_{14}H_{26}O_2$		Tetradec-9-enoic	$CH_3.[CH_2]_3.CH:CH.[CH_2]_7.COOH$†

Table 7-2. (*Continued*)

Molecular Formula	Common Name	Systematic Name	Structural Formula
$C_{16}H_{30}O_2$	Palmitoleic, zoomaric	Hexadec-9-enoic	$CH_3.[CH_2]_5.CH{:}CH.[CH_2]_7.COOH$†
$C_{18}H_{34}O_2$	Oleic	Octadec-9-enoic	$CH_3.[CH_2]_7.CH{:}CH.[CH_2]_7.COOH$
$C_{18}H_{34}O_2$	Petroselinic	Octadec-6-enoic	$CH_3.[CH_2]_{10}.CH{:}CH.[CH_2]_4.COOH$
$C_{18}H_{34}O_3$	Ricinoleic	12-Hydroxy-octadec-9-enoic	$CH_3.[CH_2]_5.CH(OH).CH_2.CH{:}CH.[CH_2]_7.COOH$†
$C_{18}H_{34}O_3$		9-Hydroxy-octadec-12-enoic	$CH_3.[CH_2]_4.CH{:}CH.[CH_2]_2.CH(OH).[CH_2]_7.COOH$†
$C_{18}H_{32}O_3$	Vernolic	12,13-Epoxy-octadec-9-enoic	$CH_3.[CH_2]_4.\overset{\displaystyle\diagdown O\diagup}{CH.CH}.CH_2.CH{:}CH.[CH_2]_7.COOH$†
$C_{19}H_{34}O_2$	Sterculic	8-(2-*n*-octyl*cyclo*prop-1-enyl)octanoic	$CH_3.[CH_2]_7.\underset{\underset{\textstyle CH_2}{\diagup\diagdown}}{C{:}C}.[CH_2]_7.COOH$†
$C_{20}H_{38}O_2$	Gadoleic	Eicos-9-enoic	$CH_3.[CH_2]_9.CH{:}CH.[CH_2]_7.COOH$†
$C_{20}H_{38}O_2$		Eicos-11-enoic	$CH_3.[CH_2]_7.CH{:}CH.[CH_2]_9.COOH$†
$C_{22}H_{42}O_2$	Cetoleic	Docos-11-enoic	$CH_3.[CH_2]_9.CH{:}CH.[CH_2]_9.COOH$
$C_{22}H_{42}O_2$	Erucic	Docos-13-enoic	$CH_3.[CH_2]_7.CH{:}CH.[CH_2]_{11}.COOH$†
$C_{24}H_{46}O_2$	Selacholeic, nervonic	Tetracos-15-enoic	$CH_3.[CH_2]_7.CH{:}CH.[CH_2]_{13}.COOH$†
$C_{26}H_{50}O_2$	Ximenic	Hexacos-17-enoic	$CH_3.[CH_2]_7.CH{:}CH.[CH_2]_{15}.COOH$†
$C_{30}H_{58}O_2$	Lumequic	Triacont-21-enoic	$CH_3.[CH_2]_7.CH{:}CH.[CH_2]_{19}.COOH$†

Mono-ethynoid acid, $C_nH_{2n-4}O_2$ or $C_mH_{2m-3}.COOH$

Molecular Formula	Common Name	Systematic Name	Structural Formula
$C_{18}H_{32}O_2$	Tariric	Octadec-6-ynoic	$CH_3.[CH]_{10}.C{:}C.[CH_2]_4.COOH$

Mono-ethenoid-diethynoid acid, $C_nH_{2n-10}O_2$ or $C_mH_{2m-9}.COOH$

Molecular Formula	Common Name	Systematic Name	Structural Formula
$C_{18}H_{26}O_2$	Isanic, erythrogenic	Octadec-17-en-9,11-di-ynoic	$CH_2{:}CH.[CH_2]_4.C{:}C.C{:}C.[CH_2]_7.COOH$†

Table 7-2. (*Continued*)

Molecular Formula	Common Name	Systematic Name	Structural Formula
		Cyclic Unsaturated Acids, $C_nH_{2n-4}O_2$ or C_mH_{2m-3}.COOH	
$C_{16}H_{28}O_2$	Hydnocarpic	11-*cyclo*Pent-2-enyl-*n*-undecanoic	CH=CH﹥CH.[CH$_2$]$_{10}$.COOH; CH$_2$-CH$_2$
$C_{18}H_{32}O_2$	Chaulmoogric	13-*cyclo*Pent-2-enyl-*n*-tridecanoic	CH=CH﹥CH.[CH$_2$]$_{12}$.COOH; CH$_2$-CH$_2$
$C_{18}H_{30}O_2$	Gorlic	13-*cyclo*Pent-2-enyl-*n*-tridec-6-enoic	CH=CH﹥CH.[CH$_2$]$_6$.CH:CH.[CH$_2$]$_4$.COOH; CH$_2$-CH$_2$
		Di-ethenoid Acids, $C_nH_{2n-4}O_2$ or C_mH_{2m-3}.COOH	
$C_{18}H_{32}O_2$	Linoleic	Octadeca-9,12-dienoic	$CH_3.[CH_2]_4.CH:CH.CH_2.CH:CH.[CH_2]_7.COOH$†
		Tri-ethenoid Acids, $C_nH_{2n-6}O_2$ or C_mH_{2m-5}.COOH	
$C_{16}H_{26}O_2$	Hiragonic	Hexadeca-6,10,14-trienoic	$CH_3.CH:CH.CH_2.CH_2.CH:CH.[CH_2]_2.CH:CH.[CH_2]_4COOH$
$C_{18}H_{30}O_2$	Linolenic	Octadeca-9,12,15-trienoic	$CH_3.CH_2.CH:CH.CH_2.CH:CH.CH_2.CH:CH.[CH_2]_7.COOH$†
$C_{18}H_{30}O_2$		Octadeca-6,9,12,-trienoic	$CH_3.[CH_2]_4.CH:CH.CH_2.CH:CH.CH_2.CH:CH.[CH_2]_4.COOH$
$C_{18}H_{30}O_2$	Elaeostearic	Octadeca-9,11,13-trienoic	$CH_3.[CH_2]_3.CH:CH.CH:CH.CH:CH.[CH_2]_7.COOH$†
$C_{18}H_{28}O_3$	Licanic	4-Keto-octadeca-9,11,13-trienoic	$CH_3.[CH_2]_3.CH:CH.CH:CH.CH:CH.[CH_2]_4.CO.[CH_2]_2.COOH$†
		Poly-ethenoid Acids	
		(i) Tetra-ethenoid	
$C_{16}H_{24}O_2$		Hexadecatetraenoic	

126

Table 7-2. (*Continued*)

Molecular Formula	Common Name	Systematic Name	Structural Formula
$C_{18}H_{28}O_2$	Parinaric	Octadeca-9,11,13,15-tetraenoic	$CH_3.CH_2.[CH.CH]_4.[CH_2]_7.COOH$†
$C_{18}H_{28}O_2$	Stearidonic	Octadecatetraenoic	
$C_{20}H_{32}O_2$	Arachidonic	Eicosa-5,8,11,14-tetraenoic	$CH_3.[CH_2]_4.CH:CH.CH_2.CH:CH.CH_2.CH:CH.CH_2.CH:CH.$ $[CH_2]_3.COOH.$
(?) $C_{22}H_{36}O_2$		Docosatetraenoic	

(ii) Penta-ethenoid

$C_{20}H_{30}O_2$		Eicosapentaenoic	
$C_{22}H_{34}O_2$	"Clupanodonic"	Docosapentaenoic	
$C_{26}H_{42}O_2$	Shibic	Hexacosapentaenoic	

(iii) Hexa-ethenoid

$C_{22}H_{32}O_2$		Docosahexaenoic	
$C_{24}H_{36}O_2$	Nisnic	Tetracosahexaenoic	
$C_{26}H_{40}O_2$	Thynnic	Hexacosahexaenoic	

127

Following this initial condensation, reduction occurs, and the ketone group is eliminated. These reactions are accomplished in three steps, two of which involve electron transfer from the pyridine nucleotides (DPNH and TPNH). These steps are illustrated below.

$$(3) \quad CH_3\overset{O}{\overset{\|}{C}}CH_2\overset{O}{\overset{\|}{C}}S\,CoA \xrightarrow{\text{DPNH + H}^+} CH_3\overset{OH}{\overset{|}{C}}HCH_2\overset{O}{\overset{\|}{C}}S\,CoA + DPN$$

$$(4) \quad CH_3\overset{OH}{\overset{|}{C}}H\overset{O}{\overset{\|}{C}}S\,CoA \longrightarrow CH_3CH{=}CH\overset{O}{\overset{\|}{C}}S\,CoA + H_2O$$

$$(5) \quad CH_3CH{=}CH\overset{O}{\overset{\|}{C}}S\,CoA \xrightarrow{\text{TPNH + H}^+} CH_3CH_2CH_2\overset{O}{\overset{\|}{C}}S\,CoA + TPN$$

Degradation of fatty acids proceeds by the stepwise removal of two-carbon units via a pathway which is essentially the reverse of that described above. There are some differences however. For example, the initial oxidative step, corresponding by analogy to step 5 above, in reverse, is mediated by the coenzyme flavine adenine dinucleotide (FAD). A second point of difference is that it does not appear that the temporary binding of CO_2 to form the malonyl derivative is involved.

The significance of the mode of fatty acid synthesis described above is that it represents an almost universal basic metabolic pathway. Therefore, all of the various fatty acids are metabolically related, and the variations in chain length, in degree of unsaturation, and even those involving terminal cyclization, are secondary.

A question of some theoretical importance is that of whether a single enzyme of low specificity is involved in the condensation of malonyl CoA with the preformed carbon chain or whether several enzymes, each with affinities for a carbon of particular length, may cooperate in the build up of a sixteen carbon fatty acid. In fact, it is possible that a different, specific enzyme exists for coupling of malonyl CoA to C_2, C_4, C_6 ... C_n residues. There is insufficient evidence on this point, to the writers' knowledge, to provide a general statement. Likewise, it is not yet known whether any specific coenzymes participate in the oxidation-reduction steps involving different carbon chain lengths, or even whether similar coenzymes but different apoenzymes participate. Crane et al. (1955) have shown that three enzymes are active in the first oxidative step in the degradation of fatty acids in pig liver, and their specificities differ for different carbon chain lengths. All three of these are flavoproteins. As indicated in Fig. 7-1, enzyme Y_1 is most active on C_8–C_{12} fatty acids, Y_2 on C_8–

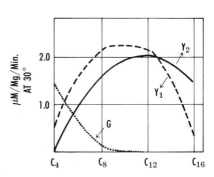

Fig. 7-1. Specificity of fatty acyl CoA dehydrogenases for sub-states of different chain length (Crane *et al.* 1955).

C_{16} fatty acids, and G (which is probably equivalent to butyryl CoA dehydrogenase) is most active on C_4 acids. The three enzymes can thus effect the degradation of fatty acids up to sixteen carbons. Moreover, these workers discovered a fourth enzyme which is specific for oxidation of the reduced forms of G, Y_1, and Y_2. The last, also a flavoprotein, was designated an "electron transferring flavoprotein." It presumably gives up electrons to some intermediate in the basic electron transport system.

In connection with the problem just posed above, a statement of Hilditch (1952) is pertinent. Hilditch noted that the fatty acids of more primitive plant and animal forms tended to represent a more complex mixture, with a simpler mixture characteristic of more advanced organisms. This could represent the evolution of enzymes with more specificity effecting more vigorous control over chain length in fatty acids. Some authors, notably McNair (1941), have considered that there is an increase in the molecular weight and the complexity of the fatty acids during the course of evolution, a viewpoint which is in part opposed to the idea of Hilditch, cited above. Goldovskii (1960) has criticized both of McNair's premises:

> Owing to the great diversity of chemical reactions, the process of fatty acid formation from its very inception must have led to a multitude of acids (polycondensation always leads to a number of polymer homologues). In fact, the simplest lower plants, in particular the algae and fungi, already possess a complex equipment of fatty acids, including high molecular ones. Nor can we agree with the idea of a rise in the degree of unsaturation in the course of evolutionary development as a whole, since even in the algae acids of a high degree of unsaturation are formed. And, on the other hand, seed fats in the Compositae, the members of which are generally taken to be at the summit of the

evolutionary development of plants, are by no means distinguished by having the highest iodine values, as might be expected if it is thought that the degree of unsaturation increases during evolution.

Another problem which must be solved in the metabolism of fatty acids is the enzymatic coupling of the acid to form an ester linkage with glycerol. If this reaction is rather unspecific, then what prevents the incorporation of shorter chain "intermediates" into triglycerides? A related question is that of the mechanism for terminating the extension of the carbon chain. One reaction has been reported which provides a partial answer to both questions. This reaction involves the acyl attachment from an acyl CoA group to phosphoglyceric acid with the liberation of CoA. The reaction proceeds more efficiently with sixteen- and eighteen-carbon acyl CoA compounds and is probably an intermediate in phosphatide (for example, lecithin) synthesis. In any case, it is clear that the presence of such enzymes could result in the capture of fatty acids of appropriate chain length as they are synthesized. Frequently, it appears that a given species tends to synthesize saturated fatty acids possessing two-carbon atoms more or less than that of the major component (Hilditch, 1952), again suggesting the possibility of less than absolute specificity for certain enzymes governing fatty acid synthesis. Perhaps this area would be particularly fruitful for comparative enzyme studies—both from the standpoint of their catalytic properties and their absolute chemical constitution (that is, amino acid sequence).

It is evident from the review by Meara (1958) that, except for the seed fats, relatively little systematic significance can be gleaned from analysis of plant fats. For example, fats of roots usually represent minor components. In a few cases, notably the sedge *Cyperus esculentus,* the oil content may be high. The fat content of bark is usually on the order of 3 per cent and in the few species examined the major fatty acid was the common oleic acid. More frequently, fruit coat fats may acquire a relatively high concentration of oil. Yet, according to Meara, "the characteristics and component fatty acids of most of the fruit coat fats, irrespective of their botanical family, are very similar."

It has generally been believed that leaf lipids and the constituents of leaf surface waxes are rather similar among different plants (Hilditch, 1956). However, since the advent of chromatographic techniques including gas chromatography, much evidence has been acquired indicating that the leaf waxes contain a quite diverse assemblage of hydrocarbons of different lengths including branched chains, alcohols, aldehydes, ketones, acids and esters. Even a new carbon-methyl flavonoid component of wax is suspected (Price, 1962). For separation of alkanes, the techniques of gas chromatography and mass spectrography are utilized together.

Purdy and Truter (1961) have compared the surface lipids of leaves of sixty three species, using thin layer chromatography to separate mixtures. Characteristic patterns were obtained for each species. It was also demonstrated that the patterns did not change with the age of the plant.

The work of Eglinton et al. (1962) is of unusual interest and indicates that wax constituents may be of exceptional taxonomic value. These workers chromatographed unfractionated extracts of alkanes, using only 40 g. of dried samples, and obtained a complete analysis of straight chain and branched chain alkanes of 23 to 35 carbons. Some of their results are shown in Fig. 7-2. The variety of patterns disclosed by their data suggests wide application of these methods in taxonomy.

The patterns of alkanes derived from individual species are apparently quite constant. A study of *Aeonium urbicum* (Crassulaceae) collected from various places and including immature and even dead

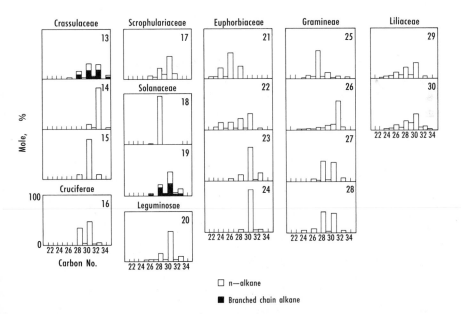

☐ n—alkane

■ Branched chain alkane

Fig. 7-2. Distribution in mole percentage of *n*- and branched chain alkanes C_{22-35} in the hydrocarbon fraction of the waxes from individual plant species. Alkane percentages less than 2 mole per cent have been omitted (Courtesy G. Eglinton).

leaves showed the pattern to be quite stable and characteristic for the species (Eglinton, 1962). However, the techniques also served to distinguish species of the same genus. Four species of the genus *Hebe,* in which hybridization frequently occurs, were compared and according to Eglinton *et al.* the four species can be immediately distinguished chemotaxonomically, e.g. *Hebe odora* has a major constituent of C_{29}; *H. parviflora* and *H. diosmifolia,* C_{31}; and *H. stricta,* C_{33}. An entirely unsuspected source of major chemical variation immediately accessible to analysis is therefore disclosed by these investigations.

The remainder of this section will be concerned with a few selected examples of fatty acids whose distributions are restricted to or characteristic of certain plant families.

FLACOURTIACEAE

Chaulmoogric (C_{16}) and hydnocarpic (C_{18}) acids occur in this family together with lower homologues in trace amounts. The distinctive characteristic of this group of acids is the presence of a cyclopentene ring. Although present in a number of genera of the Flacourtiaceae they do not occur outside the family. It is therefore evident that the distribution of these cyclic acids is of taxonomic interest.

Fatty acids with cyclic groups occur also in the genus *Sterculia* (Sterculiaceae). Thus sterculic acid (C_{19}) possesses a three-membered ring inside the chain—produced, possibly, by addition of a carbon and yielding an uneven number of carbons. Subsequently, Shenstone and Vickery (1961) have reported that, in addition to *Sterculia* and *Brachychiton* of the Sterculiaceae, certain *Malva* and *Gossypium* species (Malvaceae) produce the cyclopropene acids, sterculic acid and malvalic acid. Both families are placed in the order Malvales.

CRUCIFERAE

In this family the unsaturated acid, erucic acid (C_{22}), is quite prominent. According to Meara (1958) it is probable that many, if not most Cruciferae, contain erucic acid. Only a small proportion of the total species has been subjected to detailed analysis, however, and the statement is based partly on inferences derived from the low saponification number of the fats from a larger number of cruciferous species.

Outside the *Cruciferae,* the nasturtium (*Tropaeolum minus*), of the monogeneric family Tropaeolaceae, contains a large quantity of erucic acid. Since the Tropaeolaceae are usually placed in the Geraniales and show no obvious phylogenetic affinity to the Cruciferae, it is likely that the high erucic acid content in the two families is coincidental. It is interesting that certain relatively uncommon isothiocyanates occur in the two families (Chapter 14).

UMBELLIFERAE

A structural isomer of oleic acid, petroselinic acid, is apparently confined to a few families including the Umbelliferae where it represents a major component (for example, 75 per cent of the total fatty acids in *Petroselinum sativum*) in most of the species tested. In addition to the Umbelliferae, petroselinic acid has been found in ivy (*Hedera helix*) of the related family, Araliaceae. However, one other plant known to produce the acid as a major component is *Picrasma guassioides* of the family Simarubaceae. This family is not closely allied with the Umbelliferae though Meara (1958) states that petroselinic acid is confined to the members of the Umbelliferae and one or two members of isolated but related species. It is significant that tariric acid has been reported only from the genus *Picramnia* of the family Simarubaceae. Petroselinic acid is an octadec-6-enoic acid while tariric is an octadec-6-ynoic acid.

PALMAE

According to Hilditch (1952), "In both constancy and complexity of the mixture—the seed fats of the palm family form the outstanding instance of specificity of fatty acid composition within a single botanical family."

Within this family lauric and myristic acids (C_{12} and C_{14}) usually make up 50 per cent or more of the total fatty acid complement.

In addition shorter chain acids, such as caproic, caprylic, and capric, are generally present along with palmitic, stearic, and the unsaturated acids, oleic and linoleic. This group of acids represents remarkable diversity with respect to carbon chain length, and in addition it is indicated that the relative proportions are rather constant among different species and even among various genera within the family.

The fatty acids of the Palmae demonstrate the fact that chemical characters may be somewhat constant within a taxonomic group delimited on other grounds. This has been shown in a number of other studies involving other compounds, of course, and the fatty acids of the Palmae are distinctive only in that they involve the occurrence of rather constant *proportions* of a series of compounds. Unfortunately, the fatty acid complement of the Palmae does not provide much insight into relationships within the family or with other families.

Hilditch, a chemist, has obviously recognized that fatty acid metabolism and morphological characters are often correlated, and the following statement (Hilditch, 1952) illustrates at once the promise and the pitfalls of phytochemical systematics:

Most interesting and least understood of all is the manner in and by which species with common morphological relationships produce qualitatively the same mixtures of fatty acids in their seeds so that classification of species according to the constituent acids in their seed fats leads to much the same results as that developed by the botanical classifications of Linnaeus and his successors.

The statement quoted might elicit some justifiable criticism from systematists, most of whom envision the goal of systematics to extend beyond the mere convenient categorizing of species. A natural classification of species based solely on the constituent acids in their seed fats would bear no relationship to any present taxonomic system. While the palms would be placed into a single group, other categories would include gymnosperms, monocots and dicots together.

CARBOHYDRATES

Judging from the relatively small body of available literature it seems that the potential contribution of carbohydrates to biochemical systematics is slightly regarded, although some early work on the biochemistry of carbohydrates from the systematic aspect exists. For example, Blackman (1921) discussed in rather general terms the use of carbohydrates as phylogenetic criteria, citing specifically the accumulation of pentosan mucilages in succulent families such as the Cactaceae and Crassulaceae. Blackman cited an older work by Meyer, who arranged the flowering plants into five "classes" on the basis of their propensity to form starch. Generalizations such as a tendency for most monocots to fall into the low starch-producing classes or that the families Solanaceae and Leguminosae form starch in large amounts are not of great value in themselves. Blackman also discussed the monumental work on starch grains by Reichert (1919) which had appeared shortly before and which will be discussed in a later chapter. In his comparative study of starch grains, Reichert exposed numerous possibilities for the use of starch characters in systematics.

Carbohydrates are so diverse that one cannot relegate them *in toto* to the general categories of either basic metabolites or secondary constituents. Not only simple hexose sugars such as glucose and fructose but also the more recently familiar sugars such as ribose and sedoheptulose must now be considered as basic metabolites. In contrast, the sugars that represent the glycosidic portion of such secondary substances as pteridines, steroids, flavonoids, cyanogenetic principles, some oligo- and polysaccharides, and sugar derivatives such as the sugar alcohols, are collectively more properly considered as secondary products of metabolism.

Previously, it was stated that secondary constituents promise generally to be more useful than basic metabolites in systematic investigations. However, a basic metabolite, sedoheptulose, once considered to be restricted in occurrence to the family Crassulaceae, is now found in a number of other families (in the free, non-phosphorylated state). Since free sedoheptulose has a restricted distribution, it is potentially systematically useful. The previous generalization concerning basic metabolites is supported, however, as most of the simple sugars which are involved principally in energy relationships, for example, glucose, fructose, maltose, sucrose, and others are so widespread that they can hardly be expected to have a phyletically meaningful distribution. Some sugars and sugar derivatives which appear to be quite restricted in their occurrence may actually have a much broader distribution than expected. As in the case of sedoheptulose, screening of large numbers of species is necessary to expose meaningful patterns.

Probably many more simple sugars (up to the oligosaccharide level of complexity) and sugar derivatives exist than is generally appreciated. Because of the lack of any integrated treatment and the encyclopedic effort required to bring together data on all the different substances described to date, the present treatment is necessarily incomplete. An excellent review of the carbohydrate literature is available (Shafizadeh and Wolfrom, 1958). In the following brief account, the main purpose is to identify some of the lesser known sugars and sugar derivatives to illustrate further opportunities for phytochemical systematic investigations. In appropriate situations, phyletically meaningful distribution of a substance is noted, but in general at this time carbohydrates have not contributed nearly as much to the field of biochemical systematics as have certain other classes of compounds.

SIMPLE SUGARS (A PARTIAL LIST ONLY)

The five-carbon sugar, xylose, is frequently encountered in higher plants and is a constituent of polysaccharides such as xylan and the hemicelluloses. Other pentoses, such as arabinose and ribose are frequently found in higher plants. Ribose is associated with co-enzymes and nucleoproteins, and it is an intermediate in the dark reactions of photosynthesis. It would be indeed remarkable if ribose were absent from a higher plant. Free pentoses are often present in detectable quantities in plant tissues. Williams *et al.* (1952), who examined thirty-one different food plants, and also leaves from twenty-three trees, found free pentoses in the fruits of only the lemon and strawberry, but in the leaf material examined, free pentoses were present in about half of the species.

Of the hexoses, most are of little or no systematic significance. Although it is true that the ability to accumulate large amounts of one or another of the common hexoses may conceivably be systematically meaningful. There is no evidence that such accumulation often occurs. A chromatographic study of free sugars of twenty-seven families of seed plants and ten species of algae representing three phyla (Bidwell *et al.,* 1952) showed some differences in the relative concentrations of glucose and sucrose. Since sugar concentration may be as sensitive to conditions of growth as amino acids, quantitative differences must be evaluated conservatively. These authors reported extremely low free sugar content in the algae tested, and a similar statement appears in a report on carbohydrate accumulation by lower plants by Young (1958).

Free galactose, though uncommon, has been found in a variety of plants, and it also occurs in the sugar component of certain complex glycosides. Mannose apparently does not often occur free, yet the sugar is present in polysaccharide form (mannan) in certain palms and orchids.

Although free fructose is of slight systematic importance, the distribution of the fructose polysaccharide, inulin, appears to have some taxonomic significance. It is quite widely known that certain Compositae (for example, dandelion, Jerusalem artichoke, and *Dahlia*) store inulin. Related, but different fructose polysaccharides are apparently found in some grasses. According to Hegnauer (1958) inulin has been found in the family Boraginaceae, and Bacon (1959) found inulin in species of the Campanulaceae. Hegnauer suggests a further study of the distribution of fructosans in the plant kingdom, and Bacon infers from the presence of inulin in the Campanulaceae a close evolutionary connection between the family and the Compositae. A comprehensive survey of the Compositae for inulin would be valuable. Sporadic occurrences of inulin in two families is not necessarily indicative of a close phylogenetic relationship between the families.

Heptoses have been known to occur for many years, but it was probably Calvin's work on the dark reactions of photosynthesis that led to recognition of the biological role of certain seven-carbon sugars. Mannoketoheptose is found as a free sugar in the avocado pear. Free sedoheptulose was first reported from *Sedum spectabile* by LaForge and Hudson (1917). Subsequently, the presence of free sedoheptulose has been associated with the family Crassulaceae, and originally the sugar was considered to occur in the free state only in this family. For example, Nordal and Klevstrand (1951a; 1951b) found free sedoheptulose in all five sub-families of the Crassulaceae. However, Nordal and Oiseth (1951, 1952) examined *Primula elatior, P. vulgaris* and *P. veris* (Primulaceae) and found sedoheptulose and probably mannoheptulose. These were the first reports of sedoheptulose outside of the family Crassulaceae. The search for sedoheptulose in *P. elatior* was prompted by the identification of the seven-carbon sugar-alcohol, volemitol, from the species. Nordal and Oiseth reported the detection of sedoheptulose in several species of Saxifragaceae; *Chrysosplenium alternifolium, Parnassia palustris,* and several species of *Saxifraga* were positive for sedoheptulose. Williams *et al.* (1952) also reported heptuloses in sixteen of thirty-one plant tissues examined, and twenty-one of twenty-three species of trees had one or more heptuloses in the leaves. Recently, Brown and Hunt (1961) examined 200 species of plants representing seventy-eight families and found free sedoheptulose in at least one species of each of sixteen families. It was prevalent in the families Corylaceae and Oleaceae, but in general no clear systematic implications outside of this observation were apparent. Thus, while association of the sugar with the family Crassulaceae alone is no longer valid, and this particular phytochemical systematic correlation is negated, perhaps in a broader framework the distribution of sedoheptulose will be phylogenetically significant. In view of the basic metabolic significance of phosphorylated sedoheptulose, it is not surprising to find that free sedoheptulose occurs outside of a single family.

STRUCTURALLY MODIFIED SUGARS

Rhamnose, a methylpentose, is frequently present as a part of the glycosidic component of certain flavonoids. It does occur as the free sugar, for example, in leaves and flowers of *Rhus toxicodendron.*

Fucose, deoxygalactose, is found in the brown alga, *Laminaria digitata.* Although botanical examples of the systematic utility of fucose are lacking, there is an interesting example of genus specificity involving fucose in the sea-urchin-egg jelly coat (Vasseur and Immer, 1949). The polysaccharide of *Echinus esculentus* jelly consists entirely of galactose residues, that of *Echinocerdium cordatum* solely of fucose residues, *Strongylocentrotus draebachiensis,* fucose with galactose, and *Paracentrotus lividus,* fucose plus some glucose.

Numerous other deoxy sugars, occurring often as steroid glycosides, are known (Shafizadeh and Wolfrom, 1958; Reichstein, 1958). Deoxyribose is of ubiquitous occurrence in nucleotides of DNA.

Branched chain sugars of higher plants are somewhat rare. Apiose, illustrated below with hamamelose, are among authenticated branched pentose and hexoses respectively:

$$
\begin{array}{cc}
\text{HC}{=}\text{O} & \text{HC}{=}\text{O} \\
\text{HCOH} & \text{HOH}_2\text{CCOH} \\
\text{HOCCH}_2\text{OH} & \text{HCOH} \\
\text{HCOH} & \text{HCOH} \\
\text{H} & \text{HCOH} \\
 & \text{H} \\
\textbf{apiose} & \textbf{hamamelose}
\end{array}
$$

Hamamelose is found as a constituent of a tannin of *Hamamelis virginica,* but apiose has been identified as a free sugar in leaves of the monocot, *Posidonia australis* (Potamogetonaceae). At least it is the main sugar component following mild acid hydrolysis of leaves, so it is to be considered as only conditionally a free sugar (Bell *et al.,* 1954). Previously apiose was known only as the parsley flavone glycoside (the apioside of apigenin).

SUGAR ALCOHOLS
(ACYCLIC POLYHYDRIC ALCOHOLS)

Relatively few sugar alcohols have been identified as naturally occurring compounds. Usually the compounds are reported from a rather diverse group of plants. For example, galactitol (dulcitol) is found in certain red algae, fungi, and higher plants; sorbitol is found in algae, monocots, and dicots; mannitol, which is quite widespread,

occurs in some algae, fungi, lichens, Gnetaceae, and numerous monocot and dicot species. Others, such as volemitol, polygalitol, and
styracitol are known in only one or a very few species.

In spite of their rather broad distribution, mentioned above,
within certain delimited taxonomic groups the sugar alcohols may
have a meaningful distribution. For example, Plouvier (1948) has
shown that galactitol occurs in branches, bark, and leaves of numerous
species of the family Celastraceae, while it is absent from the related
families, Rutaceae, Simarubaceae, Meliaceae, Rhamnaceae, and
Vitaceae. It also occurs in the Lauraceae (*Cassytha filiformis*),
Scrophulariaceae (*Melampyrum species*), and Hippocrateaceae (*Pris-
timera indica*). The last example is interesting in view of the fact
that Bentham and Hooker, and others, have included members of this
family in the Celastraceae.

Among algae galactitol seems to be restricted to the red algae.
In contrast, mannitol is often found in brown algae but not, apparently, in the reds. Quillet (1957) found mannitol in seventeen species
of brown algae, sometimes comprising up to 50 per cent of the dry
weight. Volemitol was present in one species, *Pelvetia canaliculata*.
Cmelik and Marowic (1950) found mannitol in Adriatic species of
Cystosura, Sargassum, Laminaria, Dictyopteris, Fucus, and *Padina*
with a maximum accumulation at the beginning of winter. However
at no season was mannitol obtained from red or green algae. Actually,
the authors say that "practically" no mannitol was obtained from
red or green algae at any season. It is not clear whether or not
small quantities were actually detected in some. Large seasonal
variation in mannitol content sometimes occurs. Black (1948) noted
over fourfold differences in mannitol content of some *Laminaria*
species in Scotland, with the maximum concentration coming in mid
or late summer. In *L. cloustonii* the dry weight mannitol content increased from 18 per cent at one-half fathom to 36 per cent at four
fathoms.

Among flowering plants, mannitol occurs rather widely, among
so many families that a significant familial distribution is unlikely.
Mannitol is exceptionally common, however, in the family Oleaceae.

Sorbitol has a more limited distribution among angiosperm
families, e.g., the Rosaceae. According to Barker (1955) if detached
leaves of certain Rosaceae are kept in the dark to eliminate starch and
then floated in a solution of sorbitol, starch is synthesized. The leaves
cannot utilize mannitol or galactitol to form starch. Similarly, leaves of
Adonis vernalis (Ranunculaceae) and certain species of the Oleaceae
will utilize dulcitol and mannitol respectively. It would be interesting
to repeat certain of these experiments using methods of modern tissue

culture and with C^{14} labelled sugar alcohols. One could utilize liquid root-culture techniques or measure callus development from cotyledon explants upon agar with sugar alcohols as the carbohydrate source.

INOSITOL AND RELATED CYCLIC ALCOHOLS

This group of substances is arbitrarily discussed along with the other sugar alcohols. Empirically, they are close to the sugar alcohols but biosynthetic pathways leading to the synthesis of cyclic alcohols may be quite different.

The best known of the cyclic alcohols is the widely distributed inositol. Meso-inositol occurs in numerous higher plants while other isomers are more limited in distribution.

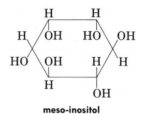

meso-inositol

Two monomethyl ethers of inositol, bornesitol and sequoyitol, occur in several families. Another monomethyl ether, pinitol, is found among a variety of conifers, in *Ephedra,* and also among a number of angiosperm families (for example, Leguminosae). Dambonitol, a dimethyl ether, occurs in a number of species of angiosperms, and the deoxyinositol, quercitol, is found in a number of angiosperm families.

The cyclitols, pinitol and quercitol, have been investigated from a systematic orientation (Dangschat, 1958; Plouvier, 1955). Despite the fact that they occur among numerous unrelated groups, within certain taxonomic groups the distribution of these compounds is definitely meaningful.

Quercitol is found in a number of families of both monocots and dicots. However Plouvier, who studied the distribution of quercitol, found that quercitol generally occurred only in one or a few representatives of a family; that is, it did not appear to be particularly characteristic of the family. In the family, Fagaceae, the compound was described from the genus *Quercus,* but Plouvier found that several species of *Fagus* and *Castanea,* of this family lacked quercitol. However, all of thirty-three species of *Quercus* investigated contained quercitol.

Thus, quercitol appears as a genus-specific character in

Quercus, but not as a family character. In contrast, pinitol is significant at the family level. While pinitol is common in the Pinaceae, it
is not the pines that provide the example to be cited, for pinitol occurs
in other families of conifers. Even in the Leguminosae, where pinitol
apparently occurs throughout most of the tribes, it is not widespread
among the tribes Vicieae and Phaseoleae (Dangschat, 1958). However,
in the Caryophyllaceae pinitol approaches a family diagnostic character. Plouvier (1954) examined forty-five species of this family representing all sub-families (Paronychioideae: four genera, five species;
Alsinoideae: six genera, thirteen species; and Silenoideae: six genera,
twenty-seven species) and found pinitol to be present in forty-three of
the forty-five species. Repeated attemps to detect pinitol in *Stellaria
media* and *Silene schafta* were negative, so one could not consider
pinitol to be infallibly diagnostic. Yet, Plouvier states:

> It appears as a constant chemical character of the Caryophyllaceae
> providing biochemical homogeneity in this morphologically hetero-
> geneous family; it establishes a connection between the three sub-
> families particularly between the Apetaly and Dialypetaly which many
> authors consider to be separate families.

Plouvier then extended his investigation to include twenty-
seven species belonging to related families, including Chenopodiaceae,
six genera; Amaranthaceae, four genera; Nyctaginaceae, two genera;
Aizoaceae, three genera; Phytolaccaceae, one genus; and Portulacaceae,
one genus. All of the above-mentioned families were included in the
Centrospermae of Engler and Diels (1936). In addition selected
families of the order Geraniales, which, according to some workers, are
phylogenetically close to the Caryophyllaceae were examined. These
included Oxalidaceae, one genus; Geraniaceae, three genera; Tropaeolaceae, one genus; Linaceae, one genus; and Zygophyllaceae, two
genera. Although the sample in each family was small, it is noteworthy that only six of the twenty-seven species contained pinitol,
and it was absent from the families Amaranthaceae and Chenopodiaceae. The six positive species were: Nyctaginaceae, *Mirabilis jalapa,*
M. longiflora, and *Bougainvillea glabra;* Phytolaccaceae, *Phytolacca
americana;* Aizoaceae, *Tetragonia expansa;* and Zygophyllaceae,
Zygophyllum fabago (in low yield). Only the last-named family is
placed in the order Geraniales. Evidence with respect to the presumed
affinity between the two orders concerned is too limited to be
significant.

Since pinitol is shown to be present in several families of the
Centrospermae however, it appears that the utilization of pinitol as a

link between the sub-families of the Caryophyllaceae is inappropriate on the same objection as noted by Mothes and Romeike (1958) concerning the isoquinoline alkaloids (to be discussed in Chapter 9); namely, that it is not proper to relate a group of families on the basis of the presence of a particular character and then, using that same character, establish a link between various sub-families. In the case of pinitol, no strong position was taken by Plouvier.

It is interesting to compare the systematic distribution of pinitol with the systematic distribution of the betacyanins discussed in Chapter 14. It may be noted that Hutchinson placed the Nyctaginaceae in the order Thymeleales which he derived from the Flacourtiaceae of the Lignosae, while deriving the Chenopodiales from the Herbaceae. The Nyctaginaceae, however, include a number of producers of betacyanins which Reznik (1957) considers to represent a diagnostic character significant at the ordinal level (Chapter 14). It is, therefore, particularly interesting to note that all of the species of Nyctaginaceae investigated by Plouvier contained pinitol. Curiously, alone among the families of the Centrospermae, the Caryophyllaceae apparently lack betacyanins yet it is this family in which pinitol is most typical. The writers do not consider that the situation described undermines in any way the validity of these biochemical data as phylogenetic criteria because the distributions of pinitol and unusual anthocyanin-like pigments in the Centrospermae, while exhibiting different patterns, at no point are in conflict, and they complement each other with respect to the placement of the somewhat disputed family, Nyctaginaceae.

Acid derivatives of inositol (not in a biosynthetic sequence relationship) include quinic and shikimic acids. Quinic acid is of quite general distribution. Shikimic acid until recently was thought to be exceedingly rare (for example, Bonner, 1950, stated that at that time it was reported only from species of *Illicium*). However, this acid, now shown to be an intermediate in the synthesis of certain amino acids as well as numerous secondary constituents (Chapter 11), is of general occurrence. Hasegawa *et al.* (1954) detected shikimic acid in a number of species of angiosperms and gymnosperms.

OLIGOSACCHARIDES

Tables 8-1 and 8-2 (Shafizadeh and Wolfrom, 1958) list the typical disaccharides, the common oligosaccharides, and some of their sources. Most disaccharides occur as glycosides and these often appear

Table 8-1. Constitution and natural origin of typical disaccharides (Shafizadeh and Wolfrom, 1958).

Common name	Constitution	Origin
Trehalose	α-D-Glucopyranosyl α-D-glucopyranoside	Fungi, mushrooms, yeast, seaweeds, trehala manna
Sucrose	α-D-Glucopyranosyl β-D-fructofuranoside α-D-Glucopyranosyl α-L-sorbofuranoside α-D-Glucopyranosyl β-D-*threo*-pentuloside	Most abundant sugar in plant saps Enzymic synthesis Enzymic synthesis
Inulobiose	1-*O*-β-D-Fructofuranosyl-D-fructose	Hydrolysis of inulin
Galactinol	1-*O*-α-D-Galactopyranosyl-D-*myo*-inositol 2-*O*-α-D-Glucopyranosyl-D-glucose	Sugar beet Enzymic synthesis
Sophorose	2-*O*-β-D-Glucopyranosyl-D-glucose 2-*O*-(α-D-Galactopyranosyl-uronic acid)-L-rhamnose 2-*O*-α-D-Xylopyranosyl-L-arabinose 2-*O*-(α-D-Glucopyranosyl-uronic acid)-D-xylose 2-*O*-(4-*O*-Methyl-α-D-glucopyranosyluronic acid)-D-xylose	Sophoraflavonoloside from *Sophora japonica* Hydrolysis of mucilages from slippery elm, flaxseed (*Plantago ovata*) and okra Hydrolysis of corn cob hemicellulose Hydrolysis of corn cob hemicellulose Hydrolysis of corn cob hemicellulose
Laminaribiose	3-*O*-β-D-Glucopyranosyl-D-glucose	Hydrolysis of *Laminaria* polysaccharide
Nigerose	3-*O*-α-D-Glucopyranosyl-D-glucose	Hydrolysis of amylopectin and the polysaccharide from *Aspergillus niger*
Turanose	3-*O*-α-D-Glucopyranosyl-D-fructose 3-*O*-β-D-Galactopyranosyl-D-galactose 3-*O*-α-D-Glucopyranosyl-L-arabinose 3-*O*-α-D-Galactopyranosyl-L-arabinose 3-*O*-β-L-Arabinopyranosyl-L-arabinose 3-*O*-α-D-Xylopyranosyl-L-arabinose	Hydrolysis of melezitose Hydrolysis of arabic acid and the gum of *Acacia pycnantha* Enzymic synthesis Autohydrolysis of arabic acid Hydrolysis of ε-galactan of larch, and gums Autohydrolysis of golden apple gum

Table 8-1. (*Continued*)

Common name	Constitution	Origin
Hyalobiuronic acid	3-*O*-(β-D-Glucopyranosyl-uronic acid)-2-amino-2-deoxy-D-glucose	Hydrolysis of hyaluronic acid
Maltose	4-*O*-α-D-Glucopyranosyl-D-glucopyranose	Hydrolysis of starch
Cellobiose	4-*O*-β-D-Glucopyranosyl-D-glucopyranose	Hydrolysis of cellulose
Lactose	4-*O*-β-D-Galactopyranosyl-D-glucopyranose	Milk of mammals
	4-*O*-α-D-Galactopyranosyl-D-galactopyranose	Hydrolysis of okra mucilage
	4-*O*-β-D-Xylopyranosyl-D-xylopyranose	Hydrolysis of xylan
	4-*O*-(α-D-Glucopyranosyl-uronic acid)-D-xylopyranose	Hydrolysis of soluble hemi-cellulose of corn cob
	4-*O*-β-D-Mannopyranosyl-D-mannopyranose	Hydrolysis of guaran poly-saccharide
	4-*O*-(α-D-Galactopyranosyl-uronic acid)-D-galacto-pyranuronic acid	Enzymic hydrolysis of pectic acid
	4-*O*-(4-*O*-Methyl-α-D-glucopyranosyluronic acid)-L-arabinopyranose	Hydrolysis of lemon gum
	4-*O*-(β-D-Glucopyranosyl-uronic acid)-D-glucopyranose	Hydrolysis of Types III and VIII *Pneumococcus* poly-saccharides
Isomaltose	6-*O*-α-D-Glucopyranosyl-D-glucose	Hydrolysis of amylopectin
Gentiobiose	6-*O*-β-D-Glucopyranosyl-D-glucose	Hydrolysis of gentianose and glycosides of amygdalin and crocin
Melibiose	6-*O*-α-D-Galactopyranosyl-D-glucose	Hydrolysis of raffinose and in plant exudates
Epimelibiose	6-*O*-α-D-Galactopyranosyl-D-mannose	Hydrolysis of guaran polysac-charide and epimerization of melibiose
Galactobiose	6-*O*-α-D-Galactopyranosyl-D-galactose	Hydrolysis of stachyose and enzymic synthesis
Planteobiose	6-*O*-α-D-Galactopyranosyl-D-fructofuranose	Hydrolysis of planteose

Table 8-1. (*Continued*)

Common name	Constitution	Origin
Rutinose	6-*O*-β-L-Rhamnopyranosyl- D-glucose	The glycoside rutin from *Ruta graveolens*
Vicianose	6-*O*-β-L-Arabinopyranosyl- D-glucose	The glycoside vicianin from *Vicia angustifolia*
Primverose	6-*O*-β-D-Xylopyranosyl- D-glucose 6-*O*-(β-D-Glucopyranosyl- uronic acid)-D-galactose	The glycoside ruberythric acid from madder root Hydrolysis of the gums obtained from many species of *Acacia*

to have a restricted distribution taxonomically, sometimes in a suggestive pattern (for example, gentiobiose is found among species of the Rosaceae). More intensive investigation of the distribution of specific disaccharides must occur before any evaluation of the systematic implications of their distributions can be made. The higher oligosaccharides are mostly products of partial hydrolysis of polysaccharides. However, several non-reducing oligosaccharides are known to occur in various parts of a number of different plant species. The important non-reducing oligosaccharides are raffinose, planteose, gentianose, stachyose, melizitose, and verbascose.

In general there is little data available on the systematic implications of the distribution of oligosaccharides. MacLeod and McCorquodale (1958) compared water-soluble carbohydrates of the Gramineae and evaluated these substances as phylogenetic criteria. Oligosaccharides were among the sugars identified. These authors were primarily concerned with the tribal disposition of certain genera. Twenty-two species, representing eleven tribes, were analysed. Since all of the species contained glucose, fructose, and sucrose, only the more complex sugars provided any useful information. The authors arranged the genera into six groups based on the presence of certain types of oligosaccharides (Table 8-2).

Raffinose is a trisaccharide (galactose-glucose-fructose) while stachyose, a tetrasaccharide, contains two galactose residues attached to glucose of a glucose-fructose unit. This difference between the two oligosaccharides may be regarded as minor. In fact, the authors note that barley embryos infiltrated with concentrated raffinose solution will form some stachyose though normally the sugar is absent.

Table 8-2. Patterns of oligosides of the Gramineae.

Group Characteristic	Genera Represented
1. Hexoses only	*Spartina*
2. Homologous series of fructosans	*Bromus*
3. Fructosans, raffinose	*Elymus* *Agropyron*
4. Raffinose	*Glyceria* *Phalaris* *Nardus* *Molinia*
5. Raffinose and Stachyose	*Brachypodium* *Poa* *Dactylis* *Cynosurus* *Arrhenatherum* *Avena* *Holcus* *Anthoxanthum* *Ammophila* *Agrostis* *Phleum*
6. Isomer of raffinose	*Festuca* *Lolium*

Nevertheless, some genera which contain much raffinose do not form stachyose.

MacLeod and McCorquodale also compared hydrolysis products of the polysaccharides. These always yielded mostly glucose but in addition, the pentoses, xylose and arabinose, were often present, and the relative per cent of xylose and arabinose differed among the genera. Finally, *Nardus* yielded 19 per cent mannose, and *Molinia* yielded 23 per cent galactose.

General appraisal by MacLeod and McCorquodale of the taxonomic significance of their findings was as follows:

(1) *Nardus* was distinctive in its high content of water-soluble mannan.

(2) The Hordeae formed a natural group, but on the basis of its content of soluble polysaccharides *Hordeum* itself is rather distinctive from the other genera examined.

Table 8-3. Constitution and origin of typical higher oligosaccharides (Shafizadeh and Wolfrom, 1958)[a].

Common name	Constitution	Origin
Maltotriose	α-D-Gp-(1 → 4)-α-D-Gp-(1 → 4)-D-Gp	Hydrolysis of starch
Panose	α-D-Gp-(1 → 6)-α-D-Gp-(1 → 4)-D-Gp	Degradation of amylopectin and enzymic synthesis from maltose
Maltose homologs	α-D-Gp-(1 → 4)-[α-D-Gp-(1 → 4)]$_{2-3}$-D-Gp	Hydrolysis of starch
Cellobiose homologs	β-D-Gp-(1 → 4)-[β-D-Gp-(1 → 4)]$_{1-5}$-D-Gp	Acetolysis of cellulose
Xylobiose homologs	β-D-Xyl$p$-(1 → 4)-[β-D-Xyl$p$-(1 → 4)]$_{1-5}$-β-D-Xyl$p$	Hydrolysis of corn cob xylan
Raffinose	α-D-Gal$p$-(1 → 6)-α-D-Gp-(1 → 2) β-D-Fru$f$	Sugar beet, cotton seed hull, other plants
Planteose	α-D-Gal$p$-(1 → 6)-β-D-Fru$f$-(2 → 1) α-D-Gp	Seeds of various *Plantago* species and tobacco
Melezitose	α-D-Gp-(1 → 3)-β-D-Fru$f$-(2 → 1) α-D-Gp	Mannas, honeydews, and exudations of several widely different plants
Gentianose	β-D-Gp-(1 → 6)-α-D-Gp-(1 → 2) β-D-Fru$f$ α-D-Gp-(1 → 4)-α-D-Gp-(1 → 2) β-D-Fru$f$	Rhizomes of several species of *Gentiana* Action of invertase on sucrose
1-Kestose	α-D-Gp-(1 → 2)-β-D-Fru$f$-(1 → 2) β-D-Fru$f$	Action of invertase and *Aspergillus niger* on sucrose
6-Kestose	α-D-Gp-(1 → 2)-β-D-Fru$f$-(6 → 2) β-D-Fru$f$	Action of yeast invertase on sucrose
Neokestose	β-D-Fru$f$-(2 → 6)-α-D-Gp-(1 → 2) β-D-Fru$f$	Action of yeast invertase on sucrose
Stachyose	α-D-Gal$p$-(1 → 6)-α-D-Gal$p$-(1 → 6)-α-D-Gp-(1 → 2) β-D-Fru$f$	*Stachys tuberifera*, soybeans, ash manna, and various plants

Table 8-3. (*Continued*)

Common name	Constitution	Origin
Verbascose	α-D-Gal$p$-(1 → 6)-α-D-Gal$p$- (1 → 6)-α-D-Gal$p$-(1 → 6)- α-D-Gp-(1 → 2) β-D-Fru$f$	Roots of the mullein, *Verbascum thapsus*
Manninotriose	α-D-Gal$p$-(1 → 6)-α-D-Gal$p$- (1 → 6)-D-Gp	Hydrolysis of stachyose; in ash manna
	α-D-Gal$p$-(1 → 6)-β-D-Man$p$- (1 → 4)-D-Man$p$	Hydrolysis of guaran
	β-D-Man$p$-(1 → 4)-β-D-Man$p$- (1 → 4)-D-Man$p$	Hydrolysis of guaran
	α-D-GpA-(1 → 4)-β-D-Xyl$p$- (1 → 4)-D-Xyl$p$	Hemicellulose-B of corn cob

[a] The following standard abbreviations are used in this table. The monosaccharide radicals are represented by the first three letters of their name, with the exception of the glucose radical, which is denoted by G. Furanose and pyranose rings are indicated by f and p, respectively. The uronic acids are shown by the suffix A as in D-GpA which indicates D-glucopyranuronic acid.

(3) The Bromeae formed a natural tribe quite distinct from the Brachypodieae, Festuceae, and Hordeae.

(4) Two genera of the Festuceae, *Lolium* and *Festuca,* were distinctive in containing an unusual trisaccharide.

(5) Two genera of the Aveneae, *Anthoxanthum* and *Holcus,* differed from the other two tested (*Avena* and *Arrhenatherum*) in that they lacked β-glucosan. According to the authors the taxonomic positions *Anthoxanthum* and *Holcus* are slightly suspect on morphological grounds, and their contents of soluble carbohydrate show affinities with the tribe Agrostideae and to a lesser extent with the *Phalarideae.*

With respect to the last statement, the biochemical data applicable to the question of the relationship within the Aveneae lack conviction. While over-all, the data appear to be suggestive, though not conclusive, the rather small number of representatives of the tribes sampled and the difficulty in appraising the biochemical significance of the data raise doubts about their true phylogenetic significance. It is difficult to evaluate the significance of an extra galactose unit on a trisaccharide with a terminal galactose or the presence or absence of a soluble β-glucosan. One is inclined to suspect that the differences alone do not represent sound biochemical criteria for adducing relationships at the tribal level and to predict that such criteria would break down in an extensive survey of species. There is no doubt that a basic problem in biochemical systematics involves the need for greater insight in the appraisal of biochemical data. The obvious fact is that some differences are apt to be more important than others.

There is an interesting paper, again involving the grass family, by Belval and de Cugnac (1941) concerning "glucides" of *Bromus* and *Festuca*. These glucides appear to be oligo- or polysaccharide in nature. The type which is characteristic of *Festuca* is phlein, found in several other grasses including *Phleum pratense*. Phlein is a fructosan, hence related to inulin. However, unlike the inulin fructosans which represent 2, 1' glycosidic linkages, the phlein type possesses 2, 6' linkages. Fructosans are laevorotatory. Belval and de Cugnac found that the specific optical rotation, (α_D), of the fructosan from *Festuca* species, before and after acid hydrolysis, was -49 and $-96°$ while that of *Bromus* species was -37 and $-84°$. These values were said to be quite consistent within the genus.

One questionable taxon, *Bromus* (or *Festuca*) *gigantea,* was particularly interesting. This species has a glucide with the optical rotation characteristic of *Festuca. Lolium perenne* and *L. multiflorum,* which contain phlein, cross with *Festuca,* and the authors suggest that the questionable taxon should be expected to cross with certain *Festuca* species although it was not possible to cross it with the two morphologically similar species, *Bromus asper* and *B. erectus.* The authors also imply that it might also cross with *Lolium.* It is pertinent to note that practically the entire argument in this case rests upon the biochemical data. In Hubbard (1954) it is noted that *Festuca gigantea* hybridizes with *F. pratense* and *F. arundinacea,* and sterile hybrids may be obtained with *Lolium perenne.*

Natural hybrids of *Festuca gigantea* and other species of *Festuca* as well as *Lolium* were known well before the Belval and de Cugnac paper (for example, Jenkins, 1933). However, there was no indication that the authors were aware of the work, and in principle it does not detract from the significance of the biochemical data.

POLYSACCHARIDES

This class of substances is referred to generally as the glycosans. Glycosans may be composed of pentoses (pentosans) or hexoses (hexosans) or even mixtures of these. In general, if a single sugar predominates in the glycosan the name is derived from the sugar involved. Although a rather large number of plant gums and mucilages of polysaccharide character (or related to polysaccharides) are known, and these may be obtained from leaves, stems, roots, and even flowers, beyond a few generalizations (for example, their association with the Leguminosae and specific genera therein such as *Acacia* and *Astragalus*), very little systematic importance is indicated for them at the present time. It is still considered likely that certain gums are synthesized by fungal or bacterial enzymes rather than via a metabolism strictly that of the host. This point is discussed briefly in the comprehensive treatment of plant gums and mucilages by Smith and Montgomery (1959).

Araban is composed of L-arabinose units. It is a common constituent of pectic materials and is very widely distributed. Xylans, whose chief constituent is xylose, occur in several forms, frequently of $1:4$ β-linked D-xylopyranose units in unbranched or branched chains. It is highly probable that the specific xylans would prove to be systematically valuable, but as yet there is inadequate knowledge from an insufficient number of species.

Galactans, which also comprise part of the pectin complex are quite common. Arabogalactans are associated with the woods of conifers, particularly various species of larch (for example, *Larix occidentalis*). Mannans are widely distributed among higher and lower organisms. Galactomannans are also known from a number of species, and according to Neumuller (1958), they are associated particularly with the family Leguminosae (for example, *Medicago sativa* produces a galactomannan with a ratio of galactose to mannose of $2:1$). Glucomannans are known from several species of *Amorphophallus* (Araceae) and seeds of certain *Iris* species.

Polyglucosides other than starch include such substances as floridean starch and laminarin. The former is formed as the reserve carbohydrate in red algae; the latter as the reserve carbohydrate in brown algae. Floridean starch has recently been studied in detail by Meeuse *et al.* (1960), who conclude that there is no basic distinction between this starch and other polysaccharides of the starch family. Floridean starch appears to have a branching pattern similar to that of glycogen, that is with somewhat more frequent, shorter $1:6$ side chains than the amylopectin component of typical starch.

Algae also produce several other unusual types of polysaccharides, some of which are little known chemically. Recently, Stoloff and Silva (1957) attempted to apply the distribution of particular water-soluble polysaccharides to the phylogenetic treatment of sixty species of red algae. The classification of the polysaccharides is based mostly on physical properties. Three types, all of which occur esterified with sulfate residues attached to galactose units, were described:

Agars   These consist of two components: agarose, a linear polymer of galactose and anhydro-galactose, and agaropectin, a sulfated poly-saccharide. Agars set to thermally reversible gels.

Carrageenans   These are also hexose-sulfate derivatives; lambda carrageenan is a galactose sulfate and kappa carrageenan is a mixture of anhydro-galactose and galactose sulfate.

Gelans   Strong gel formers similar in structure to kappa carrageenan, but with a hexose-sulfate ratio of about 0.5.

Stoloff and Silva found that all species of the same genus produced the same type of soluble polysaccharide. In general, as indicated in their paper, there are few cases of more than one type of polysaccharide occurring in the same family. Exceptions are as follows:

Gelidiaceae   *Sulina* produces gelan; four other genera, agar.

Endocladiaceae   *Glocopeltis* produces carrageenan; *Endocladia,* agar.

Phyllophoraceae   *Gymnogongrus* produces carrageenan; *Phyllophora* and *Ahnfeltia,* agar.

Stoloff (1962) has reviewed the distribution of these poly-saccharides and constructed a revised classification of the Florideae on the basis of polysaccharide type alone. According to Stoloff the taxonomist should "look up from his mounts and his microscope and make fuller use of the technological advances in related disciplines. It is not the tools but the viewpoints and objectives that should distinguish the botanist from the chemist or physicist." Later, Stoloff says, ". . . at the familial level, and certainly at the generic level of breakdown, the limits of usefulness of the evolutionary viewpoint and the value to evolutionary theory seems to have been reached." The present writers take a different view with respect to the lower taxonomic categories, for it is in these that experimental methods, cytogenetic, genetic and other macromolecular data are more applicable. In any event it is not likely that the evolutionary viewpoint will ever outlive its usefulness.

A type of polysaccharide which is somewhat difficult to classify, namely, amyloid, has been studied intensively from the systematic point of view by Kooiman (1960a) who has examined the seeds of many species of higher plants. Amyloids are complex polysaccharides which yield glucose, galactose, and xylose. Partial acid hydrolysis yields a product whose X-ray diffraction pattern resembles cellulose. The main chain of the amyloids of different species is then composed of 1-4 linked glucoses (Kooiman and Kreger, 1957). Enzymological experiments with cellulase suggest that xylose and galactose residues are attached as side chains in an undisclosed pattern. The oligosaccharides derived by cellulase hydrolysis of a number of species were the same, but their relative quantities differed (Kooiman, 1957).

The test for amyloid is a blue coloration of the amyloid solution upon exposure to I_2-KI and sodium sulphate (Kooiman, 1960b). Kooiman has tested over 2,500 species and finds certain families which are general amyloid producers. For example, in the Leguminosae, the sub-family Caesalpinioideae are a particularly rich source of amyloid. However, the positive species belong only to the tribes Cynometreae, Sclerolobieae, and Amherstieae. Numerous genera in these three tribes are amyloid containing. Galactomannan is frequently encountered as a constituent of the endosperm in the tribes Cassieae and Eucaesalpinieae.

Outside the Leguminosae amyloid was detected in sixteen dicotyledonous families, but no amyloid was found in the twenty-five monocotyledonous families examined. Some noteworthy distributions follow. In the family Acanthaceae, of the ten species known to produce amyloid all are in the tribe Justicieae. All *Paeonia* species investigated produced amyloid, but thirty other species of the family Ranunculaceae were negative. All of the investigated taxa of the order Primulales (including, according to the system of Engler, only three families: Primulaceae, Myrsinaceae, and Theophrastaceae) were found to produce amyloid. In connection with the latter observation, it seems pertinent to mention that Hutchinson's arrangement of these families differs considerably from that of Engler. Hutchinson places the predominantly herbaceous Primulaceae and Plumbaginaceae in the order Primulales and includes the woody Theophrastaceae, Myrsinaceae, and Aegicerataceae in the order Myrsinales; according to Hutchinson these orders are in different phyletic groups. It is perhaps premature to draw conclusions from the limited data available, but it is difficult to ignore the striking amyloid distribution unless one wants to assume convergence of *both* morphological and biochemical characteristics.

Whatever the ultimate disposition of the families in question, it appears likely that the carbohydrate chemistry of the groups will play some contributory role, but much additional exploratory work will be necessary before meaningful conclusions can be drawn from the amyloid data.

9 ALKALOIDS

The alkaloids include a particularly heterogeneous group of nitrogenous compounds, upwards of 1,000 in number, mostly from vascular plants (Willaman and Schubert, 1961). A few non-vascular plants and some animals synthesize alkaloids, but the compounds are rare in both of these groups. Unlike many classes of naturally occurring substances which may be defined rather precisely in chemical terms, no entirely adequate chemical definition of an alkaloid seems possible because of the variety of alkaloid types in existence. By a general operational definition an alkaloid is considered to be a pharmacologically active compound usually containing a basic group and with a heterocyclic nitrogen-containing ring.[1] It is evident, from such a definition, that alkaloids are

155

not a chemically natural group, and it likewise follows that they do not constitute a natural biological group, functionally, phylogenetically, or with respect to their biosynthesis. Therefore, few generalizations relevant to any of these above considerations are warranted. Among nitrogenous substances of plants there is almost a continuum from the universal products of metabolism to alkaloids in the strict sense, and of course nitrogen-containing secondary compounds exist which are not classified as alkaloids. Purine and pyrimidine bases and the amino acid, histidine, are alkaloids except by the physiological criterion. Betacyanins (formerly regarded as nitrogenous anthocyanins, discussed in Chapter 14), except for the absence of any obvious physiological effects, are clearly model alkaloids.

Generalizations concerning the stability of alkaloids in the plant, factors affecting their synthesis, origin within the plant, and histological distribution must also be treated conservatively because alkaloids comprise such a heterogeneous group.

Since, by definition, alkaloids are physiologically active upon animals, and many alkaloids are important drugs, the compounds are best known to the pharmacologist. Much of the voluminous literature on alkaloids is the direct or indirect result of their great economic importance. It is probable that alkaloids are less well known to most botanists than are certain compounds or classes of compounds that serve some structural or obvious functional role in the plant (for example, lignin, and plastid pigments). Consequently, a brief general discussion, including a limited treatment of the chemical affinities of the major classes of alkaloids will precede the section directly treating their sytematic significance. In this latter section no attempt is made to give a comprehensive account of alkaloid distribution or to develop any unified system of phylogenetic interpretation. Each of a number of more natural classes of alkaloids could be given such a treatment, and in fact some investigators have already done so. Certain of these latter types of studies will be described, but they have been selected mainly to provide further insight into general principles applicable to the evaluation of the systematic worth of alkaloids.

In general, discussion of biosynthetic mechanisms past the point required to clarify some point of phylogenetic interpretation is beyond the scope of this book, especially in the case of the alkaloids, wherein many classes of compounds exist, each of which may be formed by almost completely independent biosynthetic routes. The

[1] According to Elderfield (1960): "No completely satisfactory all-inclusive definition of these compounds is possible. It will be sufficient to define an alkaloid as a nitrogenous substance usually of plant origin, usually possessing basic properties, usually optically active, and usually possessing some characteristic physiological action. Such a definition is not perfect, and exceptions to all of the above criteria can be cited."

subject of alkaloid biosynthesis is rarely given comprehensive formal review, and then one is impressed with the incompleteness of knowledge and the prevalence of hypotheses supported by circumstantial evidence alone (Mothes and Romeike, 1958; Marion, 1958; and Poisson, 1958). It should be noted that numerous alkaloids show structurally a potential relationship to one or more amino acids. Consequently, it is generally regarded that alkaloid synthesis is related to amino acid synthesis. This generalization has proved helpful in seeking relationships between alkaloids otherwise difficult to interpret (discussed by Schlittler, 1956). Hegnauer (1958) has placed the major alkaloid types into amino acid "families" for purposes of disclosing useful systematic correlations. The arbitrary basis of such schemes should be remembered, however. The directness of the relationship of the biosynthesis of a particular alkaloid to a corresponding amino acid may vary greatly in different cases. Wenkert (1959) has recently suggested that we may be overemphasizing the relationship between alkaloid and amino acid biosynthesis and thereby losing sight of a potential relationship between alkaloid and carbohydrate metabolism, particularly reaction sequences leading toward or derived from aromatic synthesis.

SOME MAJOR CLASSES OF ALKALOIDS

PROTOALKALOIDS

These comprise a group of simple alkaloids lacking a heterocyclic nitrogen-containing ring. Their structure suggests a relationship to the aromatic amino acids (for example, tyrosine), and evidence exists that hordenine is formed by decarboxylation of tyrosine followed by N-methylation (Marion, 1958). Mescaline is also formed from tyrosine by decarboxylation followed by hydroxylation of the ring and methylation (Leete, 1959). These alkaloids are found in such widely separated plant families as the Gnetaceae, Gramineae, Cactaceae and Leguminosae, and their systematic value is therefore limited to considerations of intrafamilial phylogeny.

Representative types of protoalkaloids are the following:

ephedrin

hordenine

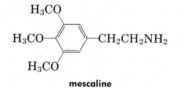

mescaline

ISOQUINOLINE ALKALOIDS

This large group of alkaloids may be considered to be derivatives of a parent substance, isoquinoline. Like the protoalkaloids they may also be regarded as, potentially, derivatives of pathways connected with aromatic amino acid synthesis.

isoquinoline

The isoquinoline alkaloids range from simple derivatives with a reduced heterocyclic ring and minor substitutions of the benzene ring to very complex alkaloids of the bis-benzylisoquinoline type. The distribution of this more or less natural class of alkaloids is of considerable interest and will be discussed in a following section. The isoquinoline alkaloids are quite characteristic of the *Papaveraceae* and certain other families. Representatives of the classes of isoquinoline derivatives are illustrated below:

(a) *Simple isoquinoline derivatives.*

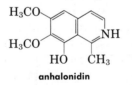

anhalonidin

(b) *Benzylisoquinoline derivatives.*

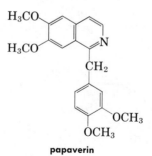

papaverin

(c) *Protoberberine derivatives.* The basic berberine ring configuration may be viewed as a benzylisoquinoline derivative in which N-methylation is followed by condensation with the free phenyl group.

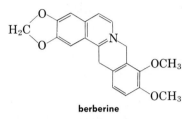

berberine

(d) *Protopine derivatives.* The protopine basic configuration may be considered to arise by opening of the original heterocyclic ring of isoquinoline in a protoberberine configuration.

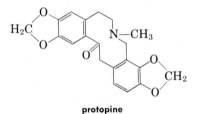

protopine

(e) *Aporphine derivatives.* These may also be regarded as derivatives of the benzylisoquinoline type in which ring closure between the free-phenyl and the isoquinoline-phenyl ring occurs.

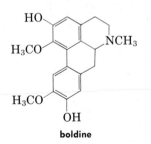

boldine

(f) *Phthalideisoquinoline derivatives.* These constitute a relatively small group which may be regarded as derivatives of benzylisoquinoline formed by a secondary ring closure to produce a five-membered, oxygen-containing ring. This group of alkaloids is found in the *Papaveraceae,* with the exception of hydrastine (below) which is found only in Berberidaceae and Ranunculaceae.

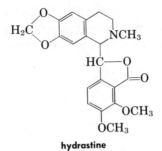

hydrastine

(g) *Bisbenzylisoquinoline derivatives.* These alkaloids consist of two benzylisoquinoline groups joined by one or more ether linkages. They are found in several families including the Magnoliaceae and Berberidaceae.

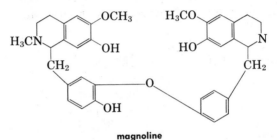

magnoline

INDOLE ALKALOIDS

This class is probably far more heterogeneous than the two previous classes. Although other mechanisms of formation of the indole nucleus doubtlessly exist, in some cases at least indole is derived from tryptophane metabolism which, in turn, is derived as an early offshoot from the pathway to the aromatic amino acids. Shikimic acid is a parent substance for both groups, and at least in the early stages of their formation all alkaloids discussed so far are likely to have metabolic connections with each other. Some simple indole alkaloids are known (for example, gramine, illustrated below), and it is not surprising to find that they too occur in a number of widely separated families.

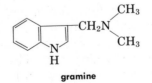

gramine

In contrast, many of the indole alkaloids such as strychnine (see below) are quite complex. Sometimes it is impossible to determine whether certain of these alkaloids are reduced indole or reduced isoquinoline derivatives (for example, some *Erythrina* alkaloids such as erysopin). Therefore, the systematic distribution may provide clues to the interpretation of the alkaloid's biosynthetic affinities. Representative indole alkaloids are the following:

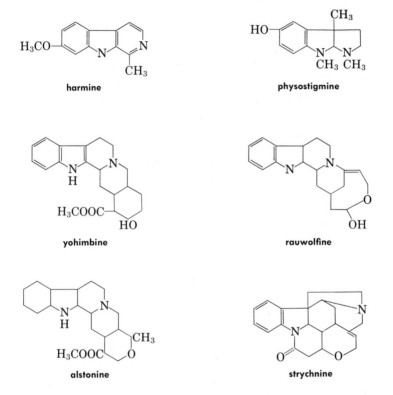

harmine

physostigmine

yohimbine

rauwolfine

alstonine

strychnine

PYRIDINE ALKALOIDS

This group includes alkaloids in which the pyridine nucleus itself is preserved as well as those with a reduced pyridine, or piperidine, nucleus. The alkaloids may be quite simple (pyridine itself is found in *Haplopappus hartwegii*) or moderately complex. Simple pyridine derivatives such as coniin are found in numerous families among gymnosperms, monocots, and dicots. Since pyridine is a part of the fundamental coenzyme complex involved in oxidative phosphorylation, repeated evolution of simple pyridine derivatives is not surprising. Although the pyridine alkaloids are widely distributed some of them are of considerable systematic importance. Representative types are illustrated below.

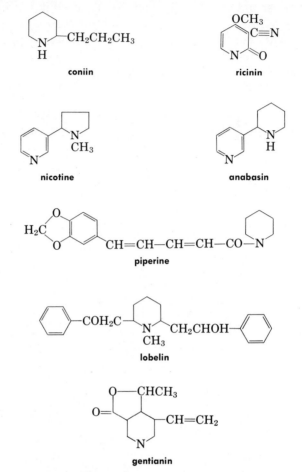

coniin

ricinin

nicotine

anabasin

piperine

lobelin

gentianin

Several minor categories are illustrated below without further comment. The term minor is used here strictly to indicate that these groups do not exhibit, in general, the diversity of subtypes encountered among the previous groups. Some of the most important and best known alkaloids will be recognized among this group however.

Quinolizine derivatives.

lupinine

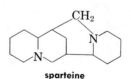

sparteine

Pyrrolidine derivatives.   *Tropane derivatives.*

hygrin

hyoscyamin

Pyrrolizidine derivatives.

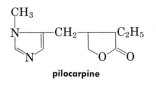

senecionine

Imidazole derivatives.   *Sterol derivatives.*

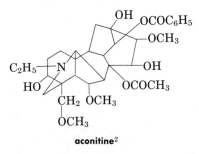

pilocarpine

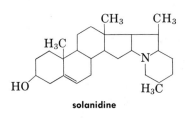

solanidine

Terpene derivatives.   *Purine derivatives.*

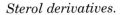

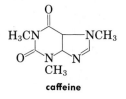

caffeine

aconitine[2]

[2] After Wiesner *et al.*, 1959 and Bachelor *et al.*, 1960.

Mothes and Romeike (1958) have summarized the major distribution of alkaloid types among orders and families of higher plants. Table 9-1 is adapted from their data. In a few places suggestive correlations in alkaloid content exist between certain families (or even groups of families as in the isoquinoline types). While certain of these correlations will be discussed in this chapter, in general the meaning of such data is not yet sufficiently clear, and the known biosynthetic relationships are too inadequate to allow meaningful speculation. The present writers believe that the diversity of alkaloid types, their complexity, and their wide distribution allow much optimism regarding their systematic importance. The taxonomic value of alkaloids is not necessarily restricted to simple correlations of distribution, but later on the basis of studies of comparative biosynthesis, enzymology, and genetic mechanisms, these compounds may yield even more substantial insight into phylogenetic problems.

Some General Considerations of
Alkaloid Distribution and Physiology

It was noted above that alkaloids are rare in animals and in lower plants. Among the former organisms alkaloids are found in such widely separate groups as sea snails (Echinodermata), sand worms (Annelida), toads[3], and sharks (Chordata). Alkaloids are apparently absent from algae, mosses, and liverworts, most fungi, and are rare among the simpler vascular plants. For example, only protoalkaloids or other relatively simple alkaloids occur in the divisions Sphenopsida and Lycopsida; alkaloids are unreported from ferns, unreported from cycads, and rare in gymnosperms in general. Thus, other than among flowering plants alkaloids are not widely distributed. Willaman and Schubert (1952) reported that about ninety-seven of the approximately 300 angiosperm families were known to have alkaloid-containing genera. Cromwell (1955) stated that forty families of flowering plants contained alkaloids. The reason for this discrepancy is not clear. Surveys of the flora of various regions provide some information about the actual percentage of alkaloid-containing species. A survey of Russian species (Orechov, 1955) yielded 10 per cent, and Australian species (Webb, 1949), yielded 20 per cent alkaloid-containing species.

---

[3] Toads (*Bufo*) are notable in that secretions from their parotoid glands contain not only alkaloids [bufotenines, also found in the plant, *Piptadenia falcata* (Giesbrecht, 1960)], but represent the only known vertebrate source of the plant sterol, phytosterol, and also contain bufagins which are similar to the cardiac aglycones found in certain plants. To our knowledge no proposal to include *Bufo* in the plant order Ranales has yet appeared, even in a chemical journal.

Table 9-1. Distribution by family of the major alkaloids of higher plants (adapted from Mothes and Romeike, 1958).

Family	Alkaloid types present (among those illustrated)
Lycopodiaceae	pyridine
Equisetaceae	protoalkaloid and pyridine
Taxaceae	protoalkaloid
Gnetaceae	protoalkaloid
Magnoliaceae	isoquinoline
Lauraceae	isoquinoline
Anonaceae	isoquinoline
Menispermaceae	isoquinoline
Ranunculaceae	isoquinoline, quinolizine, terpene
Berberidaceae	isoquinoline, quinolizine
Nymphaeaceae	terpene
Papaveraceae	isoquinoline, quinolizine, pyrrolidine
Crassulaceae	pyridine
Leguminosae	protoalkaloid, pyridine, pyrrolizidine, quinolizine, isoquinoline, indole
Theaceae	purine
Sterculiaceae	purine
Rutaceae	isoquinoline, imidazole
Celastraceae	protoalkaloid
Aquifoliaceae	purine
Malvaceae	protoalkaloid
Umbelliferae	pyridine, pyrrolidine
Piperaceae	pyridine, pyrrolidine
Moraceae	pyridine
Euphorbiaceae	pyridine
Santalaceae	pyrrolizidine
Chenopodiaceae	protoalkaloid, pyridine, quinolizine, indole
Cactaceae	protoalkaloid, isoquinoline, pyridine
Phytolaccaceae	purine
Nyctaginaceae	purine
Loganiaceae	isoquinoline, indole
Apocynaceae	indole, steroid
Asclepiadaceae	pyridine
Gentianaceae	pyridine
Convolvulaceae	pyrrolidine, tropane
Boraginaceae	pyrrolizidine
Labiatae	pyridine
Solanaceae	protoalkaloid, pyrrolidine, pyridine, pyrrolizidine, tropane, steroid
Rubiaceae	isoquinoline, indole, purine
Lobeliaceae	pyridine
Compositae	pyridine, pyrrolizidine
Liliaceae	protoalkaloid, isoquinoline, steroid, purine
Amaryllidaceae	isoquinoline
Dioscoriaceae	tropane
Gramineae	protoalkaloid, indole
Palmae	pyridine

Webb found that from 753 species in 110 families tested, 145 species from forty-one families contained alkaloids.

The distribution of alkaloids within the plant and in the cell has been discussed by James (1950). Usually, the alkaloids, which are water soluble, accumulate in the vacuoles and are rarely found in dead tissues (even the quinine of *Cinchona* bark is said to be confined to living cells). Alkaloids may be present in any part of a particular plant and very often occur in meristematic tissue. In *Baptisia leucophaea,* alkaloids have been found to be present in roots, stems, leaves, flowers, fruits, and seeds, the highest concentration occurring in the seeds. The absolute amounts and relative concentrations of the various alkaloids in *B. leucophaea* differ from one part of the plant to another (Brehm, 1962).

Synthesis of alkaloids exhibits a number of interesting variations. For example, nicotine synthesis in *Nicotiana* is initiated in the root and completed in the leaves. The lupine alkaloids, however, are produced in rapidly growing shoots. Doubtlessly, many variations are to be expected in the pattern of synthesis of such a heterogeneous group of substances.

Concerning the stability of alkaloids, James (1953) has said that

> . . . a given species always forms the same group of related alkaloids, in more or less fixed proportions and within fairly narrow limits of concentration. It has proved very difficult to modify these relations, even quantitatively, by simple experimental means.

Mothes (1955) and other workers, however, suggest that alkaloids are definitely affected by various external factors. In our analyses of individual plants of *Baptisia leucophaea* from several populations we have found a wide range in the absolute and relative concentrations of the leaf alkaloids (Fig. 9-1). We do not know yet whether or not these differences are genetic. However, even if the differences were assumed to be genetic in origin, such extensive variation would suggest a multiple gene system expressing the effects indirectly. In such circumstance (for example, wherein alkaloid synthesis is influenced by diverse internal factors) it seems likely that certain external factors would also exert some influence. A relatively small proportion of alkaloids has been studied with respect to questions of variation under experimental conditions. It is likely that the role of some alkaloids in the plant is not critical, the factor of natural selection is correspondingly presumed to be low, and therefore regulatory mechanisms controlling their synthesis would not be expected to be highly refined. Furthermore, alkaloid synthesis is somewhat closely connected

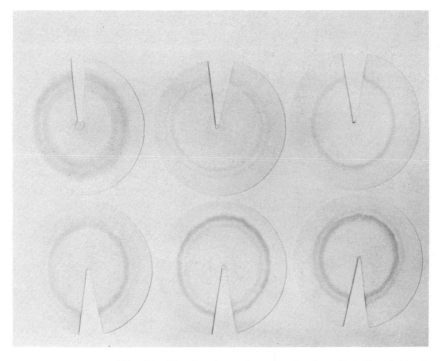

Fig. 9-1. Circular chromatograms showing alkaloid variation in individual plants of *Baptisia leucophaea* from a single population. Leaf samples were from plants of similar stage of development collected at the same time. (Courtesy of B. R. Brehm)

with amino acid metabolism, and environmental factors may have a powerful effect upon free amino acid concentrations. It is therefore understandable that alkaloids may in certain cases be quite sensitive to environmental factors.

If it were established that alkaloids served some important role in the plants in which they occur, additional systematic significance might underlie their presence; for example, the alkaloids would, in turn, be related to other special physiological attributes of the plant. However, in general, the role of alkaloids in the plant is unknown. They have been regarded as sources of protection against insects, organic waste products (detoxification products), regulatory devices, or even energy sources, but little or no direct support of any of these hypothetical functions is available. It is beyond the scope of this book to explore the possible roles of alkaloids in detail. The possibility that alkaloids serve as detoxification mechanisms in which the products are collected in vacuoles is interesting however. Alkaloids are absent from algae and aquatic plants in general. In aquatic higher plants water-soluble toxic products may be eliminated directly into the environment without the requirement of detoxification mechanisms. The aquatics which produce alkaloids are usually those with floating leaves. For example, the submerged Ceratophyllaceae lack alkaloids while the closely related Nymphaeaceae with floating leaves are alkaloid containing. [It is interesting to note that in the genus *Cabomba* (Nymphaeaceae), in which the leaves are mostly submerged, alkaloids have not to our knowledge been reported.]

Thus far there has been little or no evidence of physiological effects of alkaloids upon the plants in which they occur. Dawson (1948) has expressed skepticism that negative results effectively settle the question. Alkaloids of one species may apparently affect other species—even close relatives. Mothes (1960) noted that when belladonna or tomato was grafted onto *Nicotiana* stock, nicotine migrated into the scion and browning occurred. The browning was assumed to result from the presence of nicotine.

GENERAL CONSIDERATIONS OF THE SYSTEMATIC VALUE OF ALKALOIDS

Previously, it was noted that the protoalkaloids and nicotine had a distribution which suggested that parallel evolution accounted for their presence in certain widely separated plant groups. Rowson (1958) has noted that the distributions of anabasine, berberine, and caffeine did not closely correlate with the systematic position of the plants in which they occur. The same is true of 3-methoxypyridine (found in *Equisetum* and *Thermopsis*), the harman alkaloid types, and others. Since parallel evolution of morphological attributes is also regularly encountered, similar parallelisms among biochemical components should not be cause for excessive pessimism concerning their use. Parallel evolution is likely to be responsible for many possible misinterpretations of biochemical data.

Within an alkaloid series it is probable that alkaloid complexity is correlated generally with systematic advancement. However, McNair (1935) somewhat naively correlated the molecular weights of alkaloids with the Engler and Prantl family index number. The "percentage of frequency rule" (Chapter 4) supports the previous generalization but only within a closely knit group wherein parallel evolution for the character is minimized. It is of course important to establish better criteria of complexity than merely molecular weight. For example, the genetical basis for the synthesis of a bis-benzylisoquinoline may be no more complex than that of the smaller berberine type of isoquinoline. The former is a dimer of a simple benzylisoquinoline; the latter probably involves an N-methyl phenyl condensation of the simple benzylisoquinoline.

There seem to be an unusually large number of highly speculative statements relevant to the systematic implications of the alkaloids. Arguments based on criteria of simplicity versus complexity of the alkaloids may be quite subtle in nature. Often it is difficult to evaluate an argument fully because the logic, as applied in a chemical reference-framework, may be sound, but not in accord with the biological facts. The following discussion by Wenkert (1959) provides an example:

> On the basis of the rapidly emerging patterns of the biosynthesis of plant products, both theoretical and experimental, it is possible to categorize, albeit yet crudely, natural substances into two classes, one based to a large extent on acetate and, hence, on genetically and enzymatically easy routes, and the other founded to a major degree on non-acetate material, i.e. substances farther along in the tricarboxylic acid cycles and hence, enzymatically difficult, circuitous routes. If it be assumed that the evolution of life processes, i.e. the structure and mechanism of enzymes, through geologic time proceeded from simple to more complex patterns, a correlation of paleobotany with the chemistry of natural products would be on hand. Substances originating from acetate would be expected present in the oldest plants. On this basis the structure of *Lycopodium* alkaloid annotinine is no surprise, nor is the discovery of triterpenes from petroleum and coal deposits.

Despite specific reference to the tricarboxylic acid intermediates to illustrate the "non-acetate" pathways, we infer from the main body of the paper that Wenkert is considering the acetate-mevalonate family (Chapter 13) of compounds on the one hand and the shikimate-prephenate family (Chapter 11) on the other. The former lead to such compounds as the carotenoids, terpenes, essential oils, and sterols; the latter lead to indoles, aromatic amino acids, lignins, and tannins. In certain water-soluble plant pigments (flavonoids) there is a partial contribution from each pathway (Chapter 11). Alkaloids of both affinities are known as well as some unrelated to either (for example, the purine derivatives). Perhaps purines, by the criterion above, should be expected in the more ancient plants since it is generally believed that the earliest living organisms formed polynucleotides containing purines. However, alkaloids of the purine type are found in coffee.

While the theoretical position of Wenkert is no doubt sound, the fact is that the most "primitive" known alkaloid-containing plants are vascular plants. These plants also produce carotenoids and lignin. The mevalonate and prephenate pathways were undoubtedly well represented among lower forms possibly hundreds of millions of years before alkaloids appeared. The genetic complexity of a given alkaloid is perhaps best represented by the extent of deviation of the alkaloid from an already established basic metabolic pathway. The reasons for assuming that non-acetate pathways are more likely to involve enzymatically difficult and circuitous routes may be valid, but they are not obvious to the present writers.

SPECIFIC EXAMPLES OF ALKALOIDS OF
SYSTEMATIC SIGNIFICANCE

Alkaloids of the isoquinoline class are probably among the best examples to illustrate the application of biochemical criteria to phylogeny of the higher categories. In this case the disposition of families and perhaps even the proper delimitation of orders are involved. Nevertheless, so far the alkaloid chemistry has failed to clarify the taxonomic problems among the groups of plants concerned.

The isoquinolines, as noted above, are likely offshoots of aromatic amino acid metabolism. Hegnauer (1952, 1954, 1958) has discussed the taxonomic distribution of the entire group of related alkaloids, and our treatment is derived principally from his comprehensive account. A partial list of families containing isoquinolines follows. For later reference purposes the list is divided into the categories of Lignosae and Herbaceae (Hutchinson 1959).

Lignosae	Herbaceae
Magnoliaceae	Ranunculaceae
Anonaceae	Berberidaceae
Monimiaceae	Menispermaceae
Hernandiaceae	Papaveraceae
Rutaceae	
Aristolochiaceae	

The families listed above are recognizable as representing in general rather "primitive" families by Hutchinson's criteria, and except for the Aristolochiaceae, Rutaceae, and Papaveraceae, they represent the Ranales of Engler and Diels. Other Ranalian families (for example, Nymphaeaceae) do not contain isoquinoline alkaloids but contain other types of alkaloids. Certain families (for example, Ranunculaceae) may contain isoquinoline derivatives and in addition other types of alkaloids. Most of the families listed contain several types of isoquinolines. The Magnoliaceae contain, in addition, proto-alkaloids, the simplest group of alkaloids, which are also derived from aromatic amino acid metabolism.

General conclusions from the over-all distribution of iso-quinoline alkaloids are that their wide occurrence among the Ranales indicate phylogenetic interrelationship. Outside this group (for example, in the Amaryllidaceae) they occur infrequently, and then the specific mode of secondary ring closure differs, indicative of parallel evolution. These Amaryllidaceae alkaloids, the lycorine types, have a different type of linkage between the benzyl and heterocyclic N-containing ring of the basic benzylisoquinoline. In the Leguminosae the *Erythrina* alkaloids, regarded as possible isoquinoline derivatives, may also be interpreted as indole derivatives. An exception is the family Rutaceae wherein almost a full array of isoquinoline alkaloids of the same types as occur in the Ranales are to be found.

Gibbs (1954) has noted the striking parallelisms to be found in the alkaloids of the sub-families Papaveroideae and Fumarioideae of the Papaveraceae. (However, see Chapter 6 for the distribution of δ-acetylornithine in these sub-families.) These sub-families are con-sidered to be separate families by some systematists. It is more than a question of the common presence of isoquinolines which relates these sub-families. The extent of alkaloid *parallelism* is striking. Proto-berberines, aporphines, phthalideisoquinolines, and protopines occur widely throughout both sub-families. Phthalideisoquinolines are rare outside the Papaveraceae while protopine is found elsewhere only in *Nandina* (Berberidaceae). Gibbs states:

> We must not let the finding of protopine in a plant outside the Papaveraceae blind us to the very strong evidence from the work of Manske and others that the Papaveroideae, Hypocoideae and Fumar-ioideae are indeed very closely allied chemically. This work is one of the best examples of the worth of comparative chemistry applied to taxonomy.

Actually, demonstration of alkaloid similarities in the sub-families of Papaveraceae does not necessarily bear upon the question of whether the two taxonomic groups should be considered as sub-families or as families. The significant point is that they have been closely linked. The taxonomic position, as long as such a link is emphasized, is a matter of descretion.

Mothes and Romeike (1955) have questioned the use of isoquinoline alkaloids to relate the Papaveroideae and Fumarioideae to each other, yet by the same data to relate the Papaveroideae to other Ranalian families. They consider that such conclusions represent circular reasoning. However, there are two levels of similarity involved, and the evidence should be applied independently at different levels. For example, various types of isoquinoline alkaloids occur in the different families of the Ranalian complex, and it is merely the presence of the general isoquinoline type that ties the groups together, while, in addition, in the Papaveraceae it is the common presence of a series of specific isoquinoline derivatives, some rare, which is considered to be especially significant in adducing the relationship of the sub-families.

Comparison of certain alkaloids of the Ranunculaceae and Berberidaceae proves to be interesting. In the Ranunculaceae, *Xanthorhiza, Coptis, Thalictrum,* and *Hydrastis* produce isoquinoline alkaloids. Except in *Hydrastis* the alkaloids are relatively simple protoberberines. Species of *Hydrastis* contain hydrastine, a more complex phthalideisoquinoline, found only in *Berberis laurina* of the Berberidaceae. In the Berberidaceae, *Berberis, Mahonia,* and *Nandina* are alkaloid producers. Protopine, otherwise restricted to the Papaveraceae, is found in *Nandina,* and *Nandina* lacks the bis-benzylisoquinolines found in other Berberidaceae. It is interesting that Hutchinson (1959) and other workers have placed *Nandina* in a monotypic family, Nandinaceae. Generally, the alkaloid distribution in Berberidaceae and Ranunculaceae does not suggest any unusually close relationship between the two families. However, an interesting proposal was published in this connection by McFadden (1950). McFadden recognized a "small chromosome group" of five genera in the Berberidaceae: *Nandina, Berberis, Jeffersonia, Hydrastis,* and *Glaucidium.* Basic chromosome numbers in this group vary from $x = 6$ to $x = 14$. In the Ranunculaceae six genera also form a "small chromosome" group (Gregory, 1941): *Isopyrum, Aquilegia, Anemonella, Thalictrum, Coptis,* and *Xanthorhiza.* Basic chromosome numbers for these genera range from $x = 7$ to $x = 18$. The isoquinoline alkaloids are found, in the two families, only in the small chromosome groups. According to McFadden:

> From a morphological standpoint, treatment of this group of genera as a systematic unit is at least as tenable as their present classification. However, in grouping these genera as a taxonomic unit morphological characters would be stressed that are different from those now employed by classification of these.

Certainly, the cytological and biochemical data considered separately would not constitute strong evidence.[4] The conclusions of McFadden are not in accord with the serological data provided by Hammond (Chapter 5) who placed *Hydrastis* in the Ranunculaceae but closer to *Ranunculus* than to *Thalictrum*. Finally, the six small-chromosome genera assigned to the Ranunculaceae do not form bis-benzylisoquinolines which are typical of the Berberidaceae. Other biochemical evidence cited by McFadden was relatively meager and inconclusive, but it is quite possible that intensive biochemical studies would clarify this interesting situation.

The family Rutaceae (containing the orange) is the last to be discussed in connection with the isoquinoline alkaloids. Hegnauer (1958) noted that protoberberine, aporphine, protopine, and rare chelidonine alkaloids were all present in Rutaceae as well as in certain Ranalean families. He believes that the affinities of Rutaceae and these families are much closer than most systematic treatments imply. In Hegnauer's words:

> The exactness, not similarity, of the complex phenylisoquinoline alkaloids in both groups appear so surprising and convincing that a new investigation of the systematic position of the Rutaceae may be urgent.

In this connection it is interesting to note that Hallier presumably derived the Rutaceae from "stocks ancestral to the Berberidaceae" (Lawrence, 1951).

Another alkaloid of the Rutaceae, rutaecarpine, is a complex, indole-containing substance. Chemically related alkaloids are present in the families Apocynaceae, Loganiaceae, and Rubiaceae. No systematic bridge between these families and the Rutaceae is necessarily implied, but it is interesting that Hutchinson (1959) has proposed a relationship between Rubiaceae and the families Apocynaceae and Loganiaceae.

Other indole-alkaloids of restricted systematic distribution are those of the Amaryllidaceae. In this family over seventy alkaloids are known.[5] While there are a number of rare alkaloids in this sub-

---

[4] Kumazawa (1938) on morphological grounds provisionally included the genera *Hydrastis* and *Glaucidium* in the Ranunculaceae as the sole members of the sub-family Glaucidioideae; however, he retained *Jeffersonia* in the Berberidaceae as have nearly all subsequent workers.

[5] To indicate the increased interest in phytochemical research, it seems worth noting that only fifteen alkaloids were known in the Amaryllidaceae in 1954, the additional compounds having been acquired over a six-year period (Wildman, 1960).

family, some such as lycorine, have been found in all twenty-six of the genera of Amaryllidoideae which have been examined to date (Wildman, 1960). Pax and Hoffmann (1930), in their treatment of the Amaryllidaceae, recognized four sub-families: Agavoideae, Hypoxidoideae, Campynematoideae, and Amaryllidoideae. Most workers have treated the family similarly, but Hutchinson (1959) excluded all the sub-families, other than the Amaryllidoideae, and simultaneously transferred three tribes of the classically constituted Liliaceae to the Amaryllidaceae [including the tribe Allieae, which contains the genus *Allium* (onion)]. It is interesting to note that Hutchinson's treatment, except for the transfer of the three Liliaceous tribes (Agapantheae, Allieae, and Gilliesieae), would be compatible with the alkaloid data. However, alkaloids of the Amaryllidaceous type, while found in nearly all of the tribes of the Amaryllidoideae as classically constituted, are not found in the three transferred tribes, and therefore the family, as reconstituted by Hutchinson, is perhaps as anomalous from the standpoint of alkaloids as by the treatment of Pax and Hoffmann.

Unrelated alkaloids, of the colchicine type, have been found in five genera of three tribes of the Liliaceae. Two of the tribes (Colchiceae and Iphigenieae) appear to be fairly closely related, but the third (Uvularieae) is somewhat more distant. However, the Liliaceae is a large and varied family, and as indicated by Hutchinson (1959) it is still somewhat artificially classified, even with the removal of several of its more distinct elements. A more inclusive biochemical-morphological study might yield a better phylogenetic arrangement than exists at present. Correlations between the comparative chemistry of the alkaloids and that of other chemical groups (for example, the substituted glutamic acids, Chapter 6 and the saponins, Chapter 13) in the families Liliaceae and Amaryllidaceae should be informative.

Hegnauer (1958) considers that the occurrence of the *Senecio* alkaloids outside the family Compositae, in one instance in the Boraginaceae and in another the Leguminosae, is of phylogenetic significance. He notes the presence of inulin in both the Boraginaceae and Compositae and the flavonoid chalkone in both the Compositae and Leguminosae and concludes that,

> ... the extensive structural resemblances of the *Crotalaria, Borago* and *Senecio* alkaloids is altogether not understandable if no genetic connection can be recognized between the families, and the alkaloids are metabolic wastes.

Perhaps this is true, but parallel evolution, at least in the Leguminosae, seems to be the more likely explanation.

An interesting group of alkaloids found in the legume genus *Lupinus* and related groups may prove, eventually, to be of considerable systematic significance within the family Leguminosae. These quinolizine derivatives, represented by a relatively small number of specific types, are also known to occur in the families Berberidaceae, Chenopodiaceae, Papaveraceae, and Solanaceae, but it is the Leguminosae in which the alkaloids have been most intensively studied. In the latter family, only the tribes Genisteae, Podalyrieae, and Sophoreae of the sub-family Papilionoideae include genera which produce these alkaloids; for example, *Lupinus, Thermopsis, Baptisia, Cytisus, Sarothamnus, Genista, Sophora,* and *Podalyria.* Certain of the lupine alkaloids, such as cytisine and spartein are of quite widespread occurrence within these tribes. Biogenetic evidence plus correlated genetic studies should provide information that will yield further insight into phylogenetic problems. Intensive investigation of the lupine alkaloids using several different approaches is currently underway by Nowacki and colleagues (Kazimierski and Nowacki, 1961). Schutte and Nowacki (1959) have presented evidence that sparteine is synthesized from the amino acid, lysine, and Nowacki (1958) and Birecka *et al.* (1959) have circumstantial evidence that sparteine is converted into lupanine and then into hydroxylupanine. It is likely that some parallelism and convergence have occurred in the origin of biosynthetic mechanisms involving lupine alkaloid synthesis. To what extent these complexities can be explained in a phylogenetic sense remains to be seen. Intensive investigations of large, natural genera such as *Lupinus* should prove important in clarifying inter-generic relationships by exposing the amount and nature of variation at the infra-generic level.

Hegnauer (1958) has utilized the presence of lupinine alkaloids in the Leguminosae and Chenopodiaceae as evidence of a relationship between the orders Rosales and Ranales. In support of this Hegnauer cited Hutchinson's placement of the presumed parental stock of the Chenopodiaceae and Caryophyllaceae, adjacent to the Ranales. However, in Hutchinson's scheme the Leguminosae are in the Lignosae, allied with the woody Magnoliales, while the species producing lupine alkaloids are to be found in the herbaceous Ranunculaceae and Berberidaceae, both in Hutchinson's Herbaceae. In this instance, then, it does not seem valid to imply that the argument derives further support from Hutchinson's system.

Recently, the taxonomic significance of the steroid alkaloids of the veratrum group has been evaluated (Kupchan *et al.,* 1961). This study is representative of other similar studies which involve a group of alkaloids whose distributions within either a sub-family or

genus indicate definite taxonomic significance. This study will therefore serve as an example of the type. The veratrum alkaloids are
known, so far, from the tribe Veratreae of the Liliaceae. Numerous
individual alkaloids occur representing variations in the basic nucleus,
substitutions of the basic nucleus, and ester derivatives. Kupchan
et al. recognized two major groups, the jerveratrum group and the
ceveratrum group as follows:

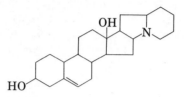

   Jerveratrum group. Veratramine, rubijervine, isorubijervine,
jervine.

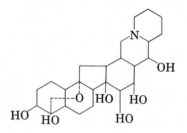

   Ceveratrum group. Zygadenine, veracevine, germine, protoverine.
  The two groups possess the C_{27} ring structure (other veratrum alkaloid types are incompletely identified). The jerveratrum
types, with few hydroxyl groups, occur as free bases or as simple
glucosides. The ceveratrum types, with seven to nine hydroxyl substitutions, usually occur esterified with various acids or ester alkaloids,
never as glycosides. Among the ceveratrum types, zygadenine and
veracevine occur as monoesters; germine and protoverine occur as tri
or tetra esters.
  The genera concerned are *Veratrum, Zygadenus, Stenanthium,
Schoenocaulon, Amianthium,* and *Melanthium. Schoenocaulon* is regarded as rather distinctive and homogeneus, *Veratrum* as relatively
homogeneous, *Stenanthium* as small and diverse, and *Zygadenus* as
quite heterogeneous possibly including several genera (as subgenera).
  The distribution of veratrum alkaloids is given in Table 9-2.

Table 9-2. Distribution of *Veratrum* alkaloids (adapted from Kupchan *et al.*, 1961).

Species	Type of alkaloids		
	jerveratrum	*cerveratrum*	*unclassified*
Veratrum album album	4	10	7
V. album oxysepalum	3	3	
V. album grandiflorum	3	2	
V. vivide	6	13	5
V. eschscholtzii	7	3	
V. stamineum	2	1	
V. fimbriatum	2	4	
V. nigrum	1	1	
Amianthium muscaetoxicum	1		1
Zygadenus venenosus venenosus		9	
Z. venenosus gramineus		1	
Z. paniculatus		5	
Schoenocaulon officinale		9	4

Kupchan *et al.* consider that alkaloid distribution supports in general the classification on morphological grounds. *Zygadenus* and *Schoenocaulon* contain only the ceveratrum alkaloids. The chemical evidence postulated as the basis for considering *Zygadenus* intermediate between *Veratrum* and *Schoenocaulon* is not particularly convincing. *Zygadenus* has a higher proportion of zygadenine esters than does *Veratrum,* and zygadenine is considered an alkaloid "hybrid" between the two ceveratrum sub-types in that it occurs as a monoester but possesses some structural similarities to the germine and protoverine types together with which it frequently occurs. In a phylogenetic sense the term "intermediate" has a connotation that *Zygadenus* was derived from *Veratrum* and gave rise to *Schoenocaulon.* However, the chemical evidence does not exclude the equally likely hypothesis that both *Schoenocaulon* and *Zygadenus* evolved either from *Veratrum* or a *Veratrum*-like ancestor. *Veratrum* as indicated appears to have a more primitive alkaloid chemistry.

Another point of taxonomic interest concerns certain *Veratrum* species. *V. album* var. *album, V. vivide,* and *V. nigrum* (Atlantic coast taxa) contain alkaloids which yield mono- or dihydroxymethylbutyrate residues upon hydrolysis. *V. album* var. *grandiflorum,* *V. eschscholtzii, V. stamineum,* and *V. fimbriatum* (Pacific coast taxa) yield angelate and tiglate upon hydrolysis.

In Table 9-2 one may note that certain taxa, such as *Veratrum album* var. *album* or *V. vivide* contain numerous alkaloids while others, for example *V. nigrum,* contain relatively few alkaloids. The apparent difference may, however, reflect merely a more intensive examination of one species. One should give more consideration to the presence of a given alkaloid then to its apparent absence. In the alkaloids, in particular, as a result of the fact that many alkaloids are drugs, designation of a species as alkaloid-containing is based upon arbitrarily designated minimum quantities. Hegnauer (1958) has recommended that an alkaloid content of 0.01 per cent dry weight represents the minimum in order for a plant to be considered alkaloid-containing. Yet, in considering the taxonomic implications of alkaloid distribution the more relevant data may be the presence of an enzymatic mechanism for synthesis of even a small amount of a particular type of alkaloid. Ability to accumulate the alkaloid in relatively large amounts may also be genetic and therefore relevant, but not necessarily as fundamental as the existence of the enzymes involved in the primary pathway. For example, in the *Solanaceae* only traces of nicotine occur in tomato and other species, but from a phylogenetic, if not physiological, point of view the trace is quite important.

In the literature of alkaloids, particularly, there are examples of rather arbitrary taxonomic revisions by chemists, based principally on chemical evidence. Thus Manske (1954) transferred *Dicranostigme franchetianum* to the genus *Stylophorum* "because its alkaloids are the same as those of *S. diphyllum.*" *Dicranostigme lactucoides* was retained "because the contained alkaloids, namely protopine, isocorydine, sanguinarine, and chelerythrine present a combination hitherto encountered only in a *Glaucium.*" Nowhere was there any discussion of the basis for the previous taxonomic dispositions of the species. The chemical evidence may be important, but it is possible that equally significant morphological or cytological evidence was ignored.

Another example of arbitrary taxonomic "revision" primarily on chemical grounds is that of Manske and Marion (1947) in *Lycopodium.* This paper appeared in the *Journal of the American Chemical Society. Lycopodium annotinum* var. *acrifolium* contained five alkaloids absent from typical *L. annotinum* (they apparently replaced a group of five alkaloids of the latter). Accordingly, *L. annotinum* var. *acrifolium* was raised to specific rank, *L. acrifolium,* with the additional comment that the newly elevated species was more different, morphologically, from *L. annotinum,* than the two species, *L. flabelliforme* and *L. complanatum* were from each other. This comparison was presumed to lend additional validity to the taxonomic disposition which otherwise was based solely on chemical data. However, Wilce, a student of *Lycopodium* has stated (personal correspondence):

So far as I know, *L. annotinum* has never been subjected to a critical study using modern taxonomic methods. Before answers can be given to the questions you ask about this species and its variety *acrifolium,* such a study should be made. I feel that it is essential to study this and other species of *Lycopodium* from a world-wide standpoint if one hopes to avoid considerable error in the interpretation and evaluation of the various characters. If after such a study were made, no distinguishing characters other than shape and texture of leaves had been found, then I would certainly hesitate to recognize var. *acrifolium* at the species level, regardless of the information given by Manske and Marion. In fact, if it were not for their biochemical evidence to support the minor morphological difference, I should be reluctant to give *acrifolium* even variatal status.

Since there is no indication that various populations of plants were examined by Manske and Marion to discover the nature of variation in alkaloid content even the chemical evidence is not established satisfactorily by the taxonomists' criteria. From our observation of plant to plant variation in *Baptisia* alkaloids, unless one has good reason to expect that variations will not occur, sampling of populations and individual plants is of critical importance.

10 CYANOGENETIC SUBSTANCES

The cyanogenetic substances of higher plants comprise a relatively small and somewhat heterogeneous group of glycosides of the cell sap. The parent substances liberate cyanide apparently enzymatically when the cells are damaged.

In recent years cyanogenetic compounds have been rather neglected. Probably the most significant recent advances have been in the elucidation of the structures of certain cyanogenetic glycosides, which have been known to exist for a number of years. Only a few new cyanogens have been disclosed since Robinson (1930) reported the existence of ten glycosides. The systematic importance of the cyanogenetic compounds cannot be denied since, although their distribution is somewhat limited, the compounds are prevalent in certain families such as the Rosaceae. However, Hegnauer (1958) concluded that at present "the taxonomic significance of the character of cyanogenesis is very limited. Its value may be more important once the cyanogenetic compounds of most of the known cyanophoric species are known." Hegnauer has alluded to a major limitation of many broad surveys of the distribution of cyanophoretic species. The tests generally utilized merely disclose whether prussic acid (HCN) is liberated by the species. The tests do not indicate the chemical nature of the parent substance. The specific type of cyanogen is known in a number of cases, but in the survey work such as that of Gibbs (1954) and others, only presence or absence of HCN is noted by use of emulsin and sodium picrate. Even with this limitation the distribution of cyanogen is often of taxonomic interest.

The most recent view of cyanogenetic compounds is that of Dillemann (1958). Cyanogenetic substances do not include numerous chemical structural analogs or modifications of the basic parent substance as do the alkaloids or flavonoids, and the limited number of the compounds reduces further their systematic significance.

According to Dillemann all the cyanogenetic substances which have been fully characterized consist of a sugar, a cyanhydric acid, and a third substance whose nature is variable. Since the number of classes of these compounds is limited, a rather complete chemical listing is possible. The following structural formulae are obtained from Dillemann, using his classification:

True cyanogenetic heterosides.

In the first group the nitrile (C≡N) group is attached to the aglycone group.

(1) Amygdaloside occurs in many species of Rosaceae.

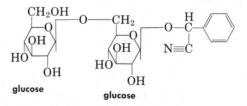

(2) Vicianoside is from *Vicia angustifolia* (Leguminosae)

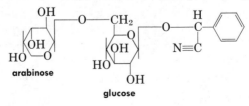

(3) A group of several closely related substances, also related to the two types illustrated above, have the basic structure phenyglycolonitrile D-glucoside-β.

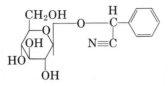

(a) Prunasine (L-phenyl) from many Rosaceae, some Myoporaceae (*Eremophila maculata*), Myrtaceae (*Eucalyptus corynocalix*) and Scrophulariaceae (*Linaria striata* and *Choenorrhinum minus*).

(b) Prulauroside (L-D-phenyl) from species of Rosaceae.

(c) Sambunigroside (D-phenyl) from *Sambucus nigra* (Caprifoliaceae), *Acacia glaucescens* (Leguminosae) and *Ximenia americana* (Oleaceae).

(d) Dhurroside, a para-OH phenyl analog of prunasine, found in *Sorghum vulgare* (Gramineae).

(e) Phyllanthoside (may be same as dhurroside) found in Euphorbiaceae (*Phyllanthus gastroemii*).

(f) Zierioside, a meta-OH phenyl analog of prunasine found in Rutaceae (*Zieria laevigata*).

(4) Linamaroside, from several legumes and others, including several species of *Dimorphotheca* (Compositae).

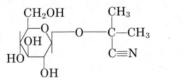

(5) Lotaustraloside is from species of *Lotus* and *Trifolium repens* (Leguminosae).

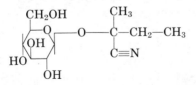

(6) Acacipetaloside is found in the legume genus, *Acacia*.

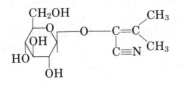

(7) Gynocardoside (the structure has not been completely established, in particular the positioning of three OH groups attached to the aglycone) is from *Gynocardium* and *Pangium* (family Flacourtiaceae).

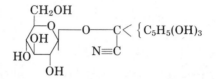

Positions of (OH) groups are doubtful.

In the second series, the nitrile group is attached to the glycosidic group.

(8) Lotusoside (lotusin) is from *Lotus arabicus.*

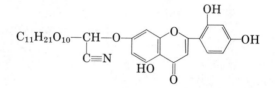

Although the formula above had been accepted for many years, work by Doporto *et al.* (1955) has established rather conclusively that the "flavone" portion is incorrectly identified. These investigators obtained some of the original samples and identified the components as a mixture of quercetin and kaempferol (flavonols).

The authors did not discuss lotusin itself, only the flavonol degradation products. If both these flavonols are derived from lotusin itself, then there must be two different lotusins present. Apparently more work is needed on the intact cyanogen.

The list of cyanogenetic compounds above agrees essentially with that of Gibbs (1954) except for two compounds, hiptagin and karakin, which Dillemann described as "pseudo-cyanogenetic" heterosides, and a third, macrozamoside, derived from several cycads including *Macrozamia spiralis.* Another substance, cycasin found in *Cycas revoluta,* consists of the same parent substance as macrozamin but is esterified with glucose (Nishidi *et al.,* 1960). These substances do not liberate HCN in hydrolysis with dilute HCl unless first treated with sodium hydroxide solution, then acidified. They are called pseudo-cyanogenetic substances by Lythgoe and Riggs (1949). According to these authors (see also Langley *et al.,* 1951, who were studying macrozamin, the substance responsible for the condition known as "wobbles" or "staggers" in Australian livestock) it is a glycoside containing the carbohydrate component, primeverose [6-(B-D-xylosido)-D-glucose].

macrozamin

Macrozamin represents one of the few known occurrences of linked nitrogen atoms in a natural product (see Chapter 6). Systematically it is interesting in that a "new" synthetic ability is associated with a primitive plant. Although such a situation should not be unexpected, it may appear to be paradoxical if one should suppose that primitiveness necessarily implies evolutionary quiescence. It is not likely that the ability of cycad species to form linked N is of recent origin, however, since the compound is found in at least three cycad genera. The important theoretical point is that macrozamin could represent a recently acquired synthetic ability even though the cycads themselves are phylogenetically old. The other pseudo-cyanogenetic compounds, hiptagin and karakin, differ from each other in the position of fusion of the nitrogen-containing group (B-nitropropionic acid: NO_2—CH_2—CH_2—$COOH$).

karakoside = 1:4:6 tri-(B-nitropropionyl)-D-glucopyranose
hiptaside = 1:5:6 tri-(B-nitropropionyl)-D-glucopyranose

Relatively little is known concerning the origin of cyanogenetic glycosides. Butler and Butler (1960) reported that when white clover was supplied with C^{14} labeled isoleucine and valine, radioactivity appeared in the aglycone portion of lotaustralin and linamarin respectively. However, radioactivity failed to appear when C^{14} labeled glycine and valine, labeled only in the 1-C, were supplied. These results suggested that isoleucine and valine are involved in the metabolism of these cyanogenetic glycosides, and that the formation of the cyanide grouping includes decarboxylation.

The role of cyanogenetic substances is unknown. Ideas that they represent protective agents, wastes, or reserve energy sources are distinctive neither by virtue of originality nor their susceptibility to direct experimentation.

Distribution of cyanogenetic substances in the plant is rather widespread although apparently the leaves are particularly rich. Green fruits in some cases are richer in cyanogenetic compounds than are the mature fruits (for example, in *Nandina domestica*). In some genera (for example, *Vicia*) only the seeds are cyanogenetic, and in others (for example, *Isopyrum*) roots as well as aerial parts are cyanogenetic.

More pertinent is the distribution of cyanogenetic compounds within the plant kingdom. According to Dillemann, except for a few isolated examples such as *Bacillus pyocyaneus,* and certain fungi, cyanogenetic substances are restricted to advanced vascular plants: about thirty species of ferns and nearly 900 species of angiosperms representing ninety-five families. Families notable for the production of cyanogenetic substances are the Rosaceae (150 species), Leguminosae (100), Gramineae (100), Araceae (50), Compositae (50), Euphorbiaceae, Passifloraceae, Ranunculaceae, and Saxifragaceae. In some families only one species is known to be cyanogenetic. Hegnauer (1959b) lists about 750 species representing sixty-two families and 250 genera of seed plants. An indication of the frequency of cyanogenesis among a broad sample of species may be obtained from results of an Australian phytochemical survey (Webb 1949). Eleven cyanogenetic species were found among 306 species representing sixty-seven families. The positive species were scattered among several families.

At the generic level, in some genera all species studied were cyanogenetic (for example, *Passiflora, Prunus, Cotoneaster, Dimorphotheca*) while in others some species were cyanogenetic and others were not. In some genera only a single species may be cyanogenetic.

There are several reports of the existence of physiological or biochemical races within a species. Thus both cyanogenetic and acyanogenetic individuals have been reported for *Trifolium repens,* and *Lotus corniculatus* (Armstrong *et al.,* 1912, 1913), *Sorghum vulgare* (Petrie, 1913), *Eucalyptus viminalis* (Finnemore *et al.,* 1938), *Euphorbia drummondii* (Seddon, 1928) *Trema aspera* (Smith and White, 1920), and other species. The subject of chemical races will be considered in more detail in Chapter 16.

In *Lotus corniculatus* a rather complex situation is encountered. In an intensive investigation in 1911 of populations of *L. corniculatus* (Armstrong *et al.,* 1912), cyanide was rarely detected. However, in the following year, in which the weather was unusually warm and dry, cyanide was rarely absent in the same populations of these perennial plants. There were populations of the species growing near each other which were markedly different in the amount of cyanide present. Futhermore, the variety *major* was always free of the cyanogen and, likewise, free of the enzyme which, in the typical *L. corniculatus,* was present.

Trione (1960), who studied the cyanogen content of flax seedlings in controlled environment, found that not only did the HCN content increase with more light but even a diurnal variation in

HCN occurred. Ermakov (1960) likewise noted that linamarin content of flax was higher under controlled conditions of lower soil moisture, low temperature, after mechanical injury, and in young growing organs, so apparently in this species cyanogen content is quite sensitive to environmental factors.

It is evident from these data that both genetic and ecological factors affect the production of the cyanogenetic compound. It would be interesting to know whether the enzyme concentration was affected similarly. The marked influence of ecological factors upon the occurrence of a biochemical component, while it may be exceptional in this instance, needs to be taken into account in the studies of physiological races either in population studies or classical genetic studies. In contrast to the situation in *Lotus corniculatus,* separate reports by Williams (1939) and Atwood and Sullivan (1943) indicate that *Trifolium repens* produces similar quantities of cyanogen under differing conditions. These authors, studying the inheritance of cyanogen production, observed plants over a period of several years and reported that individual plants always tested about the same for cyanogen.

With rare exceptions, cyanogenetic glucosides are accompanied by enzymes which catalyze their hydrolysis with liberation of HCN and sugar. A complex of enzymes is involved in the breakdown of amygdalin, but the system of enzymes is called emulsin. According to Robinson (1930) the emulsin system will liberate HCN from sambunigrin, dhurrin, vicianin, prunasin, and prulaurasin but not linamarin. Since, in all but the last-named, the linkage is quite similar, this fact is not surprising. However, reports that linase will liberate HCN from amygdalin are surprising and perhaps should be treated with some conservatism. Certain plants which do not themselves form cyanogenetic substances contain enzymes which break down amygdalin (Robinson, 1930).

Gibbs (1954) and Hegnauer (1958, 1959b) have reviewed the distribution of cyanogenetic compounds from a taxonomic viewpoint. Hegnauer investigated over 400 species and reported a number as cyanogenetic. Included were first records of the conifers *Taxus cuspidata* and *T. media.* It is unnecessary to reproduce their data in detail, for no clear-cut systematic implications are evident. The most interesting data are those in which subfamilies rich in cyanogenetic species are compared. For example:

Rosaceae: Cyanogenesis is pronounced in the Pomoideae and Prunoideae, less frequent in the Rosoideae and Spiraeoideae.

Leguminosae: Although the sub-families Mimosoideae and Caesalpinioideae contain a few cyanogenetic species, the character is best expressed in the Papilionoideae wherein most tribes contain cyanogenetic species. *Trifolium repens* contains two different types of cyanogens, apparently the only such example.

An unusual cyanogen occurs in the legume genus *Indigofera*. Morris *et al.* (1954) studying a toxic substance from the leaves of *Indigofera endecaphylla,* found it to be β-nitropropionic acid; NO_2—CH_2CH_2COOH, the aglycone of hiptagin and karakin. According to these authors they isolated the compound from several species. In a subsequent paper, Cooke (1955) studied several species of *Indigofera* with the following results:

	Concentration of β-nitropropionic acid (mg/g Fresh Weight)
Indigofera tetensis	0
I. suffruticosa	0
I. trita	0
I. dimorphophylla	0
I. subulata	7.6 (leaf)
I. endecaphylla	6.1–14.8 (leaf) 9.8 (immature leaves) 8.8 (mature leaves) 2.4 (stem)

Other workers (Schilling and Strong, 1955; Dupuy and Lees, 1956; Bell, 1962) have obtained yet another unusual nitrogenous derivative from *Lathyrus odoratus* and *Lathyrus pusillus*. This substance, β-N-(γ-L-glutamyl)-aminopropionitrile, is one of the agents producing the condition known as lathyrism (Selye, 1957), in particular the skeletal form of the disease. The active principle is β-aminopropionitrile. The compound is absent from *L. sativus, L. cicera, L. latifolius, L. strictus, L. splendens,* and others (Strong, 1956). However, most of these latter species are positive for the form known as "neurolathyrism." This fact merely confirms what has been suspected, namely, that the two forms of lathyrism result from two different agents. Among the species reported by Selye hardly any (these exceptions were also doubtful) were positive for both forms of lathyrism. More recently, Ressler *et al.* (1961) have identified a neurolathyrus factor from *L. latifolius* as L-α, γ-diamino butyric acid. This finding has led to a very interesting speculation that the two types of lathyrus factors are derived from a common precursor. Apparently, they do not occur together in a plant. The hypothetical scheme in which the lathyrus factors stem from a parent substance, asparagine, is shown in Fig. 10-1. Further support for the pathway illustrated in Fig. 10-1 was provided by the subsequent discovery of the hypothetical intermediate, β-cyano-L-alanine, in related species, *Vicia sativa* and *V. angustifolia* (Ressler, 1962).

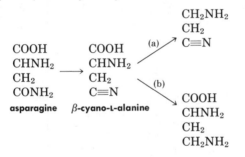

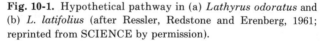

Fig. 10-1. Hypothetical pathway in (a) *Lathyrus odoratus* and (b) *L. latifolius* (after Ressler, Redstone and Erenberg, 1961; reprinted from SCIENCE by permission).

Hegnauer (1959a) has investigated the distribution of cyanogenetic substances among species of *Taxus* and certain related genera (*Cephalotaxus* and *Torreya*). The other genera were acyanogenetic as were certain species of *Taxus*. In certain cyanogenetic species, varieties were found to be either negative (*T. baccata* var. *aurea*), weakly cyanogenetic (var. *dovastoniana*), or strongly cyanogenetic (var. *baccata*). According to Hegnauer:

> It is interesting, in chemotaxonomic relationship, that the genera *Taxus* and *Cephalotaxus* are clearly phytochemically different. Both contain alkaloid but the bases are different. Cyanogenesis is found only in *Taxus*.

However, the relationship of *Cephalotaxus* to *Taxus* on morphological grounds is not considered to be close. Although formerly included in the Taxaceae, *Cephalotaxus* is now considered a separate family, Cephalotaxaceae (Buchholz, 1951). In view of this presumed lack of close relationship between *Taxus* and *Cephalotaxus* the statement by Hegnauer has less significance. Cyanogenesis in *Taxus* is not to be considered of systematic significance beyond perhaps additional support for the recognition of varieties. Hegnauer says that since separation of some of the cultivated forms of *Taxus* may be difficult, cyanogen content may serve as a useful character. This suggestion may be received with some reservation, since the character, unsupported by correlated morphological differences, is of dubious value in delimitation of anything more than a single or perhaps a few genic differences; for example, in *Trifolium repens* it has been established that a single dominant gene governs production of the cyanogenetic compound (Williams, 1939) and another gene the enzyme required to hydrolyse the cyanogen (Atwood and Sullivan, 1943). If we knew sufficiently well, the biochemistry of the species and its individuals we might regard plants as biochemical individuals just as R. J. Williams and Reichert before him regard individuals as biochemically unique.[1]

[1] Reichert, 1919. "Recently data have been rapidly accumulating along many and diverse lines of investigation which collectively indicate that every individual is a chemical entity that differs in characteristic particulars from each other."

11 PHENOLIC SUBSTANCES

This large and diversified group of compounds contains a number of classes of substances which are well known. They have been extensively investigated in spite of a relative lack of economic value within the group. Except for a few physiologically active compounds, such as phloridzin and, according to some reports, rutin, the phenolics are of little pharmacological interest.[1] Even within the plant in which they occur no physiological function is readily apparent for most phenolics, though some have been found to be effective inhibitors of seed germination

---

[1] Some isoflavones, particularly those which form a 4th ring and are therefore rather sterol-like in general configuration, exhibit estrogenic activity. A potent estrogen of this type is obtainable from *Butea superba* (Bickoff, 1961).

(de Roubaix and Lazer, 1960), and these may also be self-inhibitors in the seeds and fruits in which they occur. There are also numerous scattered reports of phenolic inhibitors of certain fungi and plant viruses (Uritani, 1961).

Although the amino acids tyrosine and dihydroxyphenyl-alanine, certain alkaloids, and other substances are phenolic in nature, customarily the term, phenolic compound, is not extended to include nitrogenous derivatives. Also, certain phenols are demonstrably related to a parent substance belonging to a different chemical group, for example terpenes, as in the case of thymol. Major categories of phenolic substances include the following: simple phenols without side chains; simple phenols with one, two, or three-carbon side chains (occurring as acids, aldehydes, ketones, or alcohols); depsides of simple phenols (for example chlorogenic acids: see Fig. 11-1); and higher polymers of simple phenols such as the important structural component of vascular plants, lignin. Another large and important group of phenolic substances is the flavonoids, which include the vacuolar pigments such as the anthocyanins and antho-xanthins, in addition to other classes. Finally, coumarins, which are unsaturated lactone derivatives (for example, coumarin and scopoletin), and which may be derived from the same biosynthetic pathway as that leading to simple phenolic compounds, are also included with the phenolic compounds. Phenolics are usually present in the plant as glycosides or esters.

Certain of the phenolics have been the objects of a large number of productive biochemical genetic studies, and also recently there have been important new advances in knowledge of the biosynthesis of these compounds. Knowledge of the genetics and biosynthesis of phenols should contribute to a clearer understanding of the meaning of some of the results of biochemical systematics studies. For this reason, brief discussions of the mode of biosynthesis and certain aspects of the genetics of flavonoids are included in this chapter.

Present knowledge of the comparative biochemistry of secondary compounds and particularly their mode of inheritance is often inadequate to provide much important insight into their systematic significance in a given instance beyond strict correlations of systematic distribution. Consequently, many biochemical systematic studies represent a rather empirical search for patterns of distribution of particular substances or groups of substances. It should be recognized, however, that for the vast majority of morphological characters used as systematic criteria, the genetic mechanisms responsible for the characters have not been revealed either. Therefore, in those cases

phloroglucinol
(*Sequoia sempervirens*)

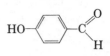

p-hydroxybenzaldehyde

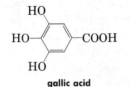

gallic acid

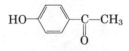

p-hydroxyacetophenone
(*Populus trichocarpa*)

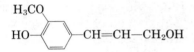

coniferyl alcohol

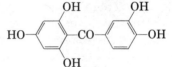

maclurin
(*Maclura tinctoria*)

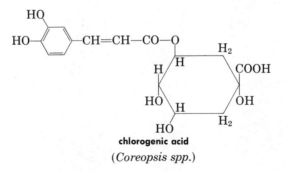

chlorogenic acid
(*Coreopsis spp.*)

Fig. 11-1. Structural formulas of some simple phenols.

wherein genetic and biochemical mechanisms governing the synthesis of certain chemical substances are yet undisclosed, it does not necessarily follow that the compounds are accordingly of little value as taxonomic criteria.

Some basic considerations of
biosynthetic pathways involved in the
production of phenolics.

The biosynthesis of phenolic compounds has been reviewed by Neish (1960) and others. A central problem, that of the initial aromatization, appears to have been solved through investigations into the biosynthesis of aromatic amino acids in microorganisms. The presently accepted biochemical pathway to tyrosine and phenylalanine is that elucidated by Davis and coworkers (Davis, 1956; Levin and Sprinson, 1960) through studies of *E. coli* biochemical mutants. The essential features of this scheme are illustrated and the pathway extended to include several classes of phenols in Fig. 11-2. Although not all evidence that these pathways are operative in higher plants is direct, isotope studies from several laboratories provide independently strongly favorable circumstantial evidence for such pathways.

There is, now, equally strong evidence from isotope studies that in the flavonoids one benzenoid portion of the molecule comes from a quite different pathway, namely head to tail condensation of three acetyl groups (Rickards, 1961). Confirmation of the theory of acetate condensation suggested by Birch and Donovan (1953) has come from studies in four different laboratories in four different countries, for example, Watkin, *et al.* in Canada (1957), Grisebach in Germany (1957), Geissman and Swain in the United States (1957), and Shibata and Yamazaki in Japan (1957). The acetate condensations are involved in the formation of the benzene ring of the flavonoid molecule customarily referred to as the "A ring" while the general pathway to phenols provides the B ring and the three carbons adjacent to the B ring (see below, formula of quercetin).

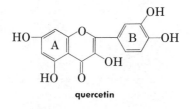

quercetin

In quercetin (and its anthocyanidin analog, cyanidin) ring B is derived from the shikimic acid pathway and ring A from the acetate pathway. This mechanism is probably generally representative of flavonoid synthesis, possibly involving a chalkone (see below) intermediate (Grisebach and Patschke, 1961). Hutchinson, *et al.* (1959)

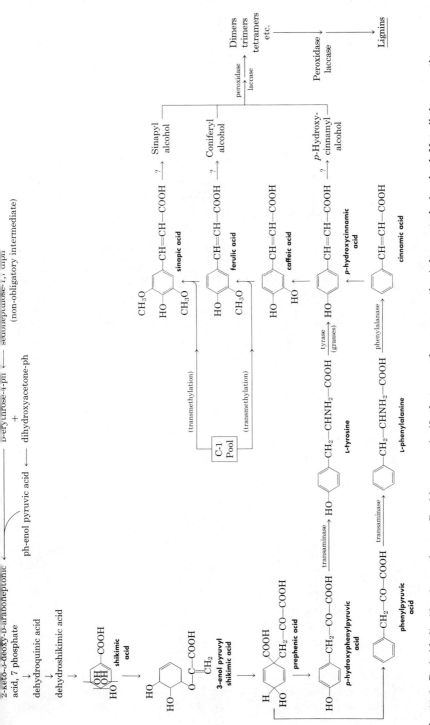

Fig. 11-2. Probable lignification pathways. Double arrows signify that more than one reaction is known to be involved. Not all these reactions occur in all species (adapted and modified from Brown, 1961). Reprinted from *Science* by permission.

195

have shown, for example, that acetate is preferentially incorporated into the A ring of phloretin by apple leaf tissue.

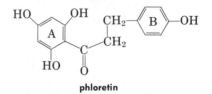

phloretin

The C_6—C_3 compounds which apparently are synthesized by way of the shikimic acid pathway are important units in the formation of lignin in addition to their roles in amino acid and flavonoid biosynthesis. While it is not appropriate to include herein a detailed discussion of lignin biosynthesis and lignin chemistry, it is pertinent to note that, although the exact structure of lignin is not known, it is believed to be a phenylpropane polymer. There is reason to believe that many different kinds of lignin exist, and a specific lignin may characterize a particular taxonomic group. The systematic implications of lignin chemistry are discussed in Chapter 14.

Coumarins comprise a particularly interesting group of phenolic compounds. There are a number of different coumarin derivatives of widespread occurrence, and some, such as scopoletin, affect plant growth. From the formula of coumarin itself, one unfamiliar with phenol chemistry may conclude that the coumarin structure is homologous with the A ring plus the heterocyclic ring of the flavonoid nucleus.

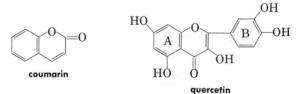

coumarin   quercetin

In such case the benzene ring of coumarin would be expected to come directly from acetate. Coumarin, however, is a lactone of o-hydroxycinnamic acid, and tracer studies support the view that coumarin synthesis follows the shikimic acid pathway (for example, labelled caffeic acid and labelled scopoletin are formed when labelled phenylalanine is provided to *Nicotiana,* Reid, 1958).

The disclosure that isoflavones are formed from phenylalanine by a mechanism which includes an aryl migration (Grisebach, 1961), in addition to relating this flavonoid group to the shikimic acid pathway, suggests that the rotenoids may also be included since rotenoids bear a structural resemblance to isoflavonoids.

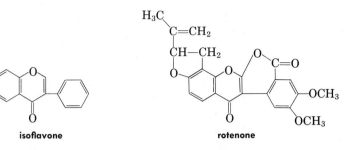

isoflavone   rotenone

Grisebach and Ollis (1961) have noted a high frequency of co-occurrence of isoflavonoids and rotenoids (see Table 11-1), and furthermore there is a rather close correlation in their group substitution patterns.

It appears that a single pathway, in reality one that is possibly as phylogenetically old as the first cellular organisms, leads to the phenolic amino acids and hence to other phenolics. Secondly, another pathway, originating also from an important basic metabolite (acetate), cooperates to yield the complex flavonoids.

Table 11-1. Distribution of flavonoids, isoflavonoids and rotenoids in selected species (*Experientia* **17:** by permission of Grisebach and Ollis, 1961).

Plant	Flavonoid	Isoflavonoid	Rotenoid
Ferreirea spectabilis (Leguminosae)	Naringenin	Biochanin-A Ferreirin Homoferreirin	– – –
Prunus puddum (Rosaceae)	Sakuranin Sakuranetin Genkwanin Taxifolin	Prunetin Padmakastin Padmakastein	– – –
Mundulea sericea (Leguminosae)	Sericetin	Mundulone Munetone	Munduserone –
Pachyrrhizus erosus (Leguminosae)	–	Pachyrrhizin Erosnin	Rotenone Pachyrrhizone
Pterocarpus angolensis (Leguminosae)	–	Muningin Angolensin	– –
Derris malaccensis (Leguminosae)	–	Toxicarol isoflavone	Rotenone Sumatrol Deguelin Toxicarol Elliptone Malaccol

In vascular plants, wherein the production of phenylpropane derivatives in lignin synthesis has been continuously (in evolutionary time) a major metabolic activity, flavonoid compounds are of general occurrence, though it is true that phenolics are far less prominent among vascular cryptogams. In thallophytes, where lignin does not occur, flavonoid pigments are practically unknown although other phenolics may be numerous. According to Blank (1947) a report of the occurrence of flavonoids in mosses is probably valid, but no algae or fungi are known to produce flavonoids. The report of flavonoids in *Chlamydomonas* (Moewus, 1950) was invalid (Kuhn and Low, 1960). Alston (1958) showed that the purple pigment of the green alga, *Zygogonium ericetorum,* was not an anthocyanin and that early reports of the occurrence of anthocyanins in filamentous algae were probably erroneous. It seems therefore that the presence of an enzyme system leading to lignin synthesis has provided an opportunity for the appearance of phenylpropane derivatives to couple with the acetate pathway to form the basic flavonoid nucleus. This step in biochemical evolution may have been acquired quite early in view of the wide distribution of flavonoids among pteridophytes, but it is also possible that it evolved repeatedly.

The next section will be devoted to biochemical genetical studies of certain classes of complex phenols, the flavonoid pigments. In order to appreciate fully the implications of such studies a brief survey of the chemistry of these compounds might prove helpful.

CHEMICAL STRUCTURES OF CLASSES
OF FLAVONOID COMPOUNDS

This group of compounds contains a C_6–C_3–C_6 carbon skeleton in which the C_3 unit links two aromatic groups. The C_3 chain is essentially the key to the different major classes of flavonoids since these classes are recognized on the basis of the oxidation state of the C_3 unit in addition to the mode of ring closure to form a heterocyclic middle ring (if ring closure ensues). Flavonoids usually occur as glycosides and sometimes also as acylated compounds, the acyl group being in many cases a phenolic acid. Glycosides are mostly formed as esters at carbons 3, 5, or 7 but some carbon glycosides at position 8 are known (Hörhammer and Wagner, 1961). Flavonoid glycosides are usually water soluble and are located in the vacuole of the cell. Classes of flavonoid compounds are discussed below:

ANTHOCYANINS

The basic aromatic unit is referred to as a phenylbenzo-pyrilium salt with the configuration shown below. This class includes most of the red and blue plant pigments.

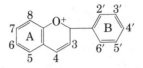

All naturally occurring anthocyanins have the 4', 3, 5, and 7 positions occupied by an hydroxyl or some substituted group. They usually occur as glycosides with the sugars attached at positions 3 or 3 and 5. Sugars commonly reported are glucose, galactose, rhamnose, and arabinose. Disaccharides (for example, rhamnoglucose) may occur as well as 3,5-dimonosides and even trisaccharides.

In acylated anthocyanins the organic acid is frequently p-hydroxybenzoic, protocatechuic, p-hydroxycinnamic or other phenolic acid. The attachment of the acyl group is apparently at a free hydroxyl in the ring or an hydroxyl group of the sugar.

The aglycone of the anthocyanin, which may be obtained by acid hydrolysis, is referred to as an anthocyanidin. Although dozens of anthocyanins have been described, only a few anthocyanidins are known, and some of these are rather rare. These compounds differ in the substitution pattern involving positions 3', 4', 5', 3, 5, and 7.

Representative anthocyanidins.

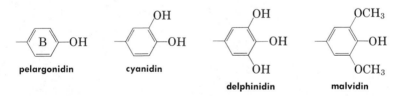

Hirsutidin is a 7-methoxy analog of malvidin. Capensinidin, a 5-methoxy analog of malvidin, has been obtained from *Plumbago capensis* (Harborne, 1962).

peonidin

Rosinidin, a 7-methoxy analog of peonidin, has been reported to occur in *Primula rosea* (Harborne, 1958).

petunidin

FLAVONOLS

These, like most of the flavonoids other than anthocyanins, are colored yellow or cream or have hardly any color. The basic flavonol nucleus is illustrated below.

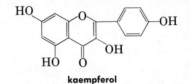

kaempferol

Substitutions, similar to some of those illustrated in the anthocyanins, also occur in the flavonol class. For example, other well known flavonols are quercetin (analogous to the anthocyanin cyanidin), and myricetin (analogous to the anthocyanin delphinidin). Flavonols are common flavonoid constituents and, like the anthocyanins, widely distributed.

FLAVONES

These are similar to flavonols but lack the 3-hydroxyl group.

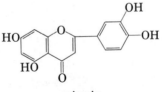

apigenin

FLAVANONES

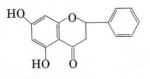

FLAVANONOLS

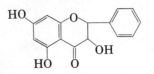

ISOFLAVONES

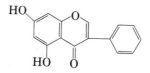

CHALKONES

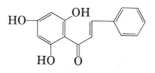

AURONES (BENZALCOUMARANONES)

This group is distinguished by the presence of a five-membered heterocyclic ring.

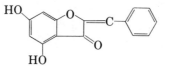

CATECHINS

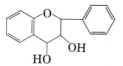

LEUCO-ANTHOCYANINS

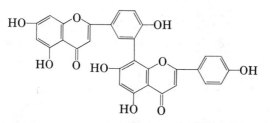

BIFLAVONYLS

In addition to the many types of flavonoids already described there are a few flavonoids substituted with isoprene units. The substances artocarpin and isoartocarpin, found in the wood of *Arto-carpus integrifolia,* are particularly interesting representatives since they also possess the rare ortho-hydroxy substitution of the B-ring (Dave *et al.,* 1962).

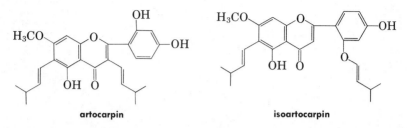

artocarpin   isoartocarpin

The isoprenoid side chains which distinguish the two compounds are linked differently, that is, C–C in artocarpin and O–C in isoarto-carpin. Yet, spatially the ortho-OH of the B-ring is close to the 3 position at which the isoprene substitution in artocarpin occurs.

Flavonoids are of special interest in that they represent a molecular composite formed via several basic pathways each of which leads to other secondary compounds: the shikimic acid pathway, mevalonic acid pathway, and acetate condensation. Other examples of phenolic-isoprenoid derivatives are known, including other flavonoids, rotenoids, coumarins, and quinones (Ollis and Sutherland, 1961).

When all the known derivatives of the classes of flavonoids including glycosides, are totaled, they number into the hundreds. Geissman and Hinreiner (1952) listed almost 200 different flavonoids already known to occur in nature, and many new types have since been described (for a recent comprehensive list see Geissman, 1962).

GENETIC STUDIES CONCERNING THE
FLAVONOID COMPOUNDS

As noted previously the inheritance of certain flavonoid pigments has been studied more intensively than perhaps any other group of chemical substances in flowering plants (Alston, 1963). The anthocyanins, particularly, have been the objects of numerous investigations extending back almost to the nineteenth century. Onslow (1916) called attention to the possibility of biochemical genetic studies of anthocyanins shortly after Willstätter had established their chemical nature. Apparently the first actual biochemical genetic investigation was that of Scott-Moncrieff (1931) who showed that in *Pelargonium zonale* a dominant gene, producing a rose-pink flower, governed the formation of a cyanidin glycoside. The double recessive, in contrast, contained a pelargonidin glycoside and was salmon-pink in color.

By 1936 a number of biochemical-genetic studies of flower

color had been completed, and Scott-Moncrieff in reviewing this work outlined several generalizations concerning the inheritance of anthocyanins, such as the fact that the more oxidized form was usually dominant to the less oxidized, and that 3-5 diglycosidic and acylated anthocyanins were dominant to the 3 monoglycosidic and nonacylated forms, respectively (Scott-Moncrieff, 1936).

Beale *et al.* (1941) in another important review of the subject concurred in general with the findings of Scott-Moncrieff. The number of species which had at that time been investigated was surprisingly large though most of the work suffered from limitations of the techniques then available. Between 1941 and the early 1950's relatively little additional work on the inheritance of flower color was reported. Haldane (1954), who apparently had interested Scott-Moncrieff in the subject, outlined some of the problems which remained unsolved at the time and deplored the declining interest in the study of the biochemical genetics of flower color. Yet, even then a number of important studies along these lines were in progress. Apparently, renewed interest stemmed in part from the introduction of paper chromatographic techniques. Before such techniques appeared, it was almost impossible to resolve the anthocyanins, yet complex mixtures of pigments were frequently encountered. The first report of the use of paper chromatography in the study of anthocyanins was that of Bate-Smith (1948), and most, if not all, of the major biochemical-genetic work on anthocyanins since has been facilitated by paper chromatographic investigations. Several significant publications on the inheritance of flower color have appeared in recent years, yet these have not answered some of the basic questions of flavonoid biosynthesis which now center on interconversions of classes of flavonoids, the point at which substitutions in the A and B rings occur, and the exact mode of union of the A and B units of the flavonoid nucleus. Some consideration will be given to these points later.

The extent of genetic investigations of flower color is emphasized by the work of Paris *et al.* (1960) who surveyed publications treating the inheritance of flower color in seventy-five different species. These workers attempted the formulation of a general inheritance scheme governing flower color. They recognized six major analogous genes on the basis of the frequency of appearance of the corresponding phenotypic effect. While it is unquestionably desirable to attempt to develop an integrated system of genetic notation in which factors known to have equivalent biochemical expression are assigned the same symbol, it is doubtful that the arbitrary recognition by these authors of six types of analogous genes based entirely on the phenotypic expression of color alone is a positive contribution. Rather, it oversimplifies the situation and conveys to the casual reader the idea that the gene categories are possibly biochemically as well as phenotypically analogous when, in fact, it is demonstrable that in numerous cases they are not.

As a result of a series of biochemical genetic studies involving numerous plants several types of biochemical differences attributable to single gene differences have been reported. (Since many of these have been confirmed several times by different workers, only cases of some special interest will be identified by citation.) In a number of instances genes are known to govern the substitution pattern of the B ring, that is, the number of hydroxyl groups present. Sometimes, for example in *Streptocarpus* (Lawrence *et al.*, 1939), a dominant gene governs the formation of malvidin instead of pelargonidin. In this case, it is possible that the gene permits the addition of one or more OH groups in the B ring (or a precursor thereof) and thus provides a site for methylation so that a single gene may appear to govern a more complex biochemical process than is actually the case. A similar situation probably occurs in *Impatiens* (Alston and Hagen, 1958). Of course, it is possible that the gene governs methoxylation, but present evidence does not permit a choice between these alternatives. It is interesting that, to the writers' knowledge, there is no report in the literature of a gene which governs substitutions in the A ring other than the glycosidic pattern. It is highly probable that such genes exist, since hirsutidin (a 7-methoxy malvidin), gossypetin (a flavonol with an 8-hydroxy substitution) and other compounds with atypical A ring substitution patterns exist.

Numerous instances of the occurrence of single genes which affect the glycosidic pattern are known, and as noted previously the diglycoside is dominant to the monoglycoside.

There are several instances known of single genes which govern acylation. Abe and Gotoh (1956) reported a dominant gene governing acylation with p-hydroxy cinnamic acid in the eggplant, and Harborne (1956) reported an interesting situation in *Solanum* in which a single gene appeared to govern three biochemical differences in the same anthocyanin: a change in substitution of the B ring, a change in the glycosidic pattern, and acylation of the glycoside with p-coumaric acid.

There are numerous examples of genetic mechanisms which involve interactions between anthocyanins and other classes of flavonoids. In *Dahlia*, the classic example of such interaction (Lawrence and Scott-Moncrieff, 1935), one factor, I, governs flavone synthesis at (apparently) the expense of anthocyanin. The authors concluded from these results that a precursor, limited in amount, was common to all the pigments. A similar type of competition is reported in *Primula* (de Winton and Haldane, 1933). In *Impatiens balsamina,* the gene L allows production of malvidin type anthocyanins and also the related flavonol, myricetin (Clevenger, 1958), yet there does not appear to be competition between anthocyanins and flavonols in this plant since a fifty-fold increase in pelargonidin content of flowers does not reduce appreciably the amount of its flavonol analog, kaempferol (Hagen, 1959). A dominant gene which effects production of two different classes of $3':4':5'$-trihydroxylated pigments is known in *Solanum phureja* and also in *Primula sinensis.* In *Dianthus* a dominant gene, R, introduces cyanidin and its flavonol analog, quercetin, while pelargonidin and its analog, kaempferol, occur in the absence of R (Geissman *et al.,* 1956).

One of the most informative examples of interaction between several classes of flavonoids is that of *Antirrhinum* (Sherratt, 1958) (Fig. 11-3). The types of flavonoids which occur in *Antirrhinum* are anthocyanins, flavonols, flavones, and aurones. In most of these classes more than one representative aglycone type is present, though not necessarily together in a single plant. Genetic control of flower color in *Antirrhinum* has been investigated by several groups independently, and the present discussion is taken from Sherratt (1958) using the genetic symbols of Dayton (1956). A factor, Y, is necessary for the formation of flavonoids. Unless certain other dominant genes are present, however, only pigments of the flavone and aurone types are found (namely, apigenin and aureusidin). In the presence of the double recessive, $I_A I_A$, aureusidin content is increased with no apparent reduction in apigenin content. In fact no other factors under consideration appear to affect apigenin. The gene, R, governs simultaneously the appearance of anthocyanins and flavonols (both classes have a 3-OH in the heterocyclic ring). Gene B governs the substitution pattern of the B ring, introducing dihydroxy rather than monohydroxy derivatives in the anthocyanins and flavonols present. Gene B does not affect the other two classes of flavonoids. The interpretation of these data is implicit in figure 11.3. Notably, it appears that the pathway to aurone synthesis is determined rather early. Jorgensen and Geissman (1955) have shown that increased anthocyanin synthesis results in some lowering of the aureusidin content however.

In *Phaseolus* a series of alleles, C^u, C and C^r influence relative quantities of flavonols and anthocyanins as well as the substitution pattern of the B ring (Feenstra, 1960). None of these substances is formed in the presence of the recessive, C^u; C along with the factor v^{lae} results in the formation of flavonols of the kaempferol type plus a small amount of the quercetin type and no anthocyanins; C^r with

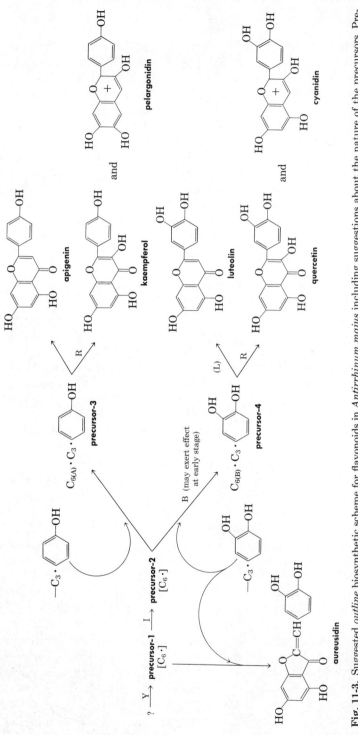

Fig. 11-3. Suggested *outline* biosynthetic scheme for flavonoids in *Antirrhinum majus* including suggestions about the nature of the precursors. Precursors 3 and 4 are common to the 4 monohydroxylated and 3′:4′-dihydroxylated pigments respectively (adapted from H. S. A. Sherratt, *Journal of Genetics* **56**: 1958).

V^{lae} results in the formation of both flavonols and anthocyanins of monohydroxy or dihydroxy types. The allele C in the presence of the dominant allele V, governs flavonols and anthocyanins mainly of the type, $3'$-$4'$-$5'$-trihydroxy, and C^r with V yields anthocyanins only, these having the trihydroxy substitution in the B ring. This case represents an unusually complex form of interaction which Feenstra interprets as indicating that a shift in the hydroxyl pattern of the B ring to the trihydroxy configuration favors anthocyanin synthesis over flavonol synthesis.

Since it has already been established that the acetate and shikimic acid pathways are involved in both anthocyanin and flavonol synthesis, it is hardly surprising to find a number of instances of interactions—in fact a number of expressions of this interaction—between classes of flavonoids. Similarly, however, the total absence of a definite instance of gene-controlled direct interconversion suggests that actual interconversion of the classes of flavonoid pigments is not the rule. In this connection it now appears that leucoanthocyanins, once thought of as likely precursors to anthocyanins, do not function in this way. Evidence is not unequivocal on this point, however. Genes affecting leucoanthocyanins are known. In *Impatiens* a gene governs the presence of a pelargonidin-type anthocyanin and, in addition, leucopelargonidin (Alston and Hagen, 1955). Feenstra (1959) reported a gene in *Phaseolus* governing the appearance of leucoanthocyanin. The leucoanthocyanins, incidentally, provide some circumstantial evidence favoring the position that methylation occurs at a late stage in anthocyanin synthesis. Methylated leucoanthocyanins are practically unknown yet leucoanthocyanins are commonly found along with methylated anthocyanins.

The quantitative inheritance of flavonoids is provided with some interesting illustrations. In some plants a rather large number of genes may influence the amount of anthocyanin. In *Primula,* for instance, at least four different loci contain dominant intensifiers for anthocyanin, and five loci contain dominant inhibitors (de Winton and Haldane, 1933). In *Dahlia* (Lawrence and Scott-Moncrieff, 1935) two loci affect the amount of anthocyanin and two others affect the amount of yellow flavonoid pigments. From studies of the physiology of anthocyanin synthesis it is clear that a host of extrinsic factors can modify anthocyanin content, in fact a number of generally harmful influences actually bring about increased anthocyanin synthesis. It is therefore to be expected that a large number of different genes would achieve a similar effect through diverse means. From a systematic viewpoint, gene homology between two factors which exert quantitative effects on anthocyanin synthesis in two different species has a low probability. The same interpretation may be expected to hold for the surprisingly large number of complex loci which affect, quantitatively, anthocyanin synthesis. Alston (1959) has discussed certain implications of the existence of such loci in a large proportion of plant species studied, and it is pertinent to note that homologies among such complex loci are considered likely to be rare.

The foregoing discussion serves to provide a perspective from which to view certain systematic investigations involving the flavonoid pigments or simpler phenols. Several illustrations have been selected which disclose that a single gene may alter several biochemical components of a plant (in one further case, the P^r allele of *Impatiens balsamina* governs not only the amount of anthocyanin in the stem, sepals, and petals, but in addition has a different qualitative expression in each plant part). Despite such examples, it seems improper to conclude, in the absence of genetic criteria, that when related anthocyanins and flavonols occur together or when similar glycosides of anthocyanins and flavonols occur together, the same enzyme (or gene) is necessarily implicated. In one such situation cited, involving *Lathyrus odoratus* (Harborne, 1960a), this assumption was made after examining a number of varieties but without benefit of genetic studies. In a previous genetic study Beale (1939) reported that the genes affecting anthocyanidin type did not influence flavonol composition in *Lathyrus odoratus*.

Just as cases are known in which one gene governs several biochemical differences, there are instances in which several different genes may affect the same biochemical character. It seems to be established that numerous gene effects are highly indirect, the primary gene effect remaining completely unsuspected.

Gene mutations affecting relatively late stages in the flavonoid biosynthetic pathway appear to be far more frequently detected than those affecting an early step. This assumption is based on the rarity of cases in which a gene is known to inhibit the total synthesis of all flavonoids (either as a dominant or recessive). Most "white" mutants involve the anthocyanins and in such mutants other types of flavonoids may still be produced. Roller (1956) who studied the flavonoids of certain white-flowered varieties of over forty species, found other types of flavonoids present in practically every instance. From two to six flavonoids were present, as a rule, with flavonols most frequent. The infrequency of cases involving mutations inhibiting total flavonoid synthesis was also noted in the discussion following a recent paper on anthocyanin genetics by Harborne (1960b).

On a priori grounds, one may predict that the earlier

in the pathway the block to the synthesis of a secondary substance occurs, the more likelihood that the metabolism of a basic metabolite is affected adversely. It follows that the early stage mutants would be eliminated more often. Modification of a terminal step is also less likely to provide the opportunity for the appearance of a new series of compounds. The question of biochemical selection is also pertinent. If selection becomes more critical, then the earlier in a sequence of reactions the change represented by the mutant occurs, the more likely is its preservation to become dependent upon the total gene pool. Thus, in general, the preservation of such a mutation rests upon a broader underlying genomic constitution than that of a mutation affecting a terminal step. Perhaps such considerations are purely academic at the moment with respect to the systematic implications of biochemical data, but they are nontheless potentially significant. Such considerations bear upon the question of whether each newly acquired synthetic ability should be given the same weight of systematic significance. In the writers' opinion they should not. Even without consideration of the actual systematic distribution of the compounds involved, the appearance of an aurone (with a five-membered heterocyclic ring) may be more significant than the appearance of a different glycosidic pattern, although in the former case the empirical chemical formula remains the same while in the latter it may be radically altered.

In summary it is evident that knowledge of the major biosynthetic route and some familiarity with the mode of inheritance of a group of related chemical constituents should allow more critical analysis and a more precise evaluation of the systematic implications of a given distributional pattern.

SYSTEMATIC ASPECTS OF THE DISTRIBUTION OF PHENOLIC COMPOUNDS

The use of phenolic substances in systematic investigations does not extend back as far as that of certain other groups of plant constituents such as alkaloids and essential oils. In the past decade a number of investigators have considered the phenolics, particularly anthocyanins, leucoanthocyanins, flavonols, and phenolic acids. Bate-Smith has stressed especially the leucoanthocyanins. In his first treatment of the systematic distribution of leucoanthocyanins (Bate-Smith and Lerner, 1954), over 500 species were surveyed for leucoanthocyanins in leaves. In general these compounds are more abundant in woody families, especially in certain groups regarded by some workers as primitive. In the predominantly herbaceous families fewer species contain leucoanthocyanins. In the family Leguminosae, which is predominantly woody, both positive and negative results were obtained, though most herbaceous members of the sub-family Papilionoideae tested negatively. Within the Papilionoideae, one tribe, Hedysareae, contains many positive species (ten out of eleven tested). Bate-Smith reported that in many legumes the seeds tested positively for leucoanthocyanins even when the leaves of the same species were negative, a fact which complicates the interpretation of distributional data.

In view of the above, Bate-Smith believes that families of Hutchinson's Herbaceae should be examined for the presence of leucoanthocyanins. It should be apparent that this application of leucoanthocyanins as systematic criteria is at the higher taxonomic levels (family, in this case). The character is not constant within a family, necessarily, or even within a genus, and its systematic value at the level indicated is somewhat questionable. Alston (unpublished) has shown that leucoanthocyanins do not, apparently, serve to clarify relationships within the genus *Prosopis*. In specific cases, however, there is no reason to doubt that leucoanthocyanins may be valuable as systematic characters particularly at lower taxonomic levels. For example, in *Iris* leucoanthocyanins are virtually restricted to the section Apogon wherein they are found in four out of seven species examined (Bate-Smith, 1958).

There is some correlation between a morphological and chemical character in the Papilionatae in that the groups having a pulvinus at the base of the leaf (the pulvinate condition is regarded as the primitive condition), including the tribes Sophoreae, Dalbergieae, Phaseoleae, and parts of Galegeae and Hedysareae, tend to be positive for leucoanthocyanins. The groups lacking a pulvinus tend to be negative for leucoanthocyanins. The pulvinate condition is also distinctly correlated with woodiness as opposed to herbaceous habit, a factor which Bate-Smith also believes to be significant. Among the herbaceous monocots, about equal numbers of positive and negative species are known. Positive species are common among gymnosperms.

With respect to qualitative aspects of leucoanthocyanins Bate-Smith (1957) reported that the leucodelphinidin was common among certain orders (for example, Rosales), but in other orders only leucocyanidin occurred (as in Ranales). In Myrtales, leucodelphinidin was quite common as was the analogous flavonol, myricetin, and the tri-hydroxy derivative ellagic acid:

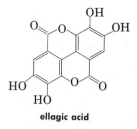

ellagic acid

Thus, in Myrtales, the tri-hydroxy configuration is expressed within several phenolic classes and is emphasized to the extent that it assumes some systematic significance. Bate-Smith noted that among the six sub-families of the Rosaceae proposed by various authors, four (Spiraeoideae, Pomoideae, Prunoideae and Rosoideae) contain only leucocyanidin while one (Chrysobalanoideae) contains both leucocyanidin and leucodelphinidin. Bate-Smith noted that the last-named sub-family had been treated as a family by at least one worker.

The situation described above emphasizes one of the most vexing problems facing the systematist, regardless of whether or not he is concerned with biochemical data, namely, the proper systematic evaluation of a particular correlation which has been established. In this case the Chrysobalanoideae as well as the other sub-families of Rosaceae have already been recognized as distinctive on morphological grounds, and in fact most have been treated as separate families on occasion (Lawrence, 1951). The question is how much additional distinctiveness is implied by the presence of leucodelphinidin in this sub-family alone (information was not available for the Neuradoideae). Unfortunately, we are not yet in a position to give unqualified opinions in many cases such as this, but conservatism with respect to the systematic evaluation of leucoanthocyanins is justifiable.

In his general article on the taxonomic aspects of phenolics Bate-Smith (1958) noted that three classes of these compounds are widespread in their distribution in leaves of higher plants. These substances are leucoanthocyanins, flavonols and hydroxycinnamic acids. He concluded that perhaps the absence of certain of these common substances might be more significant than their presence. For instance, leucoanthocyanins are for the most part absent from the orders Centrospermae, Umbelliferae, and Contortae; entirely absent from the Rhoeadales, Tubiflorae, Plantaginales and Cucurbitales; and almost entirely absent from the Campanulatae. They are also absent from many families of the Ranales. Many of these same orders do not produce flavonols. In connection with his discussion of flavonols Bate-

Smith states that among sympetalous families, those with zygomor-
phic flowers often lack flavonols in the leaves, and this fact may provide a clue to the morphological character with which the absence of
flavonols might be linked. It is important to establish any correlation
between metabolism and form since the biochemical basis of development in all its stages is so little known. However, the present writers
believe that many, if not most, secondary compounds have no critical
role in morphogenesis, and consequently correlations between a given
chemical and anatomical character may be merely coincidental.

Many biochemical studies of phenolics have emphasized the
distribution of some of the commonest phenolics, for example, flavonols and certain cinnamic acid analogs such as ferulic and caffeic
acids. This trend is natural, particularly when investigations are conducted by biologists who must rely upon relatively simple chemical
procedures. However, in many cases the actual systematic value of the
studies may not be great, particularly when minor systematic categories are being considered. As illustrations of the broad distribution
of certain phenolics, Tomaszewski (1960) surveyed 122 species of 86
families for p-hydroxybenzoic acid and other simple phenols and
found that p-hydroxybenzoic acid was present in 120 of the 122
species tested. Caffeic acid was present in all but about a dozen
species. [The author stated that caffeic acid was absent from all
gymnosperms and legumes, but none of the species investigated in
the study was named, and since, of 122 species, a total of 86 different
families was included, not many gymnosperms or legumes could have
been examined. Pecket (1959) found caffeic acid in most species of the
legume, *Lathyrus*.] Ferulic acid occurred in 63 per cent of the species.
p-Coumaric acid occurred in all but three genera, but catechol was
found only in the Salicaceae wherein it occurred in all species examined.
Takahashi *et al.* (1960) found quercetin and kaempferol to be widely
distributed in the order Coniferae, and no significant pattern was
established. The chief significance of these studies is the additional
evidence adduced for a very wide distribution of certain phenolics.
This fact does not exclude them from systematic utility within a
particular taxonomic group, since in combination with other chemical
constituents they might prove significant in individual cases.

An extension of such investigations to the more complex or
the more restricted phenolic types should yield data of more obvious
meaning, in some cases even at the infra-specific level. One excellent
example has been described by Williams (1960). Apple and pear
are significantly different in their phenolic chemistry, the distinctions remaining consistent even though individual varieties (cultivars)
of apple fruit (but not leaves) vary greatly in this respect. Apple

contains the rather uncommon dihydrochalkone, phloridzin, as its principal phenolic, while pear contains another uncommon phenolic, arbutin, a glycoside of hydroquinone. Phloridzin is absent from all pear species while arbutin is absent from apple. Even more significant is the disclosure that, among the twenty-five species of apple other than the cultivated apple (*Malus pumila*), in most species phloridzin is the dominant phenolic, but in some species phloridzin is reduced greatly in amount, and another dihydrochalkone glucoside occurs, the second containing one more phenolic hydroxyl group and with glucose attached at a different position than in phloridzin. The second compound is found, with the exception of one variant of one species, only in the four species from eastern Asia comprising the series Sieboldianae. It is difficult to ignore the phyletic significance of such data.

Other examples of the potential value of rather unusual phenolics which have a restricted distribution are the isoflavones and the rotenoids. The former are reported only from the Rosaceae, Leguminosae, Moraceae, and Iridaceae. In the first two instances, since these families are closely related and often placed in the same order, phyletic significance may be inferred while the other cases doubtlessly represent convergent evolution. The rotenoids are, to the writers' knowledge, restricted to the Leguminosae. The presence of both isoflavones and rotenoids together is further circumstantial evidence of a biosynthetic relationship between the two chemical classes as suggested on chemical grounds earlier in this chapter. It would be interesting to know if any species of Rosaceae produce rotenoids. In general the phenolic chemistry of the Rosaceae and Leguminosae are not similar (Bate-Smith, 1961).

In the genus *Iris* the distribution of isoflavones appears to be correlated with the morphological species groups delimited by taxonomists. Isoflavones are found only in the sections Evansia and Pogoniris, considered as equivalent eastern and western groups. As noted earlier, section Apogon contains most of the leucoanthocyanin-positive species. Bate-Smith noted that leucoanthocyanins are generally found in the mesic species of *Iris* and that this generalization seemed to apply to other monocots as well. Recently, Reznik and Neuhausel (1959) reported on the occurrence of colorless anthocyanins in submerged aquatics. They found that a large number of such aquatic species contained a high concentration of colorless anthocyanins, but these were not leucoanthocyanins. Rather, they were presumed to be the pseudobase form of the anthocyanin which turns red in HCl in the cold. True leucoanthocyanins must be heated in rather concentrated HCl to produce corresponding anthocyanidins.

The existence of colorless anthocyanins in numerous monocot and dicot groups was noted, though they were not detected in certain families which are predominantly aquatic, for example, Potamogetonaceae. In most cases the pigments are cyanidin derivatives, the most commonly encountered types of anthocyanins in vegetative tissue. The formation of these colorless anthocyanins may involve some type of selection which results in the appearance of a physiological state permitting the anthocyanins to exist in the pseudobase form. Possibly, some of these may have been misidentified as leucoanthocyanins.

Some recent phenolic studies having systematic implications are those of Pecket (1959, 1960a, 1960b) on *Lathyrus;* Griffiths (1960) on *Theobroma* and *Herrania;* Reznik and Egger (1960) and Egger and Reznik (1961) on Hamamelidaceae and Anacardiaceae; Bate-Smith and Whitmore (1959) on the Dipterocarpaceae; Bate-Smith (1961) on *Prunus* and *Potentilla;* Riley and Bryant (1961) on Iridaceae and Billek and Kindl (1962) on the Saxifragaceae. In each of these studies variations in patterns were observed, though the authors did not in all cases consider the systematic significance of the patterns. Perhaps more important than the establishment of taxonomic affinities at this stage of such work is the fact that species can be distinguished from other related species by the phenolic characters compared.

In the *Lathyrus* study several systematic judgments were made on the basis of the various phenolic patterns established for certain species, but the present writers, after examining the data offered, and in consideration of the general characteristics of the compounds, would be more conservative. In a genetic study of *Lathyrus odoratus* (Beale, 1939), flavonoid inheritance was shown to be quite complex with a number of chemical phenotypes represented within a single species. However, it is true that wild species, such as those studied by Pecket, tend to have fewer variations than cultivated species. If the results of studies of the comparative chemistry of the non-protein amino acids of *Lathyrus* (Chapter 6) and the toxic nitriles (Chapter 10) are integrated with the phenolic data, interesting taxonomic conclusions may be possible.

Some of these phenolic studies tend to exaggerate the systematic implications of the data. It is natural that enthusiasm will sometimes exercise a subtle influence to magnify the positive aspects of interpretation, but the occasional direct assertion that the particular biochemical data do not provide any clues to systematic relationships should be anticipated. When only a few compounds are being considered and when only a few individuals of a selected group of species are screened, such results would not be cause for repudiation of the methods, nor would they even be surprising. Studies such as that of Stoutamire (1960), though preliminary in nature, show a clear-cut rationale, and the data are evaluated conservatively. In this work several species of *Gaillardia* were analyzed for anthocyanins. Inter-specific differences involved particular cyanidin glycosides, and the patterns conformed somewhat to the sub-generic disposition. Color variations of geographic races of *G. pulchella* were found to involve only quantitative differences in the three anthocyanins present. A quite similar study of *Papaver* species was reported by Acheson *et al.* (1956) with similar conclusions. Griffiths (1960), who compared the seed polyphenols of various species of *Theobroma* and the related genus, *Herrania,* could discover no general taxonomic implications aside from the fact that he concluded that it is reasonable to suppose that the genus *Herrania* is closely related to *Theobroma.* This conclusion, based solely on the chemical data, is questionable, however, because again, only the common polyphenols were considered.

The phytochemical systematic studies of Erdtman (1956, 1958) are especially interesting. He found a distinctive combination of phenolic substances in the heartwood of the genus *Pinus* where the compounds accumulate as inert deposits. Erdtman believes that secondary constituents are generally far more useful in systematic studies than the basic metabolites such as sugars, certain common fatty acids and amino acids. This same position has been taken by others as noted elsewhere. Erdtman favors the bark and wood constituents. He states (1956):

> It is clear that compounds which occur in phylogenetically young, highly specialized organs will possess a lesser taxonomic interest especially when they take part in some of the biochemical processes specific to the organ.

If the statement given above is intended to refer to flower parts, it is more applicable to phylogenetic problems involving the higher taxonomic categories, perhaps not at all applicable to problems of systematics of the lower categories.

Phenolic compounds from the genus *Pinus* include the following:

(1) Stilbenes

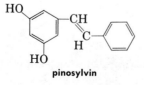

pinosylvin

pinosylvin monomethyl ether
pinosylvin dimethyl ether

(2) Dibenzyls

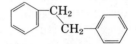

dihydropinosylvin monomethyl ether

(3) Flavanones

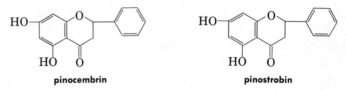

pinocembrin   pinostrobin

cryptostrobin, either 6 or 8-methyl pinocembrin

(4) Flavones

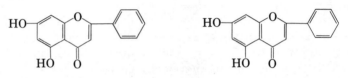

tectochrysin, 7 methoxychrysin
strobochrysin, 6 methylchrysin

(5) Flavonols

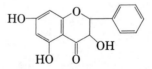

pinobanksin (2:2-dihydrogalangin)
strobobanksin 6-(8?), methyl
2:3-dihydrogalangin

(6) Flavonols: none

(7) Cyclitols: pinitol (d-inositol, sequoyitol and myoinositol reported from *P. lambertiana*)

According to Erdtman the generic sub-groups Haploxylon and Diploxylon differ chemically, but Mirov, as noted elsewhere (Chapter 13), did not find this to be a feature of the terpene chemistry of the genus. The tables in Erdtman however show clearly that the Diploxylon group has the simpler heartwood chemistry; for example, most of the compounds listed above are to be found in Haploxylon species whereas, in Diploxylon only pinosylvin, its monemthyl ether, pino-cembrin and pinobanksin occur. Erdtman states:

> The observed differences between Haploxylon and Diploxylon are of such nature that one is led to conclude that the Haploxylon pines have an oxidation-reduction system at their disposal which has disappeared or is defective in the case of the Diploxylon pines. Since "loss" muta-tions are more common than progressive mutations, it is probable that Haploxylon is more primitive than Diploxylon. Alternatively the separation has taken place already at an earlier phylogenetic stage.[2]

Furthermore, Erdtman states that "more powerful methylating systems" are characteristic of the Haploxylon pines, species of which contain carbon methylated flavones and flavanones.

Outside the genus *Pinus* some other interesting situations are discussed by Erdtman. For instance, of fourteen *Tsuga* species known, five were investigated, and all contained the lignan conidendrin, an unusual substance characteristic of *Picea*.

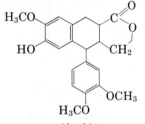

conidendrin

All *Larix* species investigated contained aromadendrin (2:3 dihydrokaempferol) and taxifolin (2:3 dihydroquercetin).

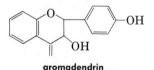

aromadendrin

Taxifolin has also been reported in *Pseudotsuga taxifolia*.

[2] The argument that Haploxylon is more primitive than Diploxylon may be valid, even on the chemical grounds, but not upon the logic that loss mutations are more fre-quent than progressive mutations, a statement which appears to be a non-sequitur. There are examples, in biochemical systematics in which a "loss" is postulated, and, accordingly, the simpler compound is regarded as phylogenetically more advanced. Thus, Gottlieb *et al.* (1959) reported that in certain *Aniba* (Lauraceae) species (for example, rosewood) four methoxylated α-pyrones occur, while in others (for example, coto) only the unsubstituted α-pyrones occur. These authors consider the plain α-pyrones of more recent phylogenetic origin, but their argument rests on the observation that current theories of the biogenesis of α-pyrones involve an expected oxygen function at position 4.

Roberts *et al.* (1958) investigated the phenolic constituents of tea varieties as well as other species of the genus *Camellia,* and their results are of considerable interest because of the type of problem involved. It is rather likely that prolonged cultivation of the tea plant may have almost obliterated the recent natural species history. In fact, according to Kingdon-Ward (1950) "wild tea" as such, no longer occurs, and despite the fact that tea taxa are recognized, the large number of cultivated "varieties" must be subjectively assigned to one of several major cultivar types or else they are classified as putative hybrids. Roberts *et al.* initiated their study on the premise that, "If the chemical compound could be shown to be a feature of one or the other of the taxa conceived by botanists, then the chemical definition could be accepted as relevant to a *natural system* of classification and need not be regarded as a special or artificial classification restricted to the circumstances of cultivation."

Tea plants are usually considered derived from *Camellia sinensis* (China tea) or *C. sinensis* var. *assamica* (Assam tea). A rather extensive phenolic complex is typical of the vegetative shoots of the species, including several catechins, depsides such as galloyl-quinic and chlorogenic acids, flavonols, anthocyanins, and leucoanthocyanins. Trihydroxy derivatives (for example, gallic acid, gallocatechin, myricetin, and leucodelphinidin) of these classes are prominent in the species. Anthocyanin is more characteristic of shoots of the China variety. In general, Assam tea lacks anthocyanin. The so-called "southern" form of Assam, in the opinion of Roberts *et al.,* has been crossed with the China variety, and this accounts for the appearance of anthocyanin in the form. It is interesting that these authors reported that leucoanthocyanins were of sporadic occurrence, sometimes absent, sometimes abundant, and it was not possible to associate them with a particular kind of tea.

These investigators further found that triglycosidic flavonols were common in the China variety but not in the Assam tea variety (except in trace amounts in some instances). An independently isolated southern form contained a substance known as IC, which gave an orange color with aluminum chloride, but which unfortunately was not further characterized. The substance was absent from all other tea varieties tested but was present in two other species of the section Thea, namely *Camellia taliensis* and *C. irrawadiensis.* The authors considered that this evidence opened the possibility that some populations of cultivated tea were derived as species hybrids. While such statements are conjectural at present, the work illustrates another possible application of biochemical data to systematics. It is noted that otherwise the three species which comprise the section Thea are

Table 11-2. Distribution of biflavonyls (Baker and Ollis, 1961; from the *Chemistry of Natural Phenolic Compounds* by permission of Pergamon Press).

Orders	Families, Genera, and Species	G.	I.	Sc.	K.	So.	H.
Cycadales	Cycadaceae *Cycas revoluta* Thunb.	–	–	–	–	•	–
Ginkgoales	Ginkgoaceae *Ginkgo biloba* L.	•	•	–	–	–	–

Coniferales	Taxaceae
	  Taxus cuspidata Sieb. and Zucc.
	  T. cuspidata var. *nana* Hort.
	  T. floriana Chap.
	  Torreya nucifera Sieb. and Zucc.
		
		–
		–
		–
		–
			
			–
			–
			–
			–
				
				•
				•
				•
				–
					
					–
					–
					–
					•
						
						–
						–
						–
						–
							
							–
							–
							–
							–

	Cephalotaxaceae
	  Cephalotaxus drupacea Sieb. and Zucc.
	  C. nana Nakai
		
		–
		–
			
			–
			–
				
				–
				–
					
					•
					•
						
						–
						–
							
							–
							–

	Podocarpaceae
	  Podocarpus macrophylla D. Don
	  P. chinensis Sweet
	  P. nagi Zoll. and Moritz
		
		–
		–
		–
			
			–
			–
			–
				
				–
				–
				–
					
					•
					•
					•
						
						–
						–
						–
							
							–
							–
							–

	Pinaceae
	  Abies firma Sieb. and Zucc.
	  A. homolepsis Sieb. and Zucc.
	  A. mariessii Mast.
	  A. veitchii Lindley
	  A. sachalinensis var. *Schmidtii* Tatewaki
	  Keteleeria davidiana Beissner
	  Pseudotsuga japonica Carriere
	  Tsuga sieboldii Carriere
	  T. diversifolia Mast.
	  Picea polita Carriere
	  P. glehnii Mast.
	  P. maximowiczii Regel
	  P. koyamai Shirasawa
	  P. bicolor Mayer
	  P. jezoensis var. *hondoensis* Rehder
	  Pseudolarix kaempferi Gordon.
	  Larix kaempferi Sargent
	  Cedrus deodara Loud.
	  Pinus densiflora Sieb. and Zucc.
	  P. koraiensis
	    (and 22 other spp. of *Pinus* not named)
		all –	all –	all –	all –	all –	all –

	Sciadopityaceae *Sciadopitys verticillata* Sieb. and Zucc.	–	–	•	–	–	–

	Taxodiaceae
	  Taxodium distichum Rich.
	  Sequoia sempervirens E.
		
		–
		–
			
			–
			–
				
				–
				–
					
					–
					•
						
						–
						–
							
							•
							•

GYMNOSPERMAE

219

Table 11-2. (*Continued*)

Orders	Families, Genera, and Species	G.	I.	Sc.	K.	So.	H.
GYMNOSPERMAE							
Coniferales	*Metasequoia glyptostroboides* Hu and Cheng	−	−	−	−	−	●
	Glyptostrobus pensilis K. Koch	−	−	−	−	−	●
	Cunninghamia lanceolata Hooker	−	−	●	●	●	●
	C. lanceolata var. *konishii* Fujita	−	−	−	●	−	●
	Taiwania cryptomerioides Hayata	−	−	−	−	−	●
	Cryptomeria japonica D. Don	−	−	●	●	●	−
	C. japonica var. *araucarioides* Hort.	−	−	●	●	●	−
	Cupressaceae						
	Callitris glauca R. Brown	−	−	−	−	−	●
	Thujopsis dolobrata Sieb. and Zucc.	−	−	●	−	●	●
	Thuja standishii C.	−	−	−	−	−	●
	T. occidentalis L.	−	−	−	−	−	●
	Biota orientalis Endl.	−	−	−	−	−	●
	Libocedrus formosana Frolin	−	−	−	−	−	●
	L. decurrens Torrey	−	−	−	−	−	●
	Cupressus funebris Endl.	−	−	−	−	−	●
	C. arizonica	−	−	−	−	−	●
	Chamaecyparis obtusa Endl.	−	−	−	−	−	●
	C. obtusa var. *breviana* Mast.	−	−	−	−	●	●
	C. pisifera Mast.	−	−	−	−	−	●
	C. pisifera var. *filifera* Mast.	−	−	−	−	−	●
	C. pisifera var. *squarrosa* Mast.	−	−	−	−	−	●
	Sabina chinensis Antoine	−	−	−	●	−	●
	S. virginiana Antoine	−	−	−	●	−	●
	S. procumbens Sieb. and Zucc.	−	−	−	●	−	●
	S. sargentii Nakai	−	−	−	●	−	●
	S. sargentii var. *kaizuka* Hort.	−	−	−	●	−	●
	Juniperis utilis Koidz.	−	−	−	●	−	●
	J. conferta Parl.	−	−	−	●	−	●
Gnetales	Ephedraceae						
	Ephedra gerardiana Wall.	−	−	−	−	−	−
ANGIOSPERMAE							
Casuarinales	Casuarinaceae						
	Casuarina stricta Ait.	−	−	−	−	−	●

G. = ginkgetin; I. = isoginkgetin; Sc. = sciadopitysin; K. = kayaflavone; So. = sotetsuflavone; H. = hinokiflavone.

chemically similar, although *C. taliensis* more closely parallels *C. sinensis*. A number of species from other sections of the genus were examined chromatographically, but their patterns did not closely resemble the Thea pattern.

In summary, phenolics may be regarded as potentially of great systematic importance because of the existence of hundreds of different types, many of which are of restricted distribution. It is probable that a comprehensive review of the chemical, biochemical, and pharmacological literature would establish a number of interesting correlations not already recognized. In most of these cases, additional work would be necessary to substantiate a systematic evaluation. Hegnauer (1956) has reviewed the comparative chemistry of an individual family, the Leguminosae and considered among other groups of compounds, the phenolics. Comprehensive chemical reviews such as that of Karrer (1958), which lists the constitution and occurrence of organic plant constituents, provide insight into attractive possibilities, for example, the distribution of the flavanone, naringenin and other flavanones and their glycosides in the genus *Acacia* and other members of the Mimosoideae. Among the commoner phenolics, specific glycoside types are likely to be more significant than the aglycone which have been more often studied.

Some of the more recently discovered flavonoids, such as the biflavonyls discussed earlier, offer opportunities for phylogenetic investigations. The biflavonyls, for example, are known to occur only in gymnosperms with the exception of *Casuarina* (Table 11-2). It is notable that biflavonyls are not yet known from Pinaceae, although numerous species have been examined. Baker and Ollis (1961), in noting the presence of biflavonyls in *Casuarina stricta,* add "This is particularly interesting because of all the angiosperms, *Casuarina* is the most closely related to the gymnosperms." That this viewpoint is far from unanimous may be quickly ascertained from Lawrence (1951). The more important question is that of how much weight ought to be given to the presence of hinokiflavone, the biflavonyl of *Casuarina,* in linking the group to gymnosperms.

In contrast to the biflavonyls, another group of recently discovered flavonoids, the C-glycosides, thus far have been reported from such widely separated plant groups as the Gramineae, Lemnaceae, Caryophyllaceae, Rosaceae, and Verbenaceae (Hörhammer and Wagner, 1961).

12 QUINONES

Three major classes of naturally occurring quinones are recognized: benzoquinones, naphthoquinones, and anthraquinones (see below). In addition a few complex substances of quinone structure occur (for example, tripterine, in *Tripterygium wilfordii,* family Celastraceae), but these last are too little known to allow much consideration of their systematic importance at this time.

The most recent treatment of the chemistry and distribution of quinones is that of Thomson (1957). He emphasized mainly quinone chemistry, but sources of all naturally occurring quinones were given.

Quinones occur in plants, animals, and micro-organisms. However, in the animal kingdom,

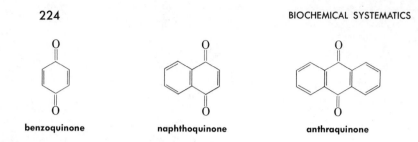

benzoquinone   naphthoquinone   anthraquinone

quinones are known to occur only in certain echinoderms and insects. They are rare in algae but common in fungi. In the vascular plants, with the exception of certain quinones which are believed to function as important coenzymes, quinones are of restricted occurrence. Although not widespread among plant families, in those families in which quinones do occur, the compounds may be characteristic for the family.

The chemical properties of quinones include relative ease of oxidation and reduction. In this connection 2-methyl,3-phytyl, 1-4-naphthoquinone (Vitamin K), found in high concentration in chloroplasts, has been proposed as a coenzyme involved in electron transport, particularly in the processes following the primary photochemical event of photosynthesis.

Recently, another group of coenzymes of a quinoid nature referred to collectively as coenzyme Q (or ubiquinone) has been described. This group is thought to participate in electron transport between cytochromes b and c. The basic structure of coenzyme Q involves a 2,3,5-tri-methyl benzoquinone substituted with isoprenoid side chains at the 6-position.

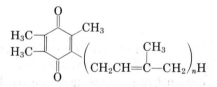

At least five naturally occurring homologues of coenzyme Q have been described, the differences involving the number of isoprene units attached. Lester and Crane (1959) studied the distribution of the coenzyme Q series in animals, plants, and microorganisms. Coenzyme Q was found in all higher plants examined (six genera) and among red, brown, and green algae. One bluegreen alga, *Anacystis nidulans,* did not yield any coenzyme Q. The higher animals and plants were found to contain, usually, coenzyme Q_{10}, with Q_9 appearing in a few cases. (The subscript refers to the number of isoprene units in the side chain.) Among microorganisms, there was considerably greater variation in the types present; for example, in ascomycetes coenzymes Q_{10}, Q_9, Q_8, Q_7, and Q_6 were present. A particular quinone found in chloroplasts having an absorption maximum at 254 mμ has been called "plastoquinone" (Crane, 1959).

The presence of a quinone coenzyme involved in an important electron transport system in plants suggests that the ability to synthesize the basic naphthoquinone nucleus is not limited but is characteristic of plants in general. Therefore, those groups of plants which accumulate naphthoquinones otherwise substituted than in the vitamin K pattern may not possess a uniquely new enzyme system for the formation of the naphthoquinone ring structure, but rather may possess a metabolic system which permits the accumulation of naphthoquinones, which, when coupled with appropriate enzymes, provide for secondary structural modifications. It is well established that some quinones are fungicidal. If then, there is some positive selective value correlated with quinone accumulation, and the basic quinone pathway pre-exists (even though production is limited) among green plants in general, it is not surprising to find distantly related plants producing the same compound. Considered in this light there is no reason to suspect cryptic phylogenetic association between taxa possessing such compounds. For example, the quinones lawsone, and its methyl ether (the latter is fungicidal) are found in *Lawsonia alba* (Lythraceae) and in *Impatiens balsamina* (Balsaminaceae) respectively. Thomson says that "it is noteworthy that such closely related quinones occur in distantly related plant families." Actually, other, even more complex quinones occur in equally distantly related families, for example, lapachol (Bignoniaceae, Verbenaceae, Sapotaceae).

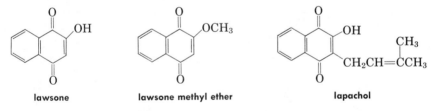

lawsone   lawsone methyl ether   lapachol

Some quinones are physiologically active (as purgatives), and others are valued as dyes. Despite their economic significance, however, relatively little is known of quinone biosynthesis, and practically no genetic studies on quinones have been reported. The favored hypothesis to account for the important anthraquinone group involves the same mechanism as that producing the A ring of flavonoid compounds, namely, the condensation of acetate units. Acetate-2-C^{14} has been used to investigate the biosynthesis of emodin by *Penicillium islandicum,* and the results suggest that head to tail condensation of eight acetate groups was involved (Friedrich, 1959). Hegnauer (1959), in contrast, emphasized the fact that compounds such as xanthones, stilbenes, chalkones, asperulosides, and so on, which may be regarded as variants of the basic C_6-C_3-C_6 flavonoid nucleus, occur in the plant families which are also notable for the production of anthraquinones. Furthermore, he notes that Trim (1955) found that asperuligenin accumulated in Rubiaceae during development, but only until the synthesis of anthraquinone began. Thus, Hegnauer believes that comparative phytochemistry points to a relationship between the C_6-C_3 and C_6-C_3-C_6 groups on the one hand and anthraquinones on the other, so that the acetate theory alone could not satisfactorily account for the facts; possibly phenol-related pathways are involved.

The simplest group of quinones, benzoquinones, are rarely found among higher plants, being better known among fungi. Although no attempt is made in this section to give a comprehensive list of the quinones and their sources, there are so few benzoquinones from higher plants, that it is practical to list them all. The following benzoquinones from higher plants are included in Thomson (1957):

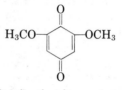

2 : 6-dimethoxybenzoquinone

Adonis vernalis, Ranunculaceae

embelin

Myrsine, Embelia and *Rapanea,* Myrsinaceae

rapanone

Rapanea maximowiczii; Myrsinaceae; *Oxalis purpurata* var. *jacquinii,* Oxalidaceae

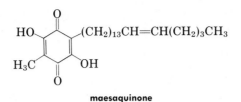

maesaquinone

Maesa javonica, Myrsinaceae

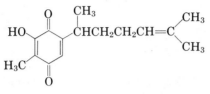

perezone

Perezia adnata, Trixis calcalioides, tribe Mutisieae of the Compositae

The Myrsinaceae seem to be particularly rich in benzoquinones, and these compounds should prove to be useful as systematic criteria. It is significant that the plants which produce benzoquinones bear no particular taxonomic affinities to those species producing the other classes of quinones.

Since these compounds are, for the most part, relatively simple derivatives of naphthoquinone, it is probable that they have arisen independently in many, if not all, of the families known to produce them.

Extensive surveys for the presence of naphthoquinones have not been made, and many naphthoquinone-containing species may remain undetected. Naphthoquinones, by present knowledge, are rather rare, and a given type usually is restricted to one or two families. The simple naphthoquinone, juglone, approaches a familial character in the Juglandaceae. Although naphthoquinones seem to be of little systematic significance above the family level, it is possible that at the lower taxonomic levels the compounds may be of systematic value.

The most complex group of quinones, the anthraquinones, is also the most widely distributed. In fact, if the three sub-types of quinones were selected to illustrate the principle of the "percentage of frequence" rule (see Fig. 4-1) the results would contradict the principle, since the least complex have the most limited taxonomic distribution. Coupled with the fact that there is little simultaneous occurrence of two or three sub-types of quinones, their general pattern of distribution implies that there is no close biosynthetic relationship between the types of quinones, and therefore this chemical class, in a biosynthetic sense, appears to be artificial. (In contrast, in the fungal genera *Penicillium* and *Aspergillus,* two and three groups, respectively, of quinones are encountered, and within a single group, a number of different quinones occur.)

The association of anthraquinones with particular families of higher plants is striking. The Rubiaceae, Polygonaceae, and Rhamnaceae are notable in this respect, with the family Rubiaceae the outstanding example (Hegnauer 1959). Anthraquinones are rare among monocots, having been reported only in the Liliaceae. Schnarf (1944) investigated the presence of aloin in tribes of the Liliaceae. In the tribe Asphodeleae, he found aloin in specialized cells in the genera *Asphodelus, Evenurus, Bulbine, Bulbinella, Bulbinopsis,* and *Alectorurus.* "Aloin cells" are otherwise found only in the tribe Aloineae (except for the presence of chrysophanol in *Xanthorrhoea* of a third tribe, Lomandreae). Moreover, the above-named genera differed in foliar anatomy and embryology from others of the Asphodeleae but resembled the Aloineae. Thus, according to Hegnauer, the biochemical evidence correlates nicely with embryological and anatomical evidence.

In a previous study, Munkner (1928) investigated extensively the tribe Aloineae and particularly the genus *Aloe.* The older technique for the detection of anthraquinones was a color test, the Bornträger test. (A slightly acidified benzene extract is shaken in a test tube with ammonia. A rose red to raspberry color indicates the presence of anthraquinone.) Since it now appears that negative tests with the Bornträger reagent are not always reliable (Hegnauer, 1959), some conclusions based on the presence or absence of anthraquinones by this test might be proven spurious. Of genera related to *Aloe,* the following results were obtained:

> *Gasteria* (seven species tested; all positive)
> *Lomatophyllum* (two species tested; both positive)
> *Apicra* (four species tested; all negative)
> *Kniphofia* (ten species tested; all negative)
> *Haworthia* (seven species tested; two positive and five negative)

One hundred and seventy eight species of *Aloe* were examined, and a large majority of the species gave a positive Bornträger reaction. However, there is little indication of a definite pattern of the distribution. For example, although nineteen species of the section Leptoaloe were negative, there were two questionable exceptions (*A. kraussii* and *A. parvula*); six of the seven remaining sections had both positive and negative species, as did all but one of the five subsections of section Eualoe.

In the family Polygonaceae, Jaretzky (1926) reported that of the two sub-families, Eriogonoideae and Polygonoideae, only the latter produced anthraquinones. Many species of the genera *Ernex, Rumex,*

Rheum, as well as species of *Atraphaxis, Oxygonum, Polygonum,* and *Muhlenbeckia* produce anthraquinones. More recently, Tsukida (1957) reported on the distribution of anthraquinones in the Polygonaceae and added several other genera to those known to produce these compounds. Jaretzky (1926, 1928) believed the presence of anthraquinones to be a primitive character since it was inversely correlated with morphological progression within the genus *Rumex* (for example, dioecious species such as *Rumex acetosa* are anthraquinone free) as well as within the sub-family as a whole (for example, *Fagopyrum* with heterostyly, is anthraquinone free). This is one of the few cases where the *presence* of a particular class of chemical substances is believed to be a primitive character. Tsukida was principally concerned with the localization of specific anthraquinones in plant organs as well as the specific anthraquinone types produced by these species, and he did not emphasize particularly the systematic implications of his data.

Heppeler (1928) studied the distribution of emodin in the genus *Rhamnus* (Rhamnaceae) and attempted a systematic arrangement of the genus based on the presence or absence of this anthraquinone in dried plants. However, Maurin (1928) in the same year reported a number of species positive which had been considered negative by Heppeler. Furthermore, Hegnauer (1959) has noted that the application of the Bornträger test to herbarium material is unreliable since a number of species judged by Heppeler to be negative have since been shown to contain anthraquinone. Hegnauer has summarized present knowledge of the occurrence of anthraquinones in the genus. Unfortunately (for purposes of phylogenetic implications), a number of the series in both the sub-genera, Frangula and Eurhamnus, which formerly had been considered negative, are now shown to be positive for anthraquinones. It appears that anthraquinones are widespread in the genus *Rhamnus* and also in a number of other genera of the Rhamnaceae. Since no distributional pattern is now recognizable, further investigation on this family is recommended by Hegnauer.

In the Leguminosae only a few genera are known to produce anthraquinones, but in one genus, *Cassia,* the compounds are widespread. The classic anthraquinone work on *Cassia* is that of Gilg and Heinemann (1926). These authors assumed that oxymethylanthraquinones were to be found only in the section Chamaesenna of the sub-genus Senna.

Within Chamaesenna the various series were analyzed for presence of emodin-like anthraquinones, yielding some interesting results. Probably the most noteworthy systematic conclusion stemming from this survey was the redisposition of the taxa belonging to the series Aphyllae, which includes only the two species,

Series	Species Examined	Results
Pachycarpae	15	(+) Emodin present
Crassirameae	1	(−) Emodin absent
Rostratae	12	(−) Emodin absent
Auriculatae	3	(−) Emodin absent
Floridae	14	(−) Emodin absent
Aculeatae	1	(−) Emodin absent
Pictae	9	(+) Emodin present
Brachycarpae	8	(+) Emodin present

C. aphylla and *C. crossiramea.* According to Gilg and Heinemann these two species are placed in Bentham's series Aphylla on a superficial character (namely, absence of leaves). Gilg and Heinemann treated *C. aphylla* as a leafless member of the series Pachycarpae, while *C. crassiamea* was placed in a newly proposed series, Crassiraea. Although these authors based their conclusions, in part, on certain morphological and geographical evidence, considerable weight was apparently given to the fact that *C. aphylla* tested positively for emodin (as did the fourteen other species tested in the series Pachycarpae) while *C. crassiramea* was negative. A similar observation was perhaps also responsible for the author's establishment of the series Aculeatae, its only species, *C. aculeatae,* which was negative for emodin, having previously been placed in the series Pictae (Bentham, 1871); the latter testing positive for those nine species examined.

However, Hegnauer (1959) has summarized more recent literature on the anthraquinones of *Cassia,* and has noted reports of a much broader distribution of anthraquinone in the genus. For example, several species of the sub-genus Fistula have been reported to contain anthraquinones: *C. fistula, C. leptophylla, C. carnaval,* and *C. javanica.* The majority of sections in the sub-genus Senna now are known to have at least one representative which produces anthraquinones, and within the section Chamaesenna, two series other than those noted by Gilg and Heinemann are included among anthraquinone producers. Finally, *C. mimosoides,* of the sub-genus Lasiorhegma (section Chamaecrista) has been found to produce anthraquinones. The situation in *Cassia* is, then, similar to that in *Rhamnus.* It is quite likely that an intensive study of the distribution of quinones in the large genus *Cassia* would disclose a pattern. Such a study would have to include a characterization of the more common quinones as well as analysis of various plant organs, for it has been demonstrated that related species may differ radically in the distribution of quinones within the plant.

13 TERPENOIDS

A rather heterogeneous group of substances is actually included under terpenoids, yet with few exceptions the compounds may be conceived as structural derivatives of the five-carbon compound, isoprene.

$$CH_2{=}\overset{\displaystyle CH_3}{\underset{\displaystyle}{C}}{-}CH{=}CH_2$$

Isoprene

Recently, the six-carbon compound, mevalonic acid, has been found to be an important precursor in cholesterol synthesis and is suspected to be involved also in the synthesis of several other classes of isoprenoid compounds such as terpenes[1] and carotenoids (Wagner and Folkers, 1961). Mevalonic acid itself apparently originates through acetate condensation. As was indicated in a previous section (Chapter 11) mevalonic acid occupies a focal position in isoprenoid synthesis somewhat analogous to that of shikimic acid in aromatic synthesis (Fig. 13-1).

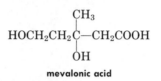

mevalonic acid

Among the simplest terpenes, the relationship to isoprene is evident at once. For example, note the monoterpene, myrcene, illustrated below:

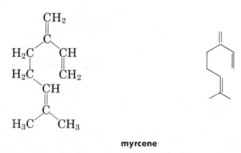

myrcene

The formula above, also of myrcene, represents the type customarily used to represent terpenoid compounds.

In addition to differences in the position of double bonds and degree of hydrogenation of a given basic terpene structure, alcohol, aldehyde, ketone, and acid derivatives of simple aliphatic terpenes exist. Geraniol, for example, is a widely distributed alcohol of this type. Furthermore, ring closure provides for simple cyclic structures. A common example of such a compound is phellandrene:

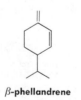

β-phellandrene

---

[1] Although Stanley (1958) has reported incorporation of C^{14} labeled mevalonic acid into α-pinene of *Pinus attenuata,* Battaile and Loomis (1961) have evidence that mevalonic acid is not incorporated into mint terpenes. These latter investigators found C^{14} from mevalonic acid in carotenoids and other compounds in the plant. Therefore, one cannot readily discount their evidence concerning terpenes on the grounds that it is negative.

It is evident that a very large number of simple terpene types are theoretically possible (and, in fact, exist). More complex terpenoid compounds, and other types of isoprenoid derivatives, also exist in abundance throughout the plant kingdom and to a more limited extent among animals. Even in simple monoterpenes internal rings may form with the elimination of a double bond, for example, as in pinene.

α-pinene

Also, additional isoprene units may be incorporated. Sesquiterpenes, for instance, represent three isoprene units (C_{15} compounds), and diterpenes represent four isoprene units. The latter are relatively uncommon. Triterpenes, with six isoprene units, are but rarely encountered in higher plants. Plant steroids are best considered allied with the terpenoid substances. Isoprene derivatives, or compounds that may be derived theoretically from isoprene, of even higher molecular weight include such compounds as the carotenoids, and high polymers such as rubber or gutta percha. Although the carotenoids may prove to be a valuable biochemical category for chemosystematic purposes, as yet little work along such lines has been done with such compounds except among the algae (Chapter 14). The phytyl group of chlorophyll is essentially a polyisoprene, and the group also occurs as part of the napthoquinone derivative, Vitamin K, discussed in Chapter 12. Such substances as these last are examples of important basic metabolic pathways and are therefore probably less useful in phytosystematic investigations.

A classic example of the application of phytochemistry to problems of phylogeny is the work of Baker and Smith (1920) on the terpenes of *Eucalyptus* oils. One might suppose that the impetus from this classic work would have encouraged considerable interest in the systematic distribution of terpenes, yet this has not occurred on a large scale. The Baker and Smith work was a remarkable achievement, but on reading the book it is nontheless evident that the immediate systematic implications of the study were quite limited. There is no doubt however that the work disclosed clearly the possibilities of phytochemical systematics. Some of the important aspects of the Baker and Smith work will be considered at this time.

One important goal of their early investigations was to determine whether or not chemical characters are dependable (or constant) enough to warrant their consideration as taxonomic characters. The examination of large numbers of individual trees over an extensive

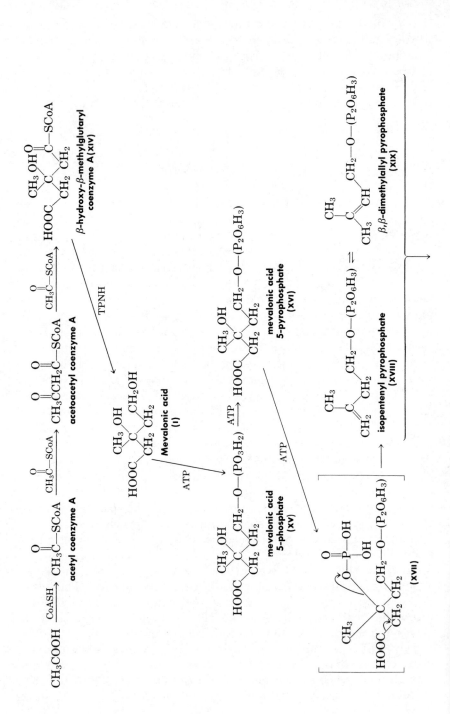

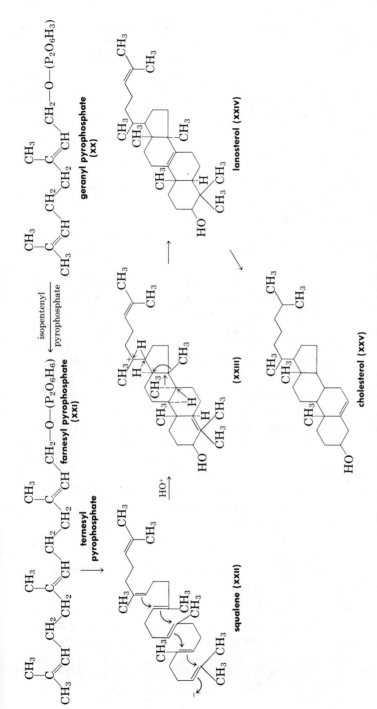

Fig. 13-1. Biosynthesis of cholesterol (Wagner and Folkers, 1961).

part of the range of the species was required to answer this question. As a result of such investigations Baker and Smith were impressed with the constancy of oil characters within a species:

> The theory has often been advanced that the chemical constituents of the same species vary in different localities, but this idea is not verified by our experiences as regards the Eucalypts, as they do not show these differences in chemical constituents that might perhaps be expected from differences of soils or localities. The reverse may possibly be accounted for by the natural selective, ecological peculiarities shown in many instances by the species themselves, as it is remarkable how a certain species will flourish on a particular geological formation and become singular to like formations, while at the same time objecting to those entirely different. However that may be, those influences do not appear to act detrimentally, or to interfere in any way with the practical constancy of results.

It is apparent now that more variation in oil character existed than was recognized by Baker and Smith, especially among the individuals of a population. For example, in discussing the oil characters of *Eucalyptus dives* they noted that the constancy of oil characters exhibited by *Eucalyptus* species generally also applied to *E. dives*. Components of *E. dives* oil are crude oil, largely phellandrene with 5 to 8 per cent cineole and some piperitone. Another fraction consisted largely of the peppermint ketone, piperitone. But, Penfold and Morrison (1927) also described major variations in the oil character of *E. dives*. Ordinarily this species yields oils with 45 to 50 per cent piperitone. Yet, some plants identical to typical *E. dives* yielded as low as 8 per cent piperitone. In fact, there had been some complaints that differences in the piperitone concentration were the fault of the distillation techniques if not the result of adulteration. The following picturesque statements from Penfold and Morrison indicate that significantly different oil characters did indeed occur in two plants which were morphologically indistinguishable:

> Then again whilst engaged in field service during the end of December, 1924, repairing a punctured tyre of the car by which we were travelling led us to examine a patch of trees of this species growing close to the Main Southern Road about 18 miles on the Sydney side of Goulburn. The observation was made of two trees growing together, indistinguishable from one another by both botanist and bushman, but each containing a different essential oil. On crushing the leaves between the fingers, one yielded the typical phellandrene-piperitone odour, whilst in the other the odour of cineol-phellandrene-terpinol was most pronounced.

A communication from another worker concerning the morphology of these plants is quoted by Penfield and Morrison:

> I tried every point to see if there is any morphological difference between these two forms, but failed to find one single character to distinguish these two trees. . . . Seedlings, young and matured foliage, buds and fruits, all agree with the other. I spent many hours over this examination that I might not miss any point."

According to Penfield and Morrison, *E. dives* is thought to be a hybrid. Thus they feel that such oil variation "seems only reasonable." Yet, why is there so little evidence in a hybrid of morphological variations? The fact that so much effort and attention was devoted to the question of whether the chemical forms of *E. dives* could be otherwise distinguished is indicative of the influence that the earlier phytochemical work had with respect to the question of chemical constancy within a species.

Baker and Smith did not apparently consider hybridization to be an important factor in the evolution of *Eucalyptus.*

> It may be now shown that most of these supposed aberrant forms are really distinct species, and in our opinion cross fertilization in the Eucalypts under natural conditions is quite exceptional, especially when we know that numerous species are growing intermixed, often flowering at the same time, and so under supposed favourable conditions for hybridization, yet preserving throughout extensive areas their specific characters with remarkable constancy.

Four types of *E. dives* were subsequently recognized, all based on oil character differences:

E. dives, type
  piperitone, 40 to 50 per cent; phellandrene, 40 per cent
E. dives, var. A
  piperitone, 5 to 15 per cent; phellandrene, 60 to 80 per cent; piperitol (small amount).
E. dives, var. B.
  piperitone, 10 to 20 per cent; cineole, 25 to 50 per cent; together with phellandrene
E. dives, var. C.
  Cineole, 45 to 75 per cent; piperitone, under 5 per cent; phellandrene, absent, or present in small quantity only.

Although Baker and Smith considered that oil characters did not usually vary greatly within a species, they found examples wherein oil characters differed among morphologically similar plants. A notable example is the species *Eucalyptus phellandra* discussed prominently by Read (1944). According to Read, *E. phellandra* had been included previously under *E. amygdalina,* and in the first edition of the Baker and Smith work (1902) it was recorded under *amygdalina.* According to Baker and Smith, "It is one of the few species of this research that has been founded almost entirely on the chemical constituents of the oil." There is then some circular reasoning if one creates a species on the basis of a difference in oil character alone, while simultaneously maintaining that constancy of oil character within a species is typical within species of the genus. As a generalization the species constancy of oil character in *Eucalyptus* is doubtlessly accurate. Physiological races are regularly encountered, and their appearance does not normally affect the integrity of the species. In *Pinus,* Mirov (1961) has found that some species vary but little in turpentine composition throughout their range while other species are quite variable in this respect.

In connection with problems of phylogeny within the genus and among other related genera, Baker and Smith noted the similarities in oil constituents of *Eucalyptus* and *Angophora* (for example, the presence of the sesquiterpene, aromadendrene, in both genera) as opposed to a third allied genus, *Tristania.* They proceeded to develop a postulated line of descent showing the supposed origin of each subgroup, the pattern stemming from correlated chemical and morphological characters. Baker and Smith recognized four major sub-divisions of the genus with distinctive chemical attributes:

(1) Those yielding oils consisting largely of the terpene pinene, either dextro-rotatory or laevo-rotatory.
(2) Those yielding oils containing varying amounts of pinene and cineole, but in which phellandrene is absent.
(3) Those yielding oils in which aromadendral is a characteristic constituent and phellandrene is usually absent.
(4) Those yielding oils in which phellandrene is a pronounced constituent with piperitone mostly present.

Since the majority of eucalypts yield oil largely of pinene and cineole without phellandrene, the authors believed that phellandrene and thus piperitone appeared later, in fact even later than aromadendral.

An interesting correlative morphological character is found among the Eucalypts. The character involves the pattern of leaf venation which seems generally to be correlated with the oil constituents. The "primitive" (*sensu* Baker and Smith) leaf venation pattern, associated with cineole and pinine oils, exhibits the following features:

(1) Angle with midrib is less acute (approaching a right angle).
(2) Marginal vein is close to edge.
(3) Reticulations between veins are prominent.

The "advanced" leaf types, associated with phellandrene and piperidine, possess the following attributes:

(1) Angles of veins with midrib acute.
(2) Marginal vein withdrawn from edge, a second marginal vein withdrawn from edge, and a third marginal vein may be in evidence (for example, *E. dives*).
(3) Reticulations between major veins are reduced, and thus more space for oil glands is present.
(4) Looping arrangement of major veins particularly noticeable in the bending of the marginal vein at positions of major lateral veins.

Elsewhere Baker and Smith stated:

> In other parts of this work we show that this alteration in leaf venation and chemical constituents is not local in its incidence, and that the specific characters of each species are practically constant over the whole range of its distribution, and numerous instances are given of this constancy.
> That the constituents of the oil have been fixed and constant for a long period of time must be evident by the fact that, to whatever extent or range any particular species has reached, it contains the same characteristic constituents, and has its botanical characters in agreement.

Baker and Smith prepared a phylogenetic tree designed to show the evolutionary relationships of over 150 species of Eucalypts. They also illustrated the general distribution of specific chemical constituents of the oil. This distribution was purported to reflect the major movement of the genus during its evolution in Australia.

The foregoing discussion may have given the impression that only a few oil constituents had been detected. In fact, even in 1920 Baker and Smith listed forty oil constituents, and at the present time it is almost a certainty that many more are known. Many of the components, however, occur in small quantities and often in only a few species and these substances may provide further taxonomically useful information.

Exceptional species such as *Eucalyptus macarthuri* and *E. citriodora,* in which the chief constituents are geranyl acetate and citronellal, were regarded as end members of sequences in which the ancestral intermediate forms have disappeared in the course of evolution (Read, 1944).

McNair (1942) attempted to correlate the morphological and chemical characteristics as reported by Baker and Smith and concluded that sometimes "primitive" morphology and "advanced" oil characters occurred together, or the opposite relationship occurred. The extent to which this is borne out is difficult to determine from the data in McNair's paper, since he presents no morphological data to compare with the chemistry. Of course, some instances of more rapid evolution in either morphology or oil chemistry are to be expected. One point made by McNair which is noteworthy is that oil constituents of the "advanced" type may appear independently in groups which otherwise show no close genetic relationships.

As noted earlier, in spite of the classic work by Baker and Smith, very little work on the biological aspects of terpene chemistry has been carried out. This is noted by Mirov in 1948 emphatically:

> ... the chemistry of essential oils to the problems of biology has been utterly neglected and very little organized work has been done in this direction. A notable exception is, of course, the classical research on the Eucalypts and their essential oils by Baker and Smith. ...

Mirov (1948) reported on the terpenes of the genus *Pinus.* He included extensive tables of data arranged according to species and following the classification of Shaw (1914). In the sub-groups Haploxylon (having a single vascular bundle in each needle with usually five needles per dwarf shoot) and Diploxylon (having a double bundle with two to three needles) there did not appear to be any significant general differences in their terpenes. For example, both groups contained dl-α-pinene as a major constituent, and other, more complex substances occurred sporadically throughout both groups.[2] However, Erdtman has shown distinctive differences in the heartwood chemistry of the two groups. (For discussion of Erdtman's work see Chapter 11.)

---

[2] However, in a discussion following presentation of a paper on the distribution of turpentine components (1958) Mirov stated that the Haploxylon group "have decidedly more sesquiterpenes" and more new substances were found in that group. Mirov believes that the two sub-groups split very early and underwent parallel evolution.

Mirov cites several instances in which closely related species have similar terpenes (for example, *Pinus muricata, P. attenuata,* and *P. radiata*), and other cases in which closely related species have quite different terpenes.

One extremely interesting situation involving pure species was reported by Mirov (1948). *Pinus ponderosa* contains β-pinene and limonene (however, the variety *scopulorum* consists mostly of α-pinene instead of β-pinene). *P. jeffreyi,* which some botanists consider a variety of *P. ponderosa,* contains no terpenes but rather heptanes. To complicate the matter further, *P. jeffreyi* in its chemical attributes approaches more closely the group Macrocarpa than the group Australia to which *P. ponderosa* belongs (heptane is found in all three species comprising the Macrocarpa group). Also, similar aldehydes are found in *P. jeffreyi* and the pines of the Macrocarpa group. Furthermore, *P. jeffreyi* crosses in nature with both *P. ponderosa* and *P. coulteri,* the latter a member of Macrocarpa. According to Mirov, *P. jeffreyi* possibly crosses more readily with *P. coulteri.*

In the genus *Mentha* rather extensive chemical investigations of the important flavoring substances have been conducted by numerous investigators. Recently, genetic studies have advanced evidence that a single pair of genes controls, directly or indirectly, the major monoterpenic chemical constituents of mint oils (Murray, 1960a, 1960b). The action of the dominant gene apparently is upon a cyclic intermediate to convert it to a spearmint (2-oxygenated-p-menthane), while in the presence of the recessive only, the cyclic intermediate is converted to the peppermint type (3-oxygenated-p-menthane) (Reitsema, 1958a, 1958b). Except for the position of the oxygen a corresponding series of compounds exists in both the peppermint and spearmint lines. No authenticated instance of the coexistence of spearmint and peppermint oils in a single plant exists. In general the spearmint oils contain more unsaturated compounds and much more saturated alcohols while odd side reaction products such as found in some peppermint oils are lacking. A third group of species, the so-called "lemon mints," do not produce cyclic derivatives but rather acyclics such as citral and linalool. Reitsema has constructed a correlative biochemical-phylogenetic sequence in which the progression is toward increasingly more reduced compounds (Fig. 13-2).

Some very interesting work on higher terpenes of the Cucurbitaceae has been reported by Enslin and Rehm (1960). These substances, not fully characterized, appear to be related to the tetracyclic triterpenes. They are bitter tasting, have a purgative action, and are referred to as "cucurbitacins." So far, eleven different cucurbitacins are known, ten of which have been crystallized and an empirical formula assigned to them. All contain two or more

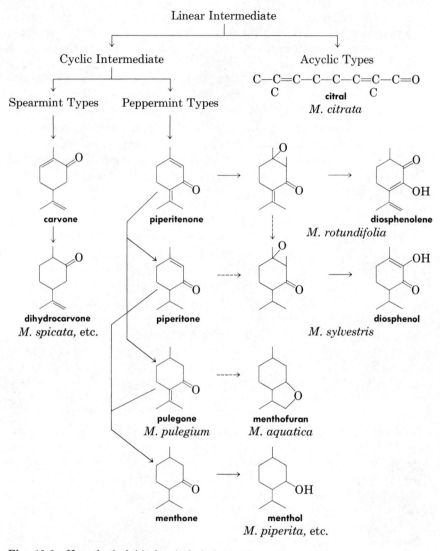

Fig. 13-2. Hypothetical biochemical-phylogenetic sequence of peppermint type oils (Reitsema in Jour. Amer. Pharm. Assoc., Sci. Ed. **47:** 268. 1958—by permission).

hydroxyl groups and several keto groups. They may be found as glycosides or aglycones in various parts of the plant, and many species contain an active glucosidase capable of hydrolysing the glycosides to aglycones. The glycosidase is apparently of somewhat low specificity since it is capable of hydrolysing steroidal saponins, the diterpene

β-D-glucoside, darutoside, and certain cardiac glycosides. Surprisingly, in one species, *Acanthosicyos horrida,* cucurbitacins occur as glycosides in the roots and as aglycones in the fruit. According to Meeuse (1954) most, if not all, genera producing the cucurbitacins are in the subfamily Cucurbitaceae (for example, *Momordica, Bryonia, Ecballium, Citrullus, Cucumis, Lagenaria, Cucurbita,* and *Sphaerosicyos*).

Two cucurbitacins, designated B and E, are thought to be the primary cucurbitacins, since other than cucurbitacin C these two are the only ones which sometimes occur alone in mature plants, and seedlings of all twenty-one species studied contained mainly B and/or E, even in species containing up to eight different cucurbitacins. The empirical formulas of B and E are given below:

$$\text{Cucurbitacin B} \quad C_{32}H_{48}O_8$$
$$\text{Cucurbitacin E} \quad C_{32}H_{44}O_8$$

Apparently the cucurbitacin content within a species may vary greatly since several genera (*Citrullus, Cucumis,* and *Lagenaria*) occur in bitter and non-bitter forms. In the case of *Cucurbita pepo* var. *ovifera* from one to eight different cucurbitacins may occur, though certain combinations are favored. Enslin and Rehm found that genetic, environmental, and developmental factors influence the cucurbitacin content.

The value of the cucurbitacin studies is further enhanced by

Table 13-1. Relative amounts of constituents in peppermint type oils[a] (Reitsema in Jour. Amer. Pharm. Assoc., Sci. Ed. **47:** 268. 1958—by permission).

	M. rotundi-folia	*M. sylvestris*	*M. pulegium*	*M. aquatica*	*M. piperita*	*M. arvensis* var. *piper-ascens*
Piperitenone	. .	*x*	. .	. .	1%	*x*
Piperitenone oxide	50%	*x*	. .	. .	. .	. .
Diosphenolene	*x*	x^b	. .	. .	. .	. .
Piperitone	x^b	. .	3%	x^b	1%	*x*
Piperitone Oxide	5%	45%	. .	. .	. .	. .
Diosphenol	x^b	3%	. .	. .	. .	. .
Pulegone	. .	. .	80%	x^b	2%	*x*
Menthofuran	. .	. .	. .	40%	2–15%	0%
Menthone	. .	. .	4%	x^b	25%	5%
Menthol	. .	. .	5%	. .	50%	80%

[a] Absence of quantitative data indicates lack of data rather than an implied absence of the compound in the oil.
[b] Identified by chromatography and ultraviolet absorption.
[x] Indicates presence without quantitative data.

investigations pertaining to enzymatic interconversion. In the fruit juice of *Lagenaria siceraria* an enzyme catalyzes efficiently the conversion of E to B while the reverse reaction occurs more slowly. The authors conclude that A is formed from B, and C from B. Enzymes occur which convert E to I, B to D, and C to F. All of these conversions involve loss of a two-carbon group. Surprisingly, the highest activity for this type of conversion is found in the fruit juice of a non-bitter Golden Hubbard squash. An alternate pathway to cucurbitacin D, from F, occurs apparently in leaves and fruits of *Cucumis angolensis*.

Emslin and Rehm summarize their evaluation of the taxonomic significance of the cucurbitacins in a brief paragraph, as follows:

> The main conclusion emerging from this study of the biogenetic interconversions is that there are only two primary bitter principles, which are chemically very labile, and easily transformed to other related substances by enzyme systems present both in bitter and non-bitter plants. It is therefore not surprising that a knowledge of the bitter principle composition of species appears to be of little value to the taxonomist.

The authors then go on to note distinctions between *Cucumis* and *Citrullus* as follows. All species of *Cucumus* investigated contained cucurbitacin B while *Citrullus* species contained only E in their seedling roots. In *Cucumis* the cucurbitacins occur mainly as aglycones while in *Citrullus* they occur as glycosides. Possibly the authors are unduly pessimistic regarding the systematic significance of these substances. Since they state that an effective paper chromatographic method is available for their study, it is likely that intensive studies of populations, particularly natural populations, would prove useful. It is not likely that cultivated varieties would offer as much promise, considering the lability of the group, as would wild species.

Another phytosystematic investigation of higher terpenes is that of Holloway (1958) who studied the diterpenes of the phyllocladene and podocarprene types. Among the former group several diterpenes, phyllocladene, rimuene, mirene, and kaurene are closely related and possibly isomers. The podocarprene group is chemically similar, and representatives of both types occur together in at least one genus, *Sciadopitys*. With the exception of *Sciadopitys* these diterpenes are confined to the tribes Araucarineae or Podocarpineae. Diterpenes of other types occur in other conifers, for example, in *Pinus*. Since, in older classifications the order Coniferales was divided into two families, the Pinaceae (including *Araucaria* and *Sciadopitys*) and the Taxaceae (including *Podocarpus*), Holloway considered that the distribution of the diterpenes was opposed to this older taxonomic disposition. *Sciadopitys*, by more recent treatments, is placed in the Taxaceae, but the genus may be somewhat closer to *Araucaria,* according to Holloway, if one uses certain criteria related to embryo development, gametophyte structure, and fertilization. He does not deny, however, the similarities between *Sciadopitys* and other genera in the Taxodineae, but he still considers it possible that the genus diverged from the main Araucarian stock at an early time. It would be interesting to know the total distribution of these diterpenes.

Holloway constructed a diagram to illustrate the relation of the occurrence of the phyllocladene and podocarprene diterpenes and conifer phylogeny (Fig. 13-3). All genera to the right of the Taxineae either have these diterpenes or are postulated to have them.

As noted in Chapter 14 the genus *Podocarpus* is biochemically distinctive in that its lignin contains some syringyl derivatives typically absent from the lignins of other conifers.

A small group of compounds of rather limited distribution on the basis of present knowledge, the tropolones, has been investigated particularly by Erdtman (1955a). Among vascular plants tropolones have been isolated only in the gymnosperms, in fact, only within the Cupressaceae. According to Erdtman (1955b), ". . . the idea that they

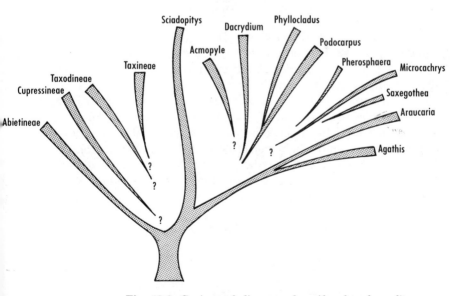

Fig. 13-3. Conjectural diagram of conifers based on diterpene content. All taxa to right of Taxineae postulated to produce diterpenes of phyllocladene or podocarprene (after Holloway, 1958).

constitute modified terpenes perhaps most probably such of carene type, seems inevitable." A naturally occurring tropolone, which may serve as an example, is nootkatin, found in the heartwood of *Chamaecyparis nootkatensis* and *Cupressus macrocarpa*.

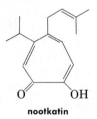

nootkatin

The tropolone nucleus itself is unusual, containing an unsaturated seven-membered ring:

tropolone

Certain tropolone derivatives (for example, puberulonic and stipitatic acids) have been described from the culture media of *Penicillium* species, but chemically they are quite distinct from tropolones of vascular plants.

The limited distribution of tropolone compounds plus the somewhat unusual seven-carbon tropolone nucleus itself combine to generate particular interest in the question of the biosynthesis of these compounds. Present knowledge of their synthesis is based principally upon the results of labeling experiments, utilizing C^{14}, followed by proposals for hypothetical mechanisms analogous to some which have been established for other substances of biological origin. Ferretti and Richards (1960), utilizing C^{14} labeled acetate, formate, and glucose, have concluded that carbons 3, 5, 8, and either 1 or 7 are derived from the two-carbon of acetate while carbons 2, 4, and 5 arise from the carboxyl of acetate.

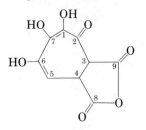

Either C-1 or C-7 may be derived from formate, and C-9 may be provided from a one-carbon pool representing carbon-1 of glucose, not however from sodium formate directly. Based on admittedly incomplete evidence, Ferretti and Richards speculated that head-to-tail condensation of three acetyl CoA units occurs followed by the acquisition of appropriate carbon side chains. These authors then postulate an oxidative ring enlargement of the six-membered ring to yield the tropolone. This work involved mold tropolones.

If this general scheme is correct, the metabolism of tropolones is related to that of benzenoid compounds rather than terpenoid, as suggested by Erdtman. It is possible that tropolone metabolism in gymnosperms bears no relationship at all to that of the mold species. There is no comparable information on the biosynthesis of the gymnosperm tropolones, but such would be of very great interest. Since there is hardly any doubt as to the independent origin of these pathways, a comparative study of biochemical routes and enzymology would be illuminating. This situation represents, theoretically at least, one suited to the study of questions of enzyme homology such as were mentioned in an earlier section.

If the mechanism for the formation of the basic tropolone nucleus is eventually established to be that proposed by Ferretti and Richards, and further, if it applies to the gymnosperm tropolones as well as to mold tropolones, then the critical step in tropolone synthesis, as it pertains to biochemical systematics, is the oxidative ring enlargement. The acetate condensation is one of major significance to a great majority of vascular plants, but this type of ring enlargement is quite rare.

The only family of higher plants known to produce tropolones, the family Cupressaceae, is represented by about fifteen genera and about 140 species. It is found throughout the world. Although relatively few species have been studied intensively, among those genera which are known to include some tropolone-containing species are *Juniperus, Chamaecyparis, Cupressus, Libocedrus, Thuja, Thujopsis,* and *Biota. Biota orientales,* which has been classified with *Thuja,* does not apparently produce tropolones. Individual species of *Thuja* contain different tropolones. Erdtman believes that the *Thuja, Thujopsis, Biota* group might be an excellent prospect for an intensive comparative biochemical study of tropolones, sesquiterpenes, and flavonoids.

The presence of tropolones in both *Chamaecyparis* and *Cupressus* is not surprising in view of the morphological similarity of the two genera. However, individual species vary in their tropolone and terpene constituents. On this basis Erdtman (1955b) states,

"Thus, obviously, the *Chamaecyparis-Cupressus* group, to the chemist appears to be less homogeneous than to the botanist."

In generally evaluating the significance of the tropolones Erdtman states, "Even at the risk of being criticized for wishful thinking, one finds it hard to avoid the belief that tropolones have some taxonomic significance." In another place he states, "The close botanical similarity between the tropolone and non-tropolone Cupressaceae leads to the suspicion that the particular chemical differences may indicate biosynthetic lability rather than botanical diversity."

Finally, Erdtman notes that, "It is possible to show chemical overlappings between almost all genera of the family Cupressaceae." He believes that this indicates that the family is an old one which has retained ancestral compounds of a "Cupressaceae type" while the individual genera and species have either lost or modified independently the pattern.

The systematic botanist may inquire, with some justification, how, in view of the preceding statements, the tropolones may make a contribution to the systematics of the Cupressaceae. It is true that the restriction of tropolones to the group is of systematic interest but not, however, illuminating with respect to the placement of the Cupressaceae. Below the family level, the tropolone content varies qualitatively within a genus and the general heartwood chemistry of *Chamaecyparis taiwanensis* and *C. obtusa,* two species which have been recorded as varieties, has been said to differ "completely" by Erdtman. Also, in genera which have tropolone-containing species, there are those which do not produce tropolones. It does not seem likely that even rigorous characterization of heartwood constituents has in this instance clarified significantly any of the relationships within the Cupressaceae. If botanical and chemical opinions are correct, and the Cupressaceae constitute an old group whose present-day genera are relicts, it is not surprising that a strictly comparative chemistry fails to solve any major phylogenetic problems of the group. The rare biflavonyls are found in Cupressaceae and may provide further taxonomic insight (Chapter 11).

Erdtman (1958) has presented a comprehensive treatment of the heartwood chemistry of the Cupressaceae, summarized in Table 13-2. Some suggestions by Erdtman, based on the data, are that *Tetraclinis* may be more closely related to the northern genera of the Cupressaceae (that is, *Heyderia*) than to the southern genera; that in the case of the two species of *Heyderia* it is tempting to separate them at the generic level. Erdtman states:

> The similarities between *Tetraclinis* and *Libocedrus decurrens* and between *Chamaecyparis nootkatinsis, Thuja, Biota* and *Libocedrus formosana,* the heterogeneity of *Chamaecyparis* and the great differ-

ences between the above *Libocedrus* species are examples where collaboration is essential. The chemist is sometimes led to feel that the calamitous phenomena of convergence may have misled the botanists.

Since Erdtman in the same article also calls attention to biochemical convergence, it is pertinent to inquire how one may determine which form of evidence reflects convergence in cases of apparently conflicting judgments. The botanist may justifiably expect the chemist to provide satisfactory proof that biochemical convergence is not providing him with spurious chemical indication of relationship.

Another group of substances some of which are terpenoid in character are the saponins. Some of the saponins are triterpenes while others are steroids. Although saponins have been known for many years there has been relatively little attention given to them in comparison with the commercially more important lower terpenes. However, in the last two decades there has been renewed interest in the steroidal saponins particularly with regard to sources which could supply substances utilizable in the synthesis of physiologically active steroids for medicinal use. A number of broad surveys have now been undertaken such as that of Ricardi *et al.* (1958) who examined 2,894 Chilean species for saponins. They found over 600 species to be saponin-producing.

Although there is now considerable knowledge of steroid metabolism in animals, there is apparently little known of plant steroidal biosynthesis. Interestingly, Heftmann *et al.* (1961) in a study of the biosynthesis of the steroidal sapogenin, diosgenin, of *Dioscorea,* found that mevalonic acid, a very efficient precursor of animal sterols, failed to become incorporated into diosgenin. It appeared that mevalonic acid was metabolized, however, and the full significance of these results is still unclear (see footnote, p. 232 of this chapter).

A number of surveys of steroidal saponins have been conducted (Marker *et al.,* 1943; Marker *et al.,* 1947; Anzaldo *et al.,* 1956, 1957). Marker and his coworkers conducted an extensive survey of over 400 Mexican and United States species and discovered a series of apparently related sapogenins of a type such as hecogenin illustrated below:

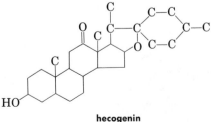

hecogenin

Table 13-2. Heartwood constituents of Cupressaceae (Erdtman, 1958 in *Biochemistry of Wood,* Pergamon Press, Inc.—with permission).

Genera and Species (Number refers to species in genus; S = Southern Hemisphere, N = Northern Hemisphere)	p-Cresol	Chamenol	Carvacrol	Carvacrol methyl ether	Hydrothymokinon	Hydroxythymoquinone monomethyl ethers	Libocedrol	Thymoquinone	Hydroxythymoquinones	Citronellic acid	Dehydrogeranic acid	Thujic acid	Shonanic acid	Chamic acid	Chaminic acid	α-Thujaplicin	β-Thujaplicin	γ-Thujaplicin	Hydroxy-β-thujaplicin
Callitris (20, S)																			
calcarata										+									
glauca										+	+								
intratropica										+									
morrisonii																			
preissii																			
propinqua																			
roei																			
rhomboidalis																			
verrucosa																			
macleayana										+									
Neocallitropsis (1, S)																			
araucarioides											+								
Widdringtonia (5, S)																			
cupressoides																			
dracomontana																			
juniperoides																			
schwarzii																			
whytei																			
Tetraclinis (1, N)																			
articulata		+			+	+		+									+		
Cupressus (15, N)																			
bakeri		+																	
macnabiana		+															+		
macrocarpa		+	+													+	+	−	
sempervirens		+	+														+		
torulosa		+														+	+		+
Chamaecyparis (7, N)																			
formosensis																−	−	−	−
lawsoniana																−	−	−	−
obtusa																−	−	−	−
nootkatensis		+	+											+	+				

250

				C15 Hydrocarbons						C15 Alcohols						C15 Acids			C20 Compounds					Flavonoids		Lignans
ρ-Dolabrin	Nootkatin	(+)-Myrtenol	(+)-Dihydromyrtenol	Cadinenes	Eudesmenes	"Cedrene"	Thujopsene	Cuparene	Nootkatene	Cadinols	Eudesmols	Cedrol	Widdrol	Guaiol	Occidentalol	Widdric acid	Cuparenic acid	Hinokiic acid	Hinokiol	Hinokion	Ferruginol	Sugiol	Manool	Aromadendrin	Taxifolin	Hinokinin
														+												
														+												
														+												
														+												
														+												
														+												
											+															
														+												
														+												
														+												
				+						+	+															
											+															
							+	+			+	+	+			+		+								
							+	+			+	+	+			+	+	+								
							+	+			+	+	+			+	+	+								
							+	+			+		+			+	+	+								
								+											+	+						
+																										
+																										
+																										
+								+					+									+				
+																						+				
−		+	+																							
−												+														
−									+										+	+	+					+
+																										

Table 13-2. (*Continued*)

Genera and Species	Various Constituents																		
(Number refers to species in genus; S = Southern Hemisphere, N = Northern Hemisphere)	p-Cresol	Chamenol	Carvacrol	Carvacrol methyl ether	Hydrothymokinon	Hydroxythymoquinone monomethyl ethers	Libocedrol	Thymoquinone	Hydroxythymoquinones	Citronellic acid	Dehydrogeranic acid	Thujic acid	Shonanic acid	Chamic acid	Chaminic acid	α-Thujaplicin	β-Thujaplicin	γ-Thujaplicin	Hydroxy-β-thujaplicin
Chamaecyparis (7, N) (*Continued*)																			
pisifera																			
taiwanensis	+	+	+							+						+	+		+
thyoides				+										+			+	+	
Juniperus (60, N)																			
communis			+																
oxycedrus																			
chinensis			+		+				++							+	+		
excelsa																			
mexicana																			
occidentalis																−	−	−	−
procera			+																
virginiana																−	−	−	−
Thuja (5, N)																			
occidentalis													+			+	+		
plicata													+			+	+	+	+
standishii																	+		
Thujopsis (1, N)																			
dolabrata			+							+						+	+		
Biota (1, N)																			
orientalis													+			+	+	+	
Fokienna (1, N)																			
hodginsii																			
Pilgerodendron (1, S)																			
uviferum																			
Calocedrus (3, N)																			
decurrens				+	+	+	+	+	+							+	+		
formosana												+	+	?	+				
Austrocedrus (1, S)																			
chilensis			+	−										?	+				

Table 13-2. (*Continued*)

				C$_{15}$ Hydrocarbons						C$_{15}$ Alcohols						C$_{15}$ Acids			C$_{20}$ Compounds					Flavonoids		Lignans
β-Dolabrin	Nootkatin	(+)-Myrtenol	(+)-Dihydromyrtenol	Cadinenes	Eudesmenes	"Cedrene"	Thujopsene	Cuparene	Nootkatene	Cadinols	Eudesmols	Cedrol	Widdrol	Guaiol	Occidentalol	Widdric acid	Cuparenic acid	Hinokiic acid	Hinokiol	Hinokion	Ferruginol	Sugiol	Manool	Aromadendrin	Taxifolin	Hinokinin
			+							+								+								
							+	+				+	+			+	+	+								
+		+		+	+	+						+	+								+	+				
+							+	+				+	+			+					+?					
						+						+														
−	−											+														
						+						+														
−	−				+	+						+														
+?											+					+										
+							+																			
							+	+						+										+	+	
										+																
		+								+																
																									+?	+

These sapogenins were encountered among numerous species of *Yucca* and *Agave* as well as other genera of the families Liliaceae (*sensu lato*), and Dioscoreaceae. Although it is not entirely clear from the text whether all species of the related family, Amaryllidaceae, were negative, a number of species of this family were examined, and the impression gained is that they were negative. Plants which tested negatively were not listed in these references, unfortunately. It was believed at the time the Marker *et al.* paper appeared that outside of monocots very few plants produced steroidal sapogenins, but more recently reports of their wider distribution, among dicot families, have occurred (Altman, 1954; Anzaldo *et al.*, 1956, 1957; Wall *et al.*, 1957). No major effort has apparently been made to evaluate the general systematic significance of the steroidal sapogenins.

Saponins of the triterpene type have been neglected more than the steroidal saponins. Simes *et al.* (1959) have recently surveyed the flowering plants of eastern Australia for saponins and found them to be widely distributed among numerous families. A few families were singled out as being especially rich in saponin-containing species, but the group does not represent a "natural" one, and its taxonomic value at this stage is probably minor.

Fontan-Candela (1957) has made a comprehensive survey of the botanical distribution of saponins, including the steroid and triterpene types. He notes that saponins in general are found throughout the plant kingdom, while the steroid types are restricted, so far as is known, to angiosperms. Although Fontan-Candela does discuss briefly phylogenetic considerations it is quickly apparent that the wide distribution of saponins among angiosperms prohibits any but the broadest generalizations concerning their systematic value. This is particularly true if one is considering only the presence or absence of saponins. Since many of the surveys do not include characterization of the specific saponins present in a species, this group of compounds suffers from a limitation similar to that of the cyanogenetic glycosides, previously discussed (Chapter 10).

One exception to the general neglect of triterpene saponins is the excellent work of Djerassi (1957) on the triterpenes of Cactaceae. Djerassi and coworkers investigated forty species representing twelve genera of the giant cacti of the Tribe Cereeae and described a number of new triterpenes. Table 13-3 summarizes the triterpene content of the species investigated. From the systematic viewpoint, it is noteworthy that alkaloids are absent or present in only minute quantity in those cacti which contain the triterpenes, while *Lophocereus*, with the highest alkaloid content, lacks triterpenes. Certain species of

Table 13-3. Triterpene composition of some giant cacti (Djerassi, 1957).

Genus	Species	Triterpene
Cereus	*jamacaru*	(β-sitosterol)
Cephalocereus	*senilis*	traces (unidentified)
Espostoa	*lanata*	none
Escontria	*chiotilla*	longispinogenin, maniladiol
Pachycereus	*marginatus*	none (see Ref. 5 for alkaloids)
	chrysomallus	traces (unidentified)
Lemaireocereus	*hollianus*	none
	hystrix	oleanolic acid, erythrodiol, betulinic acid, longispinogenin, "hystrix lactone"
	griseus	oleanolic acid, erythrodiol, longispinogenin, "hystrix lactone," betulin
	pruinosus	oleanolic acid
	longispinus	oleanolic acid, erythrodiol, longispinogenin
	chichipe	oleanolic acid, chichipegenin, longispinogenin
	aragonii	mixture of amyrins (?)
	stellatus	oleanolic acid, betulinic acid, stellatogenin, thurberogenin, oxyallobetulin
	treleasei	oleanolic acid, stellatogenin, treleasegenic acid, thurberogenin
	deficiens	traces (unidentified)
	weberi	none
	queretaroensis	oleanolic acid, queretaroic acid
	montanus	oleanolic acid, queretaroic acid (β-sitosterol)
	thurberi	oleanolic acid, thurberogenin
	laetus	none
	humilis	traces (unidentified)
	dumortieri	dumortierigenin
	beneckei	oleanolic acid, quertetaroic acid
	quevedonis	oleanolic acid, betulinic acid, longispinogenin
Machaerocereus	*gummosus*	gummosogenin, machaeric acid, machaerinic acid
	eruca	betulinic acid, stellatogenin
Nyctocereus	*guatemalensis*	none

Table 13-3. (*Continued*)

Genus	Species	Triterpene
Trichocereus	*chiloensis*	(β-sitosterol)
	cuzcoensis	(β-sitosterol)
	peruvianus	traces ("hystrix lactone"?)
Lophocereus	*schottii*	lupeol, (lophenol)
	australis	(lophenol)
	gatesii	(lophenol)
Myrtillocactus	*geometrizans*	cochalic acid, chichipegenin, myrtillogenic acid, longispinogenin
	cochal	cochalic acid, chichipegenin, myrtillogenic acid, longispinogenin
	schenckii	oleanolic acid, stellatogenin
	eichlamii	oleanolic acid, cochalic acid, chichipegenin, myrtillogenic acid, longispinogenin, maniladiol, (β-sitosterol)
	grandiareolatus	oleanolic acid, chichipegenin
Neoraimondia	*macrostibas*	none

Lemaireocereus (*L. hollianus, L. laetus,* and *L. aragonii*) lack triterpenes, and two of these, *laetus* and *aragonii,* reputedly are doubtfully included within the genus on botanical grounds.

In the genus *Myrtillocactus* the chief triterpene is chichipegenin (in every species except *M. schenckii*). Conversely, chichipegenin occurs elsewhere only in *Lemaireocereus chichipe*. Djerassi (1957) suggests that the two species may possibly have their generic assignments interchanged. While it is evident that the cactus triterpenes have provided very little insight into cactus phylogeny at the present time, the occurrence of a wide assortment of complex and somewhat characteristic components within the family suggests that an intensive chemosystematic study would be rewarding.

Another class of sapogenins or steroid glycosides (including the so-called "cardiac poisons") has been found to be of unusual systematic interest and will be discussed in some detail. The characteristic structure of these compounds may be represented by the cardinolid structure which follows:

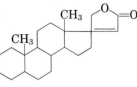

cardenolid

Some other compounds in this class are digitoxigenin, uzari-
genin, xysmalogenin, canarygenin, adynerigenin, and their glycosides.
Korte and Korte (1955b) have studied the distribution of these compounds, certain related alkaloids, and lower terpenes in the order
Contortae with some exceedingly interesting results. Within the order
the family Gentianaceae is consistent in having the terpene, gentiopikrin, present in all forms examined.

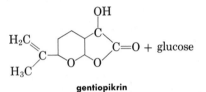

gentiopikrin

The family Menyanthaceae (sometimes classified as a sub-
family of the Gentianaceae) are separated from the Gentianaceae by
the presence of the bitter principle loganin (= meliatin) in the former
and the absence of gentiopicrin in those members of the Menyanthaceae examined.

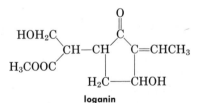

loganin

Both families include some species which produce the
alkaloid, gentianin [note that Karrer (1958) lists gentianin both as an
anthocyanin and as a xanthone, neither compound containing nitro-
gen] the structure of which is given below:

Since the Menyanthaceae share a characteristic component
of the Loganiaceae, namely, loganin, it may be deduced from these

criteria alone that they are as close to the Loganiaceae as they are to the Gentianaceae. Though the chemical correlations are interesting, they do not provide sufficient evidence to adduce family relationships.

In the family Asclepiadaceae there occur a number of glycosides, often described as "bitter principles." Korte and Korte (1955a) compared the properties of several of these substances and found that, apparently a number of substances described independently and given different names were identical to one or the other of two compounds of widespread occurrence in one of the two sub-families (Cynanchoideae). The two compounds are kondurangin, a glycoside-yielding glucose, thevatose, and cymarose, and vincetoxin, a glycoside-yielding glucose, thevatose, cymarose, and diginose. The structures of the two aglycones have not yet been fully established. These sugar combinations were otherwise known only from the cardiac poisons, and therefore these bitter principles, though not yet characterized, appear to be closely related to the cardiac poisons. As a result of the elimination of some of the chemical synonymy, a quite interesting pattern of distribution of the compounds is exposed. For example, all members of the sub-family Cynanchoideae examined contained either vincetoxin or kondurangin. The sub-family Periplocoideae do not contain either of the previously described bitter principles but rather a heart poison known as cardenolidglycoside (cardenolid, p. 257). The only genera in the Cynanchoideae to contain cardinolidglycoside are *Xysmalobium, Gomphocarpus,* and *Calotropis,* and they show no evidence of being misplaced in the sub-family. The two sub-families are well marked and are without obvious transitional forms; the Cynanchoideae occur in both hemispheres while the Periplocoideae are absent from North and South America. It is noteworthy that the related family Apocynaceae typically produces cardenolidglycoside. Korte and Korte concluded that the Apocynaceae gave rise to the Asclepiadaceae[3] and within the latter family the Periplocoideae are the most primitive sub-family. In this latter case, the morphological and biochemical transition has not been strictly parallel so that certain genera of the Cynanchoideae retain the synthesis of cardenolidglycoside. Korte and Korte conclude that the glycosides, vincetoxin and kondulangin, are truly "characteristic constituents" of the sub-family Cynanchoideae, and their conclusion seems to be well substantiated by the evidence at hand.

The family Apocynaceae has been studied in considerable de-

[3] In another paper this statement is reversed; "Die Apocynaceae, die sich wahrscheinlich phylogenetisch von den Asclepiadaceae herleiten lassen, . . ." It is not possible to determine whether this was an unintentional reversal or not since there was no further comment in the body of the text.

tail (Korte, 1955b). A comprehensive treatment of the results is presented in Table 13.4. This family is characterized by the presence of cardenolidglycosides, alkaloids, and neutral bitter principles.

The sub-family Plumieroideae is separated into several sub-tribes which, in addition to their morphological characters, may be distinguished on the basis of their chemistry. For example, *Plumiera* is characterized by the bitter principle, plumierid; *Holarrhena* through steroidal alkaloids such as conessin; and other genera through particular alkaloids. In the sub-tribe Tabernaemontaninae the alkaloid tabernimontanin is always present, but cardenolidglycosides are absent. In the second sub-family, Echitoideae, cardenolidglycosides are common, but only the sub-tribe Parsoniae produces steroid alkaloids such as conessin, and this sub-tribe appears to be, in its chemistry, more closely related to the sub-tribe Alstoniinae of the Arduineae. Conversely, the sub-tribe Melodininae appears to be related to the tribe Echitideae since the former is the only one of its sub-family producing cardenolidglycosides.

An interesting situation is presented by the family Oleaceae, included in the order Contortae by Engler and Diels (though distinguished as a separate sub-order, Oleineae). Wettstein excluded the Oleaceae from the Contortae and derived them from the order Tubiflorae. Hutchinson included the family in the order Loganiales while Hallier derived the Oleaceae from the Scrophulariaceae and the Contortae from the Linaceae. It is obvious that these proposals incorporated widely divergent views on the position of the Oleaceae on the basis of morphological data.

Korte (1954) found that the Oleaceae differed greatly, in their chemistry, from other families of the Contortae. The Oleaceae, which are usually not bitter, contain no alkaloids but rather contain the characteristic phenolics fraxin and syringin, entirely different types of substances. The other members of the Contortae do not produce fraxin or syringin and instead are prolific in the formation of bitter principles, cardiac poisons, and alkaloids. According to Korte:

> From the standpoint of their bitter substances and in agreement with the system of Wettstein the order Contortae now without doubt is subdivided into the following families: Gentianaceae, Menyanthaceae, Loganiaceae, Apocynaceae and Asclepiadaceae.

Recently, work on certain sesquiterpenes of the Compositae by Herz and coworkers has disclosed a number of taxonomically interesting correlations, and an intensive study of these compounds may provide new insights into the relationships among certain tribes of this family.

Table 13-4. Chemical constituents of the Apocynaceae as related to the systematic treatment of the family. (Korte and Korte.)

Plant		Content	
I. Sub-family: *Plumieroideae*			
Tribe	Arduinea		
Sub-tribe	Melodininae		
Genus	Acokanthera	Abyssinin = amorphes Ouabain = Carissin Acofriosid Acolongiflorosid Acovenosid A und C Ouabain = Strophantin Venenatin	Cardenolidglycoside
	Carissa	Carissin Carisson Odorosid	
Tribe	Landolphiinae		
Genus	Hancornia	Thevetin	
Tribe	Pleiocarpae	unknown	
Tribe	Plumiereae		
Sub-tribe	Alstoniinae		Bitter principles
Genus	Alstonia Plumiera	Plumierid = Agoniadin	
	Gonioma	Kamassin	Steroid alkaloids
	Holarrhena	Conamin Conessidin Conessimin Conessin Conimin Conkurchin Conkurchinin Holarrhenin Holarrhessimin Holarrhimin Holarrhin Isoconessin Kurchin	
	Alstonia	Alstonamin Alstonidin Alstonin Ditamin Echitamin Echitamidin Echitenin Lacton C und S Macralstonidin Macralstonin	Alkaloid

260

Table 13-4. (*Continued*)

Plant		Content	
	Aspidosperma	Villalstonin Aspidosamin Aspidospermatin Aspidospermicin Aspidospermin Hasslerin Hypoquebrachin Paytamin Paytin Quebrachin (= Yohimbin?)	Alkaloid
	Haplophytum	Cimicidin Haplophytin	
	Lochnera	δ-Yohimbin Pubescin	
	Vinca	Reserpin Vincarosin Vincassin Vinin	
Sub-tribe	Tabernae- montaninae		
Genus	Tabernanthe	Ibogain Tabernaemontanin	
	Geissospermum	Geissospermin Pereirin Vellosin	
	Tabernae- montana	Coronarin	
		Tabernaemontanin	Alkaloid
Sub-tribe	Rauwolfinae		
Genus	Vallesia	Aspidospermin	
	Alyxia = Gynopogon	Ajmalicin	
	Rauwolfia	Ajmalin = Rauwolfin Ajmalinin = Alkaloid C Alstonin Chalchupin A und B Isorauhimbin Raumitorin Raupin Rauwolfinin	
Genus	Rauwolfia	Rauwolscin Reserpin Sarpagin Semperflorin Seredin Serpentin Serpentinin β-Yohimbin	Alkaloid

Table 13-4. (*Continued*)

I. Sub-family: *Plumieroideae* (*Continued*)

	Plant	Content	
Sub-tribe	Cerberinae	Alkaloide	Alkaloid
Genus	Ochrosia	Alkaloide	
	Pseudochrosia	Alkaloid	
	Kopsia	Kopsin	
	Tanghinia	Acetylneriifolin = Cerberin = Veneniferin	Cardenolidglycoside
		Desacetyltanghinin	
	Cerbera	Tanghiferin	
		Tanghinin	
	Thevetia	Tanghinosid	
		Cerberin	
		= Acetylneriifolin	
		Acetylthevetin	
		Thevetin	

II. Sub-family: *Echitoideae*

	Plant	Content	
Tribe	Echitideae		
Genus	Adenium	Abobiosid	Cardenolidglycoside
		Digitalum verum	
		Honghelin	
		Honghelosid A, C, G	
		= Somalin	
		Odorosid B	
	Urechitis	Urechitin	
		Urechitonin	
		Urechitoxin	
	Apocynum	Androsin	
		Cymarin	
	Nerium	Adynerin	
		Desacetyloleandrin	
		Digitalum verum	
		Neriantin	
		Odoroside	
		Oleandrin (= Folinerin)	
		Strophanthin-K	
	Strophantus	Ambosid	Cardenolidglycoside
		Ambostrosid	
		16-Anhydrostrospesid	
		Boistrosid	
		Caudosid	
		Christyosid	
		Courmontoside	
		Cymarin	
		Cymarol	

Table 13-4. (*Continued*)

Plant		Content	
		Digitalum verum Divaricosid Emicymarin Gracilosid Honghelin Honghelosid A, C, G Inertosid Intermediosid Leptosid Millosid Musarosid Ouabain = Acokantherin = Strophantin-G Panstrosid Pauliosid Periplocymarin Pseudostrophantin Quilenglosid Sarmentocymarin Sarmentosid A und B Sarnovid Strobosid Strophantin-K Strospesid	Cardenolidglycoside
Tribe Genus	Parsonsiae Wrightia	Conessin	Steroid alkaloid
	Parsonsia Malouetia Forsteria	Guachamacin = Curarin Forsteronin	

According to Karrer (1958) five basic types of sesquiterpenes are known to occur:

1. **bisabolen type**   2. **cadinen type**   3. **eudesmol type**

263

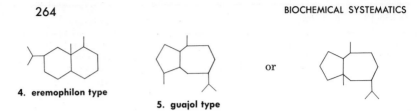

4. eremophilon type

5. guajol type

or

Sesquiterpene derivatives of type five are present in the genus *Helenium* wherein they are recognized by a bitterish taste. These compounds occur as lactones such as helenalin, or the more complex tenulin:

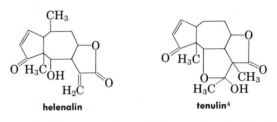

helenalin   tenulin[4]

Herz and his coworkers (Herz *et al.*, 1960; Herz and Högenaur, 1962) have been investigating certain *Helenium* species along with species of several related genera. Sesquiterpene lactones of the helenalin type occur in all three sections of *Helenium* (Table 13-5) as well as a number of other genera. Helenalin is found in *Actinospermum* also, and though helenalin itself has not been found in *Balduina,* a related substance, balduilin, is present in this genus. The close morphological similarity between *Actinospermum* and *Balduina* indicates that the presence of these similar sesquiterpenes is not coincidental. *Helenium* is placed in the tribe Helenieae while *Actinospermum* and *Balduina* are both placed in the tribe Heliantheae mainly on the basis of technical features of the capitulum. However, Rock (1957) has independently suggested (on morphological grounds) that the three genera are closely related, an interpretation which is supported by this sesquiterpene chemistry. However, sesquiterpenes also occur in a number of other genera of the family Compositae, including *Artemisia, Inula, Iva, Ambrosia, Parthenium,* and *Balsamorhiza. Artemisia* belongs to the tribe Anthemideae and *Inula* to the tribe Inuleae, while the last four genera are placed in the tribe Heliantheae. Before discussing the characteristic sesquiterpenes of the various tribes it is pertinent to note that a number of lower terpenes are found in the tribe Anthemideae, especially in *Artemisia* species: 1,8-cineole (*Artemisia*); 1-camphor (*Artemisia, Achillea*); fenchol (*Artemisia*); and thujon (*Tanacetum*) (Karrer, 1958).

[4] The structure of tenulin is modified to conform more closely to inferences derived from the revised formula of isotenulin, helenalin, and balduilin (Herz *et al.,* 1961).

Table 13-5. Distribution of sesquiterpene lactones according to sections of the genus *Helenium* and related genera.

Tribe Helenieae (As Classically Constituted)

Helenium

Sect. Helenium (One species examined)	Sect. Tetrodus (Seven species examined)
helenalin	helenalin
Sect. Leptopoda (Four species examined)	mexicanin
brevilin	tenulin
flexuosin	
helenalin	
pinnatifidin	

Tribe Heliantheae (As Classically Constituted)

Actinospermum	*Balduina*
helenalin	balduilin

Two types of lactones derived from sesquiterpenes are to be found among *Artemisia* species. Neither type is identical with the sesquiterpene lactones of *Helenium,* but both types are closely related on structural grounds. The helenalin type (I) is illustrated again for purposes of comparison with arborescin (II) and α-santonin (III).

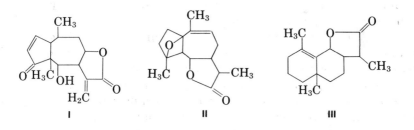

Both helenalin (I) and arborescin (II) are sesquiterpenes of the guajol type. They differ in their mode of lactone formation. To the writer's knowledge Type I is not found in Anthemideae. However, both II and III are found in the Anthemideae (in *Artemisia* species) but not the Helenieae (although tenulin may be interpreted as a lactone of type I to which a two-carbon unit adds to form an acetal). Three eudesmol type sesquiterpene lactones related to α-santonin (alantolactone, isoalanto-lactone, and dihydroisoalantolactone) occur in *Inula helenium.* Eudesmol, a non-lactone, is obtained from *Balsamorhiza,* and ivalin, a lactone of the eudesmol type, is found in *Iva.*

A non-lactone sesquiterpene of the guajol type, partheniol, is found in *Parthenium argentatum.*

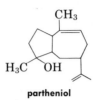

parthenioI

The presence of two similar sesquiterpenes, parthenin and ambrosin in the genera *Parthenium* and *Ambrosia,* the latter substance actually occurring in both genera, is suggestive of a relationship between the two genera not readily apparent by their taxonomic disposition (that is, they are often treated as belonging to different tribes or sub-tribes). The suggested relationship is further strengthened by the discovery of a third substance, coronopilin (1,2-dihydroparthenin) in both genera (Herz and Högenaur, 1961).

Although the eudesmol and guajol types of sesquiterpenes may not appear to be closely similar, the principal difference between the two lies in the type of cross linkage present. In the eudesmol type a C—C linkage yields a pair of six-membered rings; in the guajol type a C—C linkage yields a seven-membered and five-membered pair. This minor difference between the two types of sesquiterpenes may indicate close biosynthetic similarity. Therefore, it is not surprising to find these compounds restricted to a few rather closely related genera or even together in a single genus.

The methyl substitution at position 5 in helenalin and other guajol derivatives is considered by Herz to represent a shift from position 4 of a substance such as partheniol, illustrated above.

It is important to know whether the eudesmol or the guajol type is more primitive, but evidence is insufficient at this time to allow even useful speculation. It seems that the Anthemideae are much more versatile in terpene and sesquiterpene synthesis than other tribes of the family Compositae noted.

At least 75 different sesquiterpenes are reported from a number of different families, including those of the gymnosperms, dicots, and monocots (Karrer, 1958). However, within any closely circumscribed, natural biological group, the sesquiterpenes present fall similarly into more or less natural chemical sub-types. Thus, only the eudesmol and guajol groups of sesquiterpenes are encountered among the plant genera discussed in this section. Sesquiterpenes of the bisabolen type, which may be considered more simple in chemical terms, correspondingly have a broader and more complex distribution, not necessarily indicative of phylogenetic relationship.

The tribe Helenieae, on morphological grounds (Chapter 3) appears to be artificially circumscribed, and it should prove interesting to extend comparative biochemical studies of the sesquiterpenes to other groups of this tribe, particularly to those which are believed to have their relationship with other elements of the Compositae[5] (for example, a comparison of *Sartwellia,* currently placed in the Helenieae, with *Haplöesthes* of the Senecionieae, and so on, Turner and Johnston, 1961).

[5] Chemists may not fully understand the taxonomist's hesitancy in making such redispositions from the provocative chemical data at hand. However, evidence bearing on phylogeny is often apparently conflicting, usually circumstantial, rarely unequivocal, and basic conservatism is required. Yet taxonomic and chemical correlations reflected in the sesquiterpenes of the Compositae may eventually be utilized to decide between two conflicting points of view even when the chemical data support the more radical departure from the existing treatment of the group.

14

MISCELLANEOUS COMPOUNDS

In the 1930's and early 1940's, a series of papers by McNair appeared on the subject of biochemical systematics, for example, *Angiosperm Phylogeny on a Chemical Basis* (1932; 1934; 1935a; 1935b; 1941a; 1941b; 1943; 1945). The nature of the response to McNair's papers at the time they were published is not known, but his work has been referred to frequently by later investigators. However, some reviewers have been rather critical (for example, Turrill, 1942; Weevers, 1943).

McNair's work represented essentially a compilation of certain existing chemical data and the derivation of taxonomic generalizations therefrom. His principal thesis, that more advanced families presumably form more complex chemical substances, was valid within limits. However, he assumed the rather tenuous position that a higher molecular weight indicated a more complex substance. This idea has been attacked by Gibbs (1958) particularly with respect to the alkaloids, which may be in some cases low order polymers (for example, bisbenzylisoquinolines).

Specifically, McNair (1934) attempted to correlate the serial numbers of families of the Engler and Prantl system with the molecular weights of their alkaloids, specific gravity of their essential oils, and degree of unsaturation of their fats to support his thesis that more advanced families produce more complex substances. Despite relatively meager data, only slight positive correlation, a tenuous basic assumption with respect to what constitutes true chemical complexity, and a circular argument to begin with, he nevertheless later concluded (1935), on the basis of these criteria that:

(1) Herbs evolved from trees.
(2) Monocots are more primitive than dicots.
(3) The woody Magnoliaceae gave rise to the herbaceous Ranunculaceae.
(4) Polypetaly is more primitive than gamopetaly.
(5) Many carpels preceded few carpels.
(6) Apocarpy preceded syncarpy.
(7) Some aspects of the Bessey system are superior to the Engler and Prantl system, and some are not.

Although a number of the points listed above may actually be correct, the new evidence brought to bear on the questions by McNair will, in the final analysis, be judged as of the most trivial sort—if indeed it has any relevance whatsoever. It is possible that this rather uncritical application of biochemical information had an adverse effect upon the field, despite McNair's zealous interest in its development. Some thoughtful systematists may have concluded from these contributions that biochemistry had little to offer.

More recently, Gibbs (1945, 1954, 1958) has been particularly associated with efforts to enhance the general appreciation of biochemical systematics, along with Hegnauer, whose work has previously been discussed in other sections. Gibbs has not exaggerated the importance of the biochemical approach but rather has discussed this approach as only one of several to questions of phylogenetic relationships. In his own investigations, Gibbs has limited himself to a few relatively simple chemical characters, and it appears that in some cases these are not among the most fruitful. Some characters he has used are the presence of catechol tannins, presence of cyanogenetic substances, and the presence of raphides (a special form of calcium oxalate crystal). Catechol tannins represent a rather ill-defined group of phenolic substances, including probably the leucoanthocyanins; the mere presence or absence of this class of compounds is of dubious systematic value. Cyanogenetic substances, as noted elsewhere, have practically the same limitations. As the cyanogenetic compounds have already been discussed, there is no need to add anything further beyond the observation that it is most important to know what subclass of cyanogen is involved; Gibbs' tests for these compounds do not provide this information.

Since raphides have not been discussed elsewhere, some consideration of Gibbs' application of this criterion is appropriate here. Raphides are but one of many forms of crystals of calcium oxalate. They are recognized as bundles of acicular crystals, sometimes occurring in special mucilage-containing cells. Of raphides, Gibbs says that they represent "one of the few directly visible chemicals." However, the significance of raphides lies not merely in the fact that they are calcium oxalate (200 or more families of flowering plants and even algae, fungi, and mosses produce some form of calcium oxalate crystals) but rather that a physiological state exists in the cells leading to the deposition of calcium oxalate in the characteristic form of raphides. This latter point has been emphasized by Pobeguin (1943) in his general review of the occurrence of calcium oxalate crystals among angiosperms.

Gibbs (1958) has applied evidence from raphide distribution to the question of whether the phylogenetic position of the order Parietales (of Engler and Prantl) is closer to Laurales or to Magnoliales, the latter group being favored by Hutchinson. Gibbs notes first that several families of the Parietales have raphides: Dilleniaceae, Actinidiaceae, Marcgraviaceae, and Theaceae (all of the sub-order Theineae).[1] Members of the Ranales or Magnoliales (of Hutchinson) do not have raphides, but several families of the Laurales are said to have raphides, for example, Myristicaceae, Hernandiaceae, Gomortegaceae, Lauraceae, and Monimiaceae. Gibbs has raised the question as to whether the Dilleniaceae came from the Laurales.

Despite the importance attributed by Gibbs to criteria such as the presence of catechol tannins, cyanide, and raphides, it is the opinion of the writers that such biochemical characters are of limited value unless more specifically defined chemically. Recently, Shaw and Gibbs (1961) described the Hamamelidaceae as follows: (1) + HCl

---

[1] Raphides are uncommon in the Theaceae, occurring only in the genera *Tetramerista* and *Pelliciera*, which have been placed at times in the Marcgraviaceae, and the genus *Trematanthera* which has been placed in the Actinidiaceae (Gibbs, 1958).

methanol test, (2) + for leucanthocyanins, (3) red reaction to "syringin" test, (4) magenta with Ehrlich's reagent, (5) negative for cyanide, (6) negative to "juglone" test, (7) lacking raphides, (8) lacking glucitol and sedoheptulose, and (9) oxalis reaction + for cigarette and hot water test. Subsequently, it was stated that, "On the basis of results of these tests, one may propose an Order Hamamelidales, including the Hamamelidaceae, Platanaceae, Myrothamnaceae, and perhaps the Cunoniaceae." It is not likely that proposals for taxonomic realignment at this level based on such limited biochemical data will gather much support for biochemical systematics either from the biochemist or the classical taxonomist.

Carotenoids: In the preceding chapters certain families of compounds have been selected for special consideration, principally on the basis of their acknowledged or potential contribution to biochemical systematics. The decision to devote an entire chapter to a certain class of substances was often wholly arbitrary, though in part supported by the fact that the group of compounds concerned was prominent in the literature. The exclusion of some types of compounds was likewise arbitrary. The carotenoid pigments were not included in a separate chapter primarily because relatively little attention has been devoted to a study of their systematic distribution. Although certain carotenoids are of very wide distribution, there are nevertheless many types which are of restricted distribution, hence presumably of systematic value. Since all or almost all plants produce carotenoids, a mere presence or absence notation is meaningless. Yet, there are no simple techniques for the further characterization or separation of mixtures of carotenoids such as exist for flavonoids or even for alkaloids. Goodwin (1955a) noted that the qualitative distribution of carotenoids is rather similar among different species of angiosperms. However, xanthophylls are more complex and are of potentially greater systematic value; for example, rhodoxanthin is found in leaves only in gymnosperms. It also occurs rarely in some angiosperm fruits. Goodwin listed twenty-nine anthoxanthin pigments as occurring in higher plants, and undoubtedly a number of others remain to be described.

Goodwin (1955b) characterized completely the polyenes of twenty-three species representing eight families and concluded that the distribution of polyenes appeared to be of no obvious taxonomic significance. He stated, "The situation is so complex that many more surveys of the present type will be necessary to reveal possible taxonomic correlation."

Among bacteria and algae, in contrast to higher plants, pigments have often been used to support certain phyletic arrangements, and recognition of algal divisions in particular is based upon their chlorophyll, phycobilin, and carotenoid pigment types plus morphological criteria. As more information has become available concerning the pigments of the so-called "lower plants," the situation has become increasingly complex. The concept of characteristic pigments for particular major taxonomic categories has not been seriously affected, and the validity of pigment characters as distinguishing attributes is maintained. However, statements concerning the over-all phylogeny and the positioning of the groups relative to each other must be

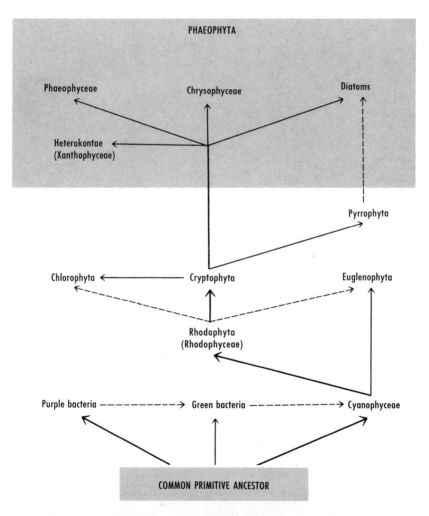

Fig. 14-1. Hypothetical phylogenetic relationships of certain bacterial and algal groups based in part on carotenoid biochemistry. (courtesy of Dr. T. W. Goodwin).

Table 14-1. Distribution of photoreactive pigments in plastids of protistan groups (Dougherty and Allen, 1960 *in* Comparative Biochemistry of Photoreactive Systems; courtesy Academic Press).[a,b,c]

Photoreactive pigments	Schizophyta		Archephyta (Cyanophyceae)	Rhodophyta (Rhodophyceae)	Cryptophyta
	Eubacteriae	Chlorobacteriae			
Chlorophylls					
Bacteriochlorophyll	+	−	−	−	−
Chlorobiochlorophyll(s)	−	+	−	−	−
Chlorophyll *a*	−	−	+	+	+
Chlorophyll *b*	−	−	−	−	−
Chlorophyll *c*	−	−	−	−	+
Chlorophyll *d*	−	−	−	±	−
Carotenoids					
Carotenes					
Lycopene	+	−	−	−	−
α-Carotene	−	−	−	+/±	+
β-Carotene	−	−	+	+(−)[d]/+	−
γ-Carotene	−	+	−	−	−
ε-Carotene	−	−	−	−	?+
Flavacene	−	−	+	−	−
Xanthophylls					
Acyclic xanthophylls (named)	+	−	−	−	−
Rubixanthin	−	+	−	−	−
Echinenone	−	−	+[e]	−	−
Myxoxanthophyll	−	−	+	−	−
Zeaxanthin	−	−	+[f]	−/±	?+[g]
Lutein	−	−	?/±	+/+	−
Violaxanthin	−	−	−	?+/−	−
Neoxanthin	−	−	−	−	−
Fucoxanthin	−	−	−	−	−
Diatoxanthin	−	−	−	−	−[g]
Diadinoxanthin	−	−	−	−	−
Flavoxanthin	−	−	−	−	−
Peridinin	−	−	−	−	−
Dinoxanthin	−	−	−	−	−
Siphonaxanthin	−	−	−	−	−
Siphonein	−	−	−	−	−
Unnamed or unidentified xanthophylls	+	−	−/+[e]	−	+
Biliproteins[h]					
Phycocyanin(s)	−	−	+(−)	+(−)	+
Phycoerythrin(s)	−	−	±	+(−)	±

[a] Based largely on the data of Goodwin and Strain; where there is disagreement between them, data of both workers are given, separated by a diagonal line—to the left for the former, to the right for the latter.

[b] The minor pigments neofucoxanthin A and B, neodiadinoxanthin, neodinoxanthin, and neoperidinin are not listed here, nor is oscillaxanthin.

[c] No information exists on the plastid pigments of the Chloromonadophyta (Chloromonadineae).

[d] Only one species without β-carotene known—*Phycodrys sinuosa*.

[e] Two "myxoxanthin-" (= echinenone-) like pigments.

[f] Not recorded by Goodwin through misprint.

[g] Probably zeaxanthin, but closely similar diatoxanthin not definitely ruled out.

[h] Several kinds of both types of bili-proteins are known; certain of these appear to be group specific, but further work is needed to clarify the over-all distribution.

Table 14-1. (*Continued*)

Heterokontae [= Xanthophyceae]	Chrysophyceae	Diatomophyceae [= Bacillariophyceae]	Phaeophyceae	Pyrrhophyta (Dinophyceae)	Chlorophyceae	Charophyceae[i]	Euglenophyta (Euglenineae)
Phaeophyta				Chlorophyta			
−	−	−	−	−	−	−	−
−	−	−	−	−	−	−	+
+	+	+	+	+	+	+	+
−	±	+	+	−	$+(-)^j$	+	−
−	−	−	−	−	−	−	−
−	−	−/±	−/±	−	$\pm^k$	+	−
+	+	+	+	+	+	+	+
−	−	−	−	−	−	+	−
−	−	+/−	−	−	$-(+)^l/-$	−	−
−	−	−	−	−	−	−	−
−	−	−	−	−	−	+	−
−	−	−	−	−	−	−	−
+/−	−	−	−	−	$-(+)^m/+$	+	?/−
−	+	?/−	?+/−	−	+	+	+
+/−	−	−	+	−	+	+	−
+/−	−	−	−	−	+	+	+/−
−	+	+	+	−	−	−	−
−	−	+	?/−	−	−	−	−
−	−	+	−	+	−/?	−	−
−	−	−	?/−	−	−	−	−
−	−	−	−	+	$-(+)^n$	−	−
−	−	−	−	−	$-(+)^n$	−	−
$-/+^o$	−	−	−	−	$-/\pm^p$	?	$-/\pm^q$
−	−	−	−	−	−(+)	−	−
−	−	−	−	−	−(+)	−	−

[i] One species studied only—*Chara fragilis.*
[j] Lacking in a few organisms only.
[k] The major carotene of most Siphonales.
[l] In Siphonales only (as trace).
[m] Major carotenoid in one species—the enigmatic *Cyanidium caldarium.*
[n] In the Siphonales only.
[o] Four unique xanthophylls claimed.
[p] One unique xanthophyll claimed to be sometimes present.
[q] Two unique xanthophylls claimed.

KEY: + = present; − = absent; ± = irregularly present or absent; +(−) = generally present, absent in a few forms; −(+) = generally absent, present in a few forms; ?+ = presence doubtful, or insufficiently verified; ? = possibly present in traces.

clearly recognized as speculative and evaluated accordingly. As indicated in Table 14-1 the distribution of carotenoid pigments among the algal groups does not provide any obvious indications of relationships among the groups. Goodwin (1962), who discussed the comparative biochemistry of carotenoids, constructed a hypothetical evolutionary scheme for the Protista based on carotenoid pigments (Fig. 14-1). However, he notes that the scheme "may have little contact with reality but insofar as it stimulates biologists to attempt to fill in the gaps which have been indicated in our knowledge of carotenoid distribution, then it will have served its purpose."

Recently, Dougherty and Allen (1960) discussed the phylogenetic relationships of the bacteria and algae. The first evolutionary level is considered by these authors to be represented by bacteria and blue-green algae, the second level by the red algae, and the third level by other algal groups. By this scheme, the red algae are assumed to have arisen from blue-green algae and in turn to have given rise to the green algae, and possibly independently, to other groups of algae. Higher plants presumably arose from green algae. Dougherty and Allen, and also Goodwin (1962), view the carotenoid (and chlorophyll) pigment distributions as generally in agreement with the broad scheme described above. At least, the data are not considered to be incompatible with the scheme proposed. Similarly, a number of alternative schemes might be accommodated by the data, for the evidence consists principally of partial overlaps in pigment complement among the various groups, and therefore a taxonomic treatment is subject to various permutations. As stated by Goodwin such schemes are valuable in stimulating future research, but they are not intended to encourage any taxonomic dogma.

Another group of pigments related to folic acid, the pteridines, comprise a potentially systematically useful group. So far, pteridines are definitely found, outside of certain animal groups, in bacteria, fungi, and certain blue-green algae, but they are suspected to occur in higher plants (Wolf, 1960). Hatfield et al. (1961) have found that the pteridine, biopterin, which occurs in many blue-green algae as a glycoside, is associated with a number of different sugars among different species, though the glycoside of a particular species is apparently constant. These authors suggest that a further study of specific glycosides of various algal species would be of taxonomic interest.

Betacyanins: A group of pigments known as betacyanins[2] provides one of the best available illustrations of the validity of

---

[2] This name was proposed by Dreiding (1961) in an important review of these compounds. The yellow pigments, presumed to be of the same type, are called betaxanthins. Both occur as glycosides.

biochemical criteria in systematics. Betacyanins have traditionally been called "nitrogenous anthocyanins." As far back as the nineteenth century these compounds were regarded as different from the typical anthocyanins. Moreover, the compounds were found only among several families of the order Centrospermae. Although further chemical properties of the pigments were described periodically, only within the past five years has there been any clear recognition that the nitrogenous anthocyanins are not true anthocyanins. Schmidt and Schonleben (1956) and Linstedt (1956) discovered the presence of acid groups in the nitrogenous anthocyanins. Wyler and Dreiding (1959) have subsequently shown that the compounds are not flavonoids. The latter authors, upon degradation of betanin, obtained indole and pyridine derivatives.

The Dreiding group has recently established the skeleton for betanidin, the aglycone of the red-violet beet pigment, betanin (Mabry et al., 1962). They have proposed the following structure for the hydrochloride of betanidin:

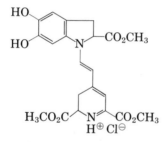

The proposed structure contains a cyanine-dye type of chromophore. Other interesting structural features include the presence of dihydroindole and dihydropyridine rings. The glucose is attached at one of the two phenolic hydroxyl groups in the natural product, betanin. Obviously, there is no relationship between the betacyanins and anthocyanins, or flavonoids in general. Despite the lack of any overt physiological activity in animals the substances may best be conceived of as alkaloids. The elucidation of the structure of this new class of natural pigments represents a significant contribution to plant chemistry and to chemical systematics.

The systematic significance of this group of compounds has been evaluated by various authors (Lawrence et al., 1941; Gibbs, 1945; Reznik, 1955, 1957; Wyler and Dreiding, 1961; Rauh and Reznik, 1961; Mabry et al., 1963). The betacyanins occur in eight families of the Centrospermae (Table 14-2). In the families Nyctaginaceae and Cactaceae the presence of betacyanins has been a factor in favor of placement of these families in the Centrospermae. Surprisingly, one major family in the classically constituted Centrospermae, Caryophyllaceae, lacks betacyanins. As noted by Dreiding (1961) this distribution raises the question of whether the Caryophyllaceae are to be considered more advanced or more primitive than other families of the order.

Table 14-2. List of genera and number of species (in parenthesis) in which betacyanins have been found (from Dreiding, 1962 and Mabry *et al.*, 1963).

CHENOPODIACEAE
  Atriplex (5)
  Beta (1)
  Chenopodium (6)
  Coriospermum (2)
  Cycloloma (1)
  Kochia (1)
  Salicornia (1)
  Suaeda (2)

AMARANTHACEAE
  Achyranthes (1)
  Aerva (1)
  Alternanthera (5)
  Amaranthus (8)
  Celosia (5)
  Froelichia (1)
  Gomphrena (4)
  Iresine (2)
  Mogiphanes (1)
  Tidestromia (1)

NYCTAGINACEAE
  Abronia (4)
  Allionia (1)
  Boerhaavia (5)
  Bougainvillea (2)
  Cryptocarpus (1)
  Cyphomeris (1)
  Mirabilis (3)
  Nyctaginia (1)
  Oxybaphus (1)

STEGNOSPERMACEAE
  Stegnosperma (1)

PORTULACACEAE
  Anacampseros (1)
  Calandrinia (1)
  Claytonia (3)
  Montia (1)
  Portulaca (4)
  Spraguea (1)

FICOIDACEAE (MESEMBRYANTHEMACEAE)
  Conophytum (17)
  Dorotheanthus (1)
  Fenestraria (1)
  Gibbaeum (2)
  Lampranthus (2)
  Lithops (1)
  Malephora (1)
  Mesembryanthemum (1)
  Pleiopilos (2)
  Sesuvium (1)
  Tetragonia (1)
  Trianthema (1)
  Trichodiadema (2)

BASELLACEAE
  Basella (2)

CACTACEAE
  Ariocarpus (1)
  Aylostera (1)
  Cereus (3)
  Chamaecereus (1)
  Cleistocactus (1)
  Hariota (1)
  Hylocereus (1)
  Gymnocalycium (3)
  Lobivia (2)
  Mammillaria (7)
  Melocactus (1)
  Monvillea (1)
  Neoporteria (1)
  Nopalxochia (1)
  Opuntia (5)
  Parodia (3)
  Pereskia (1)
  Rebutia (4)
  Selinocereus (1)
  Thelocactus (1)
  Zygocactus (1)

DIDIERACEAE
  Didiera (1)

A number of different betacyanins occur but the differences are thought to involve the nature of the glycoside rather than the basic ring structure. Betanin and amarantin are most often encountered, while certain others are at present indicated to be genus specific. In some cases the compounds are quite variable within a genus or even within a species. For example Reznik (1957) found sixteen different betacyanin type components in beets and turnips. As an illustration of the intra-specific variation, the turnip cultivar "Frankes Rekord" contained eleven different betacyanins and betaxanthins while the cultivar "Kirches Ideal" contained only two of the pigments.

It is especially interesting that there is no known case of the coexistence in the same plant of anthocyanins and betacyanins. Typical anthocyanins are common in the Caryophyllaceae. Flavonols, which are chemically quite close to the anthocyanins, are common in the betacyanin-containing species (Reznik, 1957). This distribution may indicate a functional equivalence between the brightly colored betacyanins and anthocyanins despite their chemical differences, suggestive that color rather than some cryptic metabolic role may account for the presence of anthocyanins.

One of the most unusual confirmations of the systematic importance of a group of compounds is represented by the correlations noted independently by Taylor (1940). Using rain water, gasoline from a motor boat, and other crude techniques Taylor surveyed the pigments of thirty-six species of flowering plants of Indefatigable Island in the Galapagos, and twelve species were found to contain "nitrogenous anthocyanins." Those species testing positive were in the Centrospermae.

Ordinarily, major taxonomic importance would not be accorded a single chemical character, but the totally different structures of the two types of pigments, betacyanins and anthocyanins, which indicate different synthetic pathways, their mutual exclusion, and the limited distribution of the betacyanins make the presence of betacyanins of particular taxonomic significance. In this connection, it is interesting to note that Mabry et al. (1963) suggested that the order Centrospermae (Chenopodiales), as classically constituted and including the Cactales, be reserved for the betacyanin-containing families, and that those anthocyanin-containing families such as the Caryophyllaceae and Illecebraceae be treated as a separate phyletic group whose relationship is close but not within the betacyanin producing order.

Tannins: Although tannins have been studied intensively for many years, there has been no important biochemical systematic study involving this group of compounds. Tannins are found in a wide variety of plants, including algae, fungi, mosses, and ferns. Tannins are common in seed plants. All groups of the gymnosperms, except the Gnetales, contain some tannin producers. Among angiosperms, the monocot families Palmae, Musaceae, and Iridaceae are notably tanniniferous. Dicot families of the orders Fagales, Rosales, and Myrtales are particularly rich in tannins. They are rare or absent in the families Gramineae, Caryophyllaceae, Cruciferae, Cactaceae, Chenopodiaceae, Labiatae, Umbelliferae, and Primulaceae (Skene, 1934).

Tannins are probably best considered as phenolics. In fact the non-hydrolyzable, condensed tannins are flavonoid derivatives. These are complex polymers which may form insoluble products (often called phlobaphenes). Familiar examples of condensed tannins are derivatives of catechin or gallocatechin. Their relationship to anthocyanins and leucoanthocyanins is obvious.

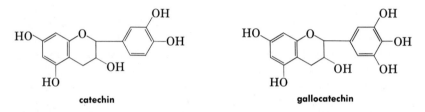

catechin   gallocatechin

The hydrolyzable tannins may occur as glycosides—the aglycone often being a phenolic acid such as gallic acid. Brief but concise recent reviews of tannin chemistry are those of Mayer (1958) and Schmidt (1955), although these reviewers did not treat at all the systematic distribution. As noted in an earlier section of this chapter Gibbs has studied the distribution of catechol tannins in the plant kingdom without, however, deriving systematic patterns of any great importance.

Lignin: Lignin is a plant product which potentially is of great systematic value, especially if technical advances occur which provide a method of analysing the sequential linkages of the building units and their cross linkages. When Freudenberg (1959a) can raise even a rhetorical question such as whether lignin is a "molecular compostheap" or consists of an orderly structure like cellulose, one clearly recognizes the present limitations of our knowledge of lignin. Even the definition of lignin is based entirely on its degradation properties: "That plant component which, when refluxed with ethanol in the presence of catalytic amounts of hydrogen chloride, gives a mixture of ethanolysis products such as α-ethoxypropioguaiacone, vanillin, and vanilloyl methyl ketone from coniferous woods, and, in addition, the corresponding syringyl derivatives from deciduous woods." (Brauns and Brauns, 1960)

Chemical degradation of lignin yields phenolic substances of the following types:

(1)

Guaiacyl or vanillyl group (typical of gymnosperms).

(2)

Syringyl group (together with (1), typical of angiosperms).

(3)

p-OH phenyl group (together with 1 + 2, typical of some monocots, e.g. certain grasses).

It is generally regarded that the precursors in lignin synthesis consist of C6—C3 units such as the above wherein R represents allyl alcohol (CH_2=$CHCH_2OH$). Thus, the possible precursor of gymnosperm lignin would be coniferyl alcohol. The scheme shown in Fig. 11-2, based on results of C^{14} labelling experiments from several laboratories, summarizes current information. Important contributions are those of Brown and Neish (1955), Brown et al. (1959), and McCalla and Neish (1959), who established the probable routes of interconversion of phenylpropane derivatives leading to such compounds as coniferyl and syringyl alcohols, and Reznik and Urban (1956) who demonstrated a very efficient incorporation of C^{14} coniferin (glucoside of coniferyl alcohol) into spruce lignin.

Less is known about the linkage of monomers in the lignin itself although Freudenberg (1959b) has obtained dimers, such as those illustrated by Fig. 14-2, and higher polymers, using an enzyme from the mushroom *Psalliota campestris* and coniferyl alcohol. Since more than one type of linkage occurred in Freudenberg's synthetic lignin, this may also be true of natural lignin. Furthermore, at least three basic building units are presently thought to be involved, and perhaps more occur. The number and sequence of monomers included in the lignin molecule may vary, cross linkages between lignin molecules probably occur, and it is likely that lignin is bound to carbohydrate constituents of the cell wall. The extent and nature of its

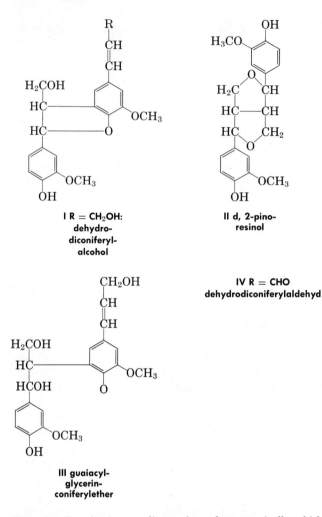

Fig. 14-2. Four lignin type dimers, formed enzymatically, which represent possible linkages of monomers in true lignin. (Freudenberg, 1959).

variation cannot be established without further technical advances in the degradation of lignin.

There is evidence that lignin varies even within a single plant. Manskaja (1959) reported that the younger parts of a plant may produce lignin with a lower methoxy content than that of the mature tissue, and Wardrop and Bland (1959) have discussed a similar situation in the genera *Eucalyptus* and *Tilia*. Since higher methoxy content is associated with a higher syringyl-guaiacyl ratio, and the higher ratio seems to be characteristic of the more advanced plants, the data provided by Manskaja may be interpreted as an example of recapitulation, or in the words of the often maligned aphorism, ontogeny recapitulates phylogeny.

As indicated above, our knowledge of lignin composition relevant to phylogeny is more or less restricted to information concerning the types and proportions of phenylpropane-type monomers. The classic work in this area is that of Creighton *et al.* (1944) who examined many gymnosperms and angiosperms. Gymnosperm lignin usually yielded only guaiacyl type derivatives. Exceptions included *Podocarpus amarus, P. pedunculatus, Tetraclinus articulata,* and species of the order Gnetales. In contrast, angiosperms contained lignin which yielded both guaiacyl and syringyl derivatives; in most, the

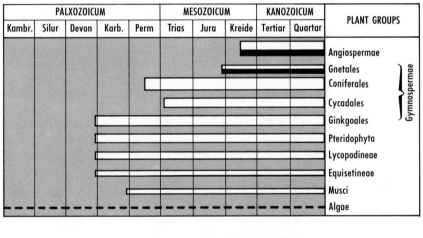

Fig. 14-3. The distribution of lignins and their aromatic monomers in plant groups in geological time. (From Manskaja, 1959).

Palxozoicum = Paleozoic...................... { Cambrium / Silurian / Devonian / Carboniferous / Permian }

Mesozoicum = Mesozoic...................... { Triassic / Jurassic / Cretaceous }

Kanozoicum = Cenozoic...................... { Tertiary / Quaternary } ratio of guaiacyl to syringyl residues was as low as 1:3, with monocots having a slightly higher ratio.

Some angiosperms regarded as primitive, for example, *Belliolum haplopus* and *Zygogynum vieillardii* (order Magnoliales) have a guaiacyl-syringyl ratio as high as approximately 1:1. This ratio is typical of the lignins of the group of gymnosperms which were noted above. *Casuarina stricta,* discussed in a previous section as possibly one of the most primitive angiosperms, has a guaiacyl-syringyl ratio of 1:0.5 (Manskaja, 1959).

It has been noted that some monocots produce lignin with p-hydroxy phenyl derivatives. Furthermore, studies of lignin biosynthesis support the presence of an enzyme mechanism in grasses which utilizes tyrosine or p-hydroxyphenylpyruvic acid. (Wright *et al.,* 1958; Acerbo *et al.,* 1958.) These facts suggest a significant difference in the lignin chemistry between monocots and dicots, but as was pointed out by Neish (1960), sampling is obviously inadequate at this time.

The members of other major vascular plant groups, for example, ferns, lycopsids, and sphenopsids, apparently produce only the guaiacyl type of lignin. Among mosses, *Sphagnum* contains phenolic compounds in the cell walls, but Manskaja (1959) has concluded that lignin itself is absent. Figure 14-3 illustrates the broad distribution of lignin and the particular monomeric building units represented among various plant groups in geological time. Presence of lignin in mosses, shown in the figure, is questionable. Fossil lignin has undergone complex chemical changes, and so far has not proven to be useful in providing insight into the actual lignin composition (Manskaja, 1960).

It is evident that most of the taxonomic inferences from lignin chemistry are presently limited to rather broad generalizations. However, Towers and Gibbs (1953) used the guaiacyl-syringyl ratio together with other evidence to suggest that box elder (*Acer negundo*) might be separable from other maples, that is, elevated to generic rank. This is one of the few examples of the actual application of lignin chemistry to a specific taxonomic problem.

Isothiocyanates: Sulfur-containing secondary compounds in higher plants are relatively few in number. By far the most important group is the mustard oils or isothiocyanates, about thirty of which have been described. The compounds occur in the living plant in the following form:

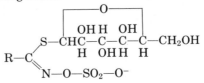

The sugar moiety of the isothiocyanate is glucose. The isothiocyanate (R—NCS) is formed enzymatically by intra-molecular rearrangement accompanied by liberation of glucose and sulfate. The enzyme, myrosinase, is relatively nonspecific for naturally occurring isothiocyanates but is highly specific in that other types of glucosidic linkages are not attacked. In some seeds the enzyme is located in special cells and the glucoside in other cells so that the isothiocyanate is produced only after the tissue is damaged. According to Kjaer (1960), three different pathways for enzymatic attack upon the *in vivo* glucosides may exist: (1) intramolecular rearrangement to isothiocyanate, (2) rearrangement to form thiocyanate, and (3) formation of nitriles and elementary sulfur with no change in the carbon skeleton. *Lepidium sativum* produces substances of Types 1 and 2, apparently enzymatically, while a related species, *L. ruderale* forms only the thiocyanate derivative.

Representative isothiocyanates are illustrated in Table 14-3. It is not unusual to find several members of a particular series occurring within a related group of plants, and representatives of more than one series may also occur together in a single species. Arrangement of the isothiocyanates into homologous series is possible, and the series are somewhat similar to those in which the cyanogenetic glycosides are arranged (Chapter 10).

Correspondence between isothiocyanates such as glucoputranjivin and cyanogenetic glycosides such as linamarin may be duplicated by other examples:

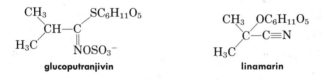

glucoputranjivin   linamarin

Also, both isothiocyanates and cyanogens are modified enzymatically upon damage to the tissue and this fact suggests that further relationships exist between the two groups. Nonetheless, little or no taxonomic overlap occurs in the distribution of cyanogenetic glycosides and isothiocyanates. Functional equivalence is suggested in the two groups, but little is known concerning either the function or mode of biosynthesis of mustard oils.

Mustard oils have been found to be common in only a few families: Cruciferae, Capparidaceae, Moringaceae, Resedaceae, and Tropaeolaceae. The compounds also occur infrequently in Caricaceae, Euphorbiaceae, Limnanthaceae, Salvadoraceae, Phytolaccaceae, and Plantaginaceae (Kjaer, 1960).

It is notable that the first four families, together with the

Table 14-3. Representative natural mustard oils.

R of Derived Isothiocyanate R-NCS	Name of Glucoside
Alkyl Compounds	
CH_3	glucocapparin
C_2H_5	glucolepidiin
$(CH_3)_2CH$	glucoputrajivin
$C_2H_5\ldots C\ldots$ $\overset{CH_3}{\underset{H}{}}$	glucocochlearin
Alkenyl Compounds	
$H_2C{=}CHCH_2$	sinigrin
$H_2C{=}CH(CH_2)_2$	gluconapin
$H_2C{=}CH(CH_2)_3$	glucobrassicanapin
Thioethers	
$CH_3S(CH_2)_3$	glucoibervirin
$CH_3S(CH_2)_4$	glucoerucin
$CH_3S(CH_2)_5$	glucoberteroin
Sulfoxides	
$CH_3SO(CH_2)_3$	glucoiberin
$CH_3SO(CH_2)_4$	glucoraphanin
$CH_3SOCH{=}CH(CH_2)_2$	glucoraphenin
$CH_3SO(CH_2)_5$	glucoalyssin
$CH_3SO(CH_2)_8$	glucohirsutin
$CH_3SO(CH_2)_9$	glucoarabin
$CH_3SO(CH_2)_{10}$	glucocamelinin
Sulfones	
$CH_3SO_2(CH_2)_3$	glucocheirolin
$CH_3SO_2(CH_2)_4$	glucoerysolin
Arylalkyl Compounds	
$C_6H_5CH_2$	glucotropaeolin
$C_6H_5(CH_2)_2$	gluconasturtiin
Phenols and Ethers	
$HO{-}C_6H_4CH_2$	sinalbin
$p\text{-}CH_3OC_6H_4CH_2$	glucoaubrietin
$m\text{-}CH_3OC_6H_4CH_2$	glucolimnanthin

Table 14-3. (*Continued*)

R of Derived Isothiocyanate R-NCS	Name of Glucoside
Aliphatic Hydroxy Compounds	
(CH₃)₂CCH₂ OH	glucoconringiin
HOCH₂CH CH₃	glucosisymbrin
H₂C=CHCHCH₂ OH	progoitrin
C₆H₅CHCH₂ OH	glucobarbarin
Esters	
CH₃OOC(CH₂)₃ C₆H₅COO(CH₂)₃	glucoerypestrin glucomalcolmiin

Papaveraceae and two other small families (Tovariaceae and Bretschneideraceae) comprise the order Rhoeodales. The Papaveraceae, so far not known to produce isothiocyanates, is a major alkaloid producer, but alkaloids are not known from the isothiocyanate-producing families of the Rhoeodales. Such examples of mutual exclusion, together with the sporadic appearance in other widely separated families of isothiocyanates identical with those of the Cruciferae should be observed. Taxonomic speculations based solely on similar correlations involving other groups of compounds need to be stated conservatively. An interesting example of such parallelisms is the occurrence of both isothiocyanates and the rare fatty acid, erucic acid, in the families Cruciferae and Tropaeolaceae. There is no obvious relationship between the two types of compounds, and the families concerned bear no obvious relationship to each other.

There is little doubt, however, of the taxonomic significance of mustard oils within the family Cruciferae. Practically all members of this family so far investigated have proven to contain isothiocyanates, and even more remarkable is the variety of different types of isothiocyanates which occur in the family. Most of the series illustrated in Table 14-3 are represented in one or another species of Cruciferae. Kjaer (1960) may be consulted for a comprehensive account of the distribution of isothiocyanates within the Cruciferae. Although much information has been accumulated concerning isothiocyanates of this family, only a few primarily systematically oriented studies have been published (for example, Kjaer and Hansen, 1958). Certainly the isothiocyanates represent a major source of taxonomic information in the Cruciferae, and since isothiocyanates can now be analyzed by paper chromatography, more studies of natural populations and their isothiocyanates content should be forthcoming.

Organic Acids: Although there are numerous organic acids found in almost all plants, most of them have either been considered elsewhere or they are so generally distributed that they offer no great utility to systematics. In the former category are the "phenolic" acids (for example, chlorogenic, cinnamic, coumaric, caffeic, and numerous others). Not all of these acids are phenols, but they are biosynthetically related to phenols and thus fit that category naturally. These acids have been discussed in Chapter 11.

Among the acids which are of such general distribution as to be of no great value in systematics are oxalic acid, lactic acid, and all those organic acids represented in the metabolic pathway leading to the oxidative breakdown of carbohydrate.

From the older literature the acids hydroxy-citric and α-hydroxyglutaric acids have been described from beet juice (Buch, 1957). Towers and Steward (1954) found evidence of the presence of α-keto-γ-methylene-glutaric acid in tulip leaves. In fact it was the most conspicuous keto acid constituent. This acid is an analog of the amino acid, γ-methyleneglutamic acid, also found in all *Tulipa* species examined by Fowden and Steward (1957). This has been discussed in Chapter 6, and the significance of the presence of the keto acid in *Tulipa* is best related to the metabolism of the corresponding amino acids. Furthermore, in the peanut (*Arachis hypogaea*), which also produces certain of the uncommon glutamic acid derivatives, Fowden and Webb (1955) detected γ-methylene-α-ketoglutaric acid in the seedlings.

Another example of considerable interest is malonic acid. This acid, a competitive inhibitor of the Krebs cycle enzyme, succinic dehydrogenase, would not normally be anticipated in large quantities, yet it has been reported to accumulate in the leaves of eighteen of twenty-seven species of the family Leguminosae, in some species of Umbelliferae, and elsewhere (Bentley, 1952). It is difficult to account for the wide occurrence of this acid, and it presents an intriguing physiological-biochemical problem.

Stafford (1959, 1961) has studied the accumulation of tartaric acid in angiosperm leaves and finds that, although many families contain some species which accumulate the acid, it is found consistently only among species in the family Vitaceae. Outside this family only two other species, of a total of forty-four tested, accumulated tartaric acid. These were *Pelargonium hortorium* (Geraniaceae) and *Phaseolus vulgaris* (Leguminosae). According to Stafford, "The genetic factors controlling this large scale accumulation must have arisen independently in each group since some closely related forms do not possess this characteristic. Within these different taxa, however, the content of tartaric acid can be used as a characteristic of taxonomic value."

There are some organic acids which are rather difficult to classify and which, because of their restricted distribution or association with particular families, appear to be of potential systematic value. One of these is the dicarboxylic acid, chelidonic acid, shown below:

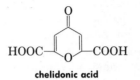

chelidonic acid

The distribution of chelidonic acid was studied by Ramstad (1945) who found only eleven positive species out of a total of 380 species representing 116 families. Ramstad (1953) extended his investigations to include 1,143 additional species representing 238 genera in nine families. Of these, 688 species (52 per cent) contained chelidonic acid. The families with numerous species producing chelidonic acid are Lobeliaceae (eight out of fifteen species were positive), Thymelaeaceae (forty-two out of 152), Rhamnaceae (twenty-six out of sixty-four), Hippocastanaceae (two out of six), Amaryllidaceae (seventy-three out of 126), Haemodoraceae (four out of seven) and Liliaceae (170 out of 576). In the family Papaveraceae only two out of 116 species were positive for chelidonic acid, though the name of the acid is derived from the genus *Chelidonium*. The wide distribution of chelidonic acid in certain families is taxonomically interesting, and in the case of the families Amaryllidaceae, Haemodoraceae, Liliaceae, and Dioscoreaceae a somewhat natural group is represented.

A number of other organic acids of a more complex nature, whose distributions are not fully investigated, may ultimately be useful as systematic criteria. Among these are abietic and neoabietic acids of the genus *Pinus,* the complex cyclic sapogenins such as betulinic and bassic acids (the latter is common in the family Sapotaceae, Haywood and Kon, 1940), and the sugar acids such as mucic and saccharic acids.

Antimicrobial Tests: Another potentially valuable biochemical approach to systematics is through surveys of antimicrobial or antifungal agents of plant species. Nickell (1959) has summarized much of these data listing the species and parts of those plants tested, type of extract used, and the groups of organisms which were affected. He also included a list of those species showing no activity, though the latter does not include reference citations. A glance at the Nickell summary is sufficient to indicate that numerous plant families contain some species with antimicrobial compounds. Skinner (1955), in his review of antibiotics in higher plants, compiled a list of the surveys of plants for antibiotic activity. His compilation included references to studies which surveyed up to 2,300 species representing 166 families (Osborn, 1943), as well as more limited surveys. In the broader surveys specific inhibitory agents were not characterized, and such studies are accordingly limited. However, a number of toxic agents have been characterized, and these fall generally into one or another of the classes of compounds which we have already taken up. Table 14-4 lists the named antibiotics and one may recognize quinones (2-methoxy-1,4-napthoquinone), flavonoids (quercetin), phenols (protocatechuic acid), alkaloids (berberine), and others. Also certain essential oils, and even fatty acids (for example, linoleic) have been reported to have some antibiotic activity. There are numerous antibiotics which do not fit readily into any of the major categories described. These probably occur in a limited number of species and, therefore, represent further possibilities for systematic use. Such compounds are first recognized by virtue of their antibiotic activities, we may conclude that, although antibiotic activity per se is meaningless, it represents a method of disclosing a new substance or class of substances which may prove to have systematic significance. For example, species of *Allium* (onion) contain several antibiotic agents, some of which are phenolic, some of which are unidentified. Garlic (*Allium sativum*), however, has been shown to contain a sulphur compound, allicin, of the following chemical structure:

$$CH_2{=}CHCH_2{-}\underset{\underset{O}{\|}}{S}{-}S{-}CH_2{-}CH{=}CH_2$$

allicin

This compound does not readily fit any of the groups previously discussed. Allicin and various allyl sulphides are characteristic of the genus *Allium*.

Two other compounds which exhibit antibiotic activity and which do not fit any of the biochemical categories previously covered are protoanemonin and anemonin, from *Anemone pulsatilla*:

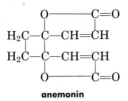

anemonin

These substances are of widespread occurrence in the Ranunculaceae.

An interesting and promising reverse application of screening of green plants for antimicrobial agents is that of the comparative response of certain algal species to specific antibiotics. Bold (1961) has utilized response to antibiotics as supplementary attributes in the taxonomy of the green algal genus *Chlorococcum*. Differential re-

Table 14-4. Named antibiotic substances on preparations and their sources (Skinner, 1955 in *Modern Methods of Plant Analysis,* Vol. 3; with permission).

Name of Antibiotic	Category (see key)	Source of Antibiotic
Allicin	A	*Allium sativum*
Anacardic acid	A	*Anacardium occidentale*
Anacardol	A	*Anacardium occidentale*
Anemonin	A	Members of *Ranunculaceae* (see *Anemone pulsatilla*)
Asiaticoside	B	*Centella asiatica*
Berberine	A	Members of *Berberidaceae* (see *Berberis* spp.)
Cardol	A	*Anacardium occidentale*
Cassic acid	A	*Cassia reticulata* (see Rhein)
Catechol	A	*Allium cepa*
Cepheranthine	B (?)	*Stephania cepherantha*
Chaksine	B	*Cassia absus*
Cheirolin	A	*Cheiranthus cheiri*
Chelerythrine	A	
Chelidonine	A	*Chelidonium majus*
Chelidoxanthine	A (?)	
Chlorophorin	B	*Chlorophora excelsa*
Conessine	A	*Holarrhena antidysenterica*
Convolvulin	A	Members of *Convolvulaceae*
Crepin	B	*Crepis taraxacifolia*
Curcumin	A	*Curcuma* spp.
Datiscetin	A	*Datisca cannabina*
Dicoumarol	A	*Melilotus spp.*
Febrifugine	B	*Dichroa febrifuga*
iso-Febrifugine	B	*Dichroa febrifuga*

Table 14-4. (*Continued*)

Name of Antibiotic	Category (see key)	Source of Antibiotic
Fulvoplumericin	B	*Plumeria acutifolia*
Gindricine	B (?)	*Stephania glabra*
Humulon	A	*Humulus lupulus*
Jalapin	B	*Ipomoea purga*
Juglone	A	*Juglans* spp.
Kawain	A	*Piper methysticum*
Lupulon	A	*Humulus lupulus*
Lycopersicin	C	*Lycopersicum* spp. (see Tomatin)
2-Methoxy-1,4-naphthaquinone	A	*Impatiens balsamina*
4-O-Methylresorcylicaldehyde	A	*Decalepis hamiltonii*
Morellins	B	*Garcinia morella*
Nimbidin	C	*Melia azadirachta*
Nordihydroguiaretic acid	A	*Larrea divaricata*
Oxyasiaticoside	B	*Centella asiatica*
Parasorbic acid	A	*Sorbus aucuparia*
Phloretin	A	*Pyrus malus*
Pinosylvine	A	*Pinus sylvestris*
Pinosylvine monomethyl ether	A	
Plumbagin	A	*Plumbago europaea*
Plumericin	B	*Plumeria multiflora*
Podophyllin	C	*Podophyllum peltatum*
Pristimerin	B	*Pristimera indica*
Protoanemonin	A	Members of *Ranunculaceae* (see *Anemone pulsatilla*)
Protocatechuic acid	A	*Allium cepa*
Pterygospermin	C	*Moringa pterygosperma*
Puchiin	C	*Eleocharis tuberosa*
Purothionin	B	*Triticum* spp.
Quercetin	A	*Quercus* spp.
Quinine	A	*Cinchona* spp. (see alkaloids)
Raphanin	B	*Raphanus sativus*
Rhein	A	Synonymous with cassic acid
Simarubidin	B	*Simaruba amara*
Solanine	A	Members of *Solanaceae* (see alkaloids)
Thujaplicins	A	*Thuja plicata*
Thujic acid	A	*Thuja plicata*
Tomatin	C	Synonymous with lycopersicin
Tomatine	B	*Lycopersicum* spp.
Tomatidine	B	*Lycopersicum* spp.
Trilobin	A	*Cocculus trilobus*
Umbellatine	B	Members of *Berberidaceae* (see *Berberis* spp.)
Vinalin	B (?)	*Prosopis ruscifolia* (see alkaloids)

KEY: A = Compound of known chemical structure; B = Isolated active substance, the structure of which is incompletely known or unknown; C = Imperfectly characterized preparation.

sponses to one or more antibiotics has been characteristic of different species or strains of this genus, and striking differences have been noted between certain taxa which are quite similar morphologically. Thus, cryptic physiological (or biochemical) differences may be disclosed, despite morphological similarity.

A related approach is that of investigations of toxic plant substances which affect higher animals. It has already been noted that cyanogenetic glycosides of the genus *Lathyrus* produce a disease in livestock known as lathyrism (Selye, 1957). The toxicity of certain plants has led to extensive chemical investigations which have disclosed information of probable systematic significance. Surveys such as those of Duncan *et al.* (1955, 1957) may therefore prove to be of indirect value through disclosing new toxic species. The information will either supplement existing knowledge to the extent that a systematic pattern is either exposed or denied, or it will encourage further chemical investigations of a group not previously known to demonstrate toxicity. A high proportion of the toxic substances disclosed by such methods are probably alkaloids which could be assayed directly with much simpler techniques. It thus appears appropriate to avoid an exaggeration of the potential of screening methods of all sorts since it is doubtful that any taxonomic conclusions of consequence can be drawn from the survey directly.

Some additional unusual approaches, which in effect are vicarious surveys, may be noted. For example, the use of arrow poisons by natives of the Americas has disclosed a much larger number of plant species which produce toxic substances than is generally known. Curare, from *Strychnos toxifera* (Loganiaceae) and other *Strychnos* species is well known, but Cheney (1931) found that species representing twenty-one different families were utilized by one or another Indian tribe. In addition to the Loganiaceae the family Ranunculaceae was well represented. Several species of *Ranunculus* and *Anemone* were employed as were those of *Aconitum* and *Delphinium*. The toxic principles in most cases are believed to be alkaloids. Cheney concluded that the Indians of a given area had succeeded in discovering and utilizing the most poisonous species indigenous to the area. Furthermore, they recognized the plant part in which the toxic principle was most concentrated and the stage of development which gave the best yield. Similarly, the use of plants as fish stupefication agents by the Tarahumar Indians of northwestern Mexico has disclosed numerous toxic plant species. Pennington (1958) lists plants of thirteen different families which were used as stupefying agents, and in these cases the toxic principles were either unknown or apparently belonged to classes such as alkaloids, cyanogenetic glycosides, or frequently saponins (for example, in *Agave schottii*).

15 BIOCHEMICAL STUDIES OF HYBRIDS

In all of modern biological science, few areas if any have provided more rewarding results than has biochemical genetics. Within a generation a few scattered reports on the Mendelian inheritance of biochemical characters (for example, flower color) have been supplemented by innumerable examples. In fact, much of our present knowledge of intermediary metabolism of amino acids results from data provided through biochemical genetics. The stimulus was furnished by the oft-cited paper of Beadle and Tatum (1941), in which they reported an analysis of biochemical mutants in the mold, *Neurospora*. For this and subsequent work these investigators shared (with Lederberg) the 1959 Nobel Prize. Now, hundreds of biochemical mutants have been detected in

295

Neurospora. In some cases mutations which appear to affect the same end product in a synthesis are found to be complementary. That is, when a mixture of the two mutant type nuclei is allowed to become established in a single mycelium, normal growth results. This result implies that the individual mutants affected a different step in a series of events leading to the synthesis or utilization of a substance. In non-complementary mutants normal growth is not restored in the presence of mixed nuclei, and one may infer that the same functional step was affected by both mutants. With more refined genetic techniques it is possible to compare a series of mutations that are non-complementary. If such non-complementary mutants are assumed to involve, by definition, the same gene, then in effect one is studying the intragenic aspects of mutation. This is not the time to engage in a discourse on modern methods of genetic fine structure analysis. Anyone not yet appreciative of the remarkable advances in this direction will find the summary by Glass (1957) and the more recent treatment by Jacob and Wolman (1961) of great value. In such a vital field new discoveries are frequent, and the non-specialist who can keep abreast of such discoveries must be indeed rare. Two smaller volumes which summarize this aspect of modern genetics in highly readable form are those by Pontecorvo (1958) and Strauss (1960).

For several reasons, microorganisms have overshadowed higher plants and animals in their contributions to progress in biochemical genetics. Notable examples are certain bacteria (*E. coli*) and fungi (other than *Neurospora,* there is for example *Aspergillus*). Populations which number in the millions, adaptability to sterile culture, and short generation time combine powerful advantages. There is also the additional advantage of haploidy, which guarantees immediate exposure of even the recessive mutant. Since recessive mutants vastly outnumber other types, this last advantage is of special significance. Consider the difficulty in disclosing the true extent of radiation-induced gene mutation in a population of human beings.

With advantages such as those cited above, it is easy to understand why biochemical genetics in higher organisms is lagging so conspicuously. Most of the biochemical mutants detected in higher plants involve secondary substances such as pigments and storage products. Recently, biochemical mutants in the small crucifer genus, *Arabidopsis,* have been studied with some success (Langridge, 1955). This plant, small enough to be grown in a test tube, thus on defined media, has a relatively short generation time and has now yielded some biochemical mutants affecting primary metabolites.

We may forecast the emergence of new techniques which will

present opportunities for the study of biochemical genetics of higher plants rivalling those of microorganisms. For example, in a recent paper, Tulecke (1960) has reported new data on the development of tissue from *Ginkgo* pollen. This tissue is basically haploid though some polyploidy appears. If extensive experimentation should lead to a practical method of deriving haploid callus growth from pollen, one major advantage is immediate. Furthermore, techniques exist for separating such clusters of cells (by pectinase, for example), and Steward *et al.* (1958) have succeeded in producing whole carrot plants, apparently from individual cells. It is not beyond possibility that clonal lines, established from single cells of dispersed haploid tissue, may someday provide the combination of advantages inherent in microorganisms.

In an earlier section it was stated that, in effect, our knowledge of biochemical pathways has emphasized the basic similarities in the metabolism of diverse organisms rather than differences. Of numerous examples supporting this view, the oxidative breakdown of carbohydrate, the structure of the nucleic acids, and the nearly universal distribution of numerous co-enzymes are particularly significant. Perhaps, partly as a consequence of a natural preoccupation with unity in metabolism, comparative biochemistry is just beginning to reveal its full potential in phylogenetic studies (for example, Florkin and Mason, 1960). It is reasonable to expect that one must establish the order before profiting fully from the study of biochemical innovation in evolution. If extensive biochemical genetic studies in higher plants become practical, we should expect an interest to develop in comparative systematic biochemistry. More effort needs to be directed toward elucidation of major metabolic pathways in the higher plants. This knowledge should be extended to include the biosynthesis of secondary substances.

One technique which may be expected to yield information of predominantly systematic importance is that of the biochemical study of hybrids. This chapter is devoted to a review of some hybrid studies which are essentially biochemical in nature. The work is widely scattered throughout the literature, and in a number of cases, the original investigation was directed to some objective which did not represent, basically, a problem in systematics. Because of this fact, and the lack of any review of the subject to use as a point of departure, the present discussion is inevitably eclectic. Many papers included in this section concern classes of compounds already discussed in previous chapters, and this pertinent background information is not repeated.

Perhaps one of the first "biochemical" studies of hybrids, or so it was thought to be at the time, happens also to be exceptional in another way. In 1914, Zade published a rather lengthy study on the serology of some legumes and grasses, including a serological comparison of three species of clover, *Trifolium repens, T. pratense* and *T. hybridum.* At that time *T. hybridum* was regarded as a hybrid of *T. repens* and *T. pratense* [in Fernald's (1950) treatment it is implied that this view no longer holds]. Zade concluded that serum interactions supported the hybrid nature of *T. hybridum.* For example, *hybridum* serum reacted more strongly with the putative parents than did reciprocal tests with serum from the parents. Chester, who discussed this work briefly in his 1937 review says, "Zade, with precipitin test, showed that *Trifolium pratense* and *T. repens* are related, but serologically distinct, their hybrid, *T. hybridum* reacts so strongly with both as to demonstrate its hybrid nature." If there had been no a priori conclusion that *T. hybridum* was actually a hybrid, the serological data may have been interpreted as indicative that *T. hybridum* was the closest of the three to some primitive *Trifolium* stock. There is then the danger of circular reasoning in the interpretation of such data.

A similar situation is that of the disputed hybrid, *Vicia leganyi* ("*Lens esculenta* × *Vicia sativa*"). Its serological properties were shown to be intermediate between the protein complexes of the "parents" (Moritz and vom Berg, 1931). Though these data alone would not serve to establish the hybrid identity of *V. leganyi,* Moritz has developed supplementary techniques to disclose hybrids through serological methods. Suppose, for example, that species A contains antigen complement a + b and species B contains antigen complement b + c. Thus, b represents the common antigenic substances. The hybrid should, therefore, possess a complement a + b + c, and a hybrid antiserum, if adsorbed with serum type A and then serum type B, should be completely neutralized. It should then give a negative response to hybrid serum. Presumably then, if a residual activity remained in the antiserum after adsorption with sera A and B, one of three explanations might hold:

(1) The plant was not a hybrid.
(2) New "hybrid-type" antigenic substances were present.
(3) Genetic heterozygosity in one or both parents led to individual differences in antigenic complement.

However, if serum of the "hybrid," completely neutralized antisera of type A and type B, this result offers strong support for the true hybrid nature of the plant in question. In the light of these refinements in technique Moritz concluded that *Vicia leganyi* was a hybrid of *Lens esculenta* and *Vicia sativa*. Despite this, its protein was not exactly equal to the summation of that of its putative parents, for some of the *Lens esculenta* protein was absent.

Authenticated hybrids involving species of *Triticum, Secale,* and *Aegilops* were serologically intermediate to the parents. Cytological studies showed these hybrids (*Aegilops ovata* × *Triticum dicoccoides* and *Triticum aestivum* × *Secale cereale*) to be amphidiploids (see Moritz, 1958).

Hall (1959) has reported an interesting study of immunoelectrophoretic properties of allopolyploid ryewheat and its parental species. Extracts of the seeds of inbred varieties of wheat and rye and the hybrid were utilized. (The method of immuno-electrophoresis is described briefly in Chapter 5.)

By use of appropriate antisera, unadsorbed, and adsorbed by selected sera, one may determine whether rye and wheat have any similar antigens, whether the hybrid has some or all of the antigens of the parents, and whether any antigens peculiar to the hybrid are present. The results of this study are, in summary, as follows:

(1) Wheat extracts contain some proteins lacking in rye but some fractions in the two extracts agree.
(2) The hybrid ryewheat contains all of the proteins recognized in wheat and all of the proteins recognized in rye except for one.

One statement by Hall is of particular significance and merits further comment:

> The formation of hybrid substances found in some species hybrids of birds (cf. Irwin 1951) was not detected in these experiments, and the protein composition of the ryewheat as far as examined was found to have originated by a more or less complete addition of the proteins of the parental species.

The observation quoted above is in accord with a point of view expressed some years ago by Moritz (1934) who said that the protein constituents of hybrids were found serologically to represent combinations of all or part of the proteins of parents without the occurrence of specifically new proteins as a result of hybridization.

Beckman *et al.* (1962) found that the protein components of hybrids of canaries and finches were essentially the summation of the components of the two parental types. However, two components, designated *A* and *B,* were always present in the hybrids but in only

half the concentration found in the parents. This result implies a possible relationship between components *A* and *B* and would, therefore,
justify further comparative study of these components. Nevertheless,
Schwartz (1960) has presented what seems to be unequivocal evidence
for the presence of a hybrid protein in maize. This work relates
to several questions of rather fundamental nature. The method, relatively simple, involves a separation of enzymes from the tissue concerned (crude extracts from endosperm, for example) by means of
starch gel zone electrophoresis. Esterases, which were the type of
enzyme studied, were then visualized by treating with a substrate
such as α-naphthyl acetate and a dye coupler.

Using different inbred genetic lines three different forms of
basic protein with esterase activity were detected and designated as
follows: S = slow moving esterase, N = normal esterase (most commonly found, with intermediate migration rate), and F = fast moving
esterase. The inbred lines contained either S, N, or F. When artificial
mixtures were utilized, no interaction occurred, and the individual
bands appeared without the formation of new bands.

When genetic lines with differing esterase components are
crossed, the hybrids produce both parental esterase types and
invariably a "hybrid esterase" running at an intermediate rate (Fig.
15-1). Furthermore when the hybrid between N and S was selfed, the
F_2 progeny segregated as follows:

Thirty-two contained N.
Fifty-five contained N, S, and hybrid esterase.
Thirty-six contained S.

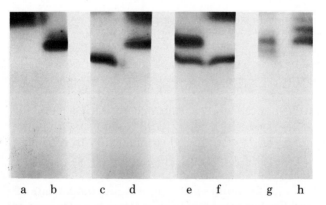

a   b   c   d   e   f   g   h

Fig. 15-1. Zymograms of endosperm extracts showing the various
esterase types; a, slow; b, normal; c, fast; d, mixture of normal and
slow; e, mixture of normal and fast; f, mixture of fast and slow; g,
N x F ♂ hybrid; h, N x S ♂ hybrid. (Schwartz, 1960).

Most of the work was carried out on endosperm tissue which is triploid, with one paternal and two maternal chromosome sets. In these cases a "maternal" effect was frequently detected; that is, the maternal bands were more concentrated than the paternal. The individual bands of the hybrids were generally less intense, indicating that the total amounts of esterases were the same.

In contrast to the endosperm, when esterases of the diploid plumule tissues of hybrid seedlings were examined, the "hybrid" esterase band was usually more intense than the parental bands.

In the words of the author, "There is no question but that the hybrid bands found in the heterozygotes represent new enzyme types not present in either parent." This work constitutes another example of allelic interaction in protein synthesis. It would be of particular interest to know whether the esterases are antigenic and, if so, whether the hybrid esterases behave as a new antigen.

The reference by Hall to hybrid substances reported from birds cited earlier relates to work summarized by Irwin (1951) and subsequent work in Irwin's laboratory. In extensive studies of serological relations in the Pearlneck dove (*Streptopelia chinensis*), the ring dove (*S. risoria*) and their hybrids, Irwin found in the hybrids all the antigens shared by the parental species and most of the characters specific to each parent. Moreover, all of the hybrids possessed a "hybrid substance" not found in either parent. Evidence was obtained that the species-specific antigens segregated in simple Mendelian fashion, indicating that each was under control of a single gene. In contrast, in backcross hybrids the "hybrid substance" behaved as though it were composed of three sub-units, each of which was linked to a separate Pearlneck chromosome. In examining Irwin's original paper (Irwin and Cumley, 1945) it is difficult to determine exactly how Irwin interprets the genetic basis of the hybrid substance. He states,

> The antigenic characters of the blood cells have been proposed to be more or less direct products or at least primary products of their causative genes. However, since the interactions of genes to produce certain antigens in some species hybrids and within a species is used to explain the experimental results it may be concluded that more than one step from gene to antigen is sometimes, if not always, involved."

The key point is that apparently all genetic elements which combine to produce the antigenic sub-units come from Pearlneck doves, but only in the hybrid is the specific hybrid-type antigen present. Irwin refers to "genes with duplicate effects in interaction located on several chromosomes of Pearlneck." It is evident that he considers it likely that the antigenic sub-units are similar.

McGibbon (1944) also found a specific hybrid-type antigen in inter-specific crosses of ducks. He was able to produce antibodies to the hybrid antigen in both parental species. Miller (1956) reported a hybrid-substance of the blood cells of inter-generic hybrids between the domestic pigeon (*Columba livia*) and the ring dove (*Streptopelia risoria*). *Columba livia* had already been determined as having several species-specific antigenic substances (A^1, B^1, C^1 and E^1) which segregated as Mendelian characters, and in backcross hybrids the hybrid substance was closely linked with the character C^1. A particularly interesting feature of this work is the fact that hybrid antisera, adsorbed with pooled cells of *S. risoria* and *C. livia* (parental species), still shows activity with a number of other related species and genera. (Specifically, "the cells of eight of thirty species of Columbidae and three other kinds of species hybrids were agglutinated strongly by the reagent for this hybrid-substance prepared from antiserum 493F4.") It is difficult to account satisfactorily for the presence of a "hybrid antigenic substance" which is closely linked with another species-specific antigenic substance (C^1 in this case). Miller appears to favor some mechanism involving allelic interaction wherein the C^1 allele and a "C-like" allele, contributed by the other species, cooperate to produce the hybrid antigen. At present no satisfactory experimental test of such an hypothesis has been contrived.

Scheinberg (1960) who studied serum antigens of pigeons, turtle doves, and ring doves corroborated the previous findings that specific antigens show Mendelian segregation. Furthermore, serum antigens of bison, cattle, and bison-cattle hybrids were tested in the conventional manner and also subjected to starch-gel electrophoresis. Their illustrations show that the starch-gel pattern of the hybrid possesses more distinguishable components than the sera of either parental species. The electrophoretic patterns of the hybrids suggested, according to the author, that the serum contained all of the proteins present in each parental serum as well as *additional components only present in the hybrid serum.* For turtle dove-ring dove hybrids whose proteins were also studied by electrophoresis it was concluded that the hybrid possessed all of the serum protein found in the sera of each of the parental species. Illustrations pertinent to this last point were not particularly good, however.

Bacharach *et al.* (1960) have also found a "hybrid" substance in hybrids of domestic fowl and pheasant. The hybrids apparently possessed most antigens specific to each species and "probably all those held in common."

To conclude references to zoological investigations of hybrids, Fox *et al.* (1961) studied the toad species, *Bufo fowleri, B. valliceps,* and their natural hybrids by means of starch-gel electrophoresis and found distinctive differences in the parental species (the actual parents of the hybrids were not available). The hybrids contained all components of both parents without any new "hybrid" substances detected. It is evident that two levels of biochemical categories are affected in hybridization. In serological studies one may be measuring substances in the general category of enzymes. Equally affected, however, as a result of hybridization will be the products of these enzymes, which may in many cases be small molecular weight basic metabolites, or secondary products. So, in hybrids, all types of substances may be affected in such a way as to increase over-all biochemical complexity. In backcrosses, furthermore, it would not be predicted that any biochemical system simpler than that of either parent would appear under normal circumstances. This generalization applies to secondary substances as well as proteins and is valid except when the original parents are complex heterozygotes. It may not necessarily be applied to secondary substances in considering an F_2 population.

Many biochemical studies other than those involving serology in nature have been conducted on hybrids. The specific substances investigated are non-protein and usually fall into the general category of secondary products of metabolism. The term secondary product refers to compounds not involved either in basic energy transfer processes or in the synthesis of metabolites essential to the life of the individual cell. Complex substances of a lipoid or carbohydrate nature, although they may possibly serve as energy sources, are considered as secondary products.

The idea of applying biochemical methods to hybrids is an old one. Perhaps the best way to illustrate this point is to use the exact words of one early investigator, Reichert, who, in 1919, published an 834 page treatise with the optimistic and visionary title of *A Biochemic Basis for the Study of Problems of Taxonomy, Heredity, Evolution, etc., with Especial Reference to the Starches and Tissues of Parent-stocks and Hybrid-stocks and the Starches and Hemoglobins of Varieties, Species, and Genera.* Most of this work by Reichert was botanical, although the author was a medical doctor. He used, primarily, starch characters in his hybrid studies. It is perhaps debatable whether the characters were truly biochemical. For example, some characters such as form, nature of hilum and lamellae, and size were morphological while others, such as iodine and aniline reactions, polariscopic and temperature reactions were more strictly biochemical.

Some of the statements from Reichert's work are truly exceptional for the period. For example, in connection with the appearance of "new" characters associated with hybrids Reichert states:

> Occasionally the hybrids of the first generation show properties which are entirely different from those of both parent species. This is particularly noticeable in the colors of the flowers. The most noteworthy example of this is the blue-blossomed hybrids of the white *Datura ferox* with the equally white species *D. laevis* and *D. straemonium bertolonia.* Instances of unexpected blossom-coloration are numerous in hybrids of species with colored flowers, in which the hybrids in no way show the coloring which one would expect from a mixture of the pigments of the parents. . . . In the crossing of races properties appear many times which do not resemble the parent form but other races of the same species. . . . The hybrid *Nicotiana rustica* × *N. paniculata* shows at times the flower coloration of *N. texana,* a foreign subspecies of *N. rustica.*

Later, in summary, referring specifically to his own work, Reichert states:

> From the records found in various parts of this work it will be noted that the starch of the hybrid exhibits, histologically, physically and physico-chemically not only both uniparental and biparental inheritance, but also individualities that are not observed in either parent; and that any given parental character that appears in the hybrid may be found in quality and quantity to be the same or practically the same as that of one parent or both parents, or of some degree of intermediateness or developed in excess or deficit of parental extremes.

And earlier, in his introduction, in connection with the excerpt immediately preceding the above he says:

> Neither the doctrine of intermediateness nor the doctrine of Mendel admits of the possibility of generating ideal organisms by crossing and selection, nor are they consistent with the development of parental characters in the hybrid beyond parental extremes; nor are they compatible with the appearance of new characters except upon the untenable assumption of such characters being latent in the parents.

It should be remembered that at the time the above was written, geneticists did not have extensive knowledge of quantitative inheritance or biochemical genetics. Such statements appear to be quite naive. When numerous genes cooperate in influencing a trait either quantitatively or qualitatively (multiple factors), when a complex series of alleles occurs, when complementary factors are involved or when a complex of other factors influences the ability of another factor to express itself phenotypically (as perhaps is the case in some penetrance effects), all of the phenomena cited above by Reichert will not only be possible, they will be inevitable. There is no reason either to expect the principles to apply only to intraspecific hybrids. Later in this section more will be said about the appearance of traits in hybrids not present in either parent. Such traits have been observed repeatedly, if sporadically, and, theoretically, inter-specific complementary genetic effects for both morphological and biochemical characters are anticipated.

Such complementary effects may not always represent the formation of a new biochemical component. For example, Bopp (1958) found that in reciprocal hybrids of *Streptocarpus wendlandii* × *S. vandeleum* flower color changed from blue-violet to red during development although the change did not occur in the parents. Bopp considered that the color change took place as the pigment, malvidin glucoside, was adsorbed onto a polysaccharide present in the hybrid. Since pH changes also affect anthocyanin coloration significantly, pH differences in cell sap of hybrids could, through modifying the visible flower color, suggest falsely the existence of a different pigment. There are known cases of single dominant genes affecting the pH of cell sap.

Earlier, it was noted that Birdsong *et al.* had suggested the possibility of complementary action in inter-specific crosses of canavanineless genera of legumes to produce a hybrid which could synthesize canavanine. In view of this it is interesting to see the full recognition of this type of phenomenon as well as other related ones as early as 1919 in the writings of Reichert.

A recent example of the appearance of a "new" substance in hybrids is that reported in *Collinsia* (Garber, 1958). Specific substances were noted in the amphidiploid, *C. concolor* × *C. sparsiflora*, which could not be detected in either parental species. The author pointed out that the different genetic background and modifier complex in the amphidiploid compared with either of the parental species permitted consideration of such a possibility. Rensch (1959) has discussed cases, involving hybrids of canaries and serins, goldfinches, linnets, and greenfinches wherein colors appeared which were absent from either parent. The colorations, however, were typical of a group of related species and are interpreted by Rensch as atavisms. Although some such phenomena are truly atavistic in that the parents have developed independently metabolic blocks at different points in a sequence of steps, it is also possible that phylogenetically "new" substances may appear in hybrids. The substance need not be previously unknown to be phylogenetically new in the sense implied above. In many cases, of course, the distinction between atavistic and non-atavistic hybrid characters will be difficult.

It is equally correct to expect hybrids to contain, frequently, constituents peculiar to one or the other parent and in fact to approximate the sum of the two parental complements. Vickery and Olson (1956), who examined the carotenoid and flavonoid pigments of a number of *Mimulus* species and their hybrids, produced data which indicate that the pigment complement of the hybrid, insofar as could be determined, was in each case the sum of the two parental complements. This was true in several different inter-specific crosses. No "hybrid" substances were reported, however. Henke (1960) found that hybrids of *Vitex* species contained the flavonoids of both parents, generally in larger quantity, though no new hybrid substances appeared.

A similar case in which the phenolic components of hybrids of apple × pear represented clearly the sum of the parental components is that of Williams (1955). Apple leaves contain the glucoside phloridzen as the principal phenolic constituent, along with some of the aglycone phloretin, a quercetin glycoside, and traces of chlorogenic acid and epicatechin. Pear leaves contain chlorogenic and isochlorogenic acids plus arbutin as the chief phenolics, with smaller amounts of catechin, epicatechin, flavonol glycosides, and hydroquinone, the aglycone of arbutin. Phloridzin is apparently quite specific for species of apple while arbutin is found in all pear species. Phloridzin is absent from pear species, and arbutin does not occur in apple species.

Among the hybrids the leaves contained phloridzin, arbutin, chlorogenic and isochlorogenic acids in large amounts together with lesser quantities of phloretin, epicatechin, and flavonol glycosides. None of the hybrids were without the typical phenolics of either parental species. According to the author,

> This apparently simple addition of the parental phenolic pattern in the hybrids contrasts with the dominant recessive relationships found with the anthocyanin coloring matter of flowers in intraspecific crosses.

No reference is cited for the final statement, but it is probably an oversimplification of the situation, since among various plants in which the inheritance of anthocyanins has been studied sometimes epistasis is apparent and sometimes several pigments, each governed by a single gene, may coexist. In any event the metabolism of one particular class of phenolics (namely, anthocyanins) is more directly interrelated than that of a series of classes of phenolics such as represented by the phenolic complements of apple and pear leaves, and the results reported are not at all surprising.

In general, hybrids tend to accumulate the compounds peculiar to both parents, but exceptions should be expected. For example, Kawatani and Asakina (1959) found that a hybrid of *Papaver orientale* and *P. somniferum* contained the alkaloids typical of both species except for oripavine, an alkaloid reportedly in *P. orientale*. A serious limitation of this study, however, is that the alkaloids of the actual parents were not examined but rather were assumed on the basis of previous reports. It is particularly important to establish that a certain compound is actually present in the parent (and consistently present in the species in question) when considering the failure of the substance to appear in the hybrid, for such instances, if authentic, may prove to be of special theoretical significance in connection with metabolic interrelationships.

There is no reason to expect that the pattern of inheritance of two biochemical characters must be similar. It is quite easy to imagine a character which becomes intermediate in the hybrid while yet another exceeds the parental extreme. Similarly, biochemical and morphological characters need show no relationship. In this connection Dillemann's (1953) discussion of the inheritance of cyanogenetic substances in natural hybrids of *Linaria vulgaris* and *L. striata* (a cyanogenetic species) is an oversimplification. Dillemann finds that the hybrid is intermediate in cyanogen content and points out that in morphological characters the hybrid is always intermediate. He then adds:

> If in interspecific crosses of *Linaria* intermediate characters are the rule in the hybrids, then it indicates that the factors which govern the characters are not dominant. Under such conditions, it is altogether normal that the same would be true for the factor of cyanogenesis.

Why one would expect the inheritance of a biochemical character to be intermediate just because most morphological characters were intermediate in the hybrid is not clear. Sometimes biochemical components are reduced in the hybrids, and sometimes they are present in increased amounts. However, there is no likelihood that any dependency upon the manner of inheritance of morphological characters exists in such cases.

Tsitsin and Lubimova (1959) described the appearance of some new "hybrid" characters in inter-generic hybrids of *Triticum* and *Agropyron*. These characters were indicated as multipistillate florets which produced double and triple kernals and cases of stamens becoming transformed into pistils. The authors come to a rather surprising conclusion from these observations:

In addition to valuable new agronomic characters, some plants of these hybrids exhibit new morphological characters not found in either of the parents. These arise as mutations and come to be inherited later. Remote hybridization acts as a kind of stimulus for the mutation process.

In some ways the results are suggestive of the classical example of cytoplasmic inheritance in *Streptocarpus* (Oehlkers, 1938). In this genus certain inter-specific hybrids have staminodia transformed into fertile carpels. While increased mutation rate represents one possible explanation of the results, it is probable that some other form of genome interaction, not necessarily involving mutation, is responsible.

Some interesting results have been reported from different sources indicating the dominance of more complex compounds over simpler ones within a general class. Related to this situation is the observation, also from several investigators working with different materials, that when two species differ in the specific representative of a biochemical class present, their hybrid contains both substances. Neither result is incompatible with generally accepted principles of biochemical genetics, nor are they mutually exclusive. At the generic level Delaveau (1961) reported that in a hybrid between *Raphanus* and *Brassica* species-specific mustard oils occurred together.

One of the most important studies of biochemical components of natural hybrids is that of Mirov (1956) who studied natural hybrids of *Pinus contorta* (lodgepole pine) and *Pinus banksiana* (jack pine). Trees intermediate between lodgepole and jack pine were discovered over part of central Alberta, representing an area roughly 150 by 200 miles. The ranges of the two species overlap in this region. Artificial hybrids have been produced (Righter and Stockwell, 1949), and these are said to be morphologically intermediate.

The significant biochemical comparisons involved the terpenoid contents of the two species and their hybrids. Lodgepole pine turpentine consists almost entirely of β-phellandrene and is levorotatory.

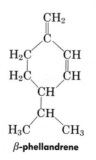

β-phellandrene

Jack pine contains a mixture of dextro- and levo-pinene with an admixture of levo-β-pinene.

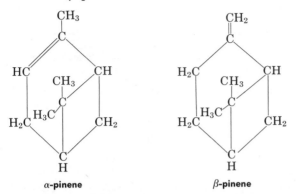

α-pinene   β-pinene

Optical rotation varies somewhat, apparently because of varying proportions of the three compounds. Although some jack pine samples are levorotatory, those from Alberta were all dextrorotatory.

Analysis of the turpentine from an artificial F_1 hybrid from California indicated 75 to 78 per cent pinenes and 20 to 22 per cent phellandrene. The conclusion, then, was that the turpentine of the hybrid was of a mixed nature. From the natural hybrid swarm Mirov collected turpentine from seventy-three individuals, including trees of an intermediate character, and those typical of the parental species. Additional samples of lodgepole and jack pine were included, presumably from regions more remote from the hybrid swarm. Analyses of the turpentine from individual trees showed extensive variation.

Estimation of the per cent of phellandrene in hybrids ranged from about 13 per cent in the artificial hybrid (data from one figure of the text give a figure of 20 to 22 per cent) to slightly above 40 per cent among certain individuals of the natural hybrid groups. Pure lodgepole gave 73 per cent phellandrene and only one morphological "hybrid" gave little or no phellandrene. A more comprehensive presentation of the biochemical and morphological data is given in the table below, adapted from Mirov (1956).

Morphological Character	Chemical Character of the Oil		
	Jack Pine	Intermediate	Lodgepole Pine
Jack pine	21	0	0
Intermediate	3	14	0
Lodgepole pine	3	17	15

It is obvious from these data that the chemical composition of turpentines from the area of overlap did not always match the morphological features of the trees from which they were derived.

An important point stressed by Mirov is what he refers to as "dominance" of the complex terpenes over the simpler phellandrene type. This does not mean strictly Mendelian dominance, merely that *more* of the pinenes appears than does phellandrene—in the artificial hybrid a 3:1 excess. In practically all of the natural hybrids there was 20 to 40 per cent phellandrene. In another example cited by Mirov, dominance of complex terpenes is implied in *Mentha* inter-specific hybrids (from Sievers, *et al.* 1945). The specific instance which Mirov has in mind must be the cross *Mentha arvensis* × *M. aquatica* wherein hybrids contained 57.6 and 60.8 per cent menthol while the *M. arvensis* parent yields 65.9 per cent menthol. (Menthol is a saturated monohydroxy derivative of phellandrene.) Yet, in the cross, *M. arvensis* × *M. spicata,* the menthol content of four plants was respectively 5.3, 7.3, 9.8, and 40.5 per cent. This seems contradictory to the point made by Mirov.

An additional interesting feature of Sievers' work was that in tetraploids of spearmint as well as an allopolyploid of *M. arvensis* × *M. spicata* the oil content was very low. A recent paper dealing with chemical changes associated with induced polyploidy (Hanson *et al.,* 1959) notes that tannin content of autotetraploids of *Lespedeza* was higher than the diploid, and allotetroploids had a higher tannin content than either parental species. Rowson (1958) has shown that polyploids in the genera *Atropa, Datura,* and *Hyoscyamus* produce more total alkaloids than their diploid counterparts, and Lukovnikova (1961) reported that polyploid potatoes accumulated larger quantities of several classes of components than did normal diploids. A further investigation of the biochemistry of polyploids is needed before any generalizations are permitted.

A particularly interesting paper on biochemical components of hybrids is that of Pryor and Bryant (1958). These investigators studied oil characters in certain *Eucalyptus* species and their hybrids. Several of the phenomena discussed previously in this section are encountered in the *Eucalyptus* work. The major segment of the study involved a detailed examination of hybrids of *Eucalyptus cinerea* × *E. macarthuri.* These plants were derived from seeds collected from two natural hybrids; thus the group represented an F_2 generation (it is not clear whether pollination was controlled or whether other trees of the parental types were nearby, but this does not affect the results of the study). The hybrids were about six years old at the time of the analyses.

Morphological differences and oil-character differences of a rather clear-cut nature exist among the two species (see chart below).

Not much specific data on the morphological character of the hybrids was available, since most tables and figures which were included related to oil characters. However, the data presented show that leaf shape among hybrids varied from one parental type to the other with most individuals falling in between. According to the authors, morphological characters show marked segregation and recombination, and hybrid individuals appeared which resembled either parent together with a series of intermediates between them.

	E. cinerea	E. macarthuri
Juvenile leaves	orbicular sessile glaucous	lanceolate sessile green
Mature leaves	sessile opposite glaucous	petiolate alternate green
Oil yield	high	low
Oil constituents	high cineole (40%)	high geranyl acetate (50%)

INHERITANCE OF OIL CHARACTERS

IN HYBRIDS OF *Eucalyptus macarthuri* $\times$ *E. cinerea:*

Oil yield, as already observed, is high in *E. cinerea* and low in *E. macarthuri*. In the hybrids, oil yield was in every case low, entirely within the range of *E. macarthuri*.

Qualitatively, the oils in the two species differ as follows (only the prominent differences are included). *E. macarthuri* produces large amounts of geranyl acetate but no cineole while *E. cinerea* produces large amounts of cineole and no geranyl acetate. Both species produce some eudesmene and sesquiterpene, and *E. macarthuri* produces significantly more eudesmol than does *E. cinerea*. Since cineole and geranyl acetate involve strict reciprocal presence-absence, these substances are studied most profitably in the hybrids.

The hybrids showed, unequivocally, recombination of the oil characters of the parents by virtue of the presence of geranyl acetate and cineole together in six cases. From Table 15-1, it appears as though, among the hybrids, these two oils were generally in lesser amounts than was typical of the respective parents. This is the case even though both do not occur together in one plant, so it is not directly the result of the presence of two oils rather than one. In contrast, certain other constituents found in lesser amounts than geranyl acetate and cineole in both parental species (for example, eudesmine, sesquiterpene, and an unidentified fluorescent compound) were more abundant in a large number of the hybrids. Another example of this sort is reported by Schwarze (1959), work to be discussed later.

Eudesmol, found in greater amount in *E. macarthuri,* is present in intermediate quantity in most of the hybrids.

The rather considerable variation observed among the hybrids is consistent with their F_2 origin. However, the fact that no hybrids were detected with oil characteristics even close to those of either parent suggests an intricate genetic basis governing both the quantitative and qualitative aspects of oil character. That in an F_2 population oil yield was not significantly above that of the low yield parent is also surprising. Since F_2 leaf shape is clustered near that of *E. cinerea* this fact tends to reduce the likelihood that the low yield typical of the F_2 results from a favoring by selection of the *E. macarthuri* genome or back crossing to *E. macarthuri.* In F_1 progeny of a cross between *E. pauciflora* and *E. dives* and also hybrids of *E. pauciflora* and *E. robertsonii* oil yield was clearly intermediate though covering a large range among the different individuals. In yet another inter-specific cross, this time between *E. maidenii* and *E. rubida,* oil yield in the hybrids was entirely within the range of the high-yield parent (*E. maidenii*). Obviously no generalizations concerning the inheritance of yield are permitted from these data.

Recombination between biochemical characters and morphological characters was also in evidence. For example, two hybrids with a leaf shape approaching *E. cinerea* were high in geranyl acetate content. According to the authors the data suggest "rather free recombination" between leaf shape and geranyl acetate content.

Additional significant findings in this research are the facts that in no case in a hybrid were both geranyl acetate and cineole absent, and one hybrid was notable in having an oil content of specific gravity and high levo-rotation, suggesting as a possibility the presence of substantial l-pinene. Aside from this observation, for which there is no additional evidence, there was no indication of the occurrence of compounds in the hybrids not present in either parent. Yet, as the authors maintain, the amounts of several components in the hybrids exceed substantially the amounts of those components in either parent (Table 15-1).

Table 15-1. Oil constituents (except Cymene and Pinenes) of *cinerea, macarthuri* and hybrids (Pryor & Bryant, 1958).

	No.	Geranyl Acetate.	Geraniol.	Cineole.	Eudesmol.	Eudesmene.	Sesquiterpene.	Fluorescent Component.
E. macarthuri.	52	× × × ×	×	−	× × ×	×	×	× × ×
	53	× × × ×	×	−	× × ×	×	×	× × ×
	54	× × × ×	×	−	× × ×	×	×	×
	55	× × × ×	×	−	× × ×	×	×	× × ×
	56	× × × ×	×	−	× × ×	×	×	× ×
	58	× × × ×	×	−	× × ×	×	×	×
	59	× × × ×	×	−	× × ×	×	×	× ×
	61	× × × ×	×	−	× × ×	×	×	× ×
	63	× × × ×	×	−	× × ×	×	×	−
	64	× × × ×	×	−	× × ×	×	×	× ×
	65	× × × ×	×	−	× × ×	×	×	−
	67	× × × ×	×	−	× × ×	×	×	×
	68	× × × ×	×	−	× × ×	×	×	×
	70	× × × ×	×	−	× × ×	×	×	$\underline{\times}$
	71	× × × ×	×	−	× × ×	×	×	× ×
	74	× × × ×	×	−	× × ×	×	×	−
	77	× × × ×	×	−	× × ×	×	×	−
	79	× × × ×	×	−	× × ×	× ×	×	−
	80	× × × ×	×	−	× × ×	×	×	−
	81	× × × ×	×	−	× × ×	×	×	−
E. cinerea.	40	−	×	× × × ×	×	−	−	−
	41	−	$\underline{\times}$	× × × ×	−	$\underline{\times}$	× ×	×
	42	−	$\underline{\times}$	× × × ×	−	$\underline{\times}$	× ×	×
	43	−	−	× × × ×	−	$\underline{\times}$	× ×	−
	45	−	−	× × × ×	−	$\underline{\times}$	× ×	−
	46	−	−	× × × ×	−	$\underline{\times}$	× ×	× ×
	47	−	−	× × × ×	−	$\underline{\times}$	× ×	−
	48	−	$\underline{\times}$	× × × ×	−	$\underline{\times}$	×	−
	49	−	−	× × × ×	−	$\underline{\times}$	×	−
	51	−	−	× × × ×	×	$\underline{\times}$	× ×	×
	85	−	−	× × × ×	−	$\underline{\times}$	× ×	−
	88	−	−	× × × ×	−	$\underline{\times}$	× ×	−
	100	−	−	× × × ×	×	$\underline{\times}$	×	$\underline{\times}$
	102	−	−	× × × ×	×	$\underline{\times}$	×	$\underline{\times}$
	104	−	×	× × × ×	$\underline{\times}$	$\underline{\times}$	×	−
	111	−	×	× × × ×	−	$\underline{\times}$	×	−
	112	−	×	× × × ×	$\underline{\times}$	$\underline{\times}$	×	×
	113	−	−	× × × ×	$\underline{\times}$	$\underline{\times}$	× ×	−
	114	−	−	× × × ×	×	$\underline{\times}$	× ×	× × ×
	?	−	×	× × × ×	×	$\underline{\times}$	×	×

Table 15-1. (*Continued*)

	No.	Geranyl Acetate.	Geraniol.	Cineole.	Eudesmol.	Eudesmene.	Sesquiterpene.	Fluorescent Component.
	1	×	–	–	×	×××	×××	×××
	3	–	–	×	×	×××	××	×××
	4	×	–	–	×	×××	××	×××
	5	××	×	–	××	××	××	×××
	8	–	×	×	$\underline{\times}$	×××	×××	×××
	11	–	×	×	$\underline{\times}$	×××	×××	×××
	12	–	–	××	$\underline{\times}$	×××	×××	×××
	13	–	×	×××	××	××	××	×××
	14	××	–	××	××	××	××	–
	15	–	×	×××	×	××	××	×××
	16	××	–	–	××	××	××	×××
	17	××	×	×	××	××	××	×××
	18	–	×	×	×	×××	××	×××
Hybrids.	21	–	××	×	×	×××	××	×××
	22	–	–	××	×	×	×××	–
	23	×××	××	–	×××	××	–	×××
	24	×	×	×××	×	××	×××	××
	25	NOT RECORDED				×××	×××	×××
	26	×	××	×××	××	×××	××	××
	27	×	×	×××	××	×××	×××	××
	29	–	$\underline{\times}$	××	×	×××	×××	××
	32	–	$\underline{\times}$	×××	×	××	×××	××
	33	×××	××	××	×	×	××	×××
	34	××	××	–	×××	×	×	××
	35	–	××	××	×	××	×××	××
	36	–	×	××	××	×××	×××	×××
	38	–	–	××××	××	××	××	××

Finally, in another cross involving the species *E. maidenii* and *E. rubida* there is an example of dominance for the absence of a component. *E. rubida* contains a fluorescent substance which is absent from *E. maidenii* and from all the F_1 hybrids (five in number).

Bannister *et al.* (1959) also reported a study of hybrids which included both morphological and chemical characters. These investigators concentrated on certain of the essential oils, such as α-pinene and β-pinene. The species involved were *Pinus attenuata, P. radiata,* and some verified and putative hybrids thereof. The method of assaying the relative content of α- and β-pinene of the oleoresin was by use of gas chromatography. This technique ought to become increasingly useful in similar studies since its advantages are basically those of paper chromatography. Thus gas chromatographic "fingerprints" of individual plants may prove to be feasible even when the available material is in small amounts.

Specimens of *P. attenuata* contained much α-pinene but practically no β-pinene. *P. radiata* had both α- and β-pinene with the latter in excess. In both artificial and putative hybrids, both pinenes were present, with α-pinene in excess. Thus the oil character of the hybrids was essentially intermediate. There was no apparent build up of minor constituents among the hybrids. Morphological characters used as criteria were not specified in detail, but the individuals with hybrid oil character were said to be morphologically intermediate.

An interesting biochemical study of *Phaseolus* hybrids has been reported by Schwarze (1960). He had previously described certain dwarfed hybrids, which appeared together with nearly normal F_1 hybrids, of *Phaseolus vulgaris* $\times$ *P. coccineus*. These dwarfed hybrids contained less chlorophyll, less protein, more peroxidase and polyphenoloxidase, less of flavonoid and simple phenylpropane derivatives, less lignification, and increased breakdown of IAA and tryptophan.

Examination of the leaf flavonoids of the two species of *Phaseolus* revealed four flavonoids in *P. vulgaris* and four different flavonoids in *P. coccineus*. The hybrids, in contrast, exhibited spots on the chromatograms equivalent to all eight parental flavonoids plus four additional spots. Schwarze stated that actually the four hybrid flavonoids did occur in minute but perceptible quantities in the *P. coccineus* parent. Young leaves were richer in flavonoids than were older leaves. The "disturbed" hybrids showed only quantitative differences (that is, lesser quantities than normal hybrids). Schwarze considered that in order for a hybrid substance to appear it must be latent or weakly expressed in one or both parents. As indicated several times in the foregoing chapters, this is not a valid assumption.

Schwarze attributed increased flavonoid synthesis to interactions, generally deleterious in effect, between *P. vulgaris* cytoplasm (female parent) and *P. coccineus* nuclear genes. It is true that generally unfavorable conditions bring about increased flavonoid synthesis. Alston (1960) has discussed this point in connection with anthocyanin pigments. One important point which seems to bear on such matters is that stress, broadly defined, must be expected to overcome normal homeostatic mechanisms, resulting in the accumulation of "useless" products—in the particular condition—via side reactions if the enzyme system is available. The stress may be extrinsic (that is, environmental) or intrinsic (that is, genetic or cytoplasmic). Schwarze also supports this hypothesis. If such a result generally occurs, one might expect the accumulation of detectable amounts of substances in hybrids which would not be found in either parent in addition to the products derived from new gene combinations.

Schwarze says in his discussion (freely translated):

> Outside of economy of metabolites and full regulation of them there are no principles of evolutionary selection. Favorable metabolic mutants thus have positive selective value, but also mutants with metabolic significance which represent neither positive or negative survival value are preserved. Metabolic economy must control their quantities. Possibly, in *Phaseolus* hybrids, in which *P. vulgaris* cytoplasm is under the influence of strange genes, formation of some useless substances occurs.

It is interesting that in the Pryor and Bryant study of *Eucalyptus* hybrids (discussed earlier), although total oil yield was generally low in the hybrids, the quantities of the minor components was, among the hybrids, very greatly increased in almost every case over that of either parent.

A biochemical study of natural hybridization in the genus *Baptisia* (Leguminosae) was initiated recently (Alston and Turner, 1959; Turner and Alston, 1959), and rather extensive biochemical documentation of hybridization in this genus has now been acquired (Alston *et al.*, 1962; Alston and Turner, 1962b; Alston and Turner, 1963). The first report dealt primarily with *Baptisia leucophaea, B. sphaerocarpa* and their assumed hybrids. Extensive hybridization between these morphologically quite different species occurs, especially near the Texas Gulf coast. By means of paper chromatography a total of six species-specific chemical components (three for each species) were detected in flower extracts. Then, chromatographic analyses of individual hybrid-type plants disclosed recombination or in some cases simple addition of the species-specific components. The same plants were adjudged hybrids or hybrid derivatives on the basis of morphological characters. The chromatographic evidence of hybridization was considered to be indisputable. Since morphology alone suggested, definitively, hybridization between the two species concerned, the biochemical evidence did not provide any further insight into that situation. However, the work firmly established the practicality of a biochemical approach to analyses of more complex hybrid situations. As will be disclosed below, it also paved the way for entirely new methods of analysis of population dynamics and gene flow in naturally hybridizing populations.

Numerous species of *Baptisia* are native to eastern North America. Inter-specific hybridization is common in the genus, and the morphological differences between species which hybridize are exceptional (Fig. 15-2, a-h). In Texas, for example, complex hybridization involving four species occurs. One population including all four species and all six of the possible different hybrid types has been located, and in various other locations hybrids between any two of the four species occur. Of the *Baptisia* species illustrated in Fig. 15-2 the following natural hybrid combinations have been definitely established through combined chromatographic and morphological analyses: a × b, a × c, a × eL, b × c, b × eL, c × eL, e × g, e × f, f × g, f × h, and g × h.

Alston and Turner (1962) executed a combined chromatographic and morphological analysis of a complicated population, near Beaumont, Texas, composed of *Baptisia leucophaea, B. sphaerocarpa, B. leucantha,* and several different types of "hybrids." Hybrids of *B. sphaerocarpa × B. leucantha* were previously reported from the same area (Larisey, 1940), but no hybrids of *B. leucophaea × B. leucantha* were known.

In the population described above the presence of three species complicated the situation sufficiently to make the population difficult to study effectively by even a painstaking morphological examination. Putative hybrids of *B. leucophaea × B. leucantha* were rare and highly conjectural, and the question was raised as to whether there was any gene exchange between the two species, perhaps with *B. sphaerocarpa* acting as a bridge for such gene exchange, since its flowering period is intermediate. Related questions of preferential hybridization, degree of fertility of particular F_1 types, backcrossing patterns, and so on, are all relevant to an understanding of the evolutionary past and future of the population, but the question raised above cannot be answered precisely in this instance through morphology (and not at all by chromosomal studies since $n = 9$ in all species concerned, and meiosis in the putative hybrids appears to be normal).

Alston and Turner selected about fifty plants, mostly hybrid types taken from a population which consisted of the three parental species about equally represented, and about 5 per cent hybrids or their derivatives. A morphological tri-hybrid index utilizing twenty characters was designed, based on examination of individuals from pure populations of each of the three species. As illustrated in Table 15-2 each plant keys out to a percentage representation of each of the three species. For example, a hybrid of A × B backcrossed to C would key out, presumably, to about 25 per cent A: 25 per cent B: 50 per cent C. It is obvious from the table that complex hybridization involving all three species in interaction was inferred from application of the morphological criteria.

Chromatographic evidence was acquired as follows. After a

Fig. 15-2. (a) *Baptisia leucophaea;* (b) *B. sphaerocarpa;* (c) *B. nuttalliana;* (d) ultra-violet photograph of leaf extract from a hybrid between *B. nuttalliana* and *B. leucantha* chromatographed in two-dimensions.

lengthy study of numerous individuals of the three species concerned, methods of two-dimensional chromatography were developed which allowed the detection (in ultra-violet light and after spraying with a general phenol-detecting reagent) of numerous compounds from leaf extracts. These compounds fell into one of four classes:

(1) substances common to two or even all three species
(2) substances which are species-specific and highly reliable because of their distinctiveness and consistent presence
(3) species-specific substances not constant for the species

Fig. 15-2 (cont.) Most spots are species-specific; (e) *B. pendula* (practically indistinguishable from *B. leucantha*); (f) *B. lanceolata;* (g) *B. perfoliata;* (h) *B. alba.*

(In text, p. 317, references to the types of interspecific hybrids involving *B. leucantha* are symbolized as "eL").

> (these are often in low concentrations and may be below
> the threshold of detection in some instances)
> (4) hybrid-specific substances

A few substances of type 4 were regularly present in hybrid types but not in the parental types. It was not possible in the original work to determine whether the "hybrid substances" were *de novo* products of the hybrid's gene combinations or accumulations of substances normally produced in small amounts in one or both parents (compare Schwarze, p. 315). Subsequently, it has been found that all four of the so-called "hybrid substances" are actually typically produced by

Table 15-2. Percentage representation of each of three species in individual plants of tri-hybrid population as indicated from morphological hybrid index, (Alston and Turner, 1962).

Plant No.	% sphaero.	% leuco.	% leu.	Plant No.	% sphaero.	% leuco.	% leu.
1	62	31	7	27	35	46	19
2	37	50	13	28	43	55	2
3	100	—	—	29	18	68	14
4	31	47	22	30	—	—	100
5	40	39	21	31	39	36	25
6	—	100	—	32	34	50	16
7	10	81	9	33	50	18	32
8	90	9	1	34	37	40	23
9	42	36	22	35	48	37	15
10	35	—	65	36	24	50	26
11	54	—	46	37	43	32	25
12	51	39	10	38	33	42	25
13	—	—	100	39	27	46	27
14	39	4	57	40	23	37	41
15	33	40	27	41	22	37	41
16	32	42	26	42	25	52	23
17	100	—	—	45	69	6	25
18	50	33	17	46	43	5	52
19	88	1	11	47	36	6	58
20	37	38	25	48	—	—	100
21	5	86	9	50	—	80	20
22	25	55	20	51	—	80	20
23	38	52	10	52	—	100	—
25	12	77	11	53	98	1	1
26	49	29	22				

B. sphaerocarpa but only in the flowers. In hybrids of *B. sphaerocarpa* × *B. leucantha* these four substances appear in unreduced amounts in leaves as well as flowers. Apparently the regulatory mechanisms which restrict the distribution of these substances in the pure species are ineffective in the hybrid. This situation does not occur in other hybrids involving *B. sphaerocarpa,* and the fact that it occurs in the *B. sphaerocarpa* × *B. leucantha* hybrid indicates that possibly a greater genome difference exists between those two species (Alston and Simmons, 1962).

A surprisingly large number of useful species-specific compounds were discovered, especially in combinations involving *B. leucantha.* For example, at least twenty reliable constituents distinguish *B. leucantha* and *B. sphaerocarpa.*

Since flower extracts yielded somewhat different two-dimensional chromatographic patterns than did the leaf extracts which were used in the earlier study, some additional species-specific compounds are now available. Other classes of compounds, detectable by other methods, are currently being investigated (for example, the anthocyanins of lower stems differ in *Baptisia* species). Figure 15-3 illustrates in comparative fashion the chromatographic patterns upon which an analysis of the "tri-hybrid" population was based. Chromatograms of individual representative hybrid types are also illustrated.

When such a large pool of useful compounds is available, it is possible to extend an analysis of hybridization to include the degree and direction of backcrossing. As a working hypothesis one may assume that a hybrid A × B contains approximately the sum of the constituents of A and B, and a backcross to B should have the compounds of B and approximately half of those of A. In a real situation the exact composition of A × B cannot be predicted because of lack of knowledge of the mode of inheritance of the specific compounds. Neither can the chemical make-up of backcross types be predicted, and in this latter situation, segregation of genetic factors in the hybrid parent provides for more individual variation among backcross types than in the hybrids themselves. However, such information can be acquired empirically by analysis of the hybrids of a large population or many populations.

To illustrate, in Fig. 15-4 data from the plants of the tri-hybrid group, ten plants of each species from pure populations plus seventeen additional *B. leucantha* × *B. sphaerocarpa* hybrids are plotted. Points in this graph for hybrids or derivations include both species-specific compounds and those compounds shared in common by the two species concerned. This type of plot makes it difficult to draw conclusions from the *B. leucophaea* × *B. sphaerocarpa* hybrids because these two species share a rather large number of compounds. In contrast, *B. leucantha* × *B. sphaerocarpa* hybrids contain mostly species-specific compounds. The hybrid types in both situations cluster at an angle near 45°, indicating, in the case of *B. leucantha* × *B. sphaerocarpa* hybrids that most of these plants are truly F_1 hybrids. Two plants, 47 and 11 (note arrows), fall sufficiently outside the area of greatest concentration to suggest that these plants may be hybrids of *B. leucantha* × *B. sphaerocarpa* backcrossed to *B. leucantha*. The morphological hybrid index suggests that they are F_1 hybrids. One of the extra *B. leucantha* × *B. sphaerocarpa* hybrids, M-1, lacks a number of major *B. leucantha* spots and may possibly be a backcross of an F_1 hybrid to *B. sphaerocarpa*.

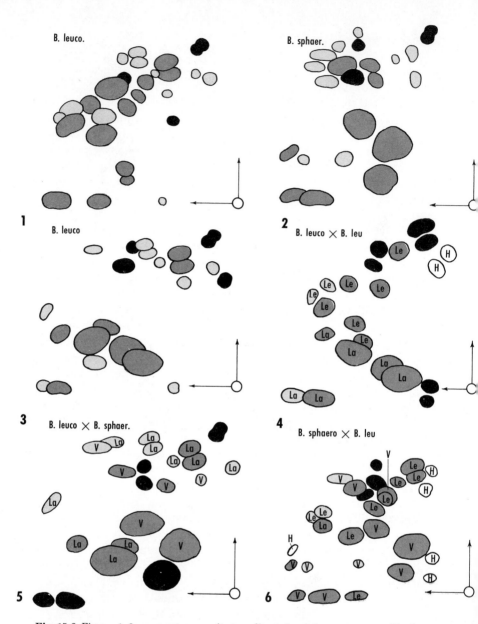

Fig. 15-3. Figures 1–3 represent composite two-dimensional chromatograms of leaf extracts of *Baptisia leucantha* (upper left), *B. sphaerocarpa* (upper right), and *B. leucophaea* (middle left). Figures 4–6 represent individual hybrids: *B. leucophaea* X *B. leucantha* (middle right); *B. leucophaea* X *B. sphaerocarpa* (lower left); *B. leucantha* X *B. sphaerocarpa* (lower right).

Black spots represent compounds of doubtful value in the cases indicated (perhaps characteristic of both parental species of a particular hybrid); dotted spots represent species-specific but minor components which are useful when present; grey (or finely stippled) spots represent major spots of greatest significance. La = *B. leucophaea* spots; Le = *B. leucantha* spots; V = *B. sphaerocarpa* spots and H = hybrid-specific spots.

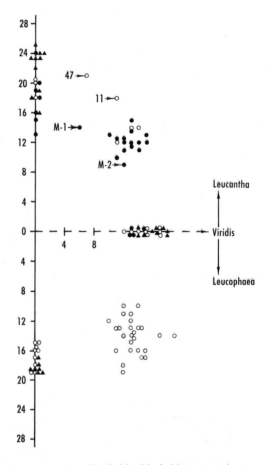

Fig. 15-4. A three-way plot of individual hybrid types and pure species. Open circles indicate plants from tri-hybrid population, closed triangles indicate miscellaneous supplementary plants from pure populations, and closed circles indicate the additional (supplementary) *Baptisia leucantha* X *B. sphaerocarpa* hybrids. Points along the X-axis represent the number of compounds recognized of *B. sphaerocarpa;* points along the Y-axis represent (above) the number of compounds recognized of *B. leucantha* and (below) the number of compounds recognized of *B. leucophaea.* Hybrids fall at some angle between the X and Y axes.

If a large population of *B. leucantha* X *B. sphaerocarpa* is analyzed by these methods the F_1's will be indicated by a primary cluster of points, backcrosses will be indicated by secondary and more diffuse clusters. The morphological discontinuity between the hybrids and pure species plus the small proportion (5 per cent) of total hybrids suggests that simple hybridization predominates in the population. The chromatographic data thus leads to conclusions quite different than expected from the previously analyzed exomorphic features. The most important difference was the fact that the biochemical data did not suggest any mixing of *B. leucophaea* and *B. leucantha* genomes.

It should be noted that the species under consideration appear to be mostly cross-fertilized, but if perchance the F_1 hybrids are self-fertile, the major concentration of points on the plot would be more diffuse, and perhaps no secondary concentrations would be noted. It is obvious that the relative sizes of the various concentrations of points provide a quantitative index of hybridization patterns. At the risk of over-extending the hypothetical possibilities of a relatively untested system, it is nevertheless theoretically valid that such a system could provide insight into the mode of inheritance of the compounds under consideration, and also, if individuals around the periphery of an area of hybridization were examined, biochemical evidence of introgression.

Generalizations which can be stated with assurance concerning *Baptisia* hybrids so far examined are the following:

(1) There is a tendency for some reduction in the amounts of many compounds present in the hybrids so that often some minor components tend to drop out.

(2) Although the hybrid tends to inherit the parental compounds additively, there are often some major spots missing.

(3) Some substances are present which, on the basis of the facts available, must be regarded as organ-specific in the hybrid only.

Substances of group 3, above, are not sporadic and capricious among the hybrids but are regularly observed.

The case of hybridization between *B. leucophaea* and *B. leucantha* is quite interesting. As noted above, no evidence of gene exchange between the two species in the tri-hybrid population was obtained, at least on the basis of the biochemical criteria. Mixed populations of *B. leucophaea* and *B. leucantha* have been examined without detection of any obvious F_1 plants, although introgression is suggested by the morphology of some of the individual plants. However, on the basis of biochemical evidence and the absence of any really intermediate morphological type, it is doubtful that the suggested introgression is real. Several unequivocal hybrids, probably F_1 between *B. leucophaea* and *B. leucantha* have now been discovered and validated chromatographically (Fig. 15-3), but it is evident that extensive hybridization between *B. leucophaea* and *B. leucantha* does not occur. However, since the peak flowering times of these two species are several weeks apart in areas where the species occur together, this time factor may account for their reproductive isolation.

Hybrids involving *Baptisia nuttalliana* and all three other species have now been discovered. *B. nuttalliana* hybridizes extensively with *B. leucophaea* in the area around Huntsville, Texas, and at other sites in Texas and Louisiana. These hybrid swarms are readily recognized, and in this case it is the biochemical corroboration which is more difficult to obtain. Of those substances available at this time *B. nuttalliana* contains a number of compounds in common with *B. leucophaea* and/or *B. sphaerocarpa*. In both types of hybrids, therefore, while *B. nuttalliana* chemical components can be documented readily, fewer species-specific contributions from the other partner are available.

Large populations of *B. sphaerocarpa* and *B. nuttalliana* have not been found together thus far, although they probably occur. Consequently, hybrids involving these two species are found in situations wherein one species (often *B. sphaerocarpa*) seems to be introduced, as along a roadside in the range of the other. Several such populations have been located, always represented by a very few plants of, usually, *B. sphaerocarpa*, some obvious hybrids, and more numerous, usually, *B. nuttalliana*. On this basis, it appears that these two species hybridize freely when they occur together. It is interesting and suggestive that the seed pods of *B. sphaerocarpa* are hard, spherical, and just about the size suited to becoming wedged into the tire grooves of vehicles.

A few definite hybrids between *B. nuttalliana* and *B. leucantha* are known; the hybrid was suspected on morphological grounds and definitely established by chromatography (Fig. 15-2d).

In the southeastern United States other complex situations involving hybridization of several species of *Baptisia* occur. In some instances chromatographic evidence is essential to establish the hybrid nature of a particular specimen. For example, two definite hybrids have been found in a population of *Baptisia lanceolata, B. alba* and *B. pendula*. The last two species are white flowered and somewhat similar morphologically, but they are chromatographically distinct. The hybrids, which involve *B. lanceolata* plus one or the other of the white flowered species, are morphologically similar. Chromatograms establish certainly the fact that one hybrid is *B. lanceolata* × *B. alba;* the other is *B. lanceolata* × *B. pendula*. (Alston et al., 1962).

Baptisia alba also hybridizes with *B. perfoliata, B. tinctoria* (Duncan, 1962) and probably certain white flowered species. Despite the striking differences between *B. alba* (Fig. 15-2h) and *B. lanceolata*

(Fig. 15-2f), the hybrids between either of these species and *B. perfoliata* (Fig. 15-2g) are difficult to distinguish when not in flower. Since these three species may be found together and hybridization between them also occurs, chromatographic evidence is not only useful but in some instances essential to the clarification of a given hybrid type or the structure of a population.

The number of species-specific compounds which may be utilized both in the study of natural hybridization in *Baptisia* and in establishing species affinities is increasing. Brehm (1962) has carried out an extensive study of variation in several categories of substances in *Baptisia leucophaea*, in different organs, at different developmental stages, in individuals of a single population, and in various populations throughout its range. Of the compounds investigated, the miscellaneous substances of leaves and flowers demonstrable in ultraviolet light, ammonia vapor, and by use of general phenol-detecting reagents are by far the most useful. The variation in the lupine-type alkaloids from plant to plant renders these compounds of relatively little use in population analyses. Surprisingly, the free amino acid patterns of seeds, stems, leaves, and flowers are not only markedly similar, but furthermore the patterns of the different species examined so far are notable for their similarities rather than differences. Thus, the free amino acids are of little use in population studies, but for unexpected reasons, since there was occasion to expect the patterns to vary rather greatly within a species (Chapter 6).

In summary we believe that biochemical comparisons have provided us with new and informative data and offer considerable promise in studies of natural hybridization and problems related thereto including perhaps a new method of documenting introgressive and transgressive hybridization. It is possible that the genus *Baptisia* is particularly well suited to such an approach and that its repository of species-specific compounds is not representative of hybridizing species in general. Even in *Baptisia* some hybrids cannot be resolved by chromatography. Although we have not discussed infra-specific chemical variation in *Baptisia*, preliminary studies indicate that in certain species (for example, *B. nuttalliana*) information can be obtained from intensive populational sampling for the presence of particular compounds found to be non-constant in the species. It is not likely that such methods may be applied as readily to species which have become established and which are suspected to be of hybrid origin. Subsequent selection of new gene combinations plus mutations may have highly modified or even obliterated the hybrid type pattern. However, it is also possible that in certain fortunate circumstances chromatographic analyses may disclose evidence of past hybridization.

GENERAL EVALUATION

Classical methods have been and continue to be
applied to specific groups of compounds by specialists. Rigorous chemical characterization of specific
compounds usually requires complex procedures for
isolation (ion-exchange, paper or column chromatography, fractional distillation or crystallization),
for establishment of structure (melting point, spectral measurement, mass spectral analysis, nuclear
magnetic resonance, elemental analysis, and so on),
and for verification (degradations, preparation of
derivatives, and synthesis if possible). Under normal
circumstances these techniques are the responsibility
of the chemist rather than the biologist. The biologist is rarely personally involved in detailed
chemical methodology, but certain techniques such

as paper and gas chromatography, spectral analysis, and so on, are now quite commonly employed by biologists, some of whom have had little formal chemical training. At present, paper chromatography is perhaps the most frequently employed single technique for screening purposes, comparisons of crude extracts, and tentative identification. Its chief advantages are its versatility and simplicity. Since excellent texts are available which describe the methods of paper chromatography, no description of methods need be included at this time. However, a few precautions may be inserted.

Normally, identification solely by paper chromatography, whether or not multiple Rf values and response to detecting reagents are utilized, is not acceptable to the chemist, and more conservative use of the technique by biologists seems justified. It is a fact, however, that after long experience with the chromatographic behavior of a limited number of compounds one can frequently recognize specific compounds by their chromatographic properties alone. It is virtually impossible to place absolute reliance upon Rf values. Not only do obvious factors such as temperature and equilibration time of the solvent affect Rf values, but more subtle influences such as the shape of the chromatographic chamber or even the number of sheets hung in a chamber and the exact method of equilibration may be sufficient to modify Rf values significantly.

Extraction procedures may grossly affect Rf values, and it is well known that compounds chromatographed from crude extracts may be affected greatly, either by physical properties of the extract or by actual chemical modification of the substances being studied. Figure 16-1 illustrates a striking effect upon the Rf values of certain pure samples of lupine alkaloids when applied so as to overlap partially a crude extract from *Baptisia* which contains similar alkaloids.

Conservatism is also advocated in the use of chromogenic sprays especially if a qualitative aspect of the color is required for identification. In the case of ninhydrin, for example, most amino acids give essentially similar colors while some, such as proline, yield radically different colors. In contrast cyclohexylamine yields a larger variety of colors with amino acids than does the ninhydrin spray, but the specific colors are hard to describe, appear differently on the two sides of the paper, and are influenced by the amount of amino acid present. It should also be recognized that the sensitivity of a given spraying reagent may vary with different compounds. For example, Dragendorff reagent, which is used for the general detection of alkaloids, exhibits large differences in sensitivity to different lupine alkaloids.

The extent to which chemical artifacts occur is dependent

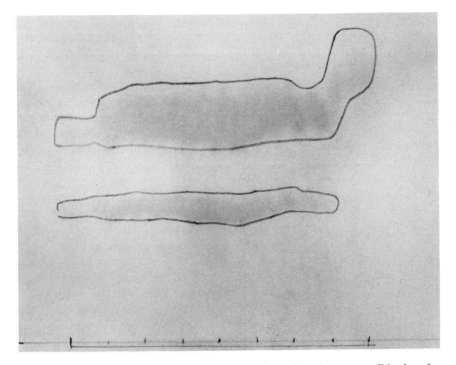

Fig. 16-1. Influence of crude extract from *Baptisia leucophaea* leaves upon Rf value of a pure sample of hydroxylupinine. The samples are co-chromatographed so as not to completely overlap. Thus, the last block on the right has 8 applications of hydroxylupinine and no *Baptisia* extract; the next block has 7 applications of hydroxylupinine and one application of *Baptisia* extract. A single application of the *Baptisia* extract is sufficient to completely alter the Rf of the pure alkaloid. The lower band is a second alkaloid present in the *Baptisia* extract. (Brehm, 1962).

upon the method of preserving, extracting, and chromatographing the sample. It is likely that such artifacts are more important than is generally recognized. Extensive changes following the harvesting of plant material have been noted variously (Yoshida, 1961) but do not necessarily occur (Dzhemukhadze and Nestyuk, 1961). Forsyth (1952) found that 80 per cent of the total polyphenols in cacao beans were removed within fifteen minutes when the beans were ground and aerated in a buffered solution. Although conditions were probably nearly optimal for the activity of oxidative enzymes, it is nevertheless important to recognize that many chemical changes may occur following harvesting, particularly influenced by the conditions at the time of death of the tissues. Volatile constituents are especially susceptible to loss while non-volatile constituents may often be light-sensitive or else subject to autocatalysis. It is possible that plant material which remains alive for a long period of time following collection will not only undergo degradative changes but may even synthesize compounds not normally produced. Also, if material remains moist after collection, invasion by molds and other microorganisms may occur. In our own work with *Baptisia* we have observed that plants which are carefully pressed and dried at 40 to 50° C then stored in a cool, dark (herbarium) cabinet apparently undergo few significant post-harvest changes. Alston and Irwin (1961) compared various drying schedules for the preservation of ninhydrin-positive and fluorescent compounds of *Cassia* species. They found that combinations of temperatures between 30° and 50° C and of drying periods between nine and forty hours yielded extracts with quite similar ninhydrin and fluorescent patterns. When some of the same *Cassia* material stored in darkness at room temperature for seven months was re-extracted, the patterns were basically unchanged. These observations need to be confirmed by more rigorous controls, but if the type of preservation suggested is found to be adequate, then plant collections such as are made for the herbarium with essentially routine collecting procedure should be suitable for limited biochemical studies.

Chromatography itself may produce certain artifacts. Harborne and Sheratt (1957) found that the pentose, arabinose, occurred as an artifact in the purification of anthocyanins if solvent mixtures containing HCl were used. This type of artifact is quite troublesome if one is investigating anthocyanins, for the positions and types of glycosides represent a major portion of the problem of identification. Of course, it is important to reduce the danger of partial or undesired hydrolysis by giving special attention to conditions during the extraction of various substances.

In addition to paper chromatography, gas chromatography can be utilized to advantage in biochemical systematic investigations, although it is still employed in highly specialized problems. Gas chromatography can be quite effective, requiring even less of a sample than does paper chromatography—in fact with high sensitivity detectors one may "see" one part per billion. Compounds which can be volatilized without degradation at temperatures up to 600° C can be chromatographed, and if the original substance is not volatile, it may be converted to a derivative that is volatile in the desired range (for example, methyl esters of fatty acids). In the hands of experienced technicians gas chromatograms may give striking results (Fig. 16-2).

It is possible that one contribution of gas chromatography to biochemical systematics will be through the use of "fingerprint"

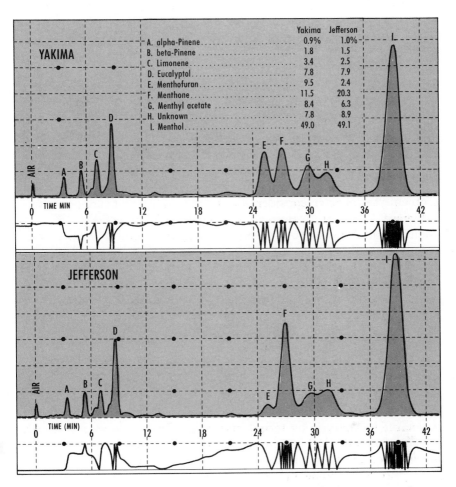

	Yakima	Jefferson
A. alpha-Pinene	0.9%	1.0%
B. beta-Pinene	1.8	1.5
C. Limonene	3.4	2.5
D. Eucalyptol	7.8	7.9
E. Menthofuran	9.5	2.4
F. Menthone	11.5	20.3
G. Menthyl acetate	8.4	6.3
H. Unknown	7.8	8.9
I. Menthol	49.0	49.1

Fig. 16-2. Chemical components of Yakima and Jefferson peppermint oils as revealed by gas chromatography (Permission of Wilkens Instrument and Research, Inc., Walnut Creek, California).

techniques. That is, relatively crude extracts may be chromatographed with different column systems, perhaps with programmed temperature control, to yield a complex chromatogram. Major peaks will be selected for comparison with extracts from other species. Even though the peaks were not immediately identified, the pool of variation thus uncovered should be subject to systematic interpretations. Such a technique should prove quite valuable in the analysis of populations and in studies of natural hybridization.

Limitations of gas chromatography at present appear to be

related not to any inherent major theoretical barriers, but rather to practical difficulties. Technical advances in the development of equipment are quite rapid at present. The area in which the most progress may be expected using gas chromatographic techniques includes the essential oils. Techniques for treating this class of compounds are highly refined.

PHYSIOLOGICAL OR CHEMICAL RACES

Chemical variation in both populations and individuals is a problem that is often considered to be of major significance—perhaps sufficient to impair seriously the general effectiveness of the biochemical approaches to systematics. Anyone slightly familiar with populations of wild flowers will perhaps recall seeing considerable variation in the flower color of certain species. (Horticultural color varieties are often truly remarkable, but these usually result from the careful preservation and propagation of many individual color mutants.) A population of spiderwort (*Tradescantia*), for example, may have dark purple, light purple, dark blue, light blue, pale pink, deep pink and white individuals, not as rare "mutants," but in large numbers, and other similar examples may be recalled. Such chemical variation, which is overt in the flower color pigments, is obviously to be encountered among other types of substances. However, only a small fraction of the compounds useful in biochemical systematics are amenable to analysis by visual inspection. In fact, some substances are so refractory that large numbers of individual plants may be required in order to get a sufficiently large sample of the compound.

It is well known that secondary substances are likely to vary in different populations, or even within individuals, of the same population, from year to year. The question of whether the variation is genetical or environmental in origin is not always easily answered though it is pertinent to biochemical systematics.

The occurrence of physiological races involving many classes of compounds has already been noted, and only a few additional examples need be cited here. Penfold and Morrison (1927) found significant differences in the piperitone content of the oil from different populations of *Eucalyptus dives*, and even earlier Armstrong, *et al.* (1913) had described populations of *Lotus corniculatus* differing markedly in their cyanogen content. Tetényi (1958) noted that individuals of *Cinnamomum camphora* sub-species *formosana* exist in at least six chemical forms; they include as major constituents borneol, camphor, cineole, linalool, safrol, and sesquiterpene.

Chemical races of *Acorus calamus* have been described (Wulff and Stahl, 1960). This species is composed of diploid, triploid, and tetraploid races. Analysis of these cytologically different populations from various locations showed significant differences in their essential oil contents (Fig. 16-3). The most striking differences were found between diploid and polyploid races. Two widely separated diploids (from Canada and Denmark) were virtually identical in their oil content, containing mostly geranyl acetate. Triploids from various European sources showed similar patterns: no geranyl acetate but a high content of asarone and traces of isoeugenol methyl ester. The tetraploids contained slightly less asarone and more isoeugenol methyl ester. It is not clear from this work whether the biochemical differences were the direct result of the cytological differences or the result of genetic selection subsequent to the formation of the cytological races.

A rather similar situation involving the mustard oils of *Brassica juncea* seeds has been reported by Hemingway *et al.* (1961). Seed samples of ninety-six individuals were collected from different parts of the world, grown in England, and analyzed for their mustard oil content. It was found that these samples could be arranged into

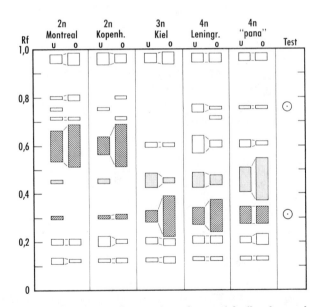

Fig. 16-3. Schematic representation of essential oils of several cultivars of *Acorus calamus*. u = upper half of leaves; o = lower half of leaves. ▨ = geranylacetate; ▢ = asarone; ▧ = isoeugenol-methylether. (After Wulff and Stahl, 1960).

three groups: (1) those with allyl isothiocyanate only; (2) those with 3-butenyl (= crotonyl) isothiocyanate only; (3) those with a mixture of the two mustard oils. Seeds from China, Japan, Nepal, and Eastern Europe were of type 1 (except for three out of forty-nine samples with traces of component 2). Seeds from India and Pakistan were either 2 or 3. Twenty-six samples from North America and Western Europe had contents compatible with their described origins. The authors considered that perhaps *Brassica juncea* had arisen independently through hybridization between *B. nigra* (which forms allyl isothiocyanate) and *B. campestris* (which forms 3-butanyl isothiocyanate). The widespread existence of chemical races renders such an hypothesis of limited value unless supported by other data.

With respect to alkaloids, Marion (1945) confirmed a report of the presence of the alkaloids, nicotine and sedamine, in *Sedum acre;* however Beyerman and Muller (1955) could not detect these two alkaloids in a European population. Instead, they found another alkaloid, sedridin. The latter results were confirmed independently by Schopf and Unger (1956) who studied a population of *Sedum acre* near Darmstadt, Germany. There is no need to cite other examples of a similar nature. To borrow a phrase from Brachet (1960), who applied it to the mitochondrion: there is one thing we know about chemical variation, it exists. In fact, serious proposals have been made to establish formal nomenclature for chemical races, and the question has been discussed in a symposium (Dillemann, 1960; Jaminet, 1960).

Since the existence of a considerable amount of variation in the chemistry of a species is established, the next question involves the extent of variation. Does chemical variation undermine the effectiveness of biochemical systematics? For every species which exhibits variation in flower color, there are numerous species whose flower color is distinctive, even diagnostic (except for the true mutant). The distinctive blue of *Commelina* flowers is contrasted with the color varieties in its close relative, *Tradescantia.* Distinctive colors, tastes, and odors, and the mere existence of drug plants should remind us that it is better not to become overly concerned about the problem of variation. Even so, chemical variation may be excessive. The variation found in the alkaloids of individual plants from various populations of *Baptisia leucophaea* (Chapter 9) is matched by the variation found in different plants within a single population. Some of the leaf coumarins are also quite variable in amounts in *B. leucophaea.* Yet, a larger number of other leaf substances including, probably, flavonoids are relatively constant and some are diagnostic for the species. No generalization can account adequately for the infinite variations in the pattern and nature of the distribution of certain chemicals.

In general, the more important a particular compound is to the survival of the species, the more effectively deficient mutations are eliminated. If the mutation frequency is quite high, however, equilibrium may be reached with a fairly high representation of the deficient type in the population. Also, the more important the compound to the survival of the species, the more likely the existence of indirect genetic buffering mechanisms which tend to inhibit drastic changes in the amount of the substance formed. This type of buffering can be effective against intrinsic (genetic recombination) or extrinsic (environmental factors) changes. Flower color in species with specific cross-pollinated vectors may represent good examples of such a situation in which pigment content of the petal is kept constant. Pigment content of stems, in contrast, may be more variable.

As noted in previous sections, although secondary substances may vary significantly, basic metabolites such as amino acids may vary as much or more, especially as a result of differing ecological factors. Pertinent to this is the recent suggestion by Jabbar and Brochmann-Hanssen (1961) that the geographical origin of opium might be traced through an analysis of the amino acid composition of the crude drug sample, the implication being that the amino acids are more valuable, by virtue of being more variable in this case, than are the alkaloids of the opium poppy. When dealing with systematic categories above the species level, however, it is not likely that common amino acids will prove of much phyletic significance. Thus, Erdtman (1956) considers the heartwood constituents to be the most reliable compounds in biochemical systematics since they are deposited over a long period of time as more or less metabolically inert substances.

Variation in the course of development and within the mature plant

It is obvious that tissues of the same plant as physically different as roots, stems, leaves, flowers, fruits, and seeds are physiologically, hence biochemically, distinctive. It should be equally apparent that overt differences such as chlorophyll, carotenoid, and anthocyanin pigment composition are matched by differences of a more subtle nature involving other classes of compounds. For example, alkaloids of leaves and stem of yohimbe differ (Paris and Letouzey, 1960); steroidal sapogenins of leaves and seeds of *Agave* differ (Wall and Fenske, 1961); and similar examples utilizing other classes of compounds could be cited.

Chemical changes in the course of growth and development are the rule. Griffiths (1958) illustrates the distribution of flavonoids and other phenols of different mature organs of *Theobroma cacao* (Table 16-1). During leaf development and maturation there is first anthocyanin and flavonol with traces of phenolic acids; then the flavonoids diminish and increased amounts of the phenolic acids appear. In the mint (*Mentha piperita*) menthol content of leaves increases with maturity while menthol content drops. Light, however, may be a factor in keeping the menthol content higher. Thus an interplay between intrinsic and extrinsic factors is present which further complicates the situation. The present writers, who have examined the fluorescent components of various species of *Prosopis* (mesquite) at different seasons, found that a large number of phenolic compounds accumulate in the leaves during the growing season—the chief increase apparently involving phenolic acids.

METHODS OF PRESENTING COMPARATIVE
BIOCHEMICAL DATA FOR SYSTEMATIC PURPOSES.

At the present time, many biochemical systematic studies involve primarily paper chromatographic screening methods. In the writers' *Baptisia* work, paper chromatography is now used to detect species-specific compounds for diagnostic purposes as well as for hybridization studies. Certain of the components originally detected by chromatography were selected for intensive study and analysis by more rigorous procedures because of their special biological or chemical properties. It is possible to obtain a great deal of useful systematic information from paper chromatographic investigations alone, even without a knowledge of the chemical nature of the spots obtained. In *Baptisia,* for example, an absolute minimum of fifty species-restricted compounds has been detected among only four species. These compounds, even without being identified, represent an important pool of variation for systematic comparisons. Of course, it is important that their presence or absence in a given species be validated. In *Baptisia* many hundreds of individual plants have now been examined. Alston and Turner (1959) referred to such data as representing a "biochemical profile." Although the original concept was rather naive, the principle is valid, and with sufficient information the idea is quite practical.

In the early stages of a chromatographic investigation, there may be little knowledge of the identity of specific substances. There is no doubt but that the identification of the chromatographic spots would add immeasurably to the elegance and inherent validity of the

Table 16-1. Distribution of phenolic and flavonoid residues in hydrolysates of mature tissues of *Theobroma cacao* (Griffiths, 1958).

Tissue	Unknown (g)	Unknown (g)	Unknown (v)	Unknown (g)	Quercetin (y)	Unknown (g)	Caffeic acid (bg)	Kaempferol (y)	Unknown (b)	Unknown (b)	p-Coumaric acid (v)	Sinapic acid (g)	Unknown (g)	Ferulic acid (b)	Unknown (v)	Cyanidin hydrochloride
R_F …	0	0·02	0·04	0·07	0·08	0·10	0·22	0·25	0·28†	0·55	0·63	0·83	0·88	0·90	0·95	0·50*
Sap wood	–	–	–	–	+	–	–	–	++	–	–	–	–	–	+	++
Heart wood	–	–	–	–	–	–	–	–	++	–	–	–	+++	–	–	+
Bark	–	–	–	++	–	–	–	–	++	–	–	–	–	–	–	++
Root	–	+	–	–	–	–	+++	–	+	–	–	–	–	–	–	+
Green stem	++	–	–	–	++	–	++	+	+	–	++	–	–	–	–	++
Leaf — Young	++	–	++	–	+	–	+++	+	++	+	+	–	–	–	–	+++
Leaf — Mature	–	++	–	++	+++	–	+++	–	+++	+	+++	+	–	–	+	++
Flower	–	++	–	–	+++	++	+	–	+	–	++	++	–	++	++	+++
Pod wall — Young Surface	–	–	–	–	+	+	++	–	++	–	+++	–	–	–	–	+++
Pod wall — Young Inner	–	–	–	–	+	–	+	–	+	–	+	–	–	–	–	++
Pod wall — Old Surface	–	–	–	–	+	+	++	–	++	–	–	–	–	++	–	++
Pod wall — Old Inner	–	–	–	–	+	–	++	–	+	–	+	–	–	–	–	++
Bean — Cotyledons	–	–	+	–	+	+	++	–	+	–	+	–	–	–	–	+++
Bean — Skin and adhering tissues	–	–	–	–	–	–	+	–	+	–	–	–	–	–	–	+

R_F values recorded (with the exception of that of cyanidin) relate to development with solvent A at 20°. Fluorescence in NH_3: b, blue; bg, blue-green; br, brown; g, green; v, violet; y, yellow.

* R_F relates to solvent B.

† This compound has now been shown to possess identical chromatographic and fluorescent properties to gentisic acid (2:5-dihydroxy-benzoic acid.)

systematic interpretations, but it would be a mistake to conclude that, lacking this knowledge, the chromatographic data are worthless. For example, after preliminary chromatographic screening and the recognition of differing spot patterns between two taxa, one may assign a unit value to each biochemical difference which is reliably established.[1] Ellison *et al.* (1962) have recently proposed this approach as a method of expressing and visualizing quantitative relationships of species using chromatographic data. The data were obtained from the genus *Bahia* and related genera. The methods of acquiring the data were by more or less standard chromatographic procedures. The number of distinct spots representative of each species was determined, spots were assigned a number, and where two or more species were assumed to have the same substance the same number was assigned (all species were chromatogrammed on the same run using identical extraction techniques). This enables one to express the relationship between any two species involved on the basis of chromatographic affinity (or presumptive biochemical affinity). The authors chose to express this relationship quantitatively as indicated below:

$$\text{paired affinity (PA)} = \frac{\text{spots in common for species A and B}}{\text{total spots in A + B}} \times 100$$

In a total of sixteen species, sixty-six different spots were utilized. Paired affinity values between a single species and each of the other species were obtained for all species tested, and the quantitative relationships were expressed in the form of polygonal graphs (Fig. 16-4). It is obvious that the greater the common area and shape shown by the polygons of any two species, the more closely the inferred biochemical relationship.

Obviously, the more crude the data the less valid the approach. Chromatographic techniques supported by other chemical methods are capable of a high degree of refinement, however, and the writers believe that the presentation of PA in the form of polygonal graphs is a practical way of communicating biochemical data derived from simple chromatographic techniques since it shows *patterns* and relative degrees of relationship that might not be apparent from mere tabular listings.

Ellison *et al.* have also presented the concept of group affinity, or GA, value. This value is the numerical expression of the summation of PA values of a given species for all species considered.

---

[1] The problem of assigning a true phylogenetic value to a particular difference will be discussed below. For the moment, it is sufficient merely to note that little more than this amount of insight is provided by the usual exomorphic differences, though one may subjectively assess the relative importance of various morphological characters.

For example, if sixteen species are under study, the maximum GA
value would be 1600, and the minimum would be 100 (that is, since
the PA of species A to species A = 100, and the PA of species A to
any other species = 0, the minimum GA value = 100). A third

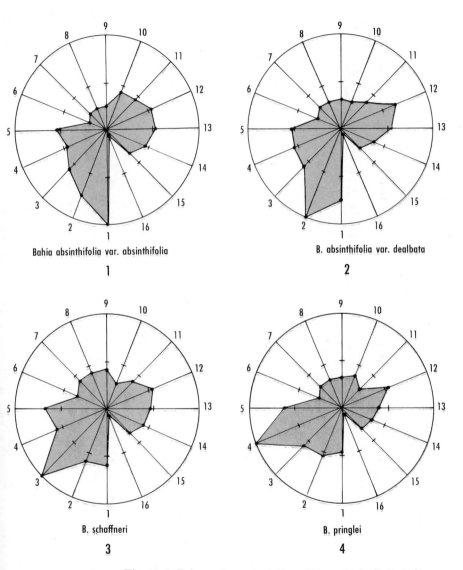

Fig. 16-4. Polygonal representation of the paired affinity indices
of each of 16 taxa to all others. Affinity indices are expressed along
the radii from 0% to 100%, beginning at the center. See text
for further explanation. (From Ellison, Alston and Turner, 1962).

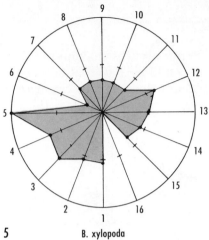

5 B. xylopoda

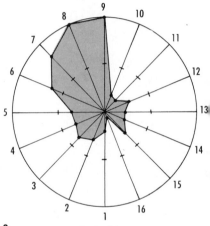

6 B. pedata

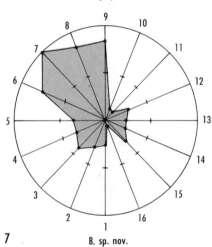

7 B. sp. nov.

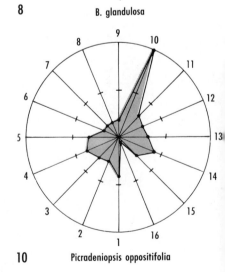

8 B. glandulosa

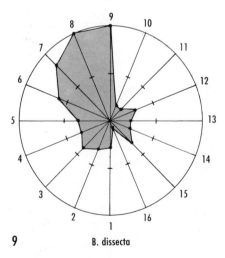

9 B. dissecta

10 Picradeniopsis oppositifolia

Fig. 16-4. (*Continued*)

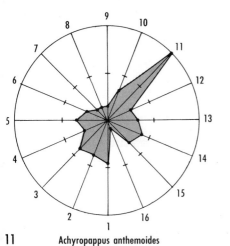

11   Achyropappus anthemoides

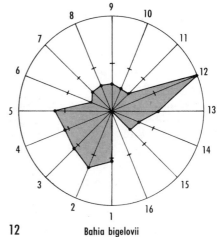

12   Bahia bigelovii

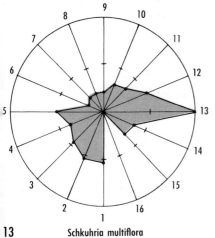

13   Schkuhria multiflora

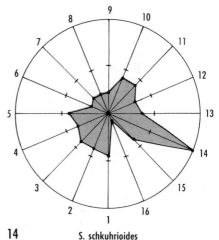

14   S. schkuhrioides

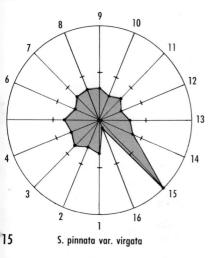

15   S. pinnata var. virgata

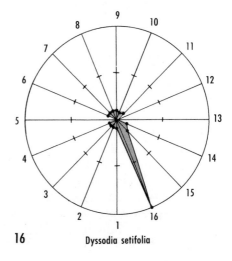

16   Dyssodia setifolia

Fig. 16-4. (*Continued*)

341

quantitative expression which is useful for certain purposes represents the number of unique compounds (in the group of species concerned) which may occur in a given taxon. This relationship has been referred to as the isolation value. Various methods of expressing the isolation value may be conceived (for example, the number of unique compounds of species A compared to the total number of compounds for the entire group, and so on).

As may be ascertained from the above, one of the advantages of the approach outlined by Ellison *et al.* is that chemical similarities or differences are expressed in a qualitative sense, and little technical experience is needed to construct and interpret such diagrams. An additional advantage is that the chromatographic data can be obtained without taxonomic bias, and this should lend considerable objectivity to the method.

EVALUATION OF SPECIFIC BIOCHEMICAL DATA

The problem of evaluating the phylogenetic significance of biochemical data is of profound importance. Failure to face this problem has been, in part, responsible for the superficiality of certain biochemical systematic investigations. According to Redfield (1936):

> If the distribution of chemical peculiarities among the natural groups of organisms is to be given an intelligent interpretation, we must first develop some satisfactory criteria by which to judge what resemblances are significant in an evolutionary sense and what are not. We need some body of chemical doctrine similar to that which embryology has given to the morphologists, by which to judge our findings. We must know not only what substances occur here and there, but also how they come to be where they are, from what they are made, and how their occurrence is determined.

Actually, through comparative biochemistry, at least some of the framework advocated by Redfield is now available, though it is primarily the basic metabolites which are best known.

It is obvious that knowledge of the biosynthesis, inheritance, and patterns of distribution of various compounds, as it accumulates, allows more and more refined interpretation of each additional fact acquired. A few examples may nevertheless give more concrete significance to the statement. Many years ago, when the distributions of anthocyanin pigments were but sketchily known, the appearance of an anthocyanin in an algal species would have been taken for granted. Now, the proven existence of an anthocyanin in an alga would be an exciting discovery. Only a few years ago, the presence of such a common anthocyanin as cyanidin in a member of the Chenopodiaceae would be of slight interest—now, the betacyanin work (Chapter 14, p. 278) has placed the matter into a totally different perspective. Again, the presence of cyanidin in general is of little significance, but since the presence of C—C glycosides has been known, a new C—C cyanidin glycoside would be of great interest. A report of a biflavonyl in an angiosperm would be exciting or a rotenone in a major plant group in which isoflavones were unknown. A 2'—OH substituted flavonoid pigment is immediately of systematic interest. Conversely, common phenolic acids such as caffeic or ferulic acids are not normally of great systematic importance, but large amounts of sinapic acid in a gymnosperm would be interesting to the systematist. The examples above are stated with as much conviction as statements bearing on the morphological features of a plant, and it indicates a serious misunderstanding of the present situation if one should assume that we do not have a background of knowledge through which we can interpret new biochemical data in systematic terms.

Earlier in this section, it was stated that in populations of *Tradescantia* one might encounter numerous flower-color forms. This phenomenon occurs in several species of the genus and, in every species examined so far, the colors of the flowers rest upon the total amount of pigment and the relative amounts of two anthocyanins, cyanidin glycoside and delphinidin glycoside. In fact, all qualitative color differences in these flowers appear to result from a minor biochemical difference, namely, a single OH substitution. Blue-flowered plants have mostly delphinidin glycoside, pink-flowered plants have mostly cyanidin glycoside, and purple-flowered plants have a mixture of the two. While the biochemical basis of flower color can be expressed rather simply, the genetic basis of flower color in this genus seems to be quite complex (Alston, unpublished). In contrast to other situations already cited in Chapter 11 (for example, Harborne, 1960b), a single gene may govern a rather complex chemical difference in the flavonoid pigments. It hardly needs to be emphasized that knowledge of the genetic basis of a biochemical difference greatly increases the possibility that the systematic significance of the biochemical difference can be determined. Since phylogenetic relationship is based on evolutionary concepts which rest principally upon genetic mechanisms, then all differences, whether biochemical or morphological, ought to be expressed in genetic terms for maximal systematic utility. Up to now, only a minute proportion of either biochemistry or morphology is understandable in a genetic sense—biochemistry best in the more fundamental reactions (that is, amino acid synthesis), morphology in some of its more trivial expressions (that is, leaf shape, pubescence, aberrations of floral morphology, and so on). If we project the present situation into the future, we conclude that there is in the final analysis a much better chance of expressing specific biochemical differences in precise genetical terms (including characterization of the enzyme involved). Therefore, although the art of assessing the phylogenetic value of morphological data is farther advanced than the art of assessing the phylogenetic value of biochemical data, and we know far less at this time about variation in the chemistry of the plant, it is probable that in fifty years this situation will be reversed. Form is so subtly, delicately, and especially so indirectly regulated that its underlying genetics and biochemistry are likely to remain among the most intractable problems in biology for a long time. In fact, an understanding of morphogenesis requires first that its biochemical basis be understood.

APPENDIX I

LIST OF NAMES CORRESPONDING TO THE NUMBERS IN FIG. 2–11, p. 33.

1. Chroococcus
2. Nostocaceae
3. Scytonemataceae
4. Tetrasporaceae
5. Mougeotia
6. Protococeae
7. Hydtrodietyaceae
8. Chrysomonadales
9. Peridinales
10. Siphonocladiales
11. Cladophora
12. Saprolegnia
13. Saccharomycetes
14. Aspergillaceae
15. Exoascus
16. Hypochreaceae
17. Exobasidium
18. Stereum
19. Vuilleminia
20. Tulostoma
21. Geaster
22. Melanogaster
23. Hymenogaster
24. Secotium
25. Hysterangium
26. Dacryomyces
27. Uredineae
28. Craterellus
29. Peniphora
30. Tremellaceae
31. Pilacre
32. Clavaria
33. Hydnum
34. Fistulina
35. Boletus
36. Cantharellus
37. Schizophyllum
38. Lentinus
39. Limacium
40. Paxillus
41. Russula
42. Clitocibe
43. Tricholoma
44. Chaetophora
45. Coleochaete
46. Fegatella
47. Pellia
48. Blasia
49. Sphagnaceae
50. Archidiaceae
51. (omitted)
52. Fossombronia
53. Chiloscyphus
54. Scapania
55. Ptilidium
56. Marsupella
57. Plagiochila
58. Madotheca
59. Georgia
60. (omitted)
61. Anthoceros
62. (omitted)
63. Hostimella
   (fossil group)
64. Asteroxylon
   (fossil group)

65. Hyenia
    (fossil group)
66. Sphenophylla
    (fossil group)
67. Calamariaceae
    (fossil group)
68. Equisetum
69. Pseudoborneales
    (fossil group)
70. Aneurophytum
    (fossil group)
71. Eofilices
    (fossil group)
72. Calloxylon
    (fossil group)
73. Mesoxylon
    (fossil group)
74. Cordaitales
    (fossil group)
75. Lepidospermae
    (fossil group)
76. Kaulfussia
77. Helminthostachys
78. Botrychium
79. Baiera (fossil group)
80. Stangeria
81. Ceratozamia
82. (omitted)
83. Cycadoidea
    (fossil group)
84. Cycadofilices
    (fossil group)
85. Marattia
86. Angiopteris
87. Todea
88. (omitted)
89. Cyathea
90. Alsophila
91. Ceratopteris
92. (omitted)
93. Blechnum
94. Aspidium
95. Cystopteris
96. (omitted)
97. (omitted)
98. Trichomanes
99. Aneimia
100. Pilularia

101. Araucaria
102. Selaginella
103. Walchia
     (fossil group)
104. (omitted)
105. (omitted)
106. Picea
107. Sciadopitys
108. Glyptostrobus
109. Pseudolarix
110. Nilsonniaceae
     (fossil group)
111. Caytoniales
     (fossil group)
112. Cyclanthaceae
113. Nymphaeaceae
114. Trochodendraceae
115. Potamogetonaceae
116. Lauraceae
117. Ranunculaceae
118. Ceratophyllaceae
119. Menispermaceae
120. Cephalotaxus
121. Podocarpus
122. Chamaecyparis
123. Butomaceae
124. Pontederiaceae
125. Dioscoriaceae
126. Iridaceae
127. Burmanniaceae
128. Orchidaceae
129. Zingiberaceae
130. Scirpoideae
131. Caricoideae
132. Restionaceae
133. Eriocaulaceae
134. Connariaceae
135. Platanaceae
136. Pittosporaceae
137. Crassulaceae
138. Thymelaeaceae
139. Elaeagnaceae
140. Halorhagaceae
141. Saxifragaceae
142. Lythraceae
143. Licythideae
144. Punicaceae
145. Araliaceae

146. Nyctaginaceae
147. Lentibulariaceae
148. Chenopodiaceae
149. Basellaceae
150. Proteaceae
151. Julianiaceae
152. Salicaceae
153. Moroideae
154. Betulaceae
155. Berberis
156. Capparidaceae
157. Dilleniaceae
158. Hydrastis
159. Lardizabaliaceae
160. Mercuriales
161. Euphorbia
162. Aceraceae
163. Rutaceae
164. Simarubaceae
165. Burseraceae
166. Empetraceae
167. Staphyleaceae
168. Hippocrateaceae
169. Linaceae
170. Erythroxylaceae
171. Tiliaceae
172. Caricaceae
173. Caryocaraceae
174. Ochnaceae
175. Oleaceae
176. Gentianaceae
177. Buddleia
178. Apocynaceae
179. Myoporaceae
180. Selaginaceae
181. Acanthaceae
182. Labiatae
183. Plantaginaceae
184. Dipsacaceae
185. Caprifoliaceae
186. Boraginaceae
187. Turneraceae
188. Droseraceae
189. Frankeniaceae
190. Styracaceae
191. Passifloraceae
192. Cucurbitaceae
193. Campanulaceae

BIBLIOGRAPHY

PREFACE AND CHAPTER 1

Anfinsen, C. B. 1959. The molecular basis of evolution. John Wiley and Sons, Inc., New York.

Clausen, J. 1953. The ecological race as a variable biotype compound in dynamic balance with its environment. I. U. B. S. symposium on genetics of population structure, Pavia, Italy (August 20–23, 1953):105–113.

Cleland, R. E. 1949. A botanical nonconformist. Sci. Monthly **48**:35–41.

Cleland, R. E. 1954. Evolution of the North American Euoenotheras: the strigosas. Proc. Amer. Phil. Soc. **98**:189–203.

Florkin, M., and H. S. Mason (eds.) 1960. Comparative biochemistry: a comprehensive treatise. Academic Press, New York.

Oparin, A. I. 1959. The origin of life on earth, 3rd ed. Oliver and Boyd, Edinburgh.

Redfield, A. C. 1936. The distribution of physiological and chemical peculiarities in the "natural" groups of organisms. Amer. Nat. **70**:110–122.

CHAPTER 2

Alston, R. E. and B. L. Turner. 1962. New techniques in analysis of complex natural hybridization. Proc. Natl. Acad. Sci. U.S. **48**:130–137.

Anderson, E. 1957. An experimental investigation of judgments concerning genera and species. Evolution **11**:260–262.

Anfinsen, C. B. 1959. The molecular basis of evolution. John Wiley and Sons, Inc., New York.

Axelrod, D. I. 1950. Evolution of desert vegetation in western North America. Publ. Carnegie Inst. Washington, No. 590.

Babcock, E. B. 1947. The genus *Crepis*. Univ. Calif. Publ. Bot. **21**:1–197.

Bailey, I. W. 1944. The development of vessels in angiosperms and its significance in morphological research. Amer. Jour. Bot. **31**:421–428.

Baker, R. T. and H. G. Smith. 1920. Research on the eucalypts especially in regard to their essential oils, 2nd ed., Sydney Techol. Mus. New South Wales, Tech. Educ. Ser. No. 13.

Banach, E. 1950. Studies in karyological differentiation of *Cardamine pratensis* L. in connection with ecology. Bull. Acad. Pol., Ser. B:197–211.

Baumann, M. G. 1946. *Myodocarpus* und die Phylogenie der Umbelliferen-Frucht. Umbelliflorin-Studien I. Ber. Schweiz. Bot. Ges. **56**:13–112.

Benson, L. 1957. Plant classification. D. C. Heath and Co., Boston.

Camp, W. H., and C. L. Gilly. 1943. The structure and origin of species. Brittonia **4**:323–335.

Chaney, R. W. 1938. Paleoecological interpretations in Cenozoic plants in western North America. Bot. Rev. **4**:371–396.

Clausen, J. 1951. Stages in the evolution of plant species. Cornell Univ. Press, Ithaca.

Constance, L. 1955. The systematics of the angiosperms. A century of progress in the natural sciences, 1853–1953, pp. 405–503. Calif. Acad. Sci., San Francisco.

Constance, L. 1960. Book review of Takhtajian, A. L., Die Evolution der Angiospermen. (Translated from the Russian by W. Höppner.) Science **131**:801–802.

Cronquist, A. 1955. Phylogeny and taxonomy of the Compositae. Amer. Midland Nat. **53**:478–511.

Cronquist, A. 1957. Outline of a new system of families and orders of dicotyledons. Bull. Jard. Bot. Bruxelles **27**:13–40.

Cronquist, A. 1960. The divisions and classes of plants. Bot. Rev. 26:425–482.

Crow, W. B. 1926. Phylogeny and the natural system. Genetics 17:6–155.

Engler, A., and L. Diels. 1936. Syllabus der Pflanzenfamilien. Aufl. 11. Berlin.

Gilmour, J. S. L. 1961. In A. M. MacLeod and L. S. Cobley [eds.], Contemporary botanical thought. Quadrangle Books, Chicago.

Grant, V. 1959. History of the phlox family. Vol. 1. Martinus Nyhoff, The Hague.

Grant, W. F. 1960. The categories of classical and experimental taxonomy and the species concept. Rev. Canadienne de Biol. 19:241–262.

Hecht, A., and S. L. Tandon. 1953. Chromosomal interchanges as a basis for the delimitation of species in Oenothera. Science 118:557–558.

Hutchinson, J. 1959. The families of flowering plants. Vol. 1 Dicotyledons. Oxford.

Just, T. 1948. Gymnosperms and the origin of angiosperms. Bot. Gaz. 110:91–103.

Lam, H. J. 1936. Phylogenetic symbols, past and present. Acta Biotheoretica 2:153–193.

Lam, H. J. 1959. Taxonomy, general principles and angiosperms. In W. B. Turrill [ed.], Vistas in Botany, Pergamon Press. New York.

Lanjouw, J. 1958. On the nomenclature of chemical strains. Taxon 7:43–44.

Lawrence, G. H. M. 1951. Taxonomy of vascular plants. Macmillan Co., New York.

Lewis, H. 1957. Genetics and cytology in relation to taxonomy. Taxon 6:42–46.

Lewis, H. and Margaret E. Lewis. 1955. The genus Clarkia. Univ. Calif. Publ. Bot. 20:241–392.

Lewis, W. 1962. Aneusomity in aneuploid populations of Claytonia virginica. Amer. Jour. Bot. 49:918–928.

Mansfeld, R. 1958. Zur Frage der Behandlung nur physiologisch, aber nicht morphologisch verschiedener Sippen in der botanischen Systematik. Taxon 7:41–43.

McNair, J. B. 1945. Some comparisons of chemical ontogeny with chemical phylogeny in vascular plants. Lloydia 8:145–169.

Rogers, D. J., and T. T. Tanimoto. 1960. A computor program for classifying plants. Science 132:1115–1118.

Rothwell, N. V. 1959. Aneuploidy in Claytonia virginica. Amer. Jour. Bot. 46:353–360.

Russell, N. H. 1962. The development of an operational approach in plant taxonomy. Systematic Zool. 10:159–167.

Simpson, G. G. 1961. Principles of animal taxonomy. Columbia Univ. Press, New York.

Sprague, T. A. 1940. Taxonomic botany with special reference to the angiosperms. *In* S. J. Huxley [ed.], The new systematics. Oxford, Clarendon Press.

Stern, K. R. 1961. Revision of *Dicentra* (Fumariaceae). Brittonia 13:1–57.

Takhtajian, A. L. 1959. Die Evolution der Angiospermen. Translated from the Russian by W. Höppner. G. Fischer, Jena.

Tétényi, P. 1958. Proposition à propos de la nomenclature des races chimiques. Taxon 7:40–41.

Turner, B. L. 1956. A cytotaxonomic study of the genus *Hymenopappus* (Compositae). Rhodora 58:163–186; 208–242; 250–269; 295–308.

Turrill, W. B. 1942. Taxonomy and phylogeny I–III. Bot. Rev. 8:247–270; 473–532; 655–707.

White, A., P. Handler, E. L. Smith, and D. Stetten, Jr. 1959. Principles of biochemistry, 2nd ed. McGraw-Hill Book Company, Inc., New York.

Williams, R. J. 1956. Biochemical individuality. The basis for the genetotrophic concept. John Wiley and Sons, Inc., New York.

CHAPTER 3

Clausen, J. 1951. Stages in the evolution of plant species. Cornell Univ. Press, Ithaca.

Constance, L. 1955. The systematics of the angiosperms. A century of progress in the natural sciences, 1853–1953, pp. 405–503. Calif. Acad. Sci., San Francisco.

Darlington, C. D. 1956. Chromosome botany. George Allen and Unwin, London.

Greene, E. L. 1909. Landmarks of botanical history. New York.

Hedberg, O. (ed.) 1958. Systematics of today. Almquist and Wiksells, Uppsala.

Heslop-Harrison, J. 1953. New concepts in flowering-plant taxonomy. Heinemann. London.

Lewis, H. 1957. Genetics and cytology in relation to taxonomy. Taxon 6:42–46.

Sachs, J. von. 1890. History of botany (1530–1860). Authorized translation by H. E. F. Garnsey, and I. B. Balfour. Oxford.

Stebbins, G. L., Jr. 1950. Variation and evolution in plants. Columbia Univ. Press, New York.

Tax, S. (ed.) 1960. Evolution after Darwin. Vol. 1, 2, Univ. of Chicago Press, Chicago.

CHAPTER 4

Abbott, Helen C. De S. 1886. Certain chemical constituents of plants considered in relation to their morphology and evolution. Bot. Gaz. **11**:270–272.

Adams, M. H. 1942. The reaction between the enzyme tyrosinase and its specific antibody. Jour. Exptl. Med. **76**:175–184.

Allison, A. C. 1959. Metabolic polymorphisms in mammals and their bearing on problems of biochemical genetics. Amer. Nat. **93**:5–16.

Alston, R. E., and B. L. Turner. 1959. Application of paper chromatography to systematics: recombination of parental biochemical components in a *Baptisia* hybrid population. Nature **184**:285–286.

Anfinsen, C. B. 1959. The molecular basis of evolution. John Wiley and Sons, New York.

Birdsong, B. A., R. E. Alston, and B. L. Turner. 1960. Distribution of canavanine in the family Leguminosae as related to phyletic groupings. Canad. Jour. Bot. **38**:499–505.

Blagoveshchenskii, A. V. 1955. Die biochemischen Grundlagen des Evolutions-prozesses der Pflanzen. Akademie-Verlag. Berlin.

Boser, H., and G. Pawelke. 1961. Zur Heterogenitat von Enzymen. II. Reindar-stellung von zwei Individuer der Malicodehydrogenase (MDH) aus Kartoffelknollen. Naturwiss. **48**:572.

Crick, F. H. C. 1958. On protein synthesis. p. 138–163. *In* Biological replication of macromolecules. Soc. Exptl. Biol. Symposia. XII. University Press, Cambridge.

Demerec, M., and Z. Hartman. 1956. Tryptophan mutants in *Salmonella thyphimurium*. *In* Genetic studies with bacteria. p. 5–33. Carnegie Institution of Washington Publication 612. Washington, D. C.

Dessauer, H. C., W. Fox, and Q. L. Hartwig. 1962. Comparative study of trans-ferrins of amphibia and reptilia using starch-gel electrophoresis and auto-radiography. Comp. Biochem. Physiol. **5**:17–29.

Erdtman, H. 1956. Organic chemistry and conifer taxonomy. p. 453–494. *In* Sir Alexander Todd [ed.], Perspectives in organic chemistry. Interscience, New York.

Esser, K., J. A. DeMoss, and D. M. Bonner. 1960. Reverse mutations and enzyme heterogeneity. Zeit. Vererbungslehre **91**:291–299.

Frederick, J. F. 1961. Immunochemical studies of phosphorylases of Cyano-phyceae. Phyton **16**:21–26.

Gibbs, R. D. 1958. Biochemistry as an aid to establishing the relationships of some families of dicotyledonous plants. Proc. Linn. Soc. London **169**: 216–230.

Glanville, E. V., and M. Demerec. 1960. Threonine, isoleucine and isoleucine-valine mutants of *Salmonella typhimurium*. Genetics 45:1359–1374.

Gregory, K. F. 1961. Introductory remarks. Conference on multiple forms of enzymes. Annals N. Y. Acad. Sci. 94:657–658.

Greshoff, M. 1909. Phytochemical investigations at Kew. Bull. Misc. Inf. Roy. Bot. Gardens, Kew 10:397–418.

Grobbelaar, N., and F. C. Steward. 1953. Pipecolic acid in *Phaseolus vulgaris:* Evidence on its derivation from lysine. Jour. Amer. Chem. Soc. 75:4341–4343.

Hansel, R. 1956. Pflanzenchemie und Pflanzenverwandtschaft. Arch. Pharm. 259/61:619–628.

Haslewood, G. A. D. 1959. Species comparison as an aid in the study of the process sterols → bile salts, p. 206–216. *In* G. E. W. Wolstenholme and M. O'Conner [eds.]. Biosynthesis of terpenes and sterols. Ciba Foundation Symp. Little, Brown and Co., New York.

Hegnauer, R. 1958. Chemotaxonomische Betrachtungen. Pharm. Acta Helvetiae 33:287–305.

Horowitz, N. H. 1950. Biochemical genetics of *Neurospora*. Adv. Genet. 3:33–71.

Hubbard, R., and R. C. St. George. 1958. The rhodopsin system of the squid. Jour. Gen. Physiol. 41:501–528.

Hubby, Jack L., and Lynn H. Throckmorton. 1960. Evolution and pteridine metabolism in the genus *Drosophila*. Proc. Nat. Acad. Sci. U.S. 46:65–78.

Ingram, V. M. 1961. Gene evolution and the haemoglobins. Nature 189:704–708.

Johnson, F. H., Y. Haneda, and E. H. C. Sie. 1960. An interphylum luciferin-luciferase reaction. Science 132:422–423.

Kaplan, N. O., and M. M. Ciotti. 1961. Evolution and differentiation of dehydrogenases. Annals N. Y. Acad. Sci. 94:701–722.

Kaplan, N. O., M. M. Ciotti, M. Hamolsky, and R. E. Bieber 1960. Molecular heterogeneity and evolution of enzymes. Science 131:392–397.

Markert, C. D., and R. D. Owens. 1954. Immunogenetic studies of tyrosine specificity. Genetics 39:818–835.

Moritz, O. 1958. Die Serologie der pflanzlichen Eiweisskorper. Encyclo. Plant Physiol. 8:356–414. Springer, Berlin.

Munkner, H. 1925. Das Vorkommen und Fehlen des Emodins bei den Arten der Gattung Aloë in Hinblick auf ihre Systematik mit einer ergänzenden Untersuchung der Aloesäftbehälter. Beitrage zur Biologie der Pflanzen 16:217–266.

Nisselbaum, J. S., M. Schlamowitz, and O. Bodansky. 1961. Immunochemical studies of functionally similar enzymes. Ann. N. Y. Acad. Sci. 94:970–987.

Paul, J., and P. F. Fottrell. 1961. Molecular variation in similar enzymes from different species. Ann. N. Y. Acad. Sci. **94**:668–677.

Smith, G. M. 1950. Fresh water algae of the United States. McGraw-Hill Book Company, New York.

Stimpfling, J. H., and M. R. Irwin. 1960a. Gene homologies in Columbidae I. Genetics **45**:233–242.

Stimpfling, J. H., and M. R. Irwin. 1960b. Evolution of cellular antigens in Columbidae. Evolution **14**:417–426.

Suskind, S. 1957. Gene function and enzyme formation. p. 123–133. *In* W. D. McElroy and B. Glass [eds.], A symposium on the chemical basis of heredity. Johns Hopkins Press, Baltimore.

Suskind, S. 1961. Studies on normal and mutationally altered tryptophan synthetase. Abstract. The fifteeth annual symposium on fundamental cancer research. Houston.

Turner, B. L. and R. E. Alston. 1959. Segregation and recombination of chemical constituents in a hybrid swarm of *Baptisia laevicaulis* × *B. viridis* and their taxonomic implication. Amer. Jour. Bot. **46**:678–686.

Van Neil, C. B. 1956. The classification and natural relationships of bacteria. Cold Spring Harbor. Symp. Quant. Biol. **11**:285–301.

Vogel, H. J. 1959a. On biochemical evolution: lysine formation in higher plants. Proc. Nat. Acad. Sci. U. S. **45**:1717–1721.

Vogel, H. J. 1959b. Lysine biosynthesis in *Chlorella* and *Euglena:* phylogenetic significance. Biochem. Biophys. Acta **34**:282–283.

Vogel, H. J. 1960. Two modes of lysine synthesis among lower fungi: evolutionary significance. Biochem. Biophys. Acta **41**:172–173.

Vogel, H. J. 1961. Lysine synthesis and phylogeny of lower fungi. Some Chytrids versus *Hypochytrium.* Nature **189**:1026–1027.

Wagner, R. P., A. N. Radhakrishnan, and E. E. Snell. 1958. The biosynthesis of isoleucine and valine in *Neurospora crassa.* Proc. Nat. Acad. Sci. U. S. **44**: 1047–1053.

Wagner, R. P., and H. K. Mitchell. 1955. Genetics and metabolism. John Wiley and Sons, New York.

Wald, George. 1947. The chemical evolution of vision. Harvey Lectures 1945–46:117–160.

Wald, George. 1960. The distribution and evolution of visual systems. *In,* M. Florkin and H. S. Mason [eds.], Comparative Biochemistry. Vol. 1. Academic Press, New York.

Wroblewski, F. (ed.). 1961. Multiple molecular forms of enzymes. Annals N. Y. Acad. Sci. **94**:657–1031.

Zuckerkandl, E., R. T. Jones, and L. Pauling. 1960. A comparison of animal hemoglobins by tryptic peptide pattern analysis. Proc. Nat. Acad. Sci. U. S. **46**:1349–1360.

CHAPTER 5

Abbott, Helen C. de S. 1886. Certain chemical constituents of plants considered in relation to their morphology and evolution. Bot. Gaz. **11**:270–272.

Abbott, Helen C. de S. 1887a. Comparative chemistry of higher and lower plants. Amer. Nat. **21**:719–800.

Abbott, Helen C. de S. 1887b. The chemical basis of plant forms. Jour. Franklin Inst. **124**:161.

Baker, R. T. and H. G. Smith. 1920. Research on the eucalypts especially in regard to their essential oils, 2nd ed. Sydney Tech. Mus., N. S. Wales Tech. Educ. Ser. No. 13.

Baldwin, I. L., E. B. Fred, and E. G. Hanstings. 1927. Grouping of legumes according to biological reactions of their seed proteins. Possible explanation of phenomenon of cross inoculation. Bot. Gaz. **83**:217–243.

Baum, W. C. 1954. Systematic serology of the family Cucurbitaceae with special reference to the genus *Cucurbita*. Serol. Mus. Bull. **13**:5–8.

Benzer, S. 1957. The elementary units of heredity. p. 70–93. *In* W. B. McElroy and B. Glass [eds.], The chemical basis of heredity. Johns Hopkins Press, Baltimore.

Boyd, W. C. 1960. The specificity of the nonspecific. Jour. Immunol. **85**:221–229.

Boyd, W. C., and R. M. J. Reguera. 1949. Hemagglutinating substances for human cells in various plants. Jour. Immunol. **62**:333–339.

Boyden, A. 1942. Systematic serology: a critical appreciation. Physiol. Zool. **15**:109–145.

Boyden, A. A., and R. J. DeFalco. 1943. Report on the use of the photron-reflectometer in serological comparisons. Physiol. Zool. **16**:229–241.

Chester, K. S. 1937a. A critique of plant serology. Part I. The nature and utilization of phytoserological procedures. Quart. Rev. Bio. **12**:19–46.

Chester, K. S. 1937b. A critique of plant serology. Part II. Application of serology to the classification of plants and the identification of plant products. Quart. Rev. Biol. **12**:165–190.

Chester, K. S. 1937c. A critique of plant serology. Part III. Phytoserology in medicine and general biology. Bibliography. Quart. Rev. Biol. **12**:294–321.

Fairbrothers, D. E., and M. A. Johnson. 1959. The precipitin reaction as an indicator of relationship in the subfamily Festucoideae of the family Poaceae (Gramineae). Abstract. Proc. IX Internat. Congr. Bot. Montreal 2:110-111.

Fairbrothers, D. E., and R. R. Boulette. 1960. Some phytoserological relationships within the Umbelliferae. Amer. Inst. Biol. Sci. Bull. 10:45.

Fox, A. S. 1949. Immunogenetic studies of *Drosophila melanogaster*. II. Genetics 34:647-664.

Gell, P. G. H., J. G. Hawkes, and S. T. C. Wright. 1960. The application of immunological methods to the taxonomy of species within the genus *Solanum*. Proc. Roy. Soc. Lond., Series B. 151:364-383.

Gemeroy, D., A. A. Boyden and R. J. De Falco. 1954. What blood is that? Bull. Ser. Mus. 15:2-3.

Gilg, E., und P. H. Schürhoff. 1927. Unsere Erfahrungen über die Brauchbarkeit der Serodiagnostik für die botanische Vervandtschaftsforschung. Ber. Deut. Bot. Ges. 45:315-330.

Hall, O. 1959. Immunoelectrophoretic analysis of allopolyploid ryewheat and its parental species. Hereditas 45:495-503.

Hammond, H. D. 1955a. A study of taxonomic relationship within the Solanaceae as revealed by the photron'er serological method. Serol. Mus. Bull. 14:3-5.

Hammond, H. D. 1955b. Systematic serological studies in Ranunculaceae. Serol. Mus. Bull. 14:1-3.

Johnson, M. A. 1953. Relationship in the Magnoliaceae as determined by the precipitin reaction. Bull. Torrey Bot. Club 80:349-350.

Johnson, M. A. 1954. The precipitin reaction as an index of relationship in the Magnoliaceae. Serol. Mus. Bul. 13:1-5.

Kloz, J. 1962. An investigation of the protein characters of four *Phaseolus* species with special reference to the question of their phylogenesis. Biol. Plant. (Praha) 4:85-90.

Kloz, Josef, V. Turková, and E. Klosová. 1960. Seriological investigations of taxonomic specificity of proteins in various plant organs in some taxons of the family Viciaceae. Biol. Plant. (Praha) 2:126-137.

Krüpe, M. 1956. Blutgruppenspezifische pflanzliche Eiweisskörper (Phytagglutinine). Ferdinand Enke Verlag. Stuttgart.

Lewis, D. 1952. Serological reactions of pollen incompatibility substances. Proc. Roy. Soc. Lond., Series B 140:127-135.

Linskens, H. F. 1960. Zur Frage der Enstehung der Abwehr-Körper bei der Inkompatibilitätsreaktion von *Petunia*. III. Mitteilung: Serologische Teste mit Leitgewebs-und Pollen-Extrakten. Zeit. für Bot. 48:126-135.

Mäkelä, Olavi. 1957. Studies in hemagglutinins of Leguminosae seeds. Helsink. Ann. Med. Exper. et Biol. Fenniae Vol. 35., Suppl. No. 11.

McLaughlin, R. P. 1933. Systematic anatomy of the woods of the Magnoliales. Trop. Woods 34:3–39.

Mez, C., and H. Ziegenspeck. 1926. Der Königsberger serodiagnostische Stammbaum. Bot. Arch. 13:483–485.

Morgan, W. T. J., and W. M. Watkins. 1956. The product of the human blood group A and B genes in individuals belonging to group AB. Nature 177: 521–522.

Moritz, O. 1958. Die Serologie der pflanzlichen Eiweisskörper. W. Ruhland [ed.], Encycl. Plant Physiol. 8:356–414. Springer, Berlin.

Moritz, O. 1960. Some variants of serological technique developed in serobotanical work. Serol. Mus. Bul. 24:1–8.

Moritz, O. and H. vom Berg. 1931. Serological Studien über das Linswicken-problem. Biol. Zentral. 51:290–307.

Nuttall, G. H. F. 1901. The new biological test for blood in relation to zoological classification. Proc. Roy. Soc. Lond., Series B 69:150–153.

Renkonen, K. O. 1948. Studies on hemagglutinins present in seeds of some representatives of the family of Leguminosae Ann. Med. Exptl. et Biol. Fenniae 26:66–72.

Rigas, D. A., R. D. Koler, and E. E. Osgood. 1955. New hemoglobin possessing a higher electrophoretic mobility than normal adult hemoglobin. Science 121:372.

Schertz, K. F., W. Jurgelsky, Jr., and W. C. Boyd. 1960. Inheritance of anti-A, hemaggluttinating activity in lima beans, *Phaseolus lunatus*. Proc. Natl. Acad. Sci. U.S. 46:529–532.

Sela, M., and Ruth Arnon. 1960. Studies on the chemical basis of the antigenicity of proteins 3. The role of rigidity in the antigenicity of polypeptidyl gelatins. Biochem. Jour. 77:394–399.

Stallcup, B. W. 1961. Relationships of some families of the Suborder Passeres (Songbirds) as indicated by comparisons of tissue proteins. Jour. Grad. Res. Center. (Southern Methodist Univ.) 29:43–65.

Stillmark, H. 1888. Über Ricin, ein giftiges Ferment aus den Samen von *Ricinus comm.* L. und einigen anderan Euphorbiaceen. Inaug. Diss. Dorpat:1888.

Watkins, W. M., and W. T. J. Morgan. 1952. Neutralization of the anti-H agglutinin in eel serum by simple sugars. Nature 169:825–826.

Wright, S. T. C. 1960. Occurrence of an organ-specific antigen associated with the microsome fraction of plant cells and its possible significance in the process of cellular differentiation. Nature 185:82–85.

CHAPTER 6

Alston, R. E., and H. S. Irwin. 1961. The comparative extent of variation of free amino acids and certain "secondary" substances among *Cassia* species Amer. Jour. Bot. **48**:35–39.

Ball, G. H., and E. W. Clark. 1953. Species differences in amino acids of *Culex* mosquitoes. Systematic Zool. **2**:138–141.

Bell, E. A. 1961. Isolation of a new amino acid from *Lathyrus tingitanus*. Biochem. Biophys. Acta **47**:602–605.

Bell, E. A. 1962a. Associations of ninhydrin-reacting compounds in the seeds of 49 species of *Lathyrus*. Biochem. Jour. **83**:225–229.

Bell, E. A. 1962b. Structure of lathyrine. Nature **194**:91–92.

Biemann, K., C. Lioret, J. Asselineau, E. Lederer, and J. Polonsky. 1960. The chemical structure of lysopine. A new amino acid isolated from the tissue of crown gall. Bull. Soc. Chim. Biol. **42**:979–991.

Birdsong, B. A., R. E. Alston, and B. L. Turner. 1960. Distribution of canavanine in the family Leguminosae as related to phyletic groupings. Can. Jour. Bot. **38**:499–505.

Blagoveshchenskii, A. V. 1960. The evolution of proteins and the evolution of flowering plants. (Translation). Biokhimiya **25**:12–16.

Buxbaum, F. 1958. Der morphologische Typus und die systematische Stellung der Gattung *Calochortus*. Beits. Biol. Pflanzen **34**:405–452.

Buzzati-Traverso, A. A. 1953. Paper chromatographic patterns of genetically different tissues: a contribution to the biochemical study of individuality. Proc. Natl. Acad. Sci. U. S. **39**:376–391.

Buzzati-Traverso, A. A., and A. B. Rechnitzer. 1953. Paper partition chromatography in taxonomic studies. Science **117**:58–59.

Carnegie, P. R. 1961. Bound amino acids of rye grass—the isolation of amphoteric peptidelike substances of low molecular weight. Biochem. Jour. **18**:697–707.

Coleman, R. G. 1957. The effect of sulphur deficiency on the free amino acids of some plants. Aust. Jour. Biol. Sci. **10**:50–56.

Consden, R., A. H. Gordon, and A. J. P. Martin. 1944. Qualitative analysis of proteins: a partition chromatographic method using paper. Biochem. Jour. **38**:224–232.

Danielsson, C. E. 1949. Seed globulins of the Gramineae Leguminosae. Biochem. Jour. **44**:387–400.

Dunn, M. S. 1943. The constitution and synthesis of the amino acids. *In* C. L. A. Schmidt [ed.], Addendum to the chemistry of the amino acids and proteins. C. C. Thomas, Springfield, Ill.

Fowden, L. 1959. Amino acids of plants with special reference to newly discovered amino acids. Symp. Soc. Exptl. Biol. 13:283-303.

Fowden, L. 1962. The non-protein amino acids of plants. Endeavour 21:35-42.

Fowden, L., and F. C. Stewart. 1957. Nitrogenous compounds and nitrogen metabolism in the Liliaceae. I. The occurrence of soluble nitrogenous compounds. Ann. Bot. 21:53-67.

Fox, Allen S. 1956. Chromatographic differences between males and females in *Drosophila melanogaster* and role of X and Y chromosomes. Physiol. Zool. 29:288-298.

Gates, R. R. A. 1918. A systematic study of the North American Melanthaceae from the genetic standpoint. Jour. Linn. Soc. Bot. 44:131-172.

Gerritsen, T. 1956. Lupin seed proteins IV. Amino acid composition of the globulins from *Lupinus angustifolius* and *Lupinus luteus*. Biochem. Biophys. Acta 22:269-273.

Gmelin, R. 1959. Die freien Aminosäuren den Samen von *Acacia willardiana* (Mimosaceae) isoliering von Willardin, eine neuen pflanzlichen aminosäure vermutlich L-Uracil-β[(α-amino-propionsäure)]-(3). Zeit. Physiol. Chem. 316:164-169.

Gmelin, R., G. Strauss, and G. Hasenmaier. 1959. Über neue Aminosäuren aus Mimosaceen. Zeit. Physiol. Chem. 314:28-32.

Gmelin, R., and P. K. Hietala. 1960. S-[B-carboxy-isopropyl]-L-cystein, eine neue Aminosäure aus den Samen von *Acacia millefolia* und *Acacia willardiana* (Mimosaceae). Zeit. für Physiol. Chem. 322:278-282.

Gray, D. O., and L. Fowden. 1961. n-Ethyl-L-asparagine—a new amino acid amide from *Ecballium*. Nature 189:401-402.

Haas, P. 1950. On certain peptides occurring in marine algae. Biochem. Jour. 46:503-505.

Hadorn, E. 1962. Fractionating the fruit fly. Sci. Amer. 206:100-110.

Hadorn, E. and H. K. Mitchell. 1951. Properties of mutants of *Drosophila melanogaster* and changes during development as revealed by paper chromatography. Proc. Natl. Acad. Sci. U. S. 37:650-655.

Hoffman, L. R. 1961. Studies of the morphology, cytology, and reproduction of *Oedogonium* and *Oedocladium*. Ph.D. Diss. Univ. of Texas, Austin, Texas.

Hutchinson, J. 1959. The families of flowering plants. Vol. 1. Dicotyledons, Oxford.

Kirk, R. L., A. R. Main, and F. G. Beyer. 1954. The use of paper partition chromatography for taxonomic studies of land snails. Biochem. Jour. 57:440-442.

Kuriyama, M., M. Takagi, and K. Murata. 1960. A new amino acid, chondrine, isolated from a red alga. Nippon Suisan Gakkaishi 26:627.

Larsen, P. O., and A. Kjaer. 1962. A new amino acid isolated from seeds of *Reseda odorata* L. Acta Chem. Scand. **16**:142.

Micks, D. W. 1954. Paper chromatography as a tool for mosquito taxonomy: the *Culex pipiens* complex. Nature **174**:217-218.

Micks, D. W. 1956. Paper chromatography in insect taxonomy. Ann. Ent. Soc. Amer. **49**:576-581.

Möhlmann, E. 1958. Chromatographische untersuchungen an verschiedenen Genotypen von *Plodia interpunctella* in vergleich mit anderen Schmetterlingsarten. Zeit. für Vererbungs. **89**:651-674.

Ownbey, M. 1940. A monograph of the genus *Calochortus*. Ann. Mo. Bot. Gard. **27**:371-558.

Pleshkov, B. P., T. B. Shmyreva, and S. Ivanko. 1959. The free amino acid content of leaves and roots of maize as related to nutritional conditions. (Translation.) Plant Physiol. (Russia) **6**:674-683.

Possingham, J. V. 1956. The effect of mineral nutrition in the content of free amino acids and amides in tomato plants I. Aust. Jour. Biol. Sci. **9**: 539-551.

Possingham, J. V. 1957. The effect of mineral nutrition in the content of free amino acids and amides in tomato plants II. Aust. Jour. Biol. Sci. **10**: 40-49.

Przybylska, J., and J. Hurich. 1960. Free amino acids in seeds of some leguminous plants. Bull. Acad. Polon. Sci., Ser. Sci. Biol. **8**:505-508.

Reuter, G. 1957. Die Hauptformen des löslichen Stickstoffs in vegetativen pflanzlichen Speicherorganen und ihre systematische Bewertbarkeit. Flora **145**:326-338.

Sibley, C. G. 1960. The electrophoretic patterns of avian egg-white proteins as taxonomic characters. Ibis **102**:215-284.

Stewart, F. C., R. M. Zacharius, and J. K. Pollard. 1955. Nitrogenous compounds in plants: recent knowledge derived from paper partition chromatography. Ann. Acad. Sci. Fennicae **60**:321-366.

Takahashi, N., and R. W. Curtis. 1961. Isolation and characterization of malformin. Plant Physiol. **36**:30-36.

Trelease, S. F., A. A. Di Somma, and A. L. Jacobs. 1960. Selenoamino acid found in *Astragalus bisulcatus*. Science **132**:618.

Tschiersch, B. 1959. Uber Canavanin. Flora **147**:405-416.

Tso, T. C., and J. E. McMurtrey Jr. 1960. Mineral deficiency and organic constituents in tobacco plants II. Amino acids. Plant Physiol. **35**:865-870.

Turner, B. L., and O. S. Fearing. 1960. Chromosome numbers in the Leguminosae. II. African species, including phyletic interpretations. Amer. Jour. Bot. **46**:49-57.

Vickery, H. B. 1941. Evidence from organic chemistry regarding the composition of protein molecules. Ann. N. Y. Acad. Sci. 41:87–120.

Virtanen, A. I., and R. Gmelin. 1959. Structure of γ-hydroxypipecolic acid isolated from green plants. Acta Chem. Scand. 13:1244–1246.

Virtanen, A. I., and E. J. Matikkala. 1960. New γ-glutamyl peptides in the onion (Allium cepa). Zeit. Physiol. Chem. 322:8–20.

Vismanathan, R., and V. K. Pillai. 1956. Paper chromatography in fish taxonomy. Proc. Ind. Acad. Sci., Sect. B 43:334–339.

Wiewiorowski, M., and J. Augustyniak. 1960. Acidic peptides from lupine seeds. Bull. Acad. Polon. Sci., Ser. Sci. Biol. 8:555–556.

Wright, C. A. 1959. The application of paper chromatography to a taxonomic study in the molluscan genus, Lymnaea. Jour. Linn. Soc. Lond. 44:222–237.

CHAPTER 7

Crane, F. L., J. G. Hauge, and H. Beinert. 1955. Flavoproteins involved in the first oxidative step of the fatty acid cycle. Biochim. Biophys. Acta 17: 292–294.

Eglinton, G., R. J. Hamilton and M. Martin-Smith. 1962. The alkane constituents of some New Zealand plants and their possible taxonomic implications. Phytochemistry. 1:137–145.

Eglinton, G. 1962. Distribution of alkanes. International Symposium on Chemical Plant Taxonomy. Oct. 4–6. Paris.

Eglinton, G., A. G. Gonzalez, R. J. Hamilton, and R. A. Raphael. 1962. Hydrocarbon constituents of the wax coatings of plant leaves: a taxonomic survey. Phytochemistry. 1:89–102.

Goldovskii, A. M. 1960. Evolutionary changes in fat biosynthesis in organisms. Russian Rev. Biol. (Translated) 50:127–141.

Hilditch, T. P. 1952. The seed and fruit fats of plants. Endeavour 11:173–182.

Hilditch, T. P. 1956. The chemical constitution of natural fats, 3rd ed. Chapman and Hall, Ltd., London.

McNair, J. B. 1941. Plant forms, the law of mass action and the production of alkaloids, cyanogenetic and organic sulphur compounds. Amer. Jour. Bot. 28:179–184.

Meara, M. L. 1958. The fats of higher plants. In W. Ruhland [ed.] Encycl. Plant Physiol. VII. Springer, Berlin.

Price, J. R. 1962. Remarks at International Symposium on Chemical Plant Taxonomy. Oct. 4–6. Paris.

Purdy, S. J. and E. V. Truter. 1961. Taxonomic significance of surface liquids of plants. Nature. **190**:554–555.

Shenstone, F. S., and J. R. Vickery. 1961. Occurrence of cyclo-propene acids in some plants of the Order Malvales. Nature **190**:168–169.

CHAPTER 8

Bacon, J. S. D. 1959. Carbohydrates of the rampion, *Campanula rapunculus* L. Nature **184**:1957.

Barker, S. A. 1955. Acyclic sugar alcohols. *In* K. Paech and V. Tracy [eds.] Modern methods of plant analysis. Vol. 2. Springer, Berlin.

Bell, D. J., F. A. Isherwood, and N. E. Hardwick. 1954. D($^+$)-Apiose from the monocotyledon, *Posidonia australis*. Jour. Chem. Soc. Lond. 3702–3706.

Belval, H., and A. de Cugnac. 1941. Le contenu glucidique des bromes et des fetuques et la classification. Bull. Soc. Chim. Biol. **23**:74–77.

Bidwell, R. G., S. G. Krotkov, and G. B. Reed. 1952. Paper chromatography of sugars in plants. Can. Jour. Bot. **30**:291–305.

Black, W. A. P. 1948. Seasonal variation in chemical constitution of some common British Laminariales. Nature **161**:174.

Blackman, F. F. 1921. The biochemistry of carbohydrate production in the higher plants from the point of view of systematic relationship. New Phyt. **21**:2–9.

Bonner, James. 1950. Plant biochemistry. Academic Press, New York.

Brown, F. L., and G. E. Hunt. 1961. Personal communication.

Cmelik, S., and Morovic. 1950. Mannitol content in some algae from the Adriatic Sea. Arkiv. Kem. **22**:228–235.

Dangschat, G. 1958. Inosite und verwandte Naturstoffe (Cyclite). *In* Encycl. of Plant Physiol. (Editor, Ruhland) VI. Springer, Berlin.

Engler, A. and L. Diehls. 1936. Syllabus der Pflanzenfamilien. Aufl. 11. Berlin.

Hasegawa, M., S. Yoshida, and T. Nakajawa. 1954. Shikimic acid in plant leaves. Kagaku **24**:421–422.

Hegnauer, R. 1958. Chemotaxonomische Betrachtungen. V. Die systematische Bedeutung des Alkaloidmerkmales. Planta Med. **6**:1–35.

Hubbard, C. E. 1954. Grasses. Penguin Books, Suffolk.

Jenkins, T. J. 1933. Interspecific and intergeneric hybrids in herbage grasses. X. Some of the breeding interactions of *Festuca gigantea*. Jour. Genet. **53**:94–99.

Kooiman, P. 1960b. A. method for the determination of amyloid in plant seeds. Recueil Travaux Chimiques Pays-Bas **79**:675–678.

Kooiman, P. 1960a. On the occurrence of amyloids in plant seeds. Acta Bot. Neerlandica 9:208–219.

Kooiman, P. 1957. Partial enzymatic degradation of *Tamarindus*-amyloid. Nature 180:201.

Kooiman, P., and D. R. Kreger. 1957. X-ray observations on *Tamarindus*-amyloid. Biochim. Biophys. Acta 26:207–208.

LaForge, F. B., and C. S. Hudson. 1917. Sedoheptulose, a new sugar from *Sedum spectabile*. Jour. Biol. Chem. 30:61–77.

MacLeod, A. M., and H. McCorquodale. 1958. Water-soluble carbohydrates of seeds of the gramineae. New Phyt. 37:168–182.

Meeuse, B. J. D., M. Andries, and J. A. Wood. 1960. Floridean starch. Jour. Exper. Bot. 11:129–140.

Mothes, K. and A. Romeike. 1958. Die Alkaloide. *In* W. Ruhland, ed., Encycl. Plant Physiol. 8:505–529.

Neumüller, G. 1958. Pentosans and hexosans (excluding celluloses). *In* W. Ruhland, [ed.], Encycl. Plant Physiol. Vol. VI. Springer, Berlin.

Nordal, A. and D. Öiseth. 1952. On the occurrence of sedoheptulose in certain species and genera of the plant family Saxifragaceae. Acta Chem. Scand. 6:446–447.

Nordal, A., and R. Klevstrand. 1951a. Studies of the constituents of Crassulacean plants. I. Acta Chem. Scand. 5:85.

Nordal, A., and R. Klevstrand. 1951b. Studies of the constituents of Crassulacean plants. II. Acta Chem. Scand. 5:898.

Nordal, A., and D. Öiseth. 1951. The occurrence of sedoheptulose in the dried root of *Primula elatior* (L.) Hill. Acta Chem. Scand. 5:1289–1292.

Plouvier, V. 1954. Sur la présence du pinitol chez les Caryophyllacées et quelques plantes de familles voisines. Compt. Rend. Acad. Sci. Paris 239:1678–1680.

Plouvier, V. 1948. Sur la recherche des itols et du saccharose chez quelques Sapindales. Compt. Rend. Acad. Sci. Paris 227:85.

Plouvier, V. 1955. Sur la recherche du d-quercitol chez quelques Fagacies et autres plantes. Compt. Rend. Acad. Sci. Paris 240:113–115.

Quillet, M. 1957. Volemitol and mannitol in the Phaeophyceae. Bull. Lab. Maritime Dinard 43:119–124.

Reichstein, T. 1958. Der zucker der herzaktiven Glykoside. Proc. IV. Inter. Cong. Biochem. Vienna. 1:124–139.

Reichert, E. T. 1919. A biochemic basis for the study of problems of taxonomy, heredity, evolution, etc., with especial reference to the starches and tissues of parent-stocks and hybrid-stocks and the starches and hemoglobins of varieties, species and genera. Carnegie Inst. of Washington Publ. 270. Part I:1-376; Part II:377-834.

Reznik, H. 1957. Die pigments der Centrospermum als systematisches Element II Untersuchungen uber das ionophoretische Verhalten. Planta. 49:406-434.

Ruhland, W. [ed.] 1958. Encyclopedia of Plant Physiology Vol. VI. Springer, Berlin.

Shafizadeh, F., and M. L. Wolfrom. 1958. Structure, properties and occurrence of the oligosaccharides. In W. Ruhland [ed.] Encycl. Plant Physiol. 6:63-86. Springer, Berlin.

Smith, F., and R. Montgomery. 1959. The chemistry of plant gums and mucilages. Reinhold, New York.

Stoloff, L. 1962. Algal classification—an aid to improved industrial utilization. Econ. Bot. 16:86-94.

Stoloff, L., and P. Silva. 1957. An attempt to determine possible taxonomic significance of the properties of water extractable polysaccharides in red algae. Econ. Bot. 11:327-330.

Vasseur, E., and J. Immers. 1949. Genus specificity of the carbohydrate component in the sea urchin egg jelly coat as revealed by paper chromatography. Arkiv Kemi 1:39-41.

Williams, K. T., E. F. Potter, and A. Bevenue. 1952. A study, by paper chromatography, of the occurrence of nonfermentable sugars in plant materials. Jour. Assoc. Off. Agric. Chem. Wash. D. C. 35:483-486.

Young, E. G. 1958. Carbohydrate accumulation by lower plants. In W. Ruhland, [ed.], Encycl. Plant Physiol. Springer, Berlin. 6:909-923.

CHAPTER 9

Bachelor, F. W., R. F. C. Brown, and G. Büchi. 1960. Tetrahedron Letters 10:1-9.

Birecka, H., Sebyla, T., and Nalborczyk, E. 1959. Changes of sparteine in white lupine (Lupinus albus) Part I. White sweet lupine. (English summary.) Acta Soc. Bot. Polon. 28:301-314.

Brehm, B. R. 1962. The distribution of alkaloids, free amino acids, flavonoids, and certain other phenolic compounds in Baptisia leucophaea Nutt. var. laevicaulis Gray, and their taxonomic significance, Ph.D. Diss. Univ. of Texas, Austin.

Cromwell, B. T. 1955. The alkaloids. In K. Paech, and M. V. Tracey, [eds.], Moderne methoden der pflanzenanalyse. Vol. IV. Springer, Berlin.

Dawson, R. F. 1948. Alkaloid biogenesis. Adv. Enzym. 8:203-251.

Elderfield, Robert C. 1960. Australian trees and high blood pressure. Amer. Sci. **48**:193–208.

Gibbs, R. D. 1954. Comparative chemistry and phylogeny of flowering plants. Trans. Roy. Soc. Canada. Sect. V. **48**:1–47.

Giesbrecht, A. M. 1960. The occurrence of bufotenine in seeds of *Piptadenia falcata* Beuth. Assoc. Braz. Quim. Ann. **19**:117–119.

Gregory, W. C. 1941. Phylogenetic and cytological studies in the Ranunculaceae. Trans. Amer. Phil. Soc. W. S. **31**:443–521.

Hegnauer, R. 1952. Botanische Betrachtungen über Alkaloide. Bull. Galenica **15**:118–136.

Hegnauer, R. 1958. Chemotaxonomische Betrachtungen. V. Die systematische Bedeutung des Alkaloidmerkmales. Planta Med. **6**:1–35.

Hegnauer, R. 1954. Gedanken über die theoretische Bedeutung der chemisch-ontogenetischen und chemisch—systematischen Betrachtung von Arznei-pflanzen. Pharm. Acta Helv. **29**:203–220.

Hutchinson, J. 1959. The families of flowering plants I and II. 2nd ed. Oxford U. P., London.

James, W. O. 1953. Alkaloids in plants. Endeavour **12**:76–79.

James, W. O. 1950. Alkaloids in the plant. *In* R. H. F. Manske, and H. L. Holmes, [eds.], The Alkaloids. Vol. I. Academic Press, New York.

Kazimierski, T., and E. Nowacki. 1961. Indigenous species of lupins regarded as initial forms of the cultivated species. *Lupinus albus* L. and *Lupinus mutabilis* Sweet. Flora **151**:202–209.

Kumazawa, M. 1938. Systematic and phylogenetic consideration on the Ranunculaceae and Berberidaceae. Bot. Mag. **52**:9–15.

Kupchan, S. M., J. H. Zimmérman, and A. Afonso. 1961. The alkaloids and taxonomy of *Veratrum* and related genera. Lloydia **24**:1–26.

Lawrence, G. H. M. 1951. Taxonomy of vascular plants. Macmillan, New York.

Leete, E. 1959. Biogenesis of mescaline. Chem. and Ind. (London), 604.

Manske, R. H. F. 1954. The alkaloids of papaveraceous plants. L. *Dicrano-stigma lacturoides* Hook. F. et Thoms. and *Bocconia pearcei* Hutchinson. Can. Jour. Chem. **32**:83–85.

Manske, R. H. F., and L. Marion. 1947. The alkaloids of *Lycopodium* species IX. *Lycopodium annotinum* var. *acrifolium* Fern. and the structure of annotinine. Jour. Amer. Chem. Soc. **69**:2126–2129.

Marion, L. 1958. La biogénèse des alcaloides. Bull. Soc. Chimique France, 109–115.

McFadden, S. E. 1950. A series of related cytological and biochemical studies of the Berberidaceae and its alliance with the Ranunculaceae. Ph.D. Diss. Univ. of Virginia.

McNair, J. B. 1935. Angiosperm phylogeny on a chemical basis. Bull. Torrey Bot. Club **62**:515–532.

Mothes, K. 1960. Alkaloids in the plant. *In* R. H. F. Manske [ed.], The Alkaloids. VI. Academic Press, New York.

Mothes, K. 1955. Physiology of alkaloids. Ann. Rev. Plant Phys. **6**:393–432.

Mothes, K., and A. Romeike. 1958. Die Alkaloide. *In* W. Ruhland [ed.] Encyclopedia of Plant Physiology. VIII.

Nowacki, E. 1958. Investigations on the synthesis of alkaloids in lupine. (English summary) Roczniki Nauk Rolniczych **79**:505–529.

Orechov. A. P. 1955. Chimija alkaloidov. (Russian.) Academic Press, Moscow.

Pax, F., and K. Hoffman. 1930. Amaryllidaceae. *In* A. Engler, and H. Prantl [eds.]. Die natürlichen Pflanzenfamilien, 2nd ed. **15a**:391–430.

Poisson, J. 1958. La biosynthese des alcaloides. Ann. Bot. **24**:395–427.

Rowson, J. M. 1958. Symposium on biochemistry and taxonomy. Alkaloids in plant taxonomy. Proc. Linn. Soc. London **169**:212–216.

Schlittler, E. 1956. Alkaloids. *In* Sir Alexander Todd [ed.] Perspectives in organic chemistry. Interscience, New York.

Schütte, H. R., and Nowacki, E. 1959. Biosynthese der Lupinenalkaloide. Naturwiss. **46**:493.

Webb, L. J. 1949. An Australian phytochemical survey. 1. Alkaloids and cyanogenetic compounds in Queensland plants. C. S. I. R. O. Bull. No. 241. 56 pp.

Wenkert, E. 1959. Alkaloid biosynthesis. Experientia **15**:165–173.

Wildman, W. C. 1960. Alkaloids of the Amaryllidaceae. *In* R. H. F. Manske [ed.], The Alkaloids. VI. Academic Press, New York.

Wiesner, K., M. Götz, D. L. Simmons, L. R. Fowler, F. W. Bachelor, R. F. C. Brown and G. Büchi. 1959. Tetrahedron Letters **2**:15.

Willaman, J. J., and B. G. Schubert. 1955. Alkaloid hunting. Econ. Bot. **9**: 141–150.

Willaman, J. J., and B. G. Schubert. 1961. Alkaloid-bearing plants and their contained alkaloids 287 p. Agric. Res. Ser. U. S. D. A. Technical Bull. No. 1234. Washington.

CHAPTER 10

Armstrong, H. E., E. F. Armstrong, and E. Horton. 1912. Herbage studies. I. *Lotus corniculatus,* a cyanophoric plant. Proc. Roy. Soc. Lond., Series B **84**:471–484.

Armstrong, H. E., E. F. Armstrong, and E. Horton. 1913. Herbage studies II. Variation in *Lotus corniculatus* and *Trifolium repens* (cyanophoric plants). Proc. Roy. Soc. Lond., Series B **86**:262–269.

Atwood, S. S., and J. T. Sullivan. 1943. Inheritance of a cyanogenetic glucoside and its hydrolysing enzyme in *Trifolium repens*. Jour. Hered. **34**:311–320.

Buchholz, J. T. 1951. Gymnosperm. Encycl. Brit. **11**:23–34.

Butler, G. W., and B. G. Butler. 1960. Biosynthesis of linamarin and lotaustralin in white clover. Nature **187**:780–781.

Cooke, A. R. 1955. The toxic constituent of *Indigofera endecaphylla*. Arch. Biochem. Biophys. **55**:114–120.

Dilleman, G. 1958. Composés cyanogénétiques. *In* W. Ruhland [ed.], Encycl. Plant Physiol. VIII Springer, Berlin.

Doporto, M. L., K. M. Gallagher, J. E. Gowan, A. C. Hughes, E. M. Philbin, T. Swain, and T. S. Wheeler. 1955. Rearrangement in the demethylation of 2′-methoxyflavons. II. Further experiments and the determination of the composition of lotoflavin. Jour. Chem. Soc. (Lond.) 4249–4256.

Dupuy, H. P., and J. G. Lee. 1956. The toxic component of the singletary pea (*Lathyrus pusillus*). Jour. Amer. Pharm. Asso. **45**:236–239.

Ermakov, A. I. 1960. The formation and quantitative change of cyanogenic glycoside in sprouting and maturing flax. Plant Physiol. (Russian) **7**: 372–375.

Finnemore, H., J. M. Cooper, and M. B. Stanley. 1938. The cyanogenetic constituents of Australian and other plants. Jour. Soc. Chem. Ind. (Translation.) **57**:162–169.

Gibbs, R. D. 1954. Comparative chemistry and phylogeny of flowering plants. Trans. Roy. Soc. Canada. Sec. V. **48**:1–47.

Hegnauer, R. 1958. Over de verspreiding van blauwzuur bij vaatplanten. Pharm. Week. **93**:801–819.

Hegnauer, R. 1959a. Die Verbreitung der Blausäure bei den Cormophyten. 2. Mitteilung. Die Cyanogenese in genus *Taxus*. Pharm. Week. **94**:241–248.

Hegnauer, R. 1959b. Die Verbreitung der Blausäure bei den Cormophyten 3. Mitteilung. Die blausäurehattigen Gattungen. Pharm. Week. **94**:248–262.

Langley, B. W., B. Lythgoe, and N. V. Riggs. 1951. Macrozamin. The aliphatic azoxystructure of the aglycone part. Jour. Chem. Soc. Lond. 2309–2316.

Lythgoe, B. and N. V. Riggs. 1949. Macrozamin. I. The identity of carbohydrate component. Jour. Chem. Soc. Lond., 2716–2718.

Morris, M. P., C. Pagán, and H. E. Warmke. 1954. Hiptagenic acid, a toxic component of *Indigofera endecaphylla*. Science **119**:322–323.

Nishidi, K., T. Nagahama, and T. Numata. 1960. Studies on cycasin, a new toxic glycoside of *cycas revoluta*. IX. Cleavage of macrozamin to cycasin. Mem. Fac. Agr. Kagoshima Univ. **4**:1–3.

Petrie, J.M. 1913. Hydrocyanic acid in plants II. Its occurrence in the grasses of N. S. Wales. Proc. Linn. Soc. N. S. Wales **38**:624–638.

Reichert, E. T. 1919. A biochemic basis for the study of problems of taxonomy, heredity, evolution, etc., with especial reference to the starches and tissues of parent-stocks and hybrid-stocks and the starches and hemoglobins of varieties, species, and genera. Carnegie Institute of Washington Publ. 270. Part I:1–376; Part II:377–834.

Ressler, C. 1962. Isolation and identification from common vetch of the neurotoxin β-cyano-L-alanine, a possible factor in neurolathyrism. Jour. Biol. Chem. **237**:733–735.

Ressler, C., P. A. Redstone and R. H. Erenberg. 1961. Isolation and identification of a neuroactive factor from *Lathyrus latifolius*. Science **134**:188–190.

Robinson, M. E. 1930. Cyanogenesis in plants. Biol. Rev. **5**:126–141.

Schilling, E. D., and F. M. Strong. 1955. Isolation, structure, and synthesis of a lathyrus factor from *L. odoratus*. Jour. Amer. Chem. Soc. **77**:2843–2845.

Seddon, H. R. 1928. Milk weed (*Euphorbia drummondi*) proved poisonous to sheep. Agric. Gaz. N. S. Wales **39**:777–782.

Selye, Hans. 1957. Lathyrism. Revue Canad. de Biol. **16**:1–82.

Smith, F., and C. T. White. 1920. The peach leaf poison bush. *Trema aspera* Blume: Its occasional toxicity. Proc. Roy. Soc. Queensland **32**:132–134.

Strong, F. M. 1956. Lathyrism and odoratism. Nut. Rev. **14**:65.

Trione, E. J. 1960. The high HCN content of flax in relation to flax wilt resistance. Phytopathology **50**:482–486.

Webb, L. J. 1949. An Australian phytochemical survey. 1. Alkaloids and cyanogenetic compounds in Queensland plants. C. S. I. R. O. Bull. No. 241. 56 pp.

Williams, R. D. 1939. Genetics of cyanogenesis in white clover (*Trifolium repens*). Jour. Genet. **38**:357–365.

CHAPTER 11

Abe, Y. and K. Gotoh. 1956. Genetic control of acylation of anthocyanin pigment in eggplant. Ann. Report Nat. Inst. Genet. (Japan) **6**:75–76.

Acheson, R. M., J. L. Harper, and I. H. McNaughton. 1956. Distribution of anthocyanin pigments in poppies. Nature **178**:1283–1284.

Alston, R. E. 1958. An investigation of the purple vacuolar pigment of *Zygogonium ericetorum* and the status of "algal anthocyanins" and "phycoporphyrins." Amer. Jour. Bot. **45**:688–692.

Alston, R. E. 1959. Physiology and the inheritance of anthocyanin pattern. Genetica **30**:261–277.

Alston, R. E. 1963. Inheritance of phenolic compounds. *In* J. B. Harborne [ed], The chemistry of phenolic compounds. Academic Press, N. Y. (In press)

Alston, R. E., and C. W. Hagen. 1955. Relation of leuco-anthocyanin to antho-cyanin synthesis. Nature **175**:990.

Alston, R. E., and C. W. Hagen, Jr. 1958. Chemical aspects of the inheritance of flower color in *Impatiens balsamina* L. Genetics **43**:35–47.

Baker, W., and W. D. Ollis. 1961. Biflavonyls. *In* W. D. Ollis. [ed] Recent developments in the chemistry of natural phenolic compounds. Pergamon, New York.

Bate-Smith, E. C. 1948. Paper chromatography of anthocyanins and related substances in petal extracts. Nature **161**:835.

Bate-Smith, E. C. 1957. Leuco-anthocyanins 3. The nature and systematic dis-tribution of tannins in dicotyledonous plants. Jour. Linn. Soc. Lond. **55**:669–705.

Bate-Smith, E. C. 1958. Symposium on biochemistry and taxonomy. Plant phenolics as taxonomic guides. Proc. Linn. Soc. Lond. **169**:198–211.

Bate-Smith, E. C. 1961. Cromatography and taxonomy of the Rosaceae, with special reference to *Potentilla* and *Prunus*. Jour. Linn. Soc. Lond. **58**:39–54.

Bate-Smith, E. C., and N. H. Lerner. 1954. Leuco-anthocyanins 2. Systematic distribution of leucoanthocyanins in leaves. Biochem. Jour. **58**:126–132.

Bate-Smith, E. C., and T. C. Whitmore. 1959. Chemistry and taxonomy in the Dipterocarpaceae. Nature **184**:795–796.

Beale, G. H., J. R. Price, and V. C. Sturgess. 1941. A survey of anthocyanins. VII. The natural selection of flower colour. Proc. Roy. Soc. Lond., Series B **130**:113–126.

Beale, G. H. 1939. Genetics and chemistry of flower colour variation in *Lathyrus odoratus*. Genetics **37**:375–388.

Bickoff, E. M. 1961. Estrogenic-like substances in plants. Conference on bio-chemistry of plant phenolic substances. Fort Collins, Colorado. (Aug. 31-Sept. 1, 1961.)

Billek, G., and H. Kindl. 1962. Über die phenolischen Inhaltsstoffe der Familie Saxifragaceae. Monats. Chem **93**:85–98.

Birch, A. J., and F. W. Donovan. 1953. Studies in relation to biosynthesis. I. Some possible routes to derivations of orcinol and phloroglucinol. Aust. Jour. Chem. **6**:360–368.

Blank, F. 1947. The anthocyanin pigments of plants. Bot. Rev. **13**:241–317.

Brown, S. A. 1961. Chemistry of lignification. Science **134**:305–312.

Clevenger, S. B. 1958. The flavonols of *Impatiens balsamina* L. Arch. Biochem. Biophys. **76**:131–138.

Dave, K. G., S. A. Telang, and K. Venkataraman. 1962. Flavonoid pigments of the heartwood of *Artocarpus integrifolia*. Tetrahedron Letters Jan. 1962, No. 1, pp. 9–14.

Dayton, T. O. 1956. The inheritance of flower colour pigments. I. The genus *Antirrhinum*. Genetics **54**:249-260.

Davis, B. D. 1956. Biochemical exploration with bacterial mutants. The Harvey Lectures, 1954-1955. Pp. 230-257. Academic Press, New York.

de Roubaix, J., and O. Lazar. 1960. The inhibitory substances contained in sugar beet glomerules. *In* J. B. Pridham. Phenolics in plants in health disease. Pergamon, New York.

de Winton, D., and J. B. S. Haldane. 1933. The genetics of *Primula sinensis*. II. Segregation and interaction of the factors in the diploid. Genetics **27**:1-44.

Egger, K., and H. Reznik. 1961. Die flavanolglykoside der Hamamelidaceen. Planta **57**:239-249.

Erdtman, H. 1956. Organic chemistry and conifer taxonomy. *In* A. R. Todd [ed.] Perspectives in organic chemistry. Interscience, New York.

Erdtman, H. 1958. Conifer chemistry and taxonomy of conifers. IVth Int. Congr. Biochem. Vienna, 1958.

Feenstra, W. J. 1960. Biochemical aspects of seedcoat colour inheritance in *Phaseolus vulgaris* L. Meded. Land. Wageningen **60**:1-53.

Feenstra, W. J. 1959. Chemical aspects of the action of three seedcoat colour genes of *Phaseolus vulgaris*. Proc. Koninkl. Nederland Akad. Wetenschap. **62**:119-130.

Geissman, T. A., and T. Swain. 1957. Biosynthesis of flavonoid compounds in higher plants. Chem. and Ind. (Lond.) 984.

Geissman, T. A., E. H. Hinreiner, and E. C. Jorgensen. 1956. Inheritance in the carnation, *Dianthus caryophyllus*. V. The Chemistry of flower color variation. II. Genetics **41**:93-97.

Geissman, T. A., and E. Hinreiner. 1952. Theories of the biogenesis of flavonoid compounds. I and II. Bot. Rev. **18**:77-244.

Gottlieb, O. R., M. T. Magalhaes, and W. B. Mors. 1959. The chemistry of rosewood V. 4-methoxyphenylcoumelin. Cont. Inst. Quím. Agríc., Rio de Janeiro **18**:37-41.

Grisebach, H. 1957. Zur biogenese des Cyanidins. I. Mitt: Versuche mit Acetat-[1-^{14}C] und Acetat-[2-^{14}C]. Zeit. Natur. **12b**:227-231.

Grisebach, H. 1961. The biosynthesis of isoflavones. *In* W. D. Ollis. [ed.] Recent developments in the chemistry of natural phenolic compounds. Pergamon, New York.

Grisebach, H., and W. D. Ollis. 1961. Biogenetic relationships between coumarins flavonoids, isoflavonoids and rotenoids. Experientia **17**:4-12.

Grisebach and L. Patschke. 1961. Zur Biogenese der Flavonoide IV. Mitt.: 2′,4′,4′,6′-tetrahydroxy-chalkon-2′-glucoside-[B-^{14}C] als Vorstoffe für Quercetin und Cyanidin Zeit. Natur. **16**:645-647.

Griffiths, L. A. 1958. Phenolic acids and flavonoids of *Theobroma cacao* L. Separation and identification by paper chromatography. Biochem. Jour. **70**:120.

Griffiths, L. A. 1960. A comparative study of the seed polyphenols of the genus *Theobroma*. Biochem. Jour. **74**:362–365.

Hagen, C. W. Jr. 1959. Influence of genes controlling flower color on relative quantities of anthocyanins and flavonols in petals of *Impatiens balsamina*. Genetics **44**:787–793.

Haldane, J. B. S. 1954. The biochemistry of genetics. George Allen and Unwin, London.

Harborne, J. B. 1956. Biochemical genetics of the acylated anthocyanins of tuberous Solanums. Biochem. Jour. **63**:30p.

Harborne, J. B. 1958. Anthocyanidins of the Primulaceae. Nature **181**:26–27.

Harborne, J. B. 1960a. Flavonoid pigments of *Lathyrus odoratus*. Nature **187**:240–241.

Harborne, J. B. 1960b. The genetic variation of anthocyanin pigments in plant tissues. *In* J. B. Pridham [ed.]. Phenolics in the plant in health and disease. Pergamon, New York.

Harborne, J. B. 1962. Plant polyphenols. 5. Occurrence of azalein and related pigments in flowers of *Plumbago* and *Rhododendron* species. Arch. Biochem. Biophys. **96**:171–178.

Hegnauer, R. 1956. Chemotaxonomische Betrachtung der Leguminosae. Arznei-pflanzen-Umschau. **5**:638–652.

Hörhammer, L. and Wagner, H. 1961. New phenolic C-glycosides in plants. *In* W. D. Ollis [ed.]. Recent developments in the chemistry of natural phenolic compounds. Pergamon, New York.

Hutchinson, A., C. D. Taper, and G. H. N. Towers. 1959. Phloridzin in *Malus*. Can. Jour. Biochem. Physiol. **37**:901–910.

Jorgensen, E. C., and T. A. Geissman. 1955. The chemistry of flower pigmentation in *Antirrhinum majus* color genotypes. III. Relative anthocyanin and aurone concentrations. Arch. Biochem. Biophys. **55**:389–402.

Karrer, W. 1958. Konstitution und Vorkommen der organischen Pflanzenstoffe (Exclusive Alkaloids). Birkhaüser, Basel.

Kingdon-Ward, F. 1950. Does wild tea exist? Nature **165**:279–299.

Kuhn, R. und Low, I. 1960. Über Flavonolglykoside von *Forsythia* und über Inhaltstoffe von *Chlamydomonas*. Chem. Ber. **93**:1009–1010.

Lawrence, G. H. M. 1951. Taxonomy of vascular plants. Macmillan, New York.

Lawrence, W. J. C., R. Scott-Moncrieff, and V. C. Sturgess. 1939. Studies on *Streptocarpus* I. Genetics and chemistry of flower colour in the garden strains. Genetics **38**:299-306.

Lawrence, W. J., C. and R. Scott-Moncrieff, 1935. The genetics and chemistry of flower colour in *Dahlia:* a new theory of specific pigmentation. Genetics **30**:155–226.

Levin, J. S., and D. B. Sprinson, 1960. Biochem. Biophys Res. Comm. **3**: 157–163.

Moewus, F. 1950. Die Bedeutung von Farbstoffen bei den Sexualprozessen der Algen und Blütenpflanzen. Ang. Chem. **62**:496–502.

Neish, A. C. 1960. Biosynthetic pathways of aromatic compounds. Ann. Rev. Plant Physiol. **11**:55–80.

Ollis, W. D., and I. O. Sutherland. 1961. Isoprenoid units in natural phenolic compounds. *In* W. D. Ollis, [ed.], Chemistry of Natural Phenolic Compounds. Pergamon, New York.

Onslow, M. W. 1916. The anthocyanin pigments of plants, 1st ed. Cambridge Univ. Press.

Paris, C. D., W. J. Haney, and G. B. Wilson. 1960. A survey of the interactions of genes for flower color. Mich. State Univ. Agri. Exp. Sta., Tech. Bull. 281.

Pecket, R. C. 1959. The constituents of leaf extracts in the genus *Lathyrus* and their bearing on taxonomy. New Phytol. **58**:182–187.

Pecket, R. C. 1960a. The nature of the variation in flower colour in the genus *Lathyrus*. New Phytol. **59**:138–144.

Pecket, R. C. 1960b. Phenolic constituents of leaves and flowers in the genus *Lathyrus. In* J. B. Pridham [ed.]. Phenolics in plants, in health and disease. Pergamon, New York.

Reid, W. W. 1958. Biosynthesis of scopoletin and caffeic acid in *Nicotiana tabacum.* Chem. and Ind. 1439–1440.

Reznik, H., and R. Neuhäusel. 1959. Farblose Anthocyanine bei submersen Wasserpflanzen. Zeit. Bot. **47**:471–489.

Reznik, H., and K. Egger. 1960. Myricetin—ein charakteristisches Flavonol der Hamamelidaceae und Anacardiaceae. Zeit. Natur. **15**:247–250.

Rickards, R. W. 1961. The biosynthesis of phenolic compounds from activated acetic acid units. *In* W. D. Ollis [ed.]. Recent development in the chemistry of natural phenolic compounds. Pergamon, New York.

Riley, H. P., and T. R. Bryant. 1961. The separation of some species of the Iridaceae by paper chromatography. Amer. Jour. Bot. **48**:133–137.

Roberts, E. A. H., W. Wright, and D. S. Wood. 1958. Paper chromatography as an aid to the taxonomy of *Thea camelleas*. New Phytol. **57**:211–225.

Roller, K. 1956. Über Flavonoide in weissen Blumenblatten. Zeit. Bot. **44**: 477–500.

Scott-Moncrieff, R. 1931. The chemical effect of a Mendelian factor for flower colour. Nature **127**:974–975.

Scott-Moncrieff, R. 1936. A biochemical survey of some Mendelian factors for flower colour. Jour. Gen. 32:117–170.

Sherratt, H. S. A. 1958. The relationship between anthocyanidins and flavonols in different genotypes of *Antirrhinum majus*. Jour. Gen. 56:28–36.

Shibata, S., and M. Yamazaki. 1957. The biogenesis of rutin. Pharm. Bull. (Tokyo) 5:501–502.

Stoutamire, W. P. 1960. The relation of anthocyanins to *Gaillardia* taxonomy. Mich. Acad. Sci. Arts and Letters 45:35–39.

Takahashi, M., T. Ito, A. Mizutari and K. Isoi. 1960. Chemical constituents of the plants of coniferae and allied orders XLIII. Distribution of flavonoids and stilbenoids. Jour. Pharm. Soc. Japan. 80:1488–1492.

Tomaszewski, M. 1960. The occurrence of p-hydroxybenzoic acid and some other simple phenols in vascular plants. Acad. Polon. Sci. B. Ser. des Sci. Biol. 8:61–65.

Uritani, Ikuzo. 1961. The role of plant phenolics in disease resistance and immunity. Conference on Biochemistry of Plant Phenolics Substances. Fort Collins, Colorado. (Aug. 31-Sept. 1, 1961.)

Watkin, J. E., E. W. Underhill, A. C. Neish, 1957. Biosynthesis of quercetin in buckwheat. II. Can. Jour. Biochem. Phys. 35:229–237.

Williams, A. H. 1960. The distribution of phenolic compounds in apple and pear trees. *In* J. B. Pridham [ed.]. Phenolics in plants in health and disease. Pergamon, New York.

CHAPTER 12

Bentham, G. 1871. Revision of the genus *Cassia*. Trans. Linn. Soc. Lond. 27:503–591.

Crane, F. L. 1959. Internal distribution of coenzyme Q in higher plants. Plant Physiol. 34:128–131.

Friedrich, H. 1959. Die Biosynthese der Anthrachinone. Planta Med. 7:383–389.

Gilg, E. and H. Heinemann. 1926. Die Beziehungen des Emodens zur Systematik der Gattung *Cassia*. Festschrift A. Tschirch-Tauchnitz, Leipzig. Pp. 52–61.

Hegnauer, R. 1959. Chemotaxonomische Betrachtungen 9. Die systematische Bedeutung des Anthrachinonen-merkmales. Planta Med. 7:344–366.

Heppeler, F. 1928. Beiträge zur Systematik der gattung *Rhamnus* mit besonderer Berüchsichtigung des Emodinvorkommens. Arch. Pharm. 266:152.

Jaretzky, R. 1928. Die Bedeutung der "Phytochemie" für die Systematik. Archiv. der Pharm. 266:602–613.

Jaretzky, R. 1926. Beiträge zur Systematik der Polygonaceae unter Berücksichtigung des Oxymethylanthrachinon-vorkommens. Fedde Rep. Spec. Nov. **22**:49.

Lester, R. L., and F. L. Crane. 1959. The natural occurrence of coenzyme Q and related compounds. Jour. Biol. Chem. **234**:2169-2175.

Maurin, E. 1928. Les Rhamnacées ā anthraquinones. Bull. Sci. Pharm. **35**:236.

Münker, H. 1928. Das Vorkommen und feblen des Emodins bei den Arten der Gattung *Alöe* in hinblick auf ihre Systematik mit einer ergänzenden Untersuchung der Alöesaftbehälter. Beitr. Biol. Pflanzen. **16**:217-266.

Thomson, R. H. 1957. Naturally occurring quinones. Academic Press, New York.

Trim, A. R. 1955. Histochemical and quantitative observations on the distribution of galiosenase in the shoots of Stellateae. Jour. Exper. Bot. **6**:100.

Schnarf, K. 1944. Ein Beitrag zur Kenntnis der Verbreitung des Aloins und ihrer systematischen Bedeutung. Österr. Bot. Zschr. **93**:113-122.

Tsukida, K. 1957. Über Derivate von Oxyanthraquinon und Oxyanthron in Pflanzen. Planta Med. **5**:97-114.

CHAPTER 13

Altman, R. F. 1954. Steroidal sapogenins in Amazonian plants. Nature **173**: 1098.

Anzaldo, F. E., J. Mararon, and S. Ancheta. 1956. Screening of Philippine plants for steroidal sapogenins. I. Philip. Jour. Sci. **85**:305-314.

Anzaldo, F. E., J. Mararon, and S. Ancheta. 1957. Screening of Philippine plants for steroidal sapogenins. II. Philip. Jour. Sci. **86**:233-239.

Baker, R. T., and H. G. Smith. 1920. Research on the eucalypts especially in regard to their essential oils, 2nd ed. Sydney Technol. Mus. N. S. Wales Tech. Educ. Ser. No. 13.

Battaile, J., and W. D. Loomis. 1961. Biosynthesis of terpenes. II. The site and sequence of terpene formation in peppermint. Biochem. Biophys. Acta **51**: 545-552.

Djerassi, Carl. 1957. Cactus triterpenes. Paper XXVI in Terpenoids. Festschrift Arthur Stoll. Birkhauser, Basel.

Enslin, P. R., and S. Rehm. 1960. The distribution and biogenesis of the cucurbitacins in relation to taxonomy of the *Cucurbitaceae*. Proc. Linn. Soc. Lond. **169**:230-238.

Erdtman, H. 1955a. The chemistry of heartwood constituents of conifers and their taxonomic importance. XIV International Congress of Pure and Applied Chemistry, Zurich: Experientia. Suppl. II. 156-180.

Erdtman, H. 1955b. Natural tropolones. *In* K. Paech, and M. V. Tracey [eds.]. Modern methods of plant analysis. Vol. III. Springer, Berlin.

Erdtman, H. 1956. Organic chemistry and conifer taxonomy. *In* Sir A. Todd. [ed.]. Perspectives in organic chemistry. Interscience.

Erdtman, H. 1958. Conifer chemistry and taxonomy of conifers. IV Internat. Congress Biochem., Vienna. II, Pergamon, New York.

Ferretti, L. O., and J. H. Richards. 1960. The biogenesis of the mold tropolones. Proc. Natl. Acad. Sci. U. S. **46**:1438–1444.

Fontan-Candela, J. L. 1957. Las saponinas y la botanica. Anales del Inst. Bot. A. J. Cavanilles de Madrid **15**:501–521.

Heftmann, E., R. D. Bennett, and J. Bonner. 1961. Biosynthesis of diosgenin in *Dioscorea* tubers. Arch. Biochem. Biophys. **92**:13–16.

Herz, W., and G. Högenaur. 1961. Isolation and structure of coronopilin, a new sesquiterpene lactone. Jour. Org. Chem. **26**:5011–5013.

Herz, W. and G. Högenaur. 1962. Ivalin, a new sesquiterpene lactone. Jour. Org. Chem. **27**:905–910.

Herz, W., P. Jayaraman, and H. Watanabe. 1960. Constituents of *Helenium* species. IX. The sesquiterpene lactones of *H. flexuosum* Raf. and *H. Campestre* Small. Jour. Amer. Chem. Soc. **82**:2276–2278.

Herz, W., M. Miyazaki, and Y. Kishida. 1961. Structures of parthenin and ambrosin. Tetrahedron Letters. **No. 2.**:82–86.

Hirose, Y., and T. Nakatsuka. 1958. Jour. Jap. Wood Res. Soc. **4**:26.

Holloway, J. T. 1958. On the phylogenetic significance of the diterpenes of the phyllocladene and podocarpene groups. New Zeal. Jour. Sci. Tech. **20**:16–20.

Karrer, W. 1958. Konstitution und Vorkommen der organischen Pflanzenstoffe. Birkhäuser, Basel.

Korte, F. 1954. Über neue glykosidische pflanzen-inhaltsstoffe. III. Mitt: Die Beziehungen zwischen Inhaltsstoffen und morphologischen Systematik in der Reihe der Contortae unter besonderer Berucksichtigung der Bitterstoffe. Zeit. für Naturforsch. **9**:354–358.

Korte, F., and I. Korte. 1955a. Charakteristische pflanzen Inhaltsstoffe VIII. Mitt: Über die Beziehung zwischen morphologischen Systematite und chemischen Inhaltsstoffen bei den Asclepiadaceen. Zeit. für Naturforsch. **10**:223–229.

Korte, F. and I. Korte. 1955b. Zur Frage der chemischen Klassifizierung höherer Pflanzen. X. Mitt.: Charakteristische Pflanzen-inhaltsstoffe. Zeit. für Naturforsch. **10**:499–503.

Marker, R. E., R. B. Wagner, P. R. Ulshafer, E. L. Wittbecker, D. P. J. Goldsmith, and C. H. Ruof. 1947. New sources for sapogenins. Jour. Amer. Chem. Soc. **69**:2242.

Marker, R. E., R. B. Wagner, P. R. Ulshafer, E. L. Wittbecker, D. P. J. Goldsmith, and C. H. Ruof. 1943. Sterols CLVII. Sapogenins LXIX. Isolation and structures of thirteen new steroidal sapogenins. New sources for known sapogenins. Jour. Amer. Chem. Soc. **65**:1199–1209.

McNair, J. B. 1942. Some chemical properties of *Eucalyptus* in relation to their evolutionary status. Madroño **6**:181–190.

Meeuse, A. D. J. 1954. Bitter substances in Cucurbitaceae. General botanical introduction. South African Ind. Chem. Pp. 69–70.

Mirov, N. T. 1961. Composition of gum turpentines of pines. U. S. D. A. Technical Bulletin No. 1239, p. 158.

Mirov, N. T. 1958. Distribution of turpentine components among species of the genus *Pinus*. *In* K. V. Thimann [ed.]. The physiology of forest trees. Ronald Press. New York.

Mirov, Nicholas T. 1948. The terpenes (in relation to the biology of genus *Pinus*). Ann. Rev. Biochem. **17**:521–540.

Murray, M. J. 1960a. The genetic basis for the conversion of methone to menthol in Japanese mint. Genetics **45**:925–929.

Murray, M. J. 1960b. The genetic basis for a third ketone group in *Mentha spicata* L. Genetics **45**:931–937.

Penfold, A. R., and F. R. Morrison. 1927. The occurrence of a number of varieties of *Eucalyptus dives* as determined by chemical analyses of the essential oils. Part I. Jour. and Proc. Roy. Soc. N. S. Wales **61**:54–67.

Read, J. 1944. Chemistry of the Australian bush. Endeavour **3**:47.

Reitsema, R. H. 1958a. Some new constituents of mint oils. Jour. Amer. Pharm. Assoc. **47**:265–266.

Reitsema, R. H. 1958b. A biogenetic arrangement of mint species. Jour. Amer. Pharm. Assoc. **47**:267–269.

Ricardi, M., C. Marticorena, M. Silva, and F. Torres. 1958. Detection of saponins in Chilean angiosperms. Bol. Soc. Biol. Conception, Chile.

Rock, H. F. L. 1957. A revision of the vernal species of *Helenium* (Compositae). Rhodora **59**:101–116; 128–158.

Shaw, G. R. 1914. The genus *Pinus*. Arnold Arboretum Pub. **5**:96.

Simes, J. J. H., J. G. Tracey, L. J. Webb, and W. J. Dunstan. 1959. An Australian phytochemical survey. III. Saponins in eastern Australian flowering plants. Aust. C. S. I. R. O. Bull. 281, 31 pp.

Stanley, R. G. 1958. Terpene formation in pine. Proceedings 4th Inter. Congr. Biochem. Vienna. Vol. II.

Turner, B. L., and M. C. Johnston. 1961. Chromosome numbers in the Compositae-III. Certain Mexican species. Brittonia **13**:64–69.

Wagner, A. F., and K. Folkers. 1961. The organic and biological chemistry of mevalonic acid. Endeavour **20**:177-187.

Wall, M. E., C. S. Fenske, H. E. Kenney, J. J. Willaman, D. S. Correll, R. G. Schubert, and H. S. Gentry. 1957. Steroidal sapogenins XLIII. Jour. Amer. Pharm. Assoc. **46**:653-686.

CHAPTER 14

Acerbo, S. N., W. J. Schubert, and F. F. Nord. 1958. Investigations on lignins and lignification. XIX. The mode of incorporation of p-hydroxyphenyl-pyruvic acid into lignin. Jour. Amer. Chem. Soc. **80**:1990-1992.

Bentley, L. E. 1952. Occurrence of malonic acid in plants Nature **170**:847-848.

Bold, H. C. 1962. Some supplementary attributes in the classification of *Chlorococcum* species. Arch. Microbiol. **42**:267-288.

Brauns, F. E., and D. A. Brauns. 1960. The chemistry of lignin. (Suppl. Volume) Academic Press, New York.

Brown, S. A. 1961. Chemistry of lignification. Science **134**:305-313.

Brown, S. A., and A. C. Neish. 1955. Studies of lignin biosynthesis using isotopic carbon. IV. Formation from some aromatic monomers. Can. Jour. Biochem. Phys. **33**:948-962.

Brown, S. A., D. Wright, and A. C. Neish. 1959. Studies of lignin biosynthesis using isotopic carbon. VII. The role of p-hydroxyphenylpyruvic acid. Can. Jour. Biochem. Phys. **37**:25-34.

Buch, M. L. 1957. Bibliography of organic acids in higher plants. U.S.D.A. Agric. Res. Ser. ARS-73-18. pp. 136.

Cheney, R. H. 1931. Geographic and taxonomic distribution of American plant arrow poisons. Amer. Jour. Bot. **18**:136-145.

Creighton, R. H. J., R. D. Gibbs, and H. Hibbert. 1944. Studies in lignin and related compounds. LXXV. Alkaline nitrobenzene oxidation of plant materials and application to taxonomic classification. Jour. Amer. Chem. Soc. **66**:32-37.

Dougherty, E. C. and M. B. Allen. 1960. Is pigmentation a clue to protistan phylogeny? *In* M. B. Allen [ed.], Comparative biochemistry of photoreactive systems. Academic Press, New York.

Dreiding, A. S. 1962. The betacyanins, a class of red pigments in the Centrospermae. *In* L. D. Ollis [ed.]. Recent developments in the chemistry of phenolic compounds. Pergamon, New York.

Duncan, W. H., P. L. Piercy, S. D. Feurt, and R. Sterling. 1955. Toxicological studies of southeastern plants. I. Leguminosae. Econ. Bot. **9**:243-255.

Duncan, W. H., P. L. Piercy, S. D. Feurt, and R. Sterling. 1957. Toxicological studies of southeastern plants. II. Compositae. Econ. Bot. **11**:75–85.

Fowden, L. and F. C. Steward. 1957. Nitrogenous compounds and nitrogen metabolism in the Liliaceae. I. The occurrence of soluble nitrogenous compounds. Ann. Bot. **21**:53–67.

Fowden, L., J. A. Webb. 1955. Evidence for the occurrence of γ-methylene-α-oxoglutaric acid in ground nut plants (*Arachis hypogaea*). Biochem. Jour. **59**:228–234.

Freudenberg, K. 1959a. Biosynthesis and constitution of lignin. Nature **183**: 1152–1155.

Freudenberg, K. 1959b. Biochemische Vorgänge bei der Holzbildung. *In* K. Kratzl and G. Billek [eds.] 4th Inter. Cong. of Biochem. Vienna Vol. II.

Gibbs, R. Darnley. 1945. Comparative chemistry as an aid to the solution of problems in systematic botany. Trans. Roy. Soc. Can. **39**:71–103.

Gibbs, R. D. 1954. Comparative chemistry and phylogeny of flowering plants. Trans. Roy. Soc. Can. **48**:1–47.

Gibbs, R. D. 1958. Chemical evolution in plants. Jour. Linn. Soc. Lond. **56**:49–57.

Goodwin, T. W. 1955a. Carotenoids. *In* K. Paech and M. V. Tracey [eds.]. Modern methods of plant analysis. Vol. III. Springer, Berlin.

Goodwin, T. W. 1955b. Studies in carotenogenesis. 19. A survey of the polyenes in a number of ripe berries. Biochem. Jour. **62**:346–352.

Goodwin, T. W. 1962. Comparative biochemistry of carotenoids *In* S. Ochoa [ed.]. Proceedings 5th Internatl. Cong. of Biochemistry, Moscow, 1961. Vol. III (in press).

Hatfield, D. L., C. Van Baalen, and H. S. Forrest. 1961. Pteridines in blue green algae. Plant Physiol. **36**:240–243.

Haywood, B. J., and G. A. R. Kon. 1940. Sapogenins. IX. Occurrence and constitution of bassic acid. Jour. Chem. Soc. 713–720.

Kjaer, A. 1960. Naturally derived isothiocyanates (mustard oils) and their parent glucosides. Progress in the chemistry of organic natural products **18**: 122–176.

Kjaer, A., and S. E. Hansen. 1958. Isothiocyanates. XXXI. The distribution of mustard oil glucosides in some *Arabis* species. A chemotaxonomic approach. Bot. Tidsskrift **54**:374–378.

Lawrence, W. J. C., J. R. Price, G. M. Robinson, and R. Robinson. 1941. The distribution of anthocyanins in flowers, fruits and leaves. Phil. Trans. B **230**:149–178.

Lindstedt, G. 1956. Electrophoresis of red beet pigments. Acta Chem. Scand. **10**:698–699.

Mabry, T. J., A. Taylor and B. L. Turner. 1963. The betacyanins and their distribution. Phytochemistry 2:61–64.

Mabry, T. J., H. Wyler, G. Sassu, M. Mercier, J. Parikh, and Andre S. Dreiding. 1962. Die Struktur des Neobetanidins. Über die Konstitution des Randenfarbstoffes Betanin. Helv. Chim. Acta 45:640–647.

Manskaya, S. M. 1960. Fossilized lignin and modern wood. Lesotekh. Akad. im S. M. Kirova Pt. 2 No. 91 Pp. 159–172. (Chem. abst. 1961. 23699i.)

Manskaja, S. M. 1959. Zur Phylogenese des Lignins, In K. Kratzl and G. Billek [eds.]. 4th Inter. Cong. Biochem. Vienna. Vol. II.

Mayer, W. 1958. Pflanzengerbstoffe. In W. Ruhland [ed.], Encycl. Plant Phys. X: Springer, Berlin.

McCalla, D. R., and A. C. Neish. 1959. Metabolism of phenylpropanoid compounds in Salvia. II. Biosynthesis of phenolic cinnamic acids. Can. Jour. Biochem. Phys. 37:536–547.

McNair, J. B. 1932. The interrelation between substances in plants: essential oils and resins, cyanogen and oxalate. Amer. Jour. Bot. 19:255–272.

McNair, J. B. 1934. The evolutionary status of plant families in relation to some chemical properties. Amer. Jour. Bot. 21:427–453.

McNair, J. B. 1935a. Angiosperm phylogeny on a chemical basis. Bull. Torrey Bot. Club 62:515–532.

McNair, J. B. 1935b. The taxonomic and climatic distribution of alkaloids. Bull. Torrey Bot. Club 62:219–226.

McNair, J. B. 1941a. Plant forms, the law of mass action and the production of alkaloids, cyanogenetic and organic sulphur compounds. Amer. Jour. Bot. 28:179–184.

McNair, J. B. 1941b. Epiphytes, parasites and geophytes and the production of alkaloids, cyanogenetic and organic sulphus compounds. Amer. Jour. Bot. 28:733–737.

McNair, J. B. 1943. Hydrophytes, xerophytes and halophytes and the production of alkaloids, cyanogenetic and organic sulphur compounds. Lloydia 6:1–17.

McNair, J. B. 1945. Some comparisons of chemical ontogeny with chemical phylogeny in vascular plants Lloydia 8:145–169.

Neish, A. C. 1960. Biosynthetic pathways to aromatic compounds Ann. Rev. Plant Physiol. 11:55–80.

Nickell, L. G. 1959. Antimicrobial activity of vascular plants. Econ. Bot. 13:281–318.

Osborn, E. M. 1943. On the occurrence of antibacterial substances in green plants. British Jour. Exptl. Path. 24:227–231.

Pennington, C. W. 1958. Tarahumar fish stupefaction plants. Econ. Bot. 11:95–102.

Pobeguin, T. 1943. Les oxalates de calcium chez quelques Angiospermes. Ann. des Sci. Nat. Bot., Ser. 11. 4:1–95.

Ramstad, E. 1945. Distribution de l'acide chelidonique dans les drogues. Pharm. Acta Helvet. 20:145–154.

Ramstad, E. 1953. Über das Vorkommen und die Verbreitung von Chelidon-säure in einigen Pflanzenfamilien. Pharm. Acta Helvet. 28:45–57.

Rauh, W., and H. Reznik. 1961. Zur Frage des systematischen Stellung der Didiereaceen. Bot. Jahrbuch 81:94–105.

Reznik, H. 1955. Die Pigmente der Centrospermen als systematisches Element. Zeit. für Bot. 43:499–530.

Reznik, H. 1957. Die Pigmente der Centrospermum als systematisches Element. II. Untersuchungen uber das ionophoretische Verhalten. Planta 49:406–434.

Reznik, H. and D. Urban. 1956. Die Aufnahme ^{14}C-markierter Ligninbausteine in Fichtennadeln. Planta 47:1–15.

Schmidt, O. T. 1955. Natürliche Gerbstoffe. In K. Paech and M. V. Tracey [eds.], Modern Methods of Plant Analysis III. Springer, Berlin.

Schmidt, O. T., and W. Schönleben. 1956. Zür Kenntnis des Farbstoffs der roten Rübe. Naturwiss. 43:159.

Selye, H. 1957. Lathyrism. Revue Canadienne de Biologie. 16:1–82.

Shaw, E., and R. D. Gibbs. 1961. Comparative chemistry and the relationship of the Hamamelidaceae. Nature 190:463.

Skene, M. 1934. The botany of the tannins. In M. Nierenstein [ed.] The nature of organic tannins. Churchill, Ltd., London.

Skinner, F. A. 1955. Antibiotics. In K. Paech and M. V. Tracey [eds.]. Modern methods of plant analysis. III: Springer, Berlin.

Stafford, H. A. 1959. Distribution of tartaric acid in the leaves of certain angio-sperms. Amer. Jour. Bot. 46:347–352.

Stafford, H. A. 1961. Distribution of tartaric acid in the Geraniaceae. Amer. Jour. Bot. 48:699–701.

Taylor, T. W. J. 1940. Plant pigments in the Galápagos Islands. Proc. Roy. Soc., Ser. B 129:230–237.

Towers, G. H. N., and F. C. Steward. 1954. Keto acids of the tulip (*Tulipa gesneriana*) with special reference to the keto analogue of γ-methylene-glutamic acid. Jour. Amer. Chem. Soc. 76:1959–61.

Towers, G. H. N., and R. D. Gibbs. 1953. Lignin chemistry and the taxonomy of higher plants. Nature 172:25–26.

Turrill, W. B. 1942. Taxonomy and phylogeny. Part I. Bot. Gaz. 8:247–270.

Turrill, W. B. 1942. Taxonomy and phylogeny. Part II. Bot. Gaz. **8**:473–532.

Turrill, W. B. 1942. Taxonomy and phylogeny. Part III. Bot. Gaz. **8**:655–707.

Wardrop, A. B., and D. E. Bland. 1959. The process of lignification in woody plants. *In* F. Brüke [ed.] Proceedings 4th Inter. Cong. Biochem. Vienna. Vol. III.

Weevers, T. 1943. The relation between taxonomy and chemistry of plants. Blumea **5**:412–422.

Wolf, F. T. 1960. Pteridine pigments in microorganisms and higher plants. *In* M. B. Allen [ed.] Comparative biochemistry of photoreactive systems. Academic Press, New York.

Wright, D., S. A. Brown and A. C. Neish. 1958. Studies of lignin biosynthesis using isotopic carbon. VI. Formation of the side chain of the phenylpropane monomer. Can. Jour. Biochem. Physiol. **36**:1037–1045.

Wyler, H. and A. S. Dreiding. 1959. Darstellung und Abbauprodukte des Betanidins über die Konstitution des randenfarbstoffes Betanin. Helv. Chim. Acta **42**:1699–1702.

Wyler, H. and A. S. Dreiding. 1961. Über Betacyane, die stichstoffhaltigen Farbstoffe der Centrospermen. Vorläufige Mitteilung. Experientia **17**: 23–25.

CHAPTER 15

Alston, R. E., 1959. Physiology and the inheritance of anthocyanin pattern. Genetica **30**:261–277.

Alston, R. E. and B. L. Turner. 1959. Applications of paper chromatography to systematics: Recombination of parental biochemical components in a *Baptisia* hybrid population. Nature **184**:285–286.

Alston, R. E., and B. L. Turner. 1962. New techniques in analysis of complex natural hybridization. Proc. Natl. Acad. Sci. U. S. **48**:130–137.

Alston, R. E., and B. L. Turner. 1963. Natural hybridization among four species of *Baptisia* (Leguminosae). Amer. Jour. Bot. **50**:159–173.

Alston, R. E., B. L. Turner, R. N. Lester, and D. Horne. 1962. Chromatographic validation of two morphologically similar hybrids of different origins. Science **137**:1048–1050.

Alston, R. E., and J. Simmons. 1962. A specific and predictable biochemical anomaly in interspecific hybrids of *Baptisia viridis* X *B. leucantha*. Nature **195**:825.

Bannister, M. H., H. V. Brewerton, and I. R. C. McDonald. 1959. Vapour phase chromatography in a study of hybridism in *Pinus*. Svenske Papperstidning **62**:567-573.

Bacharach, M. M., W. H. McGibbon, and M. R. Irwin. 1960. An interaction product of the cellular antigens in species hybrids. Jour. Hered. **51**: 122-126.

Beadle, G. W., and E. L. Tatum. 1941. Genetic control of biochemical reactions in *Neurospora*. Proc. Natl. Acad. Sci. U. S. **27**:499-506.

Beckman, L., F. Conterio, and D. Mainardi. 1962. Protein synthesis in species hybrids of birds. Nature **196**:92-93.

Bopp, M. 1958. Über den Farbwechsel von *Streptocarpus*-blüten. Zeit. Naturforsch. **136**:669-671.

Chester, K. S. 1937. A critique of plant serology. Parts I, II, and III. Quart. Rev. Biol. **12**:19-46; 165-190; 294-321.

Delaveau, P. 1961. Recherches par chromatographie sur les graines d'un Raphanobrassica, hybride intergénérique. Soc. Bot. France **108**:261-263.

Dillemann, Georges. 1953. Recherches biochimiques sur la transmission des hétérosides cyanogénétiques par hybridetion inter-spécifique dans le genre *Linaria*. Rev. Gen. Bot. **60**:338-399; 401-462.

Duncan, W. H. 1962. Evidence on hybridization of Baptisias (Leguminosae) in the Blue Ridge Province of the southeastern United States. (Abstr.) Amer. Jour. Bot. **49**:675.

Fernald, M. L. 1950. Gray's manual of botany, 8th Ed. American Book Co., New York.

Florkin, M., and H. S. Mason (eds.). 1960. Comparative biochemistry: a comprehensive treatise. Academic Press, New York.

Fox, W., H. C. Dessauer, and L. T. Maumur. 1961. Electrophoretic studies of blood proteins of two species of toads and their natural hybrids. Comp. Biochem. Physiol. **3**:52-63.

Garber, E. D. 1958. The genus *Collinsia*. VI. Distribution of pigments in the flowers. Bot. Gaz. **119**:240-243.

Glass, Bentley. 1957. A summary of the symposium on the chemical basis of heredity. *In* W. D. McElroy, and B. Glass [eds.]. A symposium on the chemical basis of heredity. Johns Hopkins University Press, Baltimore.

Hall, O. 1959. Immunoelectrophoretic analysis of allopolyploid ryewheat and its parental species. Hereditas **45**:495-503.

Hanson, C. H., W. A. Cope, and R. M. Brinkley. 1959. Chemical changes in *Lespedeza* associated with induced polyploidy. Amer. Jour. Bot. **46**:36-39.

Henke, O. 1960. Biochemische und morphologische Untersuchungen au *Vitis*-artbastarden. Züchter **30**:213-219.

Irwin, M. R. 1951. Genetics and immunology. *In* L. C. Dunn [ed.]. Genetics in the 20th century. Macmillan. New York.

Irwin, M. R., and R. W. Cumley. 1945. Suggestive evidence for duplicate genes in a species hybrid in doves. Genetics **30**:363–375.

Jacob, F., and E. L. Wolman. 1961. Sexuality and the genetics of bacteria. Academic Press, New York.

Kawatani, T., and H. Asakina. 1959. External characters and alkaloids of the artificial interspecific F₁ hybrid between *Papaver oriental L.* (♀) and *P. somniferum L.* (♂). Jap. Jour. Genet. **34**:353–362.

Langridge, J. 1955. Biochemical mutations in the crucifer. *Arabidopsis thaliana.* (L.) Heynh. Nature **176**:260.

Larisey, M. M. 1940. Analysis of a hybrid complex between *Baptisia leucantha* and *Baptisia viridis* in Texas. Amer. Jour. Bot. **27**:624–628.

Lukovnikova, G. A. 1961. Variation of the chemical composition of potato as a result of polyploidy. Biochim Plodov i Ovoshchei, Akad. Nauk. SSSR. 1961. No. 6:146–152.

McGibbon, W. H. 1944. Cellular antigens in species and species hybrids in ducks. Genetics **29**:407–419.

Miller, W. J. 1956. The hybrid-substance of the erythrocytes of the hybrids between *Columba livia* and *Streptopelia risoria*. Genetics **41**:700–714.

Mirov, N. T. 1956. Composition of turpentine of lodgepole × jack pine hybrids. Can. Jour. Bot. **34**:443–457.

Moritz, O. 1934. Die botanische Serologie. Beitr. Biol. Pflan. **22**:51–90.

Moritz, O., and H. vom Berg. 1931. Serologische Studien über das Linswichen- problem. Biol. Zbl. **51**:290–307.

Moritz, O. 1958. Die Serologie der pflanzlichen Eiweisskorper. *In*, W. Ruhland (ed.). Encyclo. Plant Physiol. VIII. Springer, Berlin.

Oehlkers, F. 1938. Bastardierungsversuche in der Gattung *Streptocarpus* Lindl. I. Plasmatische Vererbung und die Geschlechtsbestimmung von Zwitter- pflanzen. Zeit. Bot. **32**:305–393.

Pontecorvo, G. 1958. Trends in genetic analysis. Columbia University Press, New York.

Pryor, L. D., and L. H. Bryant. 1958. Inheritance of oil characters in *Eucalyptus*. Proc. Linn. Soc. N. S. Wales **83**:55–64.

Reichert, E. T. 1919. A biochemic basis for the study of problems of taxonomy, heredity, evolution, etc., with especial reference to the starches and tissues of parent-stocks and hybrid-stocks and the starches and hemoglobins of varieties, species, and genera. Carnegie Institute of Washington Publ. 270. Part I: 1–376; Part II: 377–834.

Rensch, B. 1959. Evolution above the species level. Columbia Univ. Press, New York.

Righter, F. I., W. P. Stockwell. 1949. The fertile species hybrid *Pinus murraybanksiana* Madroño 10:65–69.

Rowson, J. M. 1958. Symposium on biochemistry and taxonomy. Alkaloids in plant taxonomy. Proc. Linn. Soc. Lond. 169:212–216.

Scheinberg, S. L. 1960. Genetic studies of serum antigens in species hybrids. Genetics 45:173–188.

Schwartz, D. 1960. Genetic studies on mutant enzymes in maize: synthesis of hybrid enzymes by heterozygotes. Proc. Natl. Acad. Sci.U. S. 46:1210–1215.

Schwarze, Paul. 1959. Untersuchungen über die gesteigerte Flavonoidproduktion in *Phaseolus*-artbastarden (*Phaseolus vulgaris* × *Phaseolus coccineus*). Planta 54:152–161.

Sievers, A. F., M. S. Lowman, M. L. Ruttle. 1945. Investigations of the yield and quantity of the oils from some hybrid and tetraploid mints. Jour. Amer. Pharm. Assoc. Sci. Ed. 34:225–231.

Steward, F. C., M. A. Mapes, and J. Smith. 1958. Growth and organized development of cultured cells. I. Growth and division of freely suspended cells. Amer. Jour. Bot. 45:693–703.

Strauss, B. S. 1960. An outline of chemical genetics. W. B. Saunders Co., Philadelphia.

Tsitsin, N. V., and V. F. Lubimova. 1959. New species and forms of cereals derived from hybridizations between wheat and couch grass. Amer. Nat. 93:181–191.

Tulecke, W. S. 1960. Arginine-requiring strains of tissue derived from *Ginkgo* pollen. Plant Physiol. 35:19–24.

Turner, B. L. and R. E. Alston. 1959. Segregation and recombination of chemical constituents in a hybrid swarm of *Baptisia laevicaulis* X *B. viridis* and their taxonomic implications. Amer. Jour. Bot. 46:678–686.

Vickery, Robert K. and Richard L. Olson. 1956. Flower color inheritance in the *Mimulus cardinalis* complex. J. Heredity 47(5):195–199.

Williams, A. H. 1955. Phenolic substances of pear-apple hybrids. Nature 175:213.

Zade, A. 1914. Serologische studien au Leguminosen und Graminien. Z. Pflanzenzuchtg 2:101–151.

CHAPTER 16

Alston, R. E. and B. L. Turner. 1959. Applications of paper chromatography to systematics: Recombination of parental biochemical components in a *Baptisia* hybrid population. Nature 184:285–286.

Alston, R. E. and H. S. Irwin. 1961. The comparative extent of variation of free amino acids and certain "secondary" substances among *Cassia* species. Amer. Jour. Bot. **48**:35–39.

Armstrong, H. E., E. F. Armstrong, and E. Horton. 1913. Herbage studies II. Variation in *Lotus corniculatus* and *Trifolium repens* (cynophoric plants). Proc. Roy. Soc. London, Ser. B. **86**:262–269.

Beyerman, H., and Y. M. F. Muller. 1955. Über die Isolierung und Strukuraufklärung eines neuen Alkaloids aus *Sedum acre* L. Recueil des Travaux Chemiques des Pays-Bas **74**:1568–1571.

Brachet, J. 1957. Biochemical cytology. Academic Press, New York.

Brehm, B. G. 1962. The distribution of alkaloids, free amino acids, flavonoids, and certain other phenolic compounds in *Baptisia leucophaea* Nutt. var. *laevicaulis* Gray, and their taxonomic implications. Ph.D. Diss. Univ. of Texas, Austin.

Ellison, W. L., R. E. Alston, and B. L. Turner. 1962. Methods of presentation of crude biochemical data for systematic purposes, with particular reference to the genus *Bahia*. (Compositae.) Amer. Jour. Bot. **49**:599–604.

Erdtman, H. 1956. Organic chemistry and conifer taxonomy. *In* A. Todd (ed.), Perspectives in organic chemistry. Interscience, New York.

Dillemann, G. 1960. Infraspecific chemical differentiation. Planta Med. **8**: 263–274.

Dzhemukhadze, K. M., and M. N. Nestyuk. 1961. Changes in flavonoids of the tea leaf during drying. Doklady (Biochem. Section) **133**:153–154.

Forsyth, W. G. C. 1952. Cacao polyphenolic substances. 1. Fractionation of the fresh bean. Biochem. Jour. **51**:511–516.

Forsyth, W. G. C. 1952. Cacao polyphenolic substances. 2. Changes during fermentation. Biochem. Jour. **51**:516–520.

Griffiths, L. A. 1958. Phenolic acids and flavonoids of *Theobroma cacao* L. Separation and identification by paper chromatography. Biochem. Jour. **70**:120–125.

Harborne, J. B., and H. S. A. Sherratt. 1957. Variations in the glycosidic pattern of anthocyanins II. Experientia **13**:486.

Hemingway, J. S., H. J. Schofield, and J. B. Vaughan. 1961. Volatile mustard oils of *Brassica juncea* seeds. Nature **192**:993.

Jabbar, A., and E. Brochmann-Hanssen. 1961. Amino acids in opium. Jour. Pharm. Sciences **50**:406–408.

Jaminet, J. 1960. Infraspecific chemical differentiation: co-report. Planta Med. **8**:275–281.

Marion, L. 1945. The alkaloids of *Sedum acre* L. Can. Jour. Res. **23**:165–166.

Paris, R. R., and R. Letouzey. 1960. Distribution of alkaloids in yohimbe. Jour. Agr. Trop. Bot. Appl. **7**:256–258.

Penfold, A. R. and F. R. Morrison. 1927. The occurrence of a number of varieties of *Eucalyptus dives* as determined by chemical analyses of the essential oils. Part I. Jour. and Proc. Roy. Soc. N. S. Wales **61**:54–67.

Redfield, A. C. 1936. The distribution of physiological and chemical peculiarities in the "natural" groups of organisms. Amer. Nat. **70**:110–122.

Schopf, C., and R. Unger. 1956. Über Physiologische, durch einen Gehalten verschiedenen Alkaloiden charakterisierte Rassen von *Sedum acre* L. Experientia **12**:19–20.

Tétényi, Pierre. 1958. Proposition ā propos de la nomenclature des races chimiques. Taxon **7**:40–41.

Wall, M. E., and C. S. Fenske. 1961. Steroidal sapogenins. LXI. Steroidal sapogenin content of seeds. Econ. Bot. **15**:131–132.

Wulff, N. D., and E. Stahl. 1960. "Chemische Rassen" bei *Acorus calamus*. Naturwiss. **47**:114.

Yoshida, D. 1961. Changes of free amino acid composition in tobacco leaves during the process of "flue-curing." Plant Cell Physiol. **2**:209–211.

INDEX